THE CITY OF GOD IN JUDAISM

SOUTH FLORIDA STUDIES IN THE HISTORY OF JUDAISM

Edited by
Jacob Neusner
William Scott Green, James Strange
Darrell J. Fasching, Sara Mandell

Number 23
The City of God in Judaism

by
Jacob Neusner

THE CITY OF GOD IN JUDAISM
And Other Comparative and Methodological Studies

by
Jacob Neusner

Scholars Press
Atlanta, Georgia

BM
496.5
.N479
1991

THE CITY OF GOD IN JUDAISM
And Other Comparative and Methodological Studies

©1991
University of South Florida

Publication of this book was made possible by a grant from the Tisch Family Foundation, New York City. The University of South Florida acknowledges with thanks this important support for its scholarly projects.

Library of Congress Cataloging in Publication Data

Neusner, Jacob. 1932-
    The city of God in Judaism, and other comparative and methodological studies / by Jacob Neusner.
    p. cm. — (South Florida studies in the history of Judaism ; no. 23)
    Includes index.
    ISBN 1-55540-586-X (acid-free paper)
    1. Rabbinical literature—History and criticism. 2. Talmud—Theology. 3. Rabbinical literature—Historiography. 4. Religion and sociology. I. Title. II. Title: City of God in Judaism. III. Series.
BM496.5.N479   1991
296.1'206—dc20   91-32494
                                                                           CIP

Printed in the United States of America
on acid-free paper

Contents

Preface ix

Prologue
ON METHOD IN RELIGION AND SOCIETY: HOW WE DISCERN THE SOCIAL WORLD CONCEIVED BY FRAMERS OF ANONYMOUS AND COLLECTIVE DOCUMENTS

1. The Documentary Method in the Study of the History of Judaism in its Formative Period 3
2. Holy Writing: The Social Setting 15
3. Holy Writing: The Intellectual Setting. Analogical-Contrastive Thinking and the Problem of Dialectical Thought 33

Part One
THE CITY OF GOD IN JUDAISM: TRANSFORMATIONS OF THE SOCIAL ORDER FROM PHILOSOPHY TO RELIGION

4. The Philosophical Judaism of the Mishnah, Tosefta, and Tannaite Midrash Compilations 89
5. The Religious Judaism of the Talmud of the Land of Israel, Genesis Rabbah, and Leviticus Rabbah 105
6. The Categorical Reformation of Judaism as a Religion 117
7. From Philosophy to Religion: Systemic Integration 129
8. The City of God in the Conceptions of the Social Order of Our Sages of Blessed Memory and of St. Augustine 143

Part Two
ETERNITY AND HISTORY IN JUDAISM: COMPARATIVE STUDIES

9. How is "Eternity" To Be Understood in the Theology of Judaism? An Exercise in Comparative Theology 175
10. History in Judaism Reconsidered 189

Part Three
THE THEOLOGICAL INITIATIVE

11. Re-presenting The Torah: Sifra's Rehabilitation of Taxonomic Logic and the Judaic Conception of How through the Torah We Enter the Mind of God 199

12. The Role of Scripture in the Torah: Is Judaism a "Biblical Religion"? 221

Part Four
REPRISES AND REPLIES:
ISSUES OF METHOD

13. *Judaism in the Matrix of Christianity* Reconsidered................241

14. The Talmud of Babylonia: System or Tradition? A Reprise of Seven Monographs 279

15. Translating Rabbinic Documents: The Importance of an Analytical Reference System 297

16. Mr. Maccoby's Red Cow – and Mine: A Reply to Critics 317

17. More Orthodox Apologetics: Boyarin's Version of Midrash 327

Epilogue
ON COMPARISON

18. What Does Judaism Teach Us about Religion in General?.......333

Index 341

Preface

At the principal turnings in my work I have undertaken a labor of *haute vulgarisation* of my results, so that colleagues in neighboring fields may have easy access to results that are pertinent to their interests. Having brought to a conclusion ten years of sustained work, resting on ten prior years, in my *The Transformation of Judaism. From Philosophy to Religion*,[1] I set forth in these pages the methodological considerations and substantive issues of that prolonged study of conceptions of the social order in two distinct but interrelated bodies of writing of formative Judaism, the Mishnah and its associated Midrash compilations, ca. 200-400, and the Talmud of the Land of Israel and the concomitant Midrash compilations, ca. 400-500. Work from 1970 to 1980 was devoted to the former, from 1980-1990, the latter. In the prologue I explain the considerations that led me, in 1970, to dismiss as hopeless the received methodological consensus on how for historical purposes to study the writings of the rabbis of late antiquity ("our sages of blessed memory") and set forth the method that I devised to address the problems of those writings: what can we know? how can we know it? what is at stake in finding out? I have spent the last twenty years dealing with those three questions, and I have systematically answered them in a variety of studies and projects. Even now, I foresee another ten years of work along this same line of inquiry. I see the third and final stage in the formation of Judaism as the movement from the Talmud of the Land of Israel and its associated Midrash compilations to the Talmud of Babylonia and its companions, a transformation that reworked a religious system into a theological statement and structure. But that perspective is inchoate and general, and only after I have accomplished a considerable monographic preparation will I know in acute detail the way in which that rather

---

[1](Champaign, 1991: University of Illinois Press).

general perception works out. Chapter Three presents a prospectus of what is to come.

The particular occasion for this book of essays presented itself to me in an invitation to lecture in Madrid for the *Departamento de Estudios Hebraicos, Instituto de Filologia,* at the *Consejo superior de investigaciones cientificas.* In response to this welcome invitation, I decided to study Spanish and to try, in five lectures translated into that language, to summarize the principal results of the past twenty years of methodological reflection and substantive work, and Chapters One and Four through Eight of this book are the result. For comparative purposes, I also include my presentation of the city of God conceived by our sages of blessed memory in relationship to the city of God conceived by St. Augustine as laid out in *Transformation of Judaism.* I claim that both systems address the same issue, precipitated at the same era and by the same concatenation of events, and I also maintain that, while in no way intersecting in language or category, they in point of fact set forth the same response to the same critical and urgent questions. A second, somewhat less ambitious, comparative study is given in Chapter Nine, where I point to the necessity for a measure of caution in defining how comparison is appropriate; as shown in Chapters Four through Eight, I try to compare what I know well with that which is set forth for me by the scholarship of others, who know their subject equally well. I also insist that comparison becomes appropriate not when validated by a mere congruence of words (or alleged congruence!), but only when attempted through large-scale systemic description and analysis; and that is at the stage of systemic interpretation, as is always the case in my *oeuvre.* Chapter Ten deals with the comparison of the place of history in various Judaisms, once more underlining the difficulty addressed in Chapter Nine: on an other-than-systemic scale can we compare different religions or even systems set forth within the same religion? I once more maintain that we cannot. True, comparison proves facile when we ignore nuance and detail; but then the results prove either trivial and obvious or simply uninformed and crude. In the case at hand I show a simple fact that forms a barrier in the comparison of theological concepts. Just as eternity in the Judaism represented by the Mishnah is not congruent with eternity in the Christianity represented by Revelation, so history in Judaism is hardly the same thing as history commonly understood.

In Part Three I review some findings of mine on theological propositions (Chapter Eleven) and sources for theological truth (Chapter Twelve). These point toward the issues that I believe critical when we ask about the theology of a Judaism: the meeting with God, the sources of truth. But the dimensions of the theological

Preface xi

description of the Judaism of the Dual Torah vastly transcend these rather preliminary statements; I have much more in mind.

In Part Four I present three reprises of results of mine, Chapters Thirteen and Fourteen and Fifteen, and two replies to, or comments on the work of, critics of mine, Chapters Sixteen and Seventeen. It is clear to me that an ongoing labor of explaining to colleagues what I am doing and why, even in so fundamental a matter as providing a reference system to rabbinic texts, which until mine have had none of any consequence, is necessary. It also is an ongoing assignment to take critics seriously and to deal with their criticism. Over the last thirty years, I believe that I have reviewed every book published in my field of study, and I continue to do so. That makes unnecessary the extensive footnoting of my articles with references to work in the same general area but utterly irrelevant to what I am doing. I do my bibliographical work in other ways. Since, in the field in which I work, most books are simply not reviewed, and more than a few scholars simply decline to refer to books with which they do not concur (or which they do not understand), it remains a fundamental assignment to all reputable scholars to read and review everything of concern that appears.[2] The thirty years of *Todschweigen* – murder through ostentatious ignoring – that, in scholarship on ancient Judaism, has replaced rational, all the more so, civil, debate have served only to remove the practitioners of the ban from scholarly discourse; those who practiced silence have now fallen silent. They have stopped even repeating themselves; *Todschweigen* has now become *Selbsttodschweigen* – intellectual suicide through silence. So much for the past. Those with whom I debate – Maccoby, Sanders,[3] Boyarin – take no part in such matters and deserve to be read and taken seriously, as I do here.

---

[2] I of course have reviewed whatever has appeared out of Jerusalem in English, these being mostly handbooks, collections of this and that, reprises of work thirty years old, translation of half-century-old items, and the like. If I ignore what has appeared in modern Hebrew, it is because not a single book has appeared in twenty years that undertakes the study of Judaism in late antiquity. Since E. E. Urbach's *Sages* (1969) not a single work on the history of Judaism in the Roman and Iranian worlds has been published. Articles in Hebrew here and there have proven mainly episodic and important only for the ordinarily trivial topic that they treat, if that. That accounts for my silence on the subject.

[3] See my "Mr. Sanders's Pharisees. A Reply," *Scottish Journal of Theology*, in press for 1991. I call attention to the apology for Sanders' offensive and (in the opinion of qualified counsel) quite libelous remarks about me in his work on *Jewish Law from Jesus to the Mishnah*. It is to the credit of Trinity Press International and SCM Press that they repudiate Sanders, in their

The epilogue explains why I think people who specialize in other religions, besides Judaism, should study about Judaism, and people whose interests center upon aspects of society and culture other than the religious find fresh perspective in study about Judaism. Much more, of course, is to be said along these lines, but it seems to me a gesture of respect for colleagues to explain why what I do deserves their attention.

Since these are free-standing essays, a measure of repetition will find its way into the collection, for which I beg the reader's indulgence. I present the essays as they were originally written, free-standing and self-contained.

The University of South Florida has provided important support for my research and publication, and I express my thanks for that valuable, ongoing commitment, which is especially appreciated in a time of scarce resources. Even beyond a cordial welcome, appreciated though it is, I have found much more intellectual stimulation among my colleagues at University of South Florida, in whose achievements I take pride, than I have known elsewhere in my career. In the ascent from Rhode Island through New Jersey to Florida, Brown University, the Institute for Advanced Study, the University of South Florida – from 1988-1989, through 1989-1990, to 1990-1991 – I have not missed a step or lost a day. But conditions here prove far more favorable to sustained learning than those I have known in the past. So, drawn by inner curiosity and propelled by a perpetual dissatisfaction generated from within, I proceed apace, the unsolved problems on the forward horizon growing in proportion and density while those receding on the path now travelled lose all urgency. What I cannot account for vastly outweighs what I think I have satisfactorily explained, which, for me, surely defines the condition of a happy life.

JACOB NEUSNER

Graduate Research Professor of Religious Studies
UNIVERSITY OF SOUTH FLORIDA
Tampa, St. Petersburg, Sarasota, Lakeland, Fort Myers

December 7, 1990

735 Fourteenth Avenue Northeast
St. Petersburg, Florida 33701 USA

---

advertisements in the *Journal of the American Academy of Religion, Journal of Biblical Literature,* and elsewhere.

Prologue
ON METHOD IN RELIGION AND SOCIETY: HOW WE DISCERN THE SOCIAL WORLD CONCEIVED BY FRAMERS OF ANONYMOUS AND COLLECTIVE DOCUMENTS

1

The Documentary Method in the Study of the History of Judaism in Its Formative Period

During a long period in the history of scholarship on history of religion in general, and Judaism in particular, the premises of learning in the rabbinic literature of late antiquity joined to the received theological conviction a new historical interest. This historical interest expressed proposed to describe in historical, social context ideas that had formerly been assigned no context at all. In the theology of Judaism everything true and authoritative was, and is, equally part of the "Torah." Doctrines now were to form the history of ideas. The received theological reading of the rabbinic texts maintained that the documents of the rabbinic corpus were essentially seamless and formed one vast Dual Torah, oral and written. Of course, all attributions were valid, so that if a given authority was supposed to have made a statement, he really made it. Of course, all stories happened in concrete history precisely in the way they were told – on that day, in that way. On the basis of that received conviction, imputing inerrancy to the attributions (as well as to the storytellers) just as had many generations of the faithful, but asking questions of context and development that were supposed to add up to history, the great figures of the first three quarters of the twentieth century set forth their accounts of what they conceived to be Judaism in historical context, hence, the history of Judaism. The received consensus on the history of Judaism, formed in the nineteenth and first half of the twentieth centuries, concurred on this program: believe it all, but ask a different sort of question. The results, in English, were the great works of George F. Moore and Solomon Schechter, and their counterparts in Hebrew, culminating in E. E. Urbach.

But what if we recognize that documentary formulations play a role in the representation of compositions, so that the compositors' formulation of matters takes a critical place in the making of the documentary evidence? And what if, further, we no longer assume the historical inerrancy of the Oral Torah's writings, so that attributions are no longer taken at face value, stories no longer believed and taken at face value? Then the fundamental presuppositions of the received method of studying the history of Judaism prove null. And that fact bears in its wake the further problem: since we cannot take their answers at face value, can we pursue their questions any more? In my judgment, the answer is negative. All work in the history of the formative age of the Judaism of the Dual Torah that treats documentary lines as null, and attributions as invariably valid, must now be dismissed as a mere curiosity; a collection and arrangement of this and that, bearing no compelling argument or proposition to be dealt with by the new generation.

The question that demands a response before any historical issues can be formulated is this: How are we to determine the particular time and circumstance in which a writing took shape, and how shall we identify the generative problems, the urgent and critical questions, that informed the intellect of an authorship and framed the social world that nurtured that same authorship? Lacking answers to these questions, we find our work partial, and, if truth be told, stained by sterile academicism. Accordingly, the documentary method, which I have invented and also brought to fruition, requires us to situate the contents of writings into particular circumstances, so that we may read the contents in the context of a real time and place. How to do so? I maintain that it is by reference to the time and circumstance of the closure of a document, that is to say, the conventional assignment of a piece of writing to a particular time and place, that we proceed outward from context to matrix.

The shift from historical classification by attributions of sayings, without regard to the documentary origin of sayings, to historical classification by documents, is a considerable change in the study of the history of Judaism in its formative age. For overall, scholars have tended simply to take at face value attributions of sayings to particular authorities and then to interpret what is said as evidence of the time and place in which the cited authorities flourished. When studying topics in the Judaism of the sages of the rabbinic writings from the first through the seventh centuries, colleagues in times past have routinely cited sayings categorized by attribution rather than by document. That is to say, they treat as one group of sayings whatever is assigned to Rabbi X. This is without regard to the time of redaction of the documents in which those sayings occur or to similar considerations of literary context and documentary circumstance. The category defined by attributions to a given authority furthermore rests on the premise that the things given in the name of Rabbi X really were said by him. No other premise would justify resort to the category deriving from use of a name, that alone.

Commonly, the next step is to treat those sayings as evidence of ideas held, if not by that particular person, then by people in the age in which the cited authority lived. Once more the premise that the sayings go back to the age of the authority to whom they are attributed underpins inquiry. Accordingly, scholars cite sayings in the name of given authorities and take for granted that those sayings were said by the authority to whom they were attributed and, of course, in the time in which that authority flourished. By contrast, in my method of the documentary study of Judaism, I treat the historical sequence of sayings only in accord with the order of the documents in which they first occur. Let me expand on why I have taken the approach that I have, explain the way the method works, and then, as before, set forth an example of the method in action.[1]

---

[1] I worked on the histories of specific conceptions or problems, formulated as I think correct, out of the sequence of documents in the following works of mine:

The Idea of Purity in Ancient Judaism. The Haskell Lectures, 1972-1973 (Leiden, 1973: E. J. Brill). [This was a most preliminary work, which made me aware of the problems to be addressed later on. The documentary theory of the history of ideas was worked out only in the earlier 1980s.]

Judaism and Story: The Evidence of The Fathers According to Rabbi Nathan (Chicago, 1990: University of Chicago Press).

The Foundations of Judaism. Method, Teleology, Doctrine (Philadelphia, 1983-1985: Fortress Press). I-III. I. *Midrash in Context. Exegesis in Formative Judaism* (Second printing: Atlanta, 1988: Scholars Press for Brown Judaic Studies).

The Foundations of Judaism. Method, Teleology, Doctrine (Philadelphia, 1983-1985: Fortress Press). I-III. II. *Messiah in Context. Israel's History and Destiny in Formative Judaism* (Second printing: Lanham, 1988: University Press of America). Studies in Judaism Series.

The Foundations of Judaism. Method, Teleology, Doctrine (Philadelphia, 1983-1985: Fortress Press). I-III. III. *Torah: From Scroll to Symbol in Formative Judaism* (Second printing: Atlanta, 1988: Scholars Press for Brown Judaic Studies).

The Foundations of Judaism (Philadelphia, 1988: Fortress). Abridged edition of the foregoing trilogy.

Vanquished Nation, Broken Spirit. The Virtues of the Heart in Formative Judaism (New York, 1987: Cambridge University Press). Jewish Book Club selection, 1987.

Since many sayings are attributed to specific authorities, why not lay out the sayings in the order of the authorities to whom they are attributed, rather than in the order of the books in which these sayings occur, which forms the documentary method for the description of the matrix of texts in context? It is because the attributions cannot be validated, but the books can. What we cannot show we do not know. We cannot show that a sage really said what is assigned to him; we can show that a document reached closure at a given time and among a given set of framers or authorship. So the first of the two principles by which I describe the matrix that defines the context in which texts are framed is that we compose histories of ideas of the Judaism of the Dual Torah in accord with the sequence of documents that, in the aggregate, constitute the corpus and canon of the Judaism of the Dual Torah. And those histories set forth dimensions of the matrix in which that Judaism, through its writings, is to be situated for broader purposes of interpretation. Documents reveal the system and structure of their authorships, and, in the case of religious writing, out of a document without named authors we may compose an account of the authorship's religion: a way of life, a worldview, a social entity meant to realize both. Read one by one, documents reveal the interiority of intellect of an authorship, and that inner-facing quality of mind inheres even when an authorship imagines it speaks outward, toward and about the world beyond. Even when set side by side, moreover, documents illuminate the minds of intersecting authorships, nothing more.

In historical study, we gain access to no knowledge *a priori*. All facts derive from sources correctly situated, for example, classified, comprehensively and completely described, dispassionately analyzed, and evaluated. Nothing can be taken for granted. What we cannot show, we do not know. These simple dogmas of all historical learning derive not from this writer but go back to the very beginnings of Western

---

Editor: *Judaisms and Their Messiahs in the Beginning of Christianity* (New York, 1987: Cambridge University Press). [Edited with William Scott Green and Ernest S. Frerichs.]

Judaism in the Matrix of Christianity (Philadelphia, 1986: Fortress Press. British edition, Edinburgh, 1988, T. & T. Collins).

Judaism and Christianity in the Age of Constantine. Issues of the Initial Confrontation (Chicago, 1987: University of Chicago Press).

Judaism and its Social Metaphors. Israel in the History of Jewish Thought (New York, 1988: Cambridge University Press).

The Incarnation of God: The Character of Divinity in Formative Judaism (Philadelphia, 1988: Fortress Press).

Edited: *The Christian and Judaic Invention of History* (Atlanta, 1989: Scholars Press for American Academy of Religion). Studies in Religion Series.

critical historical scholarship, to the age of the Renaissance. But all historical and religious-historical scholarship on the documents of the Judaism of the Dual Torah in its formative age, except for mine and for that of a very few others, ignores the canons of criticism that govern academic scholarship. Everyone in the past and many even now take for granted that pretty much everything they read is true – except what they decide is not true.

They cannot and do not raise the question of whether an authorship knows what it is talking about, and they do not address the issue of the purpose of a text: historical or imaginative, for example. For them the issue always is history, namely, what really happened, and that issue was settled, so to speak, at Sinai: it is all true (except, on an episodic basis, what is not true, which the scholars somehow know instinctively). They exhibit the credulity characteristic of the believers, which in the circle of piety is called faith, and rightly so, but in the center of academic learning is mere gullibility. The fundamentalists in the talmudic academies and rabbinical seminaries and Israeli universities take not only as fact but at face value everything in the holy books. "Judaism" is special and need not undergo description, analysis, and interpretation in accord with a shared and public canon of rules of criticism. "We all know" how to do the work, and "we" do not have to explain to "outsiders" either what the work is or why it is important. It is a self-evidently important enterprise in the rehearsal of information. Knowing these things the way "we" know them explains the value of knowing these things.

Scholarship formed on the premise that the sources' stories are to be believed at face value does not merely affirm the inerrancy of attributions. That scholarship, rather, frames questions that implicitly affirm the accuracy of the holy books, asking questions, for example, that can only be answered in the assumption that the inerrant Scriptures contain the answers – therefore, as a matter of process, do not err. By extension holy books that tell stories produce history through the paraphrasing of stories into historical language: this is what happened, this is how it happened, and here are the reasons why it happened. If the Talmud says someone said something, he really said it, then and there. That premise moreover dictates their scholarly program, for it permits these faithful scholars to describe, analyze, and interpret events or ideas held in the time in which that person lived. Some of these would deny the charge, and all of them would surely point, in their writing, to evidence of a critical approach. But the premise remains the old gullibility. Specifically, the questions they frame to begin with rest on the assumption that the sources respond. The assumption that, if a story refers to a second century rabbi, then the story tells us about the second century, proves routine. And that complete reliance merely on the allegations of sayings and stories constitutes perfect faith in the facticity of fairy tales.

The operative question facing anyone who proposes to translate writing into religion – that is, accounts of "Judaism," as George F. Moore claims to give, or "The Sages," that Ephraim E. Urbach imagines he has made, is the historical one: How do you know exactly what was said and done, that is, the history that you claim to report about what happened long ago? Specifically, how do you know he really said it? And if you do not know that he really said it, how can you ask the questions that you ask, which has as its premise the claim that you can say what happened or did not happen?

The wrong, but commonplace, method is to assume that if a given document ascribes an opinion to a named authority the opinion actually was stated in that language by that sage. On this assumption a much richer history of an idea, not merely of the literary evidences of that idea, may be worked out without regard only to the date of the document at hand. Within this theory of evidence, we have the history of what individuals thought on a common topic. I have already set forth the reason that we cannot proceed to outline the sequence of ideas solely on the basis of the sequence of the sages to whom ideas are attributed. We simply cannot demonstrate that a given authority really said what a document assigns to him. Let me list the range of uncertainty that necessitates this fresh approach, which I have invented.

First, if the order of the documents were fully sound and the contents representative of rabbinical opinion, then the result would be a history of the advent of the idea at hand and the development and articulation of that idea in formative Judaism. We should then have a fairly reliable picture of ideas at hand as these unfolded in orderly sequence. But we do not know that the canonical history corresponds to the actual history of ideas. Furthermore, we cannot even be sure that the order of documents presently assumed in scholarly convention is correct. Second, if a rabbi really spoke the words attributed to him, then a given idea would have reached expression within Judaism *prior* to the redaction of the document. Dividing things up by documents will tend to give a later date and thus a different context for interpretation to opinions held earlier than we can presently demonstrate. Third, although we are focusing upon the literature produced by a particular group, again we have no clear notion of what people were thinking outside of that group. We therefore do not know how opinions held by other groups or by the Jewish people in general came to shape the vision of rabbis. When, for example, we note that there also existed poetic literature and translations of Scriptures characteristic of the synagogue worship, we cannot determine whether the poetry and most translations spoke for rabbis or for some quite different group.

For these reasons I have chosen to address the contextual question within the narrow limits of the canon. That accounts for my formulation of the episteme as "the canonical history of ideas," and explains, also, why I have carefully avoided claiming that a given idea was broadly held only at a given time and place. All I allege is that a given document underscores the presence of an idea *for that authorship* – that alone. That yields a simple exercise in maintaining that a given idea or set of ideas came prior, because it is well attested in a document that reached closure earlier on, and another idea or set of ideas came later, because it is well attested, for the first time, in a document that came to conclusion later on. Obviously, if I could in a given formulation relate the appearance of a given idea to events affecting rabbis in particular or to the life of Israel in general, the results would be exceedingly suggestive. But since we do not know for whom the documents speak, how broadly representative they are, or even how comprehensive is their evidence about rabbis' views, we must carefully define what we do and do not know. So for this early stage in research the context in which a given idea is described, analyzed, and interpreted is the canon. But this first step alone carries us to new territory. I hope that in due course others will move beyond the limits which, at the moment, seem to me to mark the farthest possible advance. Now let us turn to the specific case meant to illustrate the method.

The documentary history of ideas therefore is a mode of relating writing to religion through history through close attention to the circumstance in which writing reached closure. It is accomplished, specifically, by assessing shifts exhibited by a sequence of documents and appealing to the generally accepted dates assigned to writings in explaining those shifts. In this way I propose to confront questions of cultural order, social system and political structure, to which the texts respond explicitly and constantly. Confronting writings of a religious character, we err by asking questions of a narrowly historical character: what did X really say on a particular occasion, and why? These questions not only are not answerable on the basis of the evidence in hand. They also are trivial, irrelevant to the character of the evidence. What strikes me as I review the writings just now cited is how little of real interest and worth we should know, even if we were to concede the historical accuracy and veracity of all the many allegations of the scholars we have surveyed. How little we should know – but how much we should have *missed* if that set of questions and answers were to encompass the whole of our inquiry.

If we are to trace the unfolding, in the sources of formative Judaism, of a given theme or ideas on a given problem, the order in which we approach the several books, that is, components of the entire canon, gives us the sole guidance on sequence, order, and context, that we are apt to find. As is clear, we have no way of demonstrating that authorities to whom, in a given composition, ideas are attributed really said what is assigned to them. The sole fact in hand therefore is that the framers of a given document included in their compilation sayings imputed to named authorities. Are these dependable? Unlikely on the face of it. Why not? Since the same sayings will be imputed to diverse authorities by different groups of editors, of different books, we stand on shaky ground indeed if we rely for chronology upon the framers' claims of who said what. More important, attributions by themselves cannot be shown to be reliable. And, it goes without saying, assuming without corroboration that we have *ipssissima verba* merely because a saying is attached to a name simply contradicts the basic premises of all contemporary historical scholarship.

Since what we cannot show we do not know, we have for chronology only a single fact. It is that a document, reaching closure at a given time, contains the allegation that Rabbi X said statement Y. So we know that people at the time the document reached closure took the view that Rabbi X said statement Y. We may then assign to statement Y a position, in the order of the sequence of sayings, defined by the location of the document in the order of the sequence of documents. The several documents' dates, as is clear, all constitute guesses. But the sequence explained in the prologue, Mishnah, Tosefta, Yerushalmi, Bavli for the exegetical writings on the Mishnah is absolutely firm and beyond doubt. The sequence for the exegetical collections on Scripture Sifra, the Sifrés, Genesis Rabbah, Leviticus Rabbah, the Pesiqtas and beyond is not entirely sure. Still the position of the Sifra and the two Sifrés at the head, followed by Genesis Rabbah, then Leviticus Rabbah, then Pesiqta deRab Kahana and Lamentations Rabbati and some related collections, seems likely.

What are the canonical main beams that sustain the history of ideas as I propose to trace that history? Three principal periods presently delineate the canonical sequence, the Mishnah's, in the first two centuries; the Yerushalmi's, in the next, ca. 200-400; and the Bavli's, in the third, ca. 400-600. The formative age of Judaism is the period marked at the outset by the Mishnah, taking shape from sometime before the Common Era and reaching closure at ca. 200 C.E., and at the end by the Talmud of Babylonia, ca. 600 C.E. In between these dates, two streams of writings developed, one legal, explaining the meaning of the Mishnah, the other theological and exegetical, interpreting the sense of Scripture. The high points of the former come with tractate Abot which is the Mishnah's first apologetic, the Tosefta, a collection of supplements ca. 300 C.E., the Talmud of the Land of Israel ca. 400 C.E., followed by the Babylonian Talmud. The latter set of writings comprise compositions on Exodus, in Mekhilta Attributed to R. Ishmael and of indeterminate date, Sifra on Leviticus, Sifré on Numbers, and another Sifré, on Deuteronomy at a guess to be dated at ca. 300 C.E., then Genesis Rabbah ca. 400 C.E., Leviticus Rabbah ca. 425 C.E., and at the end, Pesiqta deRab Kahana, Lamentations Rabbati, and some other treatments of biblical books, all of them in the fifth or sixth centuries. The so-called Tannaitic Midrashim, Mekhilta, Sifra, the two Sifrés, form transitional documents, between the Mishnah and the Yerushalmi and its Midrash companions, Genesis Rabbah, Leviticus Rabbah, and Pesiqta deRab Kahana. Alongside the Bavli are its Midrash associates, Lamentations Rabbah, Song of Songs Rabbah, Esther Rabbah I, and Ruth Rabbah. These books and some minor related items together form the canon of Judaism as it had reached its definitive shape by the end of late antiquity.

If we lay out these writings in the approximate sequence in which – according to the prevailing consensus – they reached closure beginning with the Mishnah, the Tosefta, then Sifra and its associated compositions, followed by the Talmud of the Land of Israel, and alongside Genesis Rabbah and Leviticus Rabbah, then Pesiqta deRab Kahana and its companions, and finally the Talmud of Babylonia, we gain what I call "canonical history." This is, specifically, the order of the appearance of ideas when the documents, read in the outlined sequence, address a given idea or topic. The consequent history consists of the sequence in which a given statement on the topic at hand was made (early, middle, or late) in the unfolding of the canonical writings. To illustrate the process, what does the authorship of the Mishnah have to say on the theme? Then how does the compositor of Abot deal with it? Then the Tosefta's compositor's record comes into view, followed by the materials assembled in the Talmud of the Land of Israel, alongside those now found in the earlier and middle ranges of compilations of scriptural exegeses, and as always, the Talmud of Babylonia at the end. In the illustrative exercise that follows we shall read the sources in exactly the order outlined here. I produce a picture of how these sources treat an important principle of the Judaism of the Dual Torah. We shall see important shifts and changes in the unfolding of ideas on the symbol under study.

So, in sum, this story of continuity and change rests upon the notion that we can present the history of the treatment of a topical program in the canonical writings of that Judaism. I do not claim that the documents represent the state of popular or synagogue opinion. I do not know whether the history of the idea in the unfolding official texts corresponds to the history of the idea among the people who stand behind those documents. Even less do I claim to speak about the history of the topic or idea at hand outside of rabbinical circles, among the Jewish nation at large. All these larger dimensions of the matter lie wholly beyond the perspective of this book. The reason is that the evidence at hand is of a particular sort and hence permits us to investigate one category of questions and not another. The category is denied by established and universally held conventions about the order in which the canonical writings reached completion. Therefore we trace the way in which matters emerge in the sequence of writings followed here.

We trace the way in which ideas were taken up and spelled out in these successive stages in the formation of the canon. Let the purpose of the exercise be emphasized. *When we follow this procedure, we discover how, within the formation of the rabbinical canon of writings, the idea at hand came to literary expression and how it was then shaped to serve the larger purposes of the nascent canonical system as a whole.* By knowing the place and uses of the topic under study within the literary evidences of the rabbinical system, we gain a better understanding of the formative history of that system. What do we not learn? Neither the condition of the people at large nor the full range and power of the rabbinical thinkers' imagination comes to the fore. About other larger historical and intellectual matters we have no direct knowledge at all. Consequently we claim to report only what we learn about the canonical literature of a system evidenced by a limited factual base. No one who wants to know the history of a given idea in all the diverse Judaisms of late antiquity, or the role of that idea in the history of all the Jews in all parts of the world in the first seven centuries of the Common Era will find it here.

In order to understand the documentary method we must again underline the social and political character of the documentary evidence presented. These are public statements, preserved and handed on because people have adopted them as authoritative. The sources constitute a collective, and therefore official, literature. All of the documents took shape and attained a place in the canon of the rabbinical movement as a whole. None was written by an individual in such a way as to testify to personal choice or decision. Accordingly, we cannot provide an account of the theory of a given individual at a particular time and place. We have numerous references to what a given individual said about the topic at hand. But these references do not reach us in the authorship of that person, or even in his language. They come to us only in the setting of a *collection* of sayings and statements, some associated with names, others unattributed and anonymous. The collections by definition were composed under the auspices of rabbinical authority – a school or a circle. They tell us what a group of people wished to preserve and hand on as authoritative doctrine about the meaning of the Mishnah and Scripture. The compositions reach us because the larger rabbinical estate chose to copy and hand them on. Accordingly, we know the state of doctrine at the stages marked by the formation and closure of the several documents.

We follow what references we find to a topic in accord with the order of documents just now spelled out. In this study we learn the order in which ideas came to expression in the canon. We begin any survey with the Mishnah, the starting point of the canon. We proceed systematically to work our way through tractate Abot, the Mishnah's first apologetic, then the Tosefta, the Yerushalmi, and the Bavli at the end. In a single encompassing sweep, we finally deal with the entirety of the compilations of the exegeses of Scripture, arranged, to be sure, in that order that I have now explained. Let me expand on the matter of my heavy emphasis on the order of the components of the canon. The reason for that stress is simple. We have to ask not only what documents viewed whole and all at once ("Judaism") tell us about our theme. In tracing the order in which ideas make their appearance, we ask about the components in sequence ("history of Judaism") so far as we can trace the sequence. Then and only then shall we have access to issues of *history*, that is, of change and development. If our theme makes its appearance early on in one form, so one set of ideas predominate in a document that reached closure in the beginnings of the canon and then that theme drops out of public discourse or undergoes radical revision in writings in later stages of the canon, that fact may make considerable difference. Specifically, we may find it possible to speculate on where, and why a given approach proved urgent, and also on the reasons that that same approach receded from the center of interest.

In knowing the approximate sequence of documents and therefore the ideas in them (at least so far as the final point at which those ideas reached formal expression in the canon), a second possibility emerges. What if – as is the case – we find pretty much the same views, treated in the same proportion and for the same purpose, yielding the same message, early, middle, and late in the development of the canon? Then we shall have to ask why the literature remains so remarkably constant. Given the considerable shifts in the social and political condition of Israel in the Land of Israel as well as in Babylonia over a period of more than four hundred years, that evident stability in the teachings for the affective life will constitute a considerable fact for analysis and interpretation. History, including the history of religion, done rightly thus produces two possibilities, both of them demanding sustained attention. Things change. Why? Things do not change. Why not? We may well trace the relationship between the history of ideas and the history of the society that holds those same ideas. We follow the interplay between society and system – worldview, way of life, addressed to a particular social group – by developing a theory of the relationship between contents and context, between the world in which people live and the world which people create in their shared social and imaginative life. When we can frame a theory of how a system in substance relates to its setting, of the interplay between the social matrix and the mode and manner of a society's worldview and way of life, then we may develop theses of general intelligibility, theories of why this, not that, of why, and why not and how come.

The story of continuity and change rests upon the notion that we can present the history of the treatment of a topical program in the canonical writings of that Judaism. I do not claim that the documents represent the state of popular or synagogue opinion. I do not know whether the history of the idea in the unfolding official texts corresponds to the history of the idea among the people who stand behind those documents. Even less do I claim to speak about the history of the topic or idea at hand outside of rabbinical circles, among the Jewish nation at large. All these larger dimensions of the matter lie wholly beyond the perspective of this book. The reason is that the evidence at hand is of a particular sort and hence permits us to investigate one category of questions and not another. The category is defined by established and universally held conventions about the order in which the canonical writings reached completion. Therefore we trace the way in which matters emerge in the sequence of writings followed here. We trace the way in which ideas were taken up and spelled out in these successive stages in the formation of the canon. When we follow this procedure, we discover how, within the formation of the rabbinical canon of writings, the idea at hand came to literary expression and how it was then shaped to serve the larger purposes of the nascent canonical system as a whole.

2

Holy Writing: The Social Setting

Sociology in the ordinary sense – the study of society, through the data of society – of course does not define our work when, as scholars in the study of religion, we propose to define a set of questions concerning the social context of sacred texts.[1] For sociologists derive their data from actions and social interactions, which are public and bear an impact on the here and now, while, by definition, we study what people have thought up and written down, very private things indeed. And these data on which we work to begin with are not social interactions but intellectual exercises. True, they may bear upon the social order. But that is only after the fact. Accordingly, our colleagues in sociology will find somewhat odd our conception that we do sociology on texts, their texts being not in writing but in society. But colleagues in the history of ideas and literature will grasp precisely our intent. One of them, the brilliant American scholar of American literature and history, H. Jackson Wilson, with admirable precision states the task before us:

> There can be no serious history of ideas that is not also the history of the social experience of the people who have them. Apart from that experience, where their meaning is grounded, ideas may have a chronology, but not a history.[2]

Writing not on the history of formative Judaism in the first century but on the life of William Lloyd Garrison, the American abolitionist, in

---

[1] This paper was the keynote address for the International Conference on the Sociology of Sacred Texts, July 1, 1991, University of Newcastle-upon-Tyne, England.
[2] R. Jackson Wilson, *Figures of Speech. American Writers and the Literary Marketplace, from Benjamin Franklin to Emily Dickinson* (New York, 1989: Knopf), p. 122, writing about William Lloyd Garrison.

the nineteenth century, Wilson expresses the exact program that I have defined: the study of Judaisms in the context of the social world of those Jews who through those Judaisms answered the questions they found urgent: ideas in the social context of the people who have them. Setting forth self-evidently valid answers to those ineluctable questions in the worldview, way of life, and theory of themselves as the social entity, Israel, producing books deemed canonical or art regarded as fully representative, those Jews set forth their various Judaisms. So, I maintain, all meaning is grounded in those the social world of those Judaisms; apart from the compelling and urgent question raised by their encounter with the politics and society of their place and time, the canonical writings do not yield even the chronology of ideas, rather, mere dogmatic theology, and scholarship within that context provides a scarcely intelligible paraphrase of that theology.

One must immediately ask how the inquiry into the social relevance of texts and the ideas that they set forth in writing differs from the established interest in the history, including social history, that is yielded by texts. It is the fact that for more than a century, from the mid-1850s onward, in the study of the classical texts of Judaism, those composed in the first six centuries A.D., historians have read the documents and proposed to describe in historical, social context ideas that had formerly been assigned no context at all.[3] In the theology of Judaism everything true and authoritative had of course been represented as equally part of the "Torah." But doctrines now were to be re-formed into the history of ideas. The work done to date has been perhaps acceptable theology (for secularists who wanted to believe something or at least affirm that the texts were special) but bad history. It was bad history because the premises were those of credulity and gullibility concerning the allegations, as to facts, of the sources at hand. But it was good theology, of a sort. For like the received theology, this kind of "social history of ideas" treated as essentially seamless all of the various writings, whenever they reached closure.

The reason that a century of historical work on the social relevance of the sacred texts of Judaism is worthless is simple. In these studies,

---

[3]Among many results, influential in their day, that exemplify the results is Louis Finkelstein, *The Pharisees. The Sociological Background of Their Faith* (Philadelphia, 1946: Jewish Publication Society of America) I-II, and his *Aqiba, Scholar, Saint, and Martyr,* of a decade earlier, which, amazingly, has just now been reprinted (Northvale, New Jersey, 1990: Jason Aronson, Inc.) without even an introduction on the state of the question in the more than half-century since the publication of that book. Finkelstein and others of the 1930s and 1940s portrayed the Pharisees as New Deal Democrats.

Holy Writing: The Social Setting

which treated the boundaries between and among holy books as null and insisted everything was part of the same "Torah," historical differentiation would be undertaken by reference to attributions to named sages of large numbers of sayings. If a saying is attributed to an authority, without regard to date of the document containing the saying, then that person really said what is assigned to him; if stories were told, they really happened on that day, in that way.[4] On the basis of that received conviction, imputing inerrancy to the attributions (as well as to the storytellers) just as had many generations of the faithful, but asking questions of context and development that were supposed to add up to history, the great figures of the first three quarters of the twentieth century set forth their accounts of what they conceived to be Judaism in historical context, hence, the history of Judaism. The received consensus on the history of Judaism, formed in the nineteenth and first half of the twentieth centuries, concurred on this program: believe it all, but ask a different sort of question. If we could demonstrate that the attributions were valid, and that even though a document reached closure in the fifth or sixth century, what it assigned to an authority in the first century really was said in that century and by that authority, then this kind of history of ideas would bear plausible results. But what we cannot show we do not know, and the work done until very recently loses all plausibility by reason of its

---

[4]The shift from historical classification by attributions of sayings, without regard to the documentary origin of sayings, to historical classification by documents, is a considerable change in the study of the history of Judaism in its formative age. For overall, scholars have tended simply to take at face value attributions of sayings to particular authorities and then to interpret what is said as evidence of the time and place in which the cited authorities flourished. When studying topics in the Judaism of the sages of the rabbinic writings from the first through the seventh centuries, colleagues in times past have routinely cited sayings categorized by attribution rather than by document. That is to say, they treat as one group of sayings whatever is assigned to Rabbi X. This is without regard to the time of redaction of the documents in which those sayings occur or to similar considerations of literary context and documentary circumstance. The category defined by attributions to a given authority furthermore rests on the premise that the things given in the name of Rabbi X really were said by him. No other premise would justify resort to the category deriving from use of a name, that alone. Commonly, the next step is to treat those sayings as evidence of ideas held, if not by that particular person, then by people in the age in which the cited authority lived. Once more the premise that the sayings go back to the age of the authority to whom they are attributed underpins inquiry. Accordingly, scholars cite sayings in the name of given authorities and take for granted that those sayings were said by the authority to whom they were attributed and, of course, in the time in which that authority flourished.

pervasive gullibility. That is why a different kind of historical study had to be worked out, one that accorded with the critical program of the academy in the West, rather than the theological program of rabbinical seminaries.

But, as is often the case, just as our power signals our pathos, so in this instance our pathos points to our power. We cannot find out whether sages really said or did what people (later on, we know not whom) said they said and did. But the books themselves turn out to stand for collectivities – social units, and that by definition. The pathos is that we do not know who wrote the books, the power is that we do know that, on their own, the holy books represent social statements, meaning, statements not only upon the social order but by a social group that wishes to speak together and all at once.

For the problem of finding out who said what, where, and when, is complicated by the fact that the generality of religious writing, and all of the holy books of the Judaism that took shape in the first six centuries A.D., are public documents, bearing no marks of individual authorship, either explicit or (all the more so) inherent. While – to take the example of the Gospels and the writings of Paul – some of the letters attributed to Paul can be shown to have been written by him, the Gospels, it is generally held, were public documents, representative of not personal opinion but a consensus of the faithful. That is why, for example, we have learned to speak of "the school of Matthew." Then such public documents by definition provide insight into not the mentality of the person(s) who made them up but of the community that valued, preserved, and believed the documents. In writings that stand for a collectivity, not an author but an authorship, we deal with what Brian Stock felicitously labeled, "a textual community." It is writing that is, as to authorship, anonymous – and therefore authoritative; writing that is, as to sponsorship, communal – therefore socially pertinent. The beginning of our work lies in the recognition of the social sources of authorship in anonymous writing that enjoys collective sponsorship. There we hear the voice of a community, a community that speaks through the text – and only there, that is, a community of which, as a matter of fact, we have no knowledge beyond the pages of the text. The very anonymity of our documents confers upon them the status of a social statement: but in behalf of whom, and to what society?

What makes the anonymous and collective writings of Judaism subject to differentiation and analysis? It is, first of all, that authorships or editors of documents impose their judgment upon how whatever occurs in their writing should be set forth. Therefore, documentary formulations play a role in the representation of compositions, so that the compositors' formulation of matters takes a critical place in the making of the documentary evidence – and that, as a matter of fact, in this context represents a public and a social statement, not an individual and idiosyncratic one. If all work in the history of the formative age of the Judaism of the Dual Torah that treats documentary lines as null, and attributions as invariably valid, must now be dismissed as a mere curiosity, then a different kind of work can produce another sort of insight altogether, one that transforms holy books into statements upon the social order by a social group, at the very minimum, and that by definition, a textual community.

Those of us who, in studying about religion through sacred texts, deal with collective and anonymous writings rely upon one fact that, at the moment, comes to us from outside of our field, namely, the dating of these anonymous writings. Though we do not know who wrote a given document, critical literary scholarship may often tell us when that document reached closure. That place and that time then form the sole given of our work.

For example, if the Pentateuch, as we are told, reached closure in the time of Ezra, ca. 450 B.C., then we read the document as a statement about important concerns of people who lived at that time, rather than, for instance, a statement of what interested Moses and God many centuries earlier. Our work on the social setting and meaning of sacred texts then has to bear with it the stipulation: if that is the correct historical context, then this is what I think the text means in social context. In light of what (we think) we know about that time, we proceed to identify the generative problems, the urgent and critical questions, that informed the intellect of an authorship and framed the social world that nurtured that same authorship. Then we have always to stipulate, if that is not the time and circumstance of the writing, everything else we propose will be awry and wrong. But all our work is, if not speculative in an arid, academic sense, then, at least, stipulative.

Stipulating, then, that the conventionally assigned dates of closure to all of the anonymous writings of the Judaism of the Dual Torah provide us with an order in which the writings were composed and completed and a date, accurate within about a century, for those writings, I have developed my method of the documentary study of Judaism, I treat the historical sequence of sayings only in accord with the order of the documents in which they first occur. Since many sayings are attributed to specific authorities, why not lay out the sayings in the order of the authorities to whom they are attributed, rather than in the order of the books in which these sayings occur, which forms the documentary method for the description of the matrix of texts in context? It is because the attributions cannot be validated, but the books can. We cannot show that a sage really said what is assigned to him; but one can show that a document reached closure at a given time and among a given set of framers or authorship. So the first of the two principles by which I describe the matrix that defines the context in which texts are framed is that we compose histories of ideas of the Judaism of the Dual Torah in accord with the sequence of documents that, in the aggregate, constitute the corpus and canon of the Judaism of the Dual Torah. And those histories set forth dimensions of the matrix in which that Judaism, through its writings, is to be situated for broader purposes of interpretation. Documents reveal the system and structure of their authorships, and, in the case of religious writing, out of a document without named authors we may compose an account of the authorship's religion: a way of life, a worldview, a social entity meant to realize both. Read one by one, documents reveal the interiority of intellect of an authorship, and that inner-facing quality of mind inheres even when an authorship imagines it speaks outward, toward and about the world beyond. Even when set side by side, moreover, documents illuminate the minds of intersecting authorships, nothing more. All I allege is that a given document underscores the presence of an idea *for that authorship* – that alone.

The documentary history of ideas, therefore, is a mode of relating writing to the social world of religion through close attention to the circumstance in which writing reached closure. It is accomplished, specifically, by assessing shifts exhibited by a sequence of documents and appealing to the generally accepted dates assigned to writings in explaining those shifts. In this way I propose to confront questions of cultural order, social system, and political structure, to which the texts on which I work, as a matter of fact, respond explicitly and constantly. This story of continuity and change rests upon the notion that we can present the history of the treatment of a topical program in the canonical writings of that Judaism. I do not claim that the documents represent the state of popular or synagogue opinion. I do not know whether the history of the idea in the unfolding official texts corresponds to the history of the idea among the people who stand behind those documents. Even less do I claim to speak about the history of the topic or idea at hand outside of rabbinical circles, among the Jewish nation at large. All these larger dimensions of the matter lie wholly beyond the perspective of this book. The reason is that the evidence at hand is of a particular sort and, hence, permits us to investigate one category of questions and not another. The category is denied by established and universally held conventions about the order in which the canonical writings reached completion. Therefore, we

Holy Writing: The Social Setting 21

trace the way in which matters emerge in the sequence of writings followed here.

We trace the way in which ideas were taken up and spelled out in these successive stages in the formation of the canon. Let the purpose of the exercise be emphasized. *When we follow this procedure, we discover how, within the formation of the rabbinical canon of writings, the idea at hand came to literary expression and how it was then shaped to serve the larger purposes of the nascent canonical system as a whole.* By knowing the place and uses of the topic under study within the literary evidences of the rabbinical system, we gain a better understanding of the formative history of that system. What do we not learn? Neither the condition of the people at large nor the full range and power of the rabbinical thinkers' imagination comes to the fore. About other larger historical and intellectual matters we have no direct knowledge at all. Consequently, we claim to report only what we learn about the canonical literature of a system evidenced by a limited factual base. No one who wants to know the history of a given idea in all the diverse Judaisms of late antiquity, or the role of that idea in the history of all the Jews in all parts of the world in the first seven centuries of the Common Era, will find it here.

And yet – and yet in so stating, have I met Wilson's challenge or composed a mere catalogue of this and that, a different kind of paraphrase from the familiar one, but paraphrase nonetheless? To respond, I must again underline the social and political character of the documentary evidence presented. These are public statements, preserved and handed on because people have adopted them as authoritative. The sources constitute a collective, and therefore official, literature. All of the documents took shape and attained a place in the canon of the rabbinical movement as a whole. None was written by an individual in such a way as to testify to personal choice or decision. Accordingly, we cannot provide an account of the theory of a given individual at a particular time and place. We have numerous references to what a given individual said about the topic at hand. But these references do not reach us in the authorship of that person, or even in his language. They come to us only in the setting of a *collection* of sayings and statements, some associated with names, others unattributed and anonymous. The collections by definition were composed under the auspices of rabbinical authority – a school or a circle. They tell us what a group of people wished to preserve and hand on as authoritative doctrine about the meaning of the Mishnah and Scripture. The compositions reach us because the larger rabbinical estate chose to copy and hand them on. Accordingly, we know the state of doctrine at the stages marked by the formation and closure of the several documents.

We follow what references we find to a topic in accord with the order of documents just now spelled out. In this study we learn the order in which ideas came to expression in the canon. We begin any survey with the Mishnah, the starting point of the canon. We proceed systematically to work our way through tractate Abot, the Mishnah's first apologetic, then the Tosefta, the Yerushalmi, and the Bavli at the end. In a single encompassing sweep, we finally deal with the entirety of the compilations of the exegeses of Scripture, arranged, to be sure, in that order that I have now explained. In tracing the documentary order in which ideas make their appearance, we ask about the components in sequence ("history of Judaism") so far as we can trace the sequence. Then and only then shall we have access to issues of *history*, that is, of change and development. If our theme makes its appearance early on in one form, so one set of ideas predominate in a document that reached closure in the beginnings of the canon and then that theme drops out of public discourse or undergoes radical revision in writings in later stages of the canon, that fact may make considerable difference. Specifically, we may find it possible to speculate on where and why a given approach proved urgent and also on the reasons that that same approach receded from the center of interest.

In knowing the approximate sequence of documents and, therefore, the ideas in them (at least so far as the final point at which those ideas reached formal expression in the canon), a second possibility emerges. What if – as is the case – we find pretty much the same views, treated in the same proportion and for the same purpose, yielding the same message, early, middle, and late in the development of the canon? Then we shall have to ask why the literature remains so remarkably constant. Given the considerable shifts in the social and political condition of Israel in the Land of Israel as well as in Babylonia over a period of more than four hundred years, that evident stability in the teachings for the affective life will constitute a considerable fact for analysis and interpretation. History, including the history of religion, done rightly thus produces two possibilities, both of them demanding sustained attention. Things change. Why? Things do not change. Why not? We may well trace the relationship between the history of ideas and the history of the society that holds those same ideas. We follow the interplay between society and system – worldview, way of life, addressed to a particular social group – by developing a theory of the relationship between contents and context, between the world in which people live and the world which people create in their shared social and imaginative life. When we can frame a theory of how a system in substance relates to its setting, of the interplay between the social matrix and the mode and manner of a society's worldview and way of life, then we may develop theses of general intelligibility, theories of why this, not that, of why and why not, and how come.

The story of continuity and change rests upon the notion that we can present the history of the treatment of a topical program in the canonical writings of that Judaism. I do not claim that the documents represent the state of popular or synagogue opinion. I do not know whether the history of the idea in the unfolding official texts corresponds to the history of the idea among the people who stand behind those documents. Even less do I claim to speak about the history of the topic or idea at hand outside of rabbinical circles, among the Jewish nation at large. All these larger dimensions of the matter lie wholly beyond the perspective of this book. The reason is that the evidence at hand is of a particular sort and, hence, permits us to investigate one category of questions and not another. The category is defined by established and universally held conventions about the order in which the canonical writings reached completion. Therefore, we trace the way in which matters emerge in the sequence of writings followed here. We trace the way in which ideas were taken up and spelled out in these successive stages in the formation of the canon. When we follow this procedure, we discover how, within the formation of the rabbinical canon of writings, the idea at hand came to literary expression and how it was then shaped to serve the larger purposes of the nascent canonical system as a whole.

If, then, I maintain that the documents make statements upon the human condition, how am I to move from the writing to the social world imagined by the social group responsible for the writing? By what stages, specifically, do I propose to uncover the social foundations of religious texts? It is a systematic program, which I can describe, since a fair amount of the work has already been done. What I do in this reading of the canonical literature of Judaism is divided into three stages.

AUTONOMY: My work proceeds in a systematic way, document by document. I begin in the differentiation of documents by carefully describing the indicative traits of each. First, I place a document on display in its own terms, examining the text in particular and in its full particularity and immediacy. Here I describe the text from three perspectives: rhetoric, logic, and topic (the received program of literary criticism in the age at hand). Reading documents one by one represents a new approach in this field, although it is commonplace in all other humanistic fields. Ordinarily, in studying ancient Judaism people have composed studies by citing sayings attributed to diverse authorities without regard to the place in which these sayings occur. They have assumed that the sayings really were said by those to whom they are attributed, and, in consequence, the generative category is not the document but the named authority. But if we do not assume that the documentary lines are irrelevant and that the attributions are everywhere to be taken at face value, then the point of origin – the document – defines the categorical imperative, the starting point of all study.

CONNECTION: Second, I seek to move from the text to that larger context suggested by the traits of rhetoric, logic, and topic shared between one document and some other. Here I compare one text to others of its class and ask how these recurrent points of emphasis, those critical issues and generative tensions, draw attention from the limits of the text to the social world that the text's authorship proposed to address. Here, too, the notion that a document exhibits traits particular to itself is new with my work, although, overall, some have episodically noted traits of rhetoric distinctive to a given document, and, on the surface, differences as to topic – observed but not explained – have been noted. Hence, the movement from text to context and how it is effected represents a fresh initiative on my part.

CONTINUITY: Finally, so far as I can, I want to find my way outward toward the matrix in which a variety of texts find their place. In this third stage I want to move from the world of intellectuals to the world they proposed to shape and create. That inquiry defines as its generative question how the social world formed by the texts as a whole proposes to define and respond to a powerful and urgent question, that is, I read the canonical writings as response to critical and urgent questions. Relating documents to their larger political settings is not a commonplace, and, moreover, doing so in detail – with attention to the traits of logic, rhetoric, and topic – is still less familiar.

These three categories correspond, in general terms, to the study of the canonical writings as literature, religion, and theology. Read autonomously, they exhibit indicative traits. Interpreted as points of entry into the mentality of the authors, these indicators guide us toward the religious worldview of the authors. Seen as continuous with other writings of the canon, the whole then requires reading in the framework of a coherent theological discourse.

What is the relevance for the study of the interplay of religion and society through writing that I promised to describe? The answer lies in my study of the religious system that I discern in, and through, the writings, severally and jointly. This brings us to the systemic approach,[5] which, in this area, I have invented.[6] Spelling it out is not difficult. Writings such as those of the Judaic canon have been selected by the framers of a religious system, and, read all together, those writings are deemed to make a cogent and important statement of that system, hence the category, "canonical writings." I call that encompassing, canonical picture a "system," when it is composed of three necessary components: an account of a worldview, a prescription of a corresponding way of life, and a definition of the social entity that finds definition in the one and description in the other. When those three fundamental components fit together, they sustain one another in explaining the whole of a social order, hence constituting the theoretical account of a system. This is the point at which we recall my initial insistence upon seeing religion as people solving problems together. A religious system answers an urgent question with truth deemed self-evidently valid by members of the social entity that lives in accord with the way of life posited by the system and sees its society in accord with the worldview of the system and interprets its collective existence within the systemic framework as well: "'we' are 'Israel.'"

To generalize from Judaism to religions: religions form social worlds and do so through the power of their rational thought, that is, their capacity to explain data in a (to an authorship) self-evidently valid way.[7] The framers of religious documents answer urgent questions,

---

[5]See, for instance, my *First Principles of Systemic Analysis. The Case of Judaism in the History of Religion* (Lanham, 1988: University Press of America). *Studies in Judaism* Series.

[6]I, of course, do not claim to have invented the conception of religion as a cultural system, and at appropriate points in my career have devoted sustained attention to current work on that conception, e.g., in the work of Clifford Geertz and Mary Douglas. As to the former, see my *A History of the Jews in Babylonia* (Leiden, 1968: Brill). III. *A History of the Jews in Babylonia. From Shapur I to Shapur II*, where in the preface I point to Geertz as the key to a religious reading of the data on that subject; as to the latter, see my *The Idea of Purity in Ancient Judaism. The Haskell Lectures, 1972-1973* (Leiden, 1973: E. J. Brill), for which Mary Douglas kindly wrote a critique, published there.

[7]I recognize that in moving beyond specific texts into the larger worldview they join to present, I may be thought to cross the border from the humanistic study of classical texts to the anthropological reading of those same texts. I therefore emphasize that I take most seriously the particularity and specificity of each document, its program, its aesthetics, its logic. I do not propose to commit upon a classic writing an act of reductionism, reading a work of humanistic meaning merely as a sociological artifact. And, further, as between Weber and his critics, I take my place with Weber in maintaining that ideas constitute, in their context and circumstance, what sociologists call independent variables, not only responding to issues of society, but framing and giving definition to those larger issues. In this way I make a stand, in the systemic reading of the

framed in society and politics to be sure, in a manner deemed self-evidently valid by those addressed by the authorships at hand. For at stake in this *oeuvre* is a striking example of how people explain to themselves who they are as a social entity. Religion as a powerful force in human society and culture is realized in society, not only or mainly theology; religion works through the social entity that embodies that religion. Religions form social entities – "churches" or "peoples" or "holy nations" or monasteries or communities – that, in the concrete, constitute the "us," as against "the nations" or merely "them."[8] And religions carefully explain, in deeds and in words, who that "us" is – and they do it every day. To see religion in this way is to take religion seriously as a way of realizing, in classic documents, a large conception of the world. But how do we describe, analyze, and interpret a religion, and how do we relate the contents of a religion to its context? These issues of method are worked out through the reading of texts, and, I underline, through taking seriously and in their own terms the particularity and specificity of texts. This I accomplish by special reference to problems in studying Judaism in particular.

Now that I have focused upon the central role of specific documents, let me explain the movement from text to context and matrix that is signalled by use of the word "system." For reading a text in its context and as a statement of a larger matrix of meaning, I propose to ask larger questions of systemic description of a religious system represented by the particular text and its encompassing canon. Colleagues who work on issues of religion and society will find familiar the program I am trying to work out.[9] But, I underline, the success of that program is measured by its power to make the texts into documents of general intelligibility for the humanities, to read the text at hand in such a way as to understand its statement within, and of, the human condition. That seems to me not only the opposite of reductionism but also a profoundly rationalist mode of inquiry.

---

classic writings of Judaism in its formative age, with those who insist upon the ultimate rationality of discourse.
[8]In the case of a Judaism, this will be expressed in the theory of the social entity, "Israel": what it is, who it is. See my *Judaism and its Social Metaphors. Israel in the History of Jewish Thought* (New York, 1988: Cambridge University Press).
[9]*Religious Writings and Religious Systems. Systemic Analysis of Holy Books in Christianity, Islam, Buddhism, Greco-Roman Religions, Ancient Israel, and Judaism* (Atlanta, 1989: Scholars Press for Brown Studies in Religion). Volume I. *Islam, Buddhism, Greco-Roman Religions, Ancient Israel, and Judaism.* Volume II. *Christianity.* [Edited with Ernest S. Frerichs and A. J. Levine.]

Systems begin in the social entity, whether one or two persons or two hundred or ten thousand – there and not in their canonical writings, which come only afterward, or even in their politics. The social group, however formed, frames the system; the system then defines its canon within, and addresses the larger setting, the *polis*, without. We describe systems from their end products, the writings. But we have then to work our way back from canon to system, not to imagine either that the canon is the system, or that the canon creates the system. The canonical writings speak, in particular, to those who can hear, that is, to the members of the community, who, on account of that perspicacity of hearing, constitute the social entity or systemic community. The community then comprises that social group the system of which is recapitulated by the selected canon. The group's exegesis of the canon in terms of the everyday imparts to the system the power to sustain the community in a reciprocal and self-nourishing process. The community through its exegesis then imposes continuity and unity on whatever is in its canon.

While, therefore, we cannot account for the origin of a successful religious-social system, we can explain its power to persist. It is a symbolic transaction, as I said just now, in which social change comes to expression in symbol-change. That symbolic transaction, specifically, takes place in its exegesis of the systemic canon, which, in literary terms, constitutes the social entity's statement of itself. So, once more, the texts recapitulate the system. The system does not recapitulate the texts. The system comes before the texts and defines the canon. The exegesis of the canon then forms that ongoing social action that sustains the whole. A system does not recapitulate its texts, it selects and orders them. A religious system imputes to them as a whole cogency, one to the next, that their original authorships have not expressed in and through the parts, and through them a religious system expresses its deepest logic, *and it also frames that just fit that joins system to circumstance.*

The whole works its way out through exegesis, and the history of any religious system – that is to say, the history of religion writ small – is the exegesis of its exegesis. And the first rule of the exegesis of systems is the simplest, and the one with which I conclude: *the system does not recapitulate the canon. The canon recapitulates the system.* The system forms a statement of a social entity, specifying its world view and way of life in such a way that, to the participants in the system, the whole makes sound sense, beyond argument. So in the beginning are not words of inner and intrinsic affinity, but (as Philo would want us to say) the Word: the transitive logic, the system, all together, all at once, complete, whole, finished – the word awaiting only that labor of exposition and articulation that the faithful, for centuries to come, will lavish at the altar of the faith. A religious system, therefore, presents a fact not of history but of immediacy, of the social present.

The issue of why a system originates and survives, if it does, or fails, if it does, by itself proves impertinent to the analysis of a system but of course necessary to our interpretation of it. A system on its own is like a language. A language forms an example of language if it produces communication through rules of syntax and verbal arrangement. That paradigm serves full well however many people speak the language or however long the language serves. Two people who understand each other form a language community, even, or especially, if no one understands them. So, too, by definition religions address the living, constitute societies, frame and compose cultures. For however long, at whatever moment in historic time, a religious system always grows up in the perpetual present, an artifact of its day, whether today or a long-ago time. The only appropriate tense for a religious system is the present. A religious system always *is*, whatever it was, whatever it will be. Why so? Because its traits address a condition of humanity in society, a circumstance of an hour – however brief or protracted the hour and the circumstance.

When we ask that a religious composition speak to a society with a message of the *is* and the *ought* and with a meaning for the everyday, we focus on the power of that system to hold the whole together: the society the system addresses, the individuals who compose the society, the ordinary lives they lead, in ascending order of consequence. And that system then forms a whole and well-composed structure. Yes, the structure stands somewhere, and, yes, the place where it stands will secure for the system either an extended or an ephemeral span of life. But the system, for however long it lasts, serves. And that focus on the eternal present justifies my interest in analyzing why a system works (the urgent agenda of issues it successfully solves for those for whom it solves those problems) when it does, and why it ceases to work (loses self-evidence, is bereft of its "Israel," for example) when it no longer works. The phrase, the *history* of a *system*, presents us with an oxymoron. Systems endure – and their classic texts with them – in that eternal present that they create. They evoke precedent, they do not have a history. A system relates to context, but, as I have stressed, exists in an enduring moment (which, to be sure, changes all the time). We capture the system in a moment, the worm consumes it an hour later. That is the way of mortality, whether for us one by one, in all mortality, or for the works of humanity in society. But systemic analysis and interpretation requires us to ask questions of history and comparison, not merely description of structure and cogency. So in this exercise we undertake first description, that is, the text, then analysis, that is, the context, and finally, interpretation, that is, the matrix, in which a system has its being.

It follows that I am trying to find out how to describe a Judaism in a manner consonant with the historical character of the evidence, therefore in the synchronic context of society and politics, and not solely or mainly in the diachronic context of theology which, until now, has defined matters. The inherited descriptions of the Judaism of the Dual Torah (or merely "Judaism") have treated as uniform the whole corpus of writing called "the Oral Torah." The time and place of the authorship of a document played no role in our use of the allegations, as to fact, of the writers of that document. All documents have ordinarily been treated as part of a single coherent whole, so that anything we find in any writing held to be canonical might be cited as evidence of views on a given doctrinal, legal, or ethical topic. "Judaism" then was described by applying to all of the canonical writings the categories found imperative, for example, beliefs about God, life after death, revelation, and the like. So far as historical circumstance played a role in that description, it was assumed that everything in any document applied pretty much to all cases, and historical facts derived from sayings and stories pretty much as the former were cited and the latter told.

This brings me back, at the end, to the intellectual bankruptcy of historical method, succeeded by the one I have outlined here. It is time to say quite simply that much that the inherited agenda of learning has produced is trivial, merely antiquarian, not much worth knowing. The so-called critical historical method rarely led historians to ask what is at stake in their inquiries and, consequently, celebrate self-validating knowledge ("for its own sake"). I should want my contribution assessed by the weight of the questions I have formulated: in the case I make, the arguments I amass, and the evidence I adduce, are the stakes trivial or high? So if I had to specify a single charge against the received scholarly tradition, it would not be intellectual incompetence, on the one side, or mere gullibility, on the other, but rather something much simpler: triviality. If they all are right in everything they say, so what? And my answer: so nothing.

I offer in place a history of a Judaism in its historical and social setting. I am not alone in undertaking the social study of Judaisms – the way in which a Judaism sets forth its conception of the social order. Many now recognize that systems of thought concerning the social order work out a cogent picture, self-evidently true for those who make them up, of *how* things are correctly to be sorted out and fitted together, of *why* things are done in one way, rather than in some other, and of *who* they are that do and understand matters in this particular way. These systems of thought then are composed of three elements: ethics, ethos, and ethnos, that is, worldview, way of life, and an account of the social entity at hand. Such systems need not fall into the category of religion or invariably be held to form religions, and it is the fact that not all religions set forth accounts of the social order. But when, as has often been the case, people invoke God as the foundation for their worldview, maintaining that their way of life corresponds to what God wants of them, projecting their social entity in a particular relationship to God, then we have a system that is, as a matter of fact. And when, finally, a religious system appeals as an important part of its authoritative literature or canon to the Hebrew Scriptures of ancient Israel or "Old Testament," we have a Judaism.[10]

In the renewal of the academic engagement with the study of religion, we find our purpose for the study of formative Judaism. When we ask that a religious composition such as the Mishnah or a Midrash compilation or one of the Talmuds speak to a society with a message of the *is* and the *ought* and with a meaning for the everyday, we focus on the power of that system to hold the whole together: the society the system addresses, the individuals who compose the society, the ordinary lives they lead, in ascending order of consequence. And that system then forms a whole and well-composed structure. I conceive this project of the social study of the formation of Judaism to form a chapter in the study of the rise of Western civilization. Just as Max Weber understood the issue, why has the West defined the world, so I want to explain in what ways Judaism has formed a Western religion, and in what ways it has not. Just as Weber asked questions of comparison and contrast in finding out what is particular and what common, so I want to find points of commonality and difference in the study of Judaisms. The given of my inquiry is that religion is what social science calls an independent variable, that is to say, a factor that explains other things but is not explained by other things. Religion I see as the single

---

[10]*Judaism in the Matrix of Christianity* (Philadelphia, 1986: Fortress Press. British edition, Edinburgh, 1988: T. & T. Collins); *Judaism and Christianity in the Age of Constantine. Issues of the Initial Confrontation* (Chicago, 1987: University of Chicago Press); *Death and Birth of Judaism. The Impact of Christianity, Secularism, and the Holocaust on Jewish Faith* (New York, 1987: Basic Books); and *Self-Fulfilling Prophecy: Exile and Return in the History of Judaism* (Boston, 1987: Beacon Press) altogether form a complete "field theory" of the history of Judaism within the theory of the systemic approach to the study of a religion, in this case, of Judaisms. Not one of these books was reviewed in any journal of Judaic studies.

most powerful force in the making of human civilization: it is why we are what we are, for good or ill. When I describe, analyze, and interpret the evidence of Judaisms in late antiquity, therefore, I work my way into the formative power in the life of Israel, the Jewish people, and I furthermore aim at setting forth the Judaic part of the world-defining power of Western civilization, which is the creation of Judaism, Christianity, and Islam.

Why do I conceive this work to demand continuators in the twenty-first century? The reason is simple. At issue in academic debate in the next half century will be the place of the West in the world. Since, as a matter of fact, everywhere in the world, people aspire to those material advantages that flow, uniquely I think, from the modes of social organization that the West has devised – the West's economics, its science and technology, and also – let us say it straight out – its politics and also its philosophy as modes of thought and inquiry, I think it is time to stop apologizing and start analyzing what has made Western civilization the world-defining power that it has become. When Weber asked why no capitalism in India, China, or Judaism, he opened, in that exemplary manner, a much broader set of questions. When, nowadays, people rightly want to find a place, in the study of civilization that the academy sustains, for Africa, Asia, peoples indigenous to every region and land, we all need to frame a global program of thought and reflection. And if we are not merely to rehearse the facts of this one and that one, we shall require modes of comparison and in particular the comparative study of rationalities.

Hence sustaining questions, applying to all areas because of their ubiquitous relevance, why this, not that?, have to come to definition. And since the simple fact of world civilization is that the West has now defined the world's economy, politics, and philosophy, and since all social systems measure themselves by Western civilization in its capacity to afford to large masses of people both the goods of material wealth and the services of political power, the indicative traits of the West demand close study. These are, I think, in politics, mass distribution of power in political structures and systems, in economics, capitalism, and in philosophy, the modes of thought and inquiry we call scientific. That explains why I have now undertaken to revise the entire program of the study of the Jews and Judaism. And, it is self-evident, what I mean to do is provide a model for others to follow in the study of all other social entities and their social systems. So the stakes in this scholarly program of mine are as high as I can make them.

3

Holy Writing:
The Intellectual Setting.
Analogical-Contrastive Thinking and the Problem of Dialectical Thought
Or:
When Is a List a Series?

Entire chapters of the Bavli work in detail on accumulating evidence in behalf of a single, unarticulated but always stipulated, proposition.[1] The Babylonian Talmud's exposition of Mishnah-tractate Zebahim 5:1-2 in a systematic and amazingly orderly way sets forth principles of comparison and contrast within the discipline of dialectical thinking. As we follow the chapter, we shall see how beneath the surface – but not very far – the issue of the dialectics of analogical-contrastive thought, that is, the question facing us is the logic of a series. Then I shall spell out in detail the context in which the metapropositional statement before us is made and show what is remarkable and fresh in the thought of the Bavli's framers. As we shall see, they are trying to show the logic, and limits, of a series, or, as I shall explain, if A=B and B=C, then does A=C, and, if so, why? Let us first consider the documentary evidence in my form-analytical translation, then turn to investigate the metapropositional inquiry

---

[1] References to "Freedman" in this article allude to *Hebrew-English Edition of the Babylonian Talmud. The Babylonian Talmud. Zebahim.* Translated into English with notes, glossary, and indices by H. Freedman. *Under the editorship of* Rabbi Dr. I. Epstein (London, 1989: The Soncino Press). While the translation is my own, I refer line by line to Freedman's excellent presentation.

that I claim is before us. I indent material that occupies a subordinate position in the exposition at hand; in a contemporary re-presentation, what is indented would be a footnote or an appendix; such secondary and supplementary material forms only a tiny proportion of the whole.[2]

Mishnah-tractate Zebahim 5:1

A. What is the place [in which the act of sacrifice] of animal-offerings [takes place]?
B. Most Holy Things [the whole-offering, sin-offering, and guilt-offering] – the act of slaughtering them is carried out at the north [side of the altar].
C. The bullock and the he-goat of the Day of Atonement – the act slaughtering them is at the north.
D. And the receiving of their blood is carried out in a utensil of service, at the north [side of the altar].
E. And their blood requires sprinkling over the space between the bars [of the ark], and on the veil, and on the golden altar.
F. One act of placing of their [blood] [if improperly done] impairs [atonement].
G. And the remnants of the blood did one pour out at the western base of the outer altar.
H. [But] if he did not place [the remnants of their blood at the stated location], he did not impair [atonement].

5:2

A. Bullocks which are to be burned and he-goats which are to be burned –
B. The act of slaughtering them is at the north [side of the altar].
C. And the receiving of their blood is in a utensil of service at the north.
D. And their blood requires sprinkling on the veil and on the golden altar.
E. [47B] [The improper sprinkling of] one act of placing of their [blood] impairs [atonement].
F The remnants of their blood did one pour out on the western base of the outer altar.
G. If he did not place [the remnants of the blood at the stated location], he did not impair [atonement].
H. These and those are burned in the ash pit.

I.1 A. *But why should the Tannaite author of the passage not state in the opening clause [A-B] as he does later on [Cff.]:* **And the**

---

[2]I explain this matter at some length in my *The Rules of Composition of the Talmud of Babylonia. The Cogency of the Bavli's Composite* (Atlanta, 1991: Scholars Press for South Florida Studies in the History of Judaism).

Analogical-Contrastive Thinking and the Problem of Dialectical Thought 35

        receiving of their blood is carried out in a utensil of service, at the north [side of the altar]!

B. *Since there is the matter of the guilt-offering presented by the person healed of the skin ailment [which is classified also as Most Holy Things], the blood of which is received in the hand [not in a utensil of service], he leaves out that item.*

C. *But is the blood not received in a utensil of service? And lo, it is taught later on,* The peace-offerings of the congregation and the guilt-offerings – What are the guilt-offerings? (1) The guilt-offering for false dealing, and (2) the guilt-offering for acts of sacrilege, and (3) the guilt-offering [because of intercourse with] a betrothed bondwoman, and (4) the guilt-offering of a Nazir, and the (5) guilt-offering of the person healed of the skin ailment, and (6) the suspensive guilt-offering – the act of slaughtering them is at the north [side of the altar]. And the receiving of their blood is with a utensil of service at the north [M. 5:5]!

D. *To begin with he took the position that the receiving of the blood was to be done by hand. So he omitted reference to the item here [just as has been explained]. But when he realized that the collection of the blood cannot be done unless a utensil is used, he included it later on. For it has been taught on Tannaite authority:*

E. "And the priest shall take of the blood of the guilt-offering" – might one think that this is done with a utensil?

F. Scripture states, "and the priest shall put it" (Lev. 14:14) – just as the putting on of the blood is to be done by the priest's hand itself, so the taking of the blood also should be done by the priest's hand itself.

G. Might one suppose that that is the same for the altar [so that blood to be sprinkled on the altar is received not in a utensil but in the hand]?

H. Scripture states, "For as the sin-offering so is the guilt-offering" (Lev. 14:13) – just as the sin-offering requires a utensil for receiving the blood, so the guilt-offering requires a utensil for receiving the blood.

I. You must then draw the conclusion that two priests received the blood of the guilt-offering of the one healed of the skin ailment, one in his hand, the other in a utensil. The one who received the blood in a utensil went to the altar and put the blood there, and the one who received it in his hand went to the person who had been healed of the skin ailment and put it on the specified parts of his body.

II.1 A. [48A] Bullocks which are to be burned and he-goats which are to be burned – the act of slaughtering them is carried out at the north side of the altar. And the receiving of their blood is in a utensil of service at the north. And their blood requires sprinkling on the veil and on the golden altar:

    B. *Now take note that the requirement that the rite be carried out at the north side of the altar is written in regard to the burnt-offering,*

>   so let the framer of the passage formulate the rule by making reference first of all to the burnt-offering.
>
> C. [The reason that he treats the sin-offering first is that] since the rule covering the sin-offering derives from exegesis of Scripture [rather than being stated explicitly therein], it is regarded by him as of greater value.
>
> D. But then let him present the rules governing the sin-offerings that are offered on the outer altar!
>
> E. Since the blood of those listed first is taken into the inner sanctum, it is regarded by him as of greater value.

We open with two entirely conventional questions, namely, analysis of the formulation of the Mishnah's rule, within the premise that the wording in all of its patterns yields meaning. The solution of the initial problem, in appeal to a verse of Scripture, provides only a routine demonstration of the metaproposition that Scripture forms the court of final appeal. The second entry follows suit. Now begins the chapters great, sustained project.

> II.2 A. Where in Scripture is reference made to the rule governing the burnt-offering?
>
> B. "And he shall kill it on the side of the altar at the north" (Lev. 1:11).
>
> C. So we have found the explicit rule that treats a beast deriving from the flock. How do we know that the same rule governs what comes of the herd?
>
> D. Scripture states, "And if his offering be of the flock," and the word "and" continues the preceding statement, with the result that the subject that is prior may be deduced from the one given following. [Freedman: When a passage commences with 'and' the conjunction links it with the previous portion, and a law stated in one applies to the other, too. Here the subject above is the burnt-offering of the herd and the subject below is the flock.]
>
> E. That answer is satisfactory for him who takes the view that one may indeed derive a rule governing a prior subject from one that is given later on, but from the perspective of him who denies that fact, what is to be said?

The question before us is startling. In the prior chapter, and in the materials just now examined, no one has told us that there are rules of exegesis, which provide sign posts on the road from Scripture to the Mishnah, or from Scripture to the law. Now we encounter the first of the chapter's sustained and systematic discussions of rules of reading Scripture.

> F. For it has been taught on Tannaite authority:
>
> G. "'And if any one [commits a breach of faith and sins unwittingly in any of the Holy Things of the Lord]' (Lev. 5:15) – this ["and if"] serves to impose liability for a suspensive guilt-offering in the

case of an act of sacrilege that is subject to doubt," the words of R. Aqiba.
H. And sages declare him exempt.
I. *May not one say that this is what is subject to dispute: R. Aqiba takes the view that we derive the rule for a prior matter from one that is mentioned later on, and rabbis maintain that we do not derive the rule governing a prior matter from a matter that is mentioned later on.* [The prior matter is the one regarding sacrilege, the one that follows deals with the suspensive guilt-offering, so Lev. 5:17: If any one sins, doing any of the things that the Lord has commanded not to be done, though he does not know it, yet he is guilty and shall bear his iniquity." Aqiba then derives the rule governing the case of an act of sacrilege that is subject to doubt from the rule governing unwitting sins that are subject to doubt, and consequently requires a suspensive guilt-offering, and that explains his position: **R. Aqiba declares [a person] liable to a suspensive guilt-offering in the case of a matter of doubt regarding acts of sacrilege.** Sages do not read the rule of the latter passage into the definition of the former.]
J. Said R. Pappa, *"All parties concur that we derive the rule for a prior topic from one that comes later on,* [B. Ker. 22B adds:] *for otherwise we should have no basis for the law that the bullock has to be slaughtered on the north side of the altar* [for that rule derives from the fact that while the rule on the bullock-offerings, Lev. 1:3-4, comes prior to the rule on offering small cattle, Lev. 1:10f., and only the latter requires the slaughter to take place on the north side of the altar, we do indeed slaughter the bullock-offerings on the north side of the altar as well]. *But this is the reason for the position of rabbis, who declare one exempt [from having to present a suspensive guilt-offering in the case of a matter of doubt regarding acts of sacrilege]: they derive a verbal analogy to a sin-offering based on the appearance of the word 'commandments' with reference to both matters.* There [at Lev. 4:27, with reference to a sin-offering] there is an offense for which one is liable to extirpation in the case of a deliberate violation of the law, and to a sin-offering in the case of an inadvertent violation of the law, and to a suspensive guilt-offering in the case of doubt. So in every case, for which one is liable to extirpation in the case of a deliberate violation of the law, and to a sin-offering in the case of an inadvertent violation of the law, and to a suspensive guilt-offering in the case of doubt, the same rule applies; *but this excludes sacrilege, for in that case,* a deliberate violation of the law does not bring on the penalty of extirpation." [B. Ker. 22B adds: *For it has been taught on Tannaite authority*, He who deliberately committed an act of sacrilege – Rabbi says, "He is subject to the death penalty." And sages say, "He is subject to an admonition."]
K. And how about the position of R. Aqiba?
L. *He maintains that when we draw a verbal analogy between the reference here to "commandments" and the reference to*

"commandments" with regard to the sin-offering [thus yielding the position outlined at E], it serves for the eating of prohibited fat and accomplishes the following purpose: Just as in that matter, reference is made to a sacrifice of fixed value, so all of the sacrifices must be of fixed value, *thus excluding sacrifices of variable value [such as those listed at Lev. 5:1-13], for example, a sin-offering brought on account of imparting uncleanness to the sanctuary and its Holy Things, which is expiated by an offering of variable value.*

M. *And rabbis?*

N. They take the view that one may not derive from an argument by analogy established through the use of a word in common only a limited repertoire of conclusions [but once the analogy is drawn, then all of the traits of one case apply to the other].

Now we find something that captures our attention, which is evidence of a sustained and systematic inquiry. First we have introduced our guideline on moving from Scripture to law. Then, second and by consequence, we have introduced a refinement on the guide line. At stake is the limits of analogy: is something like something else in one way analogous in all other ways, so that every rule pertaining to the one thing applies also to the other? Or is an analogy limited, determinate only for itself? That seems to me a question of sufficient abstraction to impress the thinkers behind the propositions we gained in Chapter One of this same tractate, since it has to do with, not the rules of argument or guidelines in an exegetical venture, but the rules of thought and guidelines on right reason. Once people think in a deep system of analogy and contrast, the issue before us becomes urgent and unavoidable.

O. *Then does it follow that* R. Aqiba holds that one may derive from an argument by analogy established through the use of a word in common only a limited repertoire of conclusions? [Not at all.] *All parties concur that* one may not derive from an argument by analogy established through the use of a word in common only a limited repertoire of conclusions [but once the analogy is drawn, then all of the traits of one case apply to the other].

P. *And this is the operative consideration for the position of R. Aqiba:* Scripture has said, "And if any one," with the result that the use of the "if" serves to complement the matter that is treated first and to impose upon that matter a rule that is presented only later on. [Thus: "'And if any one [commits a breach of faith and sins unwittingly in any of the Holy Things of the Lord]' (Lev. 5:15) – this 'and if' serves to impose liability for a suspensive guilt-offering in the case of an act of sacrilege that is subject to doubt," the words of R. Aqiba.]

Q. *Now surely rabbis have to take account of the fact that* Scripture has said, "And if any one," [with the result that the use of the "if"

Analogical-Contrastive Thinking and the Problem of Dialectical Thought 39

R.   serves to complement the matter that is treated first and to impose upon that matter a rule that is presented only later on].
R.   *May one propose that it is in the following point that they differ:*
S.   *One authority maintains that proof supplied by analogy [here: the analogy sustained by the use of "and" to join the two subjects] takes priority, and the other party maintains that the proof supplied by the demonstration of a totality of congruence among salient traits takes precedence. Rabbis prefer the latter, Aqiba the former position.]*
T.   *Not at all! All parties concur that proof supplied by analogy [here: the analogy sustained by the use of "and" to join the two subjects] takes priority. But rabbis in this context will say to you that the rule governing the subject treated below derives from the rule governing the subject treated above, so that the guilt-offering must be worth at least two silver sheqels. This is established so that you should not argue that the doubt cannot be more stringent than the matter of certainty, and just as where there is certainty of having committed a sin, one has to present a sin-offering that may be worth even so little as a sixth of a zuz in value, so if there is a matter of doubt, the guilt-offering worth only a sixth of a zuz would suffice.*

What I said a moment ago pertains here as well. The same issue is now restated and refined. Do we have to show that things that are alike are alike in all respects, or is it sufficient to show likeness in only salient, therefore indicative and determinative, ones?

U.   *And how does R. Aqiba derive that same theory?*
V.   *He derives it from the verse, "And this is the Torah of the guilt-offering" (Lev. 7:1), meaning, there is a single Torah that covers all guilt-offerings.*
W.   *You may then leave off considering the issue from the view of him who maintains that "Torah" is to be interpreted in that way, but on the view of him who maintains that "Torah" is not to be interpreted in that way, what is to be said?*
X.   *Such a one derives the matter from the use of "according to your valuation" at Lev. 5:15 and Lev. 5:18 [and that yields a verbal analogy based on congruence of shared traits].*
Y.   *That poses no problems in the context in which "according to your valuation" occurs, but what about the guilt-offering that is presented in the case of the violation of a maidservant who has been promised in marriage (Lev. 19:20-22), in which no reference is made to "according to your valuation"?*
Z.   *There we find the repetition of "with the lamb" (Lev. 5:16 and 19:22) [which yields the same rule on the minimum value of the beast offered for this purpose].*

It suffices at this point to observe that this rather long and complex inquiry is cogent, and the cogency is both on the surface and underneath. The sustained sequence of moving questions and answers ("dialectic"), with a question's answer raising its own question, carries the surface discourse from point to point, beginning to end. But at the deep structure is also a program of inquiry, exemplified at the surface, and the inquiry concerns principles of the reading of Scripture, which can obviously serve for the reading of any other writing to which the standing and stylistic power of Scripture are imputed, within a logic of comparison and contrast. What we want to know in the subtext (if that is the right term for the here-articulated program exemplified by the text) is that logic: if we find similarity, what conclusions do we draw from that similarity?

III.1 A. [Supply: **Most Holy Things (...sin-offering...) – the act of slaughtering them is carried out at the north side of the altar:**]
B. *How on the basis of Scripture do we know that the sin-offering has to be prepared at the north side of the altar?*
C. *As it is written, "And he shall kill the sin-offering in the place of the burnt-offering" (Lev. 4:24).*
D. *So we have found that the act of slaughter must take place in the designated place, but how on the basis of Scripture do we know that the same rule applies to the act of receiving the blood?*
E. *As it is written, "And the priest shall take of the blood of the sin-offering" (Lev. 4:25). ["...take" means to receive the blood, and the "and" joins this to the immediately preceding verse (Freedman)].*
F. *What about the rule governing the location of the priest himself who receives the blood? How on the basis of Scripture do we know that rule?*
G. *Said Scripture, "And he shall take to himself" [in the place where the blood is received, that is, at the north of the altar].*
H. *So we have found the manner in which the religious duty is optimally carried out. But how do we know that these rules are absolutely indispensable to the rite [so that if they are not observed, the offering is ruined]?*
I. *A further verse of Scripture states, "And he shall kill it for a sin-offering in the place where they kill the burnt-offering" (Lev. 4:33), and it has been taught on Tannaite authority:*
J. *Where is the burnt-offering slaughtered? It is in the north. This too [the sin-offering] also is slaughtered in the north.*
K. *[48B] Now is it from this verse that the rule is to be derived? Is it not in point of fact stated, "In the place where the burnt-offering is killed shall the sin-offering be killed" (Lev. 6:18) [referring to all sin-offerings]? So why is this [sin-offering presented by a ruler] singled out? It is to establish the place in which it is to be killed, so to prove that if one did not slaughter it in the north, it is invalid [and that repetition teaches the rule just now stated, yielding the fact that keeping these rules is indispensable to the valid performance of the rite].*

Analogical-Contrastive Thinking and the Problem of Dialectical Thought 41

L. You maintain that that is the reason that the matter has been singled out. But perhaps it is not the case, but rather to indicate that this offering alone [the ruler's sin-offering] is the only one that requires the north, but no other sin-offering has to be killed at the north side of the altar? Therefore Scripture states, "And he shall kill the sin-offering in the place of the burnt-offering," so stating an encompassing rule in regard to all sin-offerings: all have to be slaughtered in the north.

M. *So we have found the rule governing the sin-offering presented by the ruler: It is both described as properly carried out in this way and also prescribed as indispensably carried out in this way. And we also know that other sin-offerings are properly carried out in this way. But how do we know that it is necessary to carry out other sin-offerings in this way [so that if they are not slaughtered at the north, they are invalid]?*

N. Because the same requirement is specified in Scripture in regard to both the lamb (Lev. 4:33) and the she-goat (Lev. 4:29).

Here is a model of the familiar inquiry into the linkage between Scripture and the law presented in the Mishnah. What we now are beginning to perceive is that our entire chapter is going to tell us the answer to the one question: What is the scriptural basis for the rule before us? Why the subject matter of this chapter of the Mishnah persuades the framers of the Talmud to the chapter of the Mishnah that the issue of scriptural sources of the law in the Mishnah is a compelling and dominant theme is clear: the question can be asked, because, on this subject, Scripture is prolix and abundant, rich in rules, prolix in their formulation. Consequently, where the question can be asked, it is asked; our authors would have had a very difficult time pursuing the same question in connection with, for example, writs of divorce, where a couple of verses of Scripture pertain, all the more so the many Mishnah tractates to which no verses of Scripture allude at all. It is because the subject matter of the Mishnah chapter coincides with numerous and well-articulated verses of Scripture that we are able to address what I claim to be the deeper issues throughout: not only exegesis or rules of exegesis, but rather, analogical-contrastive thinking and the rules of the logic of comparison and contrast. It is the point at which these deeper issues of thought are articulated that the Talmud moves away from the obvious program of linking law to Scripture; and that same point, moreover, concerns not rules of exegesis at all, but rules of right thinking.

III.2 A. [As to the verse, "And he shall kill *it* for a sin-offering in the place where they kill the burnt-offering" (Lev. 4:33),] what is the purpose of the word "it"?

B. *It is required in line with that which has been taught on Tannaite authority:*

C. "...it..." is slaughtered at the north side of the altar, but the goat presented by Nahshon is not slaughtered at the north side of the altar [that is, the goats brought as a sin-offering at the consecration of the altar, Num. 7:17. These are not really sin-offerings at all.]

D. *And it has been taught on Tannaite authority:*

E. "'And he shall lay his hand upon the head of the goat' (Lev. 4:24) [the goat brought by the ruler] – this encompasses the goat brought by Nahshon under the rule of the laying on of hands," the words of R. Judah.

F. R. Simeon says, "It serves to encompass under the rule of laying on of hands the goats brought on account of inadvertent idolatry."

G. *[Reverting to the question of A,] You might have supposed that since they are encompassed under the rule of laying on of hands, they also are encompassed under the rule of being slaughtered in the north. So we are informed to the contrary.*

H. *To this proposition Rabina objected, "That conclusion serves full well for R. Judah, but from R. Simeon's perspective, what is there to be said?"* [Freedman: He does not include it in respect of laying hands, so a text is not required to show that the north does not apply to it].

What follows is of special interest, because it articulates another (rather obvious) rule of analogical thinking, which is, rules can be derived not only by appeal to Scripture but also by reference to analogy not made explicit by the verbal formulations of Scripture. The main point here is that, once an analogy serves, it serves everywhere an analogy can be drawn; there is no a priori that limits the power of an analogy to govern all like cases.

I. *Said Mar Zutra b. R. Mari to Rabina, "And does that conclusion serve so well for R. Judah anyhow? Where it is included under the law, it is included under the law, where not, not [so no verse of Scripture is required]. And should you say that if Scripture had not included the matter, we should have reached the same conclusion by argument for analogy, then if that is the case, we can infer by analogy also the rule on laying on of hands. So you must answer that a temporary sacrifice [done once, as with Nahshon's] cannot derive its law by inference from a permanent one, and so here, too, a sacrifice brought only on a special occasion cannot find its rule by analogy to the rule governing a sacrifice that is permanent. [There is no reason to suppose that the sin-offering of Nahshon, which was for an occasion, had to be done at the north, and therefore why is a text needed to exclude it? So we do not know the answer to our question, As to the verse, 'And he shall kill it for a sin-offering in the place where they kill the burnt-offering' (Lev. 4:33), what is the purpose of the word 'it'?]*

J. *"Rather: 'It' is slaughtered in the north, but the one who does the slaughtering does not have to stand in the north."*

Analogical-Contrastive Thinking and the Problem of Dialectical Thought   43

K. *But the law on the slaughterer derives from what R. Ahia said. For it has been taught on Tannaite authority:*

L. R. Ahia says, "'And he shall kill it on the side of the altar at the north': Why is this stated? It is because we find that the priest who receives the blood must stand in the north and also must receive the blood in the north. If he stood in the south and received the blood in the north, the offering is invalid. So you might have thought that the same rule governs slaughtering the animal. Scripture says, 'And he shall kill it,' meaning, 'it' must be in the north, while the one who does the act of slaughter need not be in the north."

M. [Reverting again to the question of A,] "it" must be killed in the north, but a bird does not have to be killed in the north [when the neck of the bird is wrung to kill it as a sacrifice]. *For it has been taught on Tannaite authority:*

N. Might one suppose that killing a bird-offering must be done in the north?

O. That conclusion, after all, stands to reason, for if killing a lamb, which does not have to be done by a priest, must be done in the north, killing a bird, which does have to be done by a priest, surely should be done in the north!

P. Accordingly, it is necessary to specify "it," to bear the meaning, "it" must be killed in the north, but a bird does not have to be killed in the north.

Q. No, what is particular to the lamb is that Scripture has required the use of a utensil in killing it [while no knife is required for a bird]!

R. Rather, [reverting again to the question of A,] "it" must be killed in the north, but a Passover-offering does not have to be slaughtered in the north. *For it has been taught on Tannaite authority:*

S. R. Eliezer b. Jacob says, "Might one suppose that slaughtering the Passover-offering must take place in the north? For it stands to reason. If Scripture required that the burnt-offering be slaughtered at the north, though it did not specify a fixed time for slaughtering the burnt-offering, surely the Passover-offering, for which Scripture prescribed a fixed time for slaughter, surely should have to be slaughtered in the north.

T. "Accordingly, it is necessary to specify 'it,' to bear the meaning, 'it' must be killed in the north, but a Passover-offering does not have to be killed in the north."

U. Not at all. The distinctive trait of the burnt-offering is that it is wholly burned up.

V. Then derive the matter from the sin-offering [which is not wholly burnt up but yields meat to the priest].

W. What is distinctive about the sin-offering is that it achieves atonement for those who are liable to the penalty of extirpation.

X. Then derive the matter from the guilt-offering.

Y. What is distinctive about the guilt-offering is that it falls into the classification of Most Holy Things, and, as a matter of fact, you cannot derive the rule from the cases of the burnt-offering, guilt-offering, or sin-offerings, for all of them are in the classification of Most Holy Things.

Z. *So, in the end, it must be as we originally said:*

AA. "It" is slaughtered in the north, but the one who does the slaughtering does not have to stand in the north."

BB. *And as to the question that you raised based on what R. Ahia said* [R. Ahia says, "'And he shall kill it on the side of the altar at the north': why is this stated? It is because we find that the priest who receives the blood must stand in the north and also must receive the blood in the north. If he stood in the south and received the blood in the north, the offering is invalid. So you might have thought that the same rule governs slaughtering the animal. Scripture says, 'And he shall kill it,' meaning, 'it' must be in the north, while the one who does the act of slaughter need not be in the north."] – *The answer is, the sense is not to exclude the slaughterer from the requirement that the rite be done in the north, but rather,* "While the one who does the slaughtering need not be in the north, the one who receives the blood must be in the north."

CC. *The receiver? But surely that is deduced from the language,* "and he shall take," *meaning,* "let him take himself to the north"!

DD. The authority at hand does not accept the sense, "and he shall take," meaning, "let him take himself to the north."

It is hardly necessary to remind ourselves that we are dealing with a sustained and continuous exposition, one that holds together from start to finish: the same question, addressed in sequence to successive statements of the same base text (the Mishnah's paragraph), and answered in a consistent way throughout.

III.3 A. *So we have found that, so far as fulfilling the religious duty, the act of slaughtering of the burnt-offering must be done in the north, and the act of receiving, so far as fulfilling the religious duty, must be done in the north. How do we know that it is indispensable that the act of slaughtering and receiving the blood be done in the north [and if not, the offering is invalid]?*

B. Said R. Adda b. Ahbah – others say, Rabbah b. Shila, "It is an argument a fortiori: If slaughtering and receiving the blood at the north form an indispensable part of the rite of offering the sin-offering, the rule of which in any event is derived from the rule governing the burnt-offering, then surely it is reasonable to suppose that these same procedures' being done in the north are indispensable in the case of the burnt-offering, from which the rules governing the sin-offering derive!"

C. But the distinctive trait of the sin-offering is that it effects atonement for those who are liable to extirpation.

D. *Said Rabina,* "[*The reason that nonetheless Adda utilizes the argument a fortiori is as follows:*] *This is what R. Adda bar Ahbah found troubling: Do we ever find the rule governing a derivative matter more stringent than the rule governing the primary matter?"* [The sin-offering here is secondary to the burnt-offering, since the requirement of offering the sacrifice at the northern side of the altar occurs primarily in connection with the burnt-offering (Freedman)].

E. Said Mar Zutra b. R. Mari to Rabina, "Do we not find such a case? [49A] Lo, there is the matter of second tithe, which itself can be redeemed, while what is purchased with money exchanged for produce in the status of second tithe cannot be redeemed. *For we have learned in the Mishnah:* [Produce] purchased with coins [in the status] of second tithe, which becomes unclean [and therefore may not be eaten as second tithe] – let it be redeemed. R. Judah says, "Let it be buried." They said to R. Judah, "If it is the case that when produce which is designated as second tithe itself becomes unclean, lo, it must be redeemed, is it not logical that produce purchased with coins in the status of second tithe which becomes unclean also should be redeemed?" He said to them, "No! If you say this in regard to [produce designated as] second tithe itself, which, if in a state of cleanness, may be redeemed when it is outside Jerusalem, can you say so as regards produce purchased with coins [in the status of second tithe which, when it is [in a state of] cleanness, may not be redeemed when outside Jerusalem?" [M. M.S. 3:10].

F. *In that case the power of the sanctification is insufficient to govern its redemption.* [Freedman: An object must possess a certain degree of sanctity before the sanctity can be transferred to something else, while the sanctity of this is too light to permit such a transfer. Hence Judah's ruling arises out of the lesser, not the greater, sanctity of what has been purchased.]

G. *And lo, there is the case of a beast declared as a substitute for a consecrated beast, for while an act of consecration does not affect a beast that is permanently blemished, an act of substitution does affect a beast that is permanently blemished!*

H. *The consecration of the beast declared as a substitute derives from the consecration of the consecrated beast itself, while the sanctification of a consecrated animal for its part derives from its originally unconsecrated status.* [Another animal already has been sanctified.]

I. *And lo, there is the case of the Passover, which itself does not require the laying on of hands, drink-offerings, and the waving of the breast and shoulder, while a beast purchased with the remainder of funds set aside for the purchase of a Passover-offering, when it is offered up on that occasion, does require the laying on of hands, drink-offerings, and the waving of the breast and shoulder.*

J. *But the animal purchased with the remainder of funds set aside for the purchase of a Passover-offering during the rest of the year is classified simply as a peace-offering* [and it is not a Passover-offering at all; it is a different sacrifice, subject to its own rules (Freedman)].

K. *If you prefer, I shall say,* Scripture has said, "the burnt-offerings," meaning, "it must be in its appointed place." [That means doing so in the northern area is essential to the rite, not merely recommended.]

IV.1 A [Supply: **Most Holy Things (...guilt-offering) – the act of slaughtering them is carried out at the north side of the altar**].

Here we go again: How on the basis of Scripture do we know the law that the Mishnah has stated without a prooftext?

B. *How on the basis of Scripture do we know that the guilt-offering has to be prepared at the north side of the altar?*
C. *As it is written,* "In the place in which they kill the burnt-offering shall they kill the guilt-offering" (Lev. 7:1).
D. *So we have found that the act of slaughter of the guilt-offering must take place at the northern side of the altar. How on the basis of Scripture do we know that the collecting of the blood also must take place there?*
E. "And the blood thereof shall be dashed" (Lev. 7:2).
F. *So the receiving of the blood must also be in the north. How about the location of the one who receives the blood?*
G. *That is indicated by the use of the <u>accusative particle et</u> [which extends the law to the one who receives the blood] in the verse,* "And the blood thereof shall be dashed" (Lev. 7:2).
H. *So we have found that that is the recommended manner of carrying out the rite. But how do we know that it is indispensable to the proper performance of the rite that matters be done in this way?*
I. *There is another verse that is written in this same connection:* "And he shall kill the he-lamb in the place where they kill the sin-offering and the burnt-offering" (Lev. 14:13) [repeating the rule in regard to another guilt-offering shows that it is indispensable to the proper carrying out of the rite].

IV.2 A *But does the cited verse really serve the stated purpose in particular? Surely it serves another purpose altogether, as has been taught on Tannaite authority:*
B. *If a matter was covered by an encompassing rule but then was singled out for some innovative purpose, you have not got the right to restore the matter to the rubric of the encompassing rule unless Scripture itself explicitly does so.*
C. *How so?*
D. "And he shall kill the lamb in the place where they kill the sin-offering and the burnt-offering, in the holy place; for the guilt-offering, like the sin-offering, belongs to the priest; it is most holy" (Lev. 14:13) –
E. *Now what need does Scripture have to state, "for the guilt-offering, like the sin-offering"?* [Freedman: For if it is to teach that it is slaughtered in the north, that follows from the first half of the verse; if it teaches that sprinkling of the blood and eating the meat follow the rules of the sin-offering, that is superfluous, since

Analogical-Contrastive Thinking and the Problem of Dialectical Thought 47

it is covered by the general regulations on guilt-offerings given at Lev. 7:1-10]. And why does Scripture state, "for the guilt-offering, like the sin-offering"?

F. The reason is that the guilt-offering presented by the person healed of the skin ailment was singled out for the innovative purpose of indicating the following:

G. In regard to the thumb of the hand, big toe of the foot, and right ear, you might have thought that the rite does not require the presentation of the blood of the offering and the parts to be burned up on the altar. Scripture therefore states, "for the guilt-offering, like the sin-offering," to show that just as the sin-offering's blood and sacrificial parts have to be presented on the altar, so the blood and sacrificial parts of the guilt-offering presented by the person healed of the skin ailment have to be presented on the altar.

H. *If [you claim that the purpose of the verse is as stated and not to teach that doing the rite at the north is indispensable, as originally proposed,] then Scripture should have stated only the rule governing the rite for the one healed from the skin ailment but not the earlier version of the rule.*

I. *Quite so — if we take the view that when something becomes the subject of a new law, it cannot then be covered by an encompassing rule that otherwise would apply,* **[49B]** *while the encompassing rule still can be derived from that special case. But if we take the view that when something becomes the subject of a new law, then it cannot be covered by an encompassing rule that otherwise would apply, and the encompassing rule also cannot be derived from that special place, then the law [Lev. 7:1-10, indicating that the guilt-offering must be killed in the north] is needed for its own purpose!*

J. Since Scripture has restored the matter to the rubric of the encompassing rule explicitly, that restoration has taken place.

K. Said Mar Zutra b. R. Mari to Rabina, "But why not say, when Scripture restored the matter to the rubric of the encompassing rule, that was solely in regard to having to present the blood and the sacrificial parts on the altar, since the priest is necessary to perform that rite. But as to slaughtering the animal, which does not have to be done by a priest, that does not have to be done at the northern side of the altar?"

L. [He said to him,] "If so, Scripture should say simply, 'for it is like the sin-offering.' Why say, 'or the guilt-offering, like the sin-offering'? It is to teach, let it be like other guilt-offerings [that must be slaughtered at the northern side of the altar]."

IV.3 A. *Why must a verbal analogy [for the burnt-offering] be drawn to both a sin-offering and also a guilt-offering?*

B. *Said Rabina, "Both are necessary. If a verbal analogy had been drawn to a sin-offering but not to a burnt-offering, I should have reached this conclusion: From what source did we derive the rule that a sin-offering is slaughtered at the north side of the altar? It is on the basis of the analogy to the burnt-offering. The consequence is that a rule that has been derived by analogy in* turn generates another rule through analogy [so to avoid such a circularity, Scripture adds the matter of the burnt-offering, to prove that that is not the case]."

C. Said Mar Zutra b. R. Mari to Rabina, "Then draw the analogy to the burnt-offering and omit reference to a verbal analogy to the sin-offering altogether!"

Now we come to one of the great moments of our chapter: the truly dialectical question, that is generated by the dialectical mode of thought. What we want to know, stated narrowly, is the limits of verbal analogy. To explain what is at issue, we have to proceed in a moving argument, hence, the issue is the dialectics of analogy. Specifically: I have two items, A and B. I claim that B is like A, therefore the rule governing A applies also to B. Now I turn forward, to C. C is not analogous to A; there are no points of congruence or (in the exegetical formulation that our authors use) verbal intersection. But C is like B. It is like B because there is an analogy by reason of verbal intersection (the same word being used in reference to C and B.) The question is, may I apply to C, by reason of the verbal intersection between C and B, the lesson that I have learned in regard to B only by reason of B's similarity by reason of congruence, not verbal intersection, to A? This is formulated (as best as I can translate the Hebrew/Aramaic) as, "Can a conclusion that is derived on the basis of a verbal analogy go and impart a lesson by reason of analogy to a third item?" This issue is going to occupy us for quite some time.

D. [He said to him,] "Then I might reach the conclusion that [elsewhere] what is derived on the basis of a verbal analogy turns around and imparts a lesson by means of a verbal analogy [and there would be nothing in the text to show the contrary (Freedman)]. And if you should say, then draw the analogy to a sin-offering, I would reply: Scripture prefers to draw the analogy to what is primary rather than to what is secondary [and the sin-offering is the primary source of the law, since that is where the requirement that the rite take place at the north is specified, and the sin-offering is derivative of the burnt-offering]. That is why the analogy is drawn to the sin-offering and also to the burnt-offering, bearing the sense that that which is derived on the basis of a verbal analogy does not in turn go and impart a lesson by means of a verbal analogy."

IV.4 A. Raba said, "[The proposition that that which is derived on the basis of a verbal analogy does not in turn go and impart a lesson by means of a verbal analogy] derives from the following proof:

B. "It is written, 'As is taken off from the ox of the sacrifice of peace-offerings' (Lev. 4:10) [namely, the sacrificial parts of the anointed priest's bullock brought for a sin-offering] – now for what purpose is this detail given? That the lobe of the liver and the two kidneys are to be burned on the altar [as is the case with those of the sin-

Analogical-Contrastive Thinking and the Problem of Dialectical Thought 49

offering], that fact is specified in the body of the verse itself. But the purpose is to intimate that the burning of the lobe of the liver and the two kidneys of the he-goats brought as sin-offerings for idolatry are to be derived by analogy from the bullock of the community brought on account of an inadvertent sin. That law is not explicitly stated in the passage on the bullock that is brought for an inadvertent sin, but is derived from the rule governing the bullock of the anointed priest. 'As is taken off' is required so that it might be treated as something written in that very passage [on the bullock of inadvertence, being superfluous in its own context], not as something derived on the basis of a verbal analogy does not in turn go and impart a lesson by means of a verbal analogy."

C. Said R. Pappa to Raba, "Then let Scripture inscribe the rule in that very passage, and not trouble to draw a verbal analogy to the bullock of the anointed priest at all."

D. "If the rule had been inscribed in its own context and not been presented by means of a verbal analogy to the bullock of the anointed priest, I might have said that that which is derived on the basis of a verbal analogy does in turn go and impart a lesson by means of a verbal analogy. And if you should object, 'Then let Scripture present the rule by analogy without making it explicit,' I could answer that Scripture prefers to make an explicit statement in the proper context rather than to present a law through a verbal analogy. Scripture therefore inscribed the matter in the passage dealing with the anointed priest and established the analogy so as to demonstrate that that which is derived on the basis of a verbal analogy does not in turn go and impart a lesson by means of a verbal analogy."

My claim that this chapter is systematic and orderly, composed with a broader program in mind and not narrowly limited to the exegesis of phrases of the Mishnah read in sequence, is now demonstrated by what is to follow. We have proven one point. It bears a consequence. We go on to the consequence. The mode of thought is dialectical not only in form, but also in substance: if A, then B. If B, then what about C? But we see that matters are not only continued, but also refined. It is one thing to have shown that if B is like A, and C, unlike A, is rendered comparable to B by a verbal analogy, then may I take the next step and draw into the framework of B and C, joined by verbal analogy and assigned a common rule by B's congruent analogy to A, also D, E, F, and G, that is, other classes of things joined to C by verbal analogy – but not necessarily the same verbal analogy that has joined C to B? That indeed is the obvious next step to be taken, and it is now taken.

IV.5 A. Now it is a fact that that which is derived on the basis of a verbal analogy does in turn go and impart a lesson by means of a verbal analogy, *demonstrated whether in the manner of Raba or in the manner of Rabina.*

B. Is it the rule, however, that *that which is derived on the basis of a verbal analogy may in turn go and impart a lesson by means of an argument on the basis of congruence?* [Freedman: Thus the law stated in A is applied to B by analogy. Can that law then be applied to C because of congruence between B and C?]

C. [Indeed it can.] *Come and take note:* R. Nathan b. Abetolomos says, "How on the basis of Scripture do we know that when there is a spreading of disease signs [of Lev. 13-14] in clothing, [if it covers the entire garment], it is ruled to be clean? The words 'baldness on the back of the head' and 'baldness on the front of the head' are stated in respect to man, and 'baldness on the back' and 'baldness on the front' are mentioned in connection with clothing. Just as is in the former case, if the baldness spread throughout the whole, the man is clean, so here, too, if the baldness spread throughout the whole, the garment is clean."

D. And in that context how do we know the rule [that that which spreads and covers the whole head is clean, since Lev. 13:12-13 refers to what is on the skin, not the head? And furthermore, the symptoms differ (Freedman)]? Because it is written, "And if the skin ailment...cover all the skin...from his head even to his feet" (Lev. 13:12) – so the head is treated as analogous to the feet. Just as if the feet have all turned white, the ailment has spread over the whole of the body, the man is clean, so here, too, when it spreads over the whole of the head and beard, he is clean. [Thus we derive the rule by a verbal analogy that the specified marks covering the whole head are clean, and then the same rule is applied to the garments by the argument resting on congruence, as stated at C (Freedman)].

E. [To the contrary,] said R. Yohanan, "Throughout the Torah we infer one rule from another that has itself been derived by inference, except for the matter of consecration, in which we do not derive a rule from another that has itself been inferred."

F. *Now if it were the fact that we did so, then let the reference to "north" not be stated in the context of the guilt-offering at all, and it could be inferred from the rule governing sin-offerings, by means of the argument based on the congruence of the language, "It is most Holy" [which is stated in the setting of the sin-offering at Lev. 7:18 and the guilt-offering at Lev. 7:1]! Does that not bear the implication that that which is derived on the basis of a verbal analogy may not in turn go and impart a lesson by means of an argument on the basis of congruence?*

G. *But perhaps the reason that we do not learn the lesson at that passage is that there is an ample refutation: the reason that the sin-offering has to be offered in the north is that it achieves atonement for those who are liable to the penalty of extirpation?*

H. *Still, in context, there is nonetheless a superfluous reference to "most Holy" [at Num. 18:9]. [Freedman: Since this is superfluous, an argument from congruence is plausible, even though the guilt-offering is dissimilar to the sin-offering; the fact that we do not do so proves that in the case of sacrifices that which is derived on the*

Analogical-Contrastive Thinking and the Problem of Dialectical Thought 51

basis of a verbal analogy may not in turn go and impart a lesson by means of an argument on the basis of congruence.]

What follows simply proceeds to the logically next question: we have now linked B to C via a verbal analogy. C stands in relationship to other classes of things, but not for the same reason that it stands in relationship to B, that is, through other than verbal analogical relationships. It forms a relationship a fortiori, for instance, with D, E, and F. If something applies to C, the lesser, it surely should apply to D, the greater. So now we want to know the permissible grounds for drawing relationships – comparisons and contrasts – of classes of things. The deeper issue of comparative-contrasting thinking is now right on the surface: what constitutes the proper basis for establishing the plausibility of comparison and contrast anyhow? We obviously do not want to compare things that do not bear comparison because they are not species of the same genus, but distinct genera. But then on what basis do we move from species to species and uncover the genera of which they form a part (if they do form a part)? Is it only verbal correspondence or intersection, as has been implicit to this point? Or are there more abstract bases for the same work of genus construction (in our language: category formation and re-formation)? This simple issue is going to keep us busy from here to nearly the end of the chapter, because there is a rich repertoire of principles that establish of discrete data classes of data and that then link one class to another. The first was, we recall, deriving a rule by analogy and then moving on to transmit the rule to classes linked by not analogy but rather verbal intersection. We proceed to the next problem, which is, whether or not a rule shown to apply to two or more classes of things linked by verbal analogy may then be applied to further classes of things that relate to the foregoing by not verbal analogy but a relationship a fortiori.

IV.6 A. That which is learned by a verbal analogy may in turn go and impart a rule by an argument a fortiori.
     B. [50A] That is in line with that which the Tannaite authority of the household of R. Ishmael set forth.

IV.7 A. Can that which is learned by verbal analogy in turn go and impart a rule by an analogy based on the congruence of other shared traits [but not verbal ones in context]? [This mode of argument depends not on verbal analogy supplied by Scripture but an analogy drawn from similarity of the traits of two subjects.]
     B. *Said R. Jeremiah, "Let Scripture omit reference to slaughtering the guilt-offering at the north of the altar, and that rule can have been inferred by appeal to an analogy based on the congruence of other shared traits [but not verbal ones in context] from the rule governing a sin-offering. [Both offerings expiate sin. So the rule governing the one will pertain to the other.]*

C. "So why has Scripture stated that law? Is it not to indicate that that which is learned by verbal analogy may not in turn go and impart a rule by an analogy based on the congruence of other shared traits [but not verbal ones in context]?"

D. But in accord with your reasoning, let the rule be inferred by an analogy based on the congruence of other shared traits [but not verbal ones in context] from the one governing a burnt-offering! [The rule is explicitly stated in that context, and the intermediate analogy based on verbal similarities is not required at all (Freedman).]

E. So why is it not inferred in that way?

F. It is because one may present the following challenge: The distinguishing trait of the burnt-offering is indeed that it is turned to ashes on the altar! [That is not the case of the guilt-offering.]

G. In reference to the sin-offering, one may also present a challenge, namely: The distinguishing trait of the sin-offering is that it expiates sins that bear the sanction of extirpation.

H. While, therefore, admittedly one cannot learn the rule on a one-to-one basis, why not derive the rule by imputing to the third classification the law governing two other classifications of sacrifice [so that Scripture can have intimated that slaughter at the north is required for two of the three classifications, and by an argument based on the congruence of other shared traits, we should derive the rule governing the third of the three]?

I. From which two of the three can the rule have been derived for the third? If Scripture had not written the rule in connection with the burnt-offering, you might have derived the rule for that classification from the one covering the sin-offering and the guilt-offering.

J. Not at all, for the distinguishing trait of these is that they effect atonement [which is not accomplished by the burnt-offering].

K. Then let Scripture not state the rule in connection with the sin-offering, and derive it from the other two.

L. Not at all, for the distinguishing trait of these is that they require male animals [which is not the case of the sin-offering, which is a female].

M. Then let Scripture not state the rule in connection with the guilt-offering, and derive it from the other two.

N. Not at all, for the distinguishing trait of these is that they may be brought as much in behalf of the community as in behalf of an individual. [A guilt-offering is presented only by an individual.]

Not surprisingly, we now move forward once more – but by taking a step backward. We have shown that we may move from a class of things joined to another through analogy based on congruence, that is, from A to B, onward to other classes of things joined to the foregoing by verbal analogy or intersection, that is, from B to C and beyond. But can we then move from C, linked to B via verbal analogy, to D, linked to C, but not to A or B, by congruence, for example, comparable and shared traits of a salient order? The issue then, is may we move forward to

Analogical-Contrastive Thinking and the Problem of Dialectical Thought 53

further classes of things by moving "backward," to a principle of linkage of classes that has served to bring us to this point, in other words, reversing the course of principles of linkage? What our framers then want to know is a very logical question: are there fixed rules that govern the order or sequence by which we move from one class of things to another, so that, if we propose to link classes of things, we can move only from A to B by one principle (comparison and contrast of salient traits), and from B to C by a necessarily consequent and always second principle (verbal intersection); then we may move (by this theory) from C to D only by verbal intersection but not by appeal to congruence. Why not? Because, after all, if C is linked to B only by verbal intersection but not by congruence, bearing no relationship to A at all, then how claim that D stands in a series begun at A, if it has neither verbal connection, nor, as a matter of fact, congruence to link it to anything in the series? Is then a series substantive, in that we ask that there be some "natural logic" holding the parts together, a "natural logic" that derives from the sequence of operative principles of comparison and contrast? Or is a series merely formal, in that if we can link D to C in one way but D to A in no ways, D still has been shown, in the course of argument but not by the reason or internal logic of the argument, to relate to A at all? This enormously engaging question dictates everything that is coming, and I do not have to repeat the point, since there is no grasping a line from here to nearly the end of the chapter if we do not understand that what our sages are trying to find out is whether a series is a series because of its external form alone or because of its internal, inherent traits as well. If I were a mathematician, I could appeal to the issue of whether the symbolic representation of, for example, spatial relations is limited by tests out there, as Euclid supposed, so that we move from data to symbol, or may there be a symbolic representation of "things" for which there is not "out there" there, as non-Euclidean geometries claim. But I am not a mathematician.

IV.8 A. Can a rule that is derived by analogy based on the congruence of other shared traits [but not verbal ones in context] turn around and teach a lesson through an analogy based on verbal analogy?

      B. *Said R. Pappa, "'This is the law of the sacrifice of peace-offerings...if he offers it for a thanksgiving-offering' (Lev. 7:11ff.): in this verse we learn the rule that funds for the purchase of an animal offered for a thanksgiving-offering may derive from money exchanged for produce in the status of second tithe, since we find, in point of fact, that peace-offerings themselves [into the class of which the cited verse assimilates thanksgiving-offerings] may be purchased from money exchanged for produce in the status of second tithe."*

		On Method in Religion and Society

C. *And how do we know, as a matter of fact, that peace-offerings themselves [into the class of which the cited verse assimilates thanksgiving-offerings] may be purchased from money exchanged for produce in the status of second tithe?*

D. *The reason is that the word "there" is written in the context of both a beast purchased for use as a peace-offering and also second tithe [at Deut. 27:7 and Deut. 14:23, respectively]. [It follows that the rule governing the peace-offering derives from an argument based on an analogy established through verbal congruence, and that rule is then applied to a thanksgiving-offering by an analogy based on other than verbal congruence.]*

E. *Said Mar Zutra b. R. Mari to Rabina, "But tithe of grain is in the status of unconsecrated food in general [but the issue at hand addresses tithe of the corral, which is in the status of Holy Things]!"*

F. *He said to him, "Who has claimed that that to which a rule is transferred [by means of the exegetical principle at hand] must be in the class of Holy Things and that that from which a rule is transferred likewise must be in the class of Holy Things?"*

IV.9 A. Can a rule that is derived by an analogy based on the congruence of other shared traits [but not verbal ones in context] turn around and teach a lesson through an analogy based on the congruence of [other] shared traits?

B. Said Rami bar Hama, "It has been taught on Tannaite authority:

C. "'"Of fine flour soaked" (Lev. 7:12) – this teaches that the soaked cake [one that is made of boiled flour] must be made of fine flour.

D. "'How do we know the rule that applies to the ordinary unleavened cakes [*hallot*]?

E. "'Scripture in both contexts [speaking of the cakes that are soaked as well as the unleavened ones] speaks of *hallot*.

F. "'How do we know that the same rule applies to thin wafers?

G. "'Because Scripture in both contexts speaks of unleavened bread.'" [Freedman: Thus we first learn by an analogy based on shared traits that the ordinary unleavened cakes must be made of fine flour, and then by a further such argument we learn from the ordinary unleavened cakes that the thin wafers likewise must be of fine flour.]

H. *Said to him Rabina, "How do you know that he derives the rule governing unleavened cakes from the one governing ordinary unleavened cakes? Perhaps he derives the rule from the law governing oven-baked cakes [Lev. 2:4] [without appeal to the analogy that has been drawn here]?"*

I. Rather, said Raba, "It has been taught on Tannaite authority:

J. "'"And its innards and its dung, even the whole bullock shall he carry forth outside of the camp" (Lev. 4:11) – this teaches that they carry it out whole.

K. "'Might one suppose that they burn it whole?

L. "'Here we find a reference to "its head and its legs," and elsewhere [Lev. 1:8-9, 12-13] we find reference also to "its head and its legs." Just as in that other case, this is done only after cutting up the beast, so here, too, it means only after cutting up the beast.

Analogical-Contrastive Thinking and the Problem of Dialectical Thought 55

M. "'If so, then just as there is this after flaying the hide, so here, too, is it to be after flaying the hide? Scripture states, "and its innards and its dung."'"

N. *What conclusion is supposed to be drawn here?*

O. Said R. Pappa, "Just as its dung is kept within the innards, so the meat must be held within the hide."

P. *And so, too, it has been taught on Tannaite authority:*

Q. Rabbi says, "Here [with reference to the bullock and he goat of the Day of Atonement] we find a reference to 'hide and meat and dung,' [50B] and elsewhere, we find a reference to hide and meat and dung [in connection with the bullock of the anointed priest]. Just as there, the beast was burned only after being cut up, but without flaying the hide, so here, too, the beast was burned only after being cut up, but without flaying the hide." [Thus the result of one such argument is transferred to another case by another such argument (Freedman)].

IV.10 A. Can a rule that is derived by an analogy based on the congruence of other shared traits [but not verbal ones in context] go and teach a lesson through an argument a fortiori?

B. Indeed so, by reason of an argument a fortiori:

C. If an argument deriving from an analogy based on verbal congruence, which cannot go and, by an argument based on verbal congruence, impart its rule to some other class – *as has been shown by either Raba's or Rabina's demonstration* – nonetheless can go and by an argument a fortiori impart its rule to some other class – *as has been shown by the Tannaite authority of the household of R. Ishmael* – then a rule that is derived by an argument based on analogy based on other than verbal congruence, which can for its part go and impart its lesson by an argument based on an analogy resting on verbal congruity – *as has been shown by R. Pappa* – surely can in turn teach its lesson by an argument a fortiori to yet another case!

D. *That position poses no problems to one who takes the view that R. Pappa's case has been made. But for one who takes the view that R. Pappa's case has not been made, what is to be said?*

E. *Rather, this is an argument a fortiori in favor of the same point:*

F. If an argument deriving from an analogy based on verbal congruence, which cannot go and, by an argument based on verbal congruence, impart its rule to some other class – *as has been shown by either Raba's or Rabina's demonstration* – nonetheless can go and by an argument a fortiori impart its rule to some other class – *as has been shown by the Tannaite authority of the household of R. Ishmael* – then a rule that is derived by an argument based on analogy based on other than verbal congruence, which can for its part go and impart its lesson by an argument based on an analogy resting on verbal congruity which is like itself – *as has been shown by Rami bar Hama* – surely can in turn teach its lesson by an argument a fortiori to yet another case!

IV.11 A. Can a rule that is derived by an analogy based on the congruence of other shared traits [but not verbal ones in context] go and teach a lesson through an argument constructed by analogy based on the congruence of other shared traits among two or more classifications of things?

B. *That question must stand.*

IV.12 A. Can a rule derived by an argument a fortiori go and teach a rule established through analogy of verbal usage?

B. The affirmative derives from an argument a fortiori:

C. If an argument deriving from an analogy based on points of other than verbal congruence, which cannot go and, by an argument based on verbal congruence, impart its rule to some other class – *as has been shown by R. Pappa's demonstration* – then a rule that is derived by an argument a fortiori, which can be derived by an argument based on the shared verbal traits of two things – *as has been shown by the Tannaite authority of the house of R. Ishmael* – surely should be able to impart its rule to another classification of things by reason of an argument based on a verbal analogy!

D. *That position poses no problems to one who takes the view that R. Pappa's case has been made. But for one who takes the view that R. Pappa's case has not been made, what is to be said?*

E. *The question then must stand.*

IV.13 A. Can a rule that is derived by an argument a fortiori go and teach a lesson through an argument based on the congruence of other shared traits [but not verbal ones in context]?

B. The affirmative derives from an argument a fortiori:

C. If an argument deriving from an analogy based on points of other than verbal congruence, which cannot be derived from an argument based on verbal congruence, imparts its rule to some other class – *as has been shown by R. Yohanan's demonstration* – and can go and teach a lesson by an argument based on an analogy established through other than verbal traits, *as has been shown by Rami bar Hama* – a rule based on an argument a fortiori, which can be derived by an argument based on an analogy resting on verbal coincidence, surely should be able to impart its rule to another classification of things by reason of an argument based on an other than verbal analogy!

IV.14 A. Can a rule based on an argument a fortiori turn around and teach a lesson through an argument based on an argument a fortiori?

B. Indeed so, and the affirmative derives from an argument a fortiori:

C. If an argument deriving from an analogy based on points of other than verbal congruence, which cannot be derived from an argument based on verbal congruence, imparts its rule to some other class – *as has been shown by R. Yohanan's demonstration* – and can go and teach a lesson by an argument a fortiori, as we have just pointed out, then an argument that can be derived from an analogy based on verbal congruence – *as has been shown by the Tannaite authority of the household of R. Ishmael* – surely should be able to impart its rule by an argument a fortiori!

D. But would this then would represent what we are talking about, namely, a rule deriving from an argument a fortiori that has been applied to another case by means of an argument a fortiori?

Analogical-Contrastive Thinking and the Problem of Dialectical Thought 57

	Surely this is nothing more than a secondary derivation produced by an argument a fortiori!
E.	Rather, argue in the following way:
F.	Indeed so, and the affirmative derives from an argument a fortiori:
G.	If an argument based on an analogy of a verbal character cannot be derived from another such argument based on an analogy between two classes of things that rest upon a verbal congruence – *in accordance with the proofs of either Raba or Rabina* – nonetheless can then go and impart its lesson by an argument a fortiori – *in accordance with the proof of the Tannaite authority of the household of R. Ishmael* – then an argument a fortiori, which can serve to transfer a lesson originally learned through an argument based upon verbal congruence, *in accordance with the proof of the Tannaite authority of the household of R. Ishmael* – surely should be able to impart its lesson to yet another classification of things through an argument a fortiori.
H.	And this does represent what we are talking about, namely, a rule deriving from an argument a fortiori that has been applied to another case by means of an argument a fortiori.

IV.15 A. Can a rule based on an argument a fortiori turn around and teach a rule through an argument constructed on the basis of shared traits of an other-than-verbal character among two classifications of things?

B. *Said R. Jeremiah, "Come and take note:* [If] one pinched off the neck and [the bird] turned out to be terefah – R. Meir says, "It does not impart uncleanness of the gullet [since slaughtering a beast is wholly equivalent to pinching the neck of a bird]." R. Judah says, "It does impart uncleanness of the gullet." [Birds and beasts in no way are comparable; neither slaughtering an unconsecrated clean bird nor pinching the neck of a consecrated one will exempt from uncleanness a bird which turns out to be terefah.] Said R. Meir, "It is an argument a fortiori: now if in the case of the carrion of a beast, which imparts uncleanness through contact and through carrying, proper slaughter renders clean from its uncleanness that which was terefah, [in the case of] the carrion of fowl, which to begin with does not impart uncleanness through contact and through carrying, it should logically follow that its proper slaughter should render clean from its uncleanness that which was terefah. Just as we find that its proper slaughter [in the case of a bird or beast] renders it valid for eating [51A] and renders it clean from its uncleanness in the case of terefah, so proper pinching of the neck, which renders it valid for eating, should render it clean from its uncleanness in the case of terefah." R. Yosé says, "It is sufficient that it [the slaughtering of the bird] be equivalent to the carrion of a beast: its [a beast's or a bird's] slaughtering renders clean [what is terefah], but the pinching of the neck [of a bird does] not [render clean what

58   On Method in Religion and Society

is terefah]" [M. Zeb. 7:6]. [The language "Just as we find" then represents an argument based on shared traits of two distinct classifications of things, and so we see that a rule derived by an argument a fortiori then through such an argument based on shared traits is transferred to another class of things altogether.]"

C. But that is not so. For even if we concede that that is the case there, then still the rule derives from the act of slaughter of unconsecrated beasts [Freedman].

IV.16 A. Can a rule derived by an argument based on shared traits of an other than verbal character shared among two classes of things then turn around and teach a lesson by an argument based on an analogy of a verbal character, an analogy not of a verbal character, an argument a fortiori, or an argument based on shared traits?

B. Solve at least one of those problems by appeal to the following:

C. On what account have they said that if blood of an offering is left overnight on the altar, it is fit? Because if the sacrificial parts are kept overnight on the altar, they are fit. And why if the sacrificial parts are kept overnight on the altar are they fit? Because if the meat of the offering is kept overnight on the altar it is fit. [Freedman: Thus the rule governing the sacrificial parts is derived by an appeal to an argument based on shared traits of an other than verbal character shared among two classes of things, and that rule in turn is applied to the case of the blood by another such argument based on shared traits of an other than verbal character shared among two classes of things].

D. What about the rule governing meat that is taken outside of the Temple court? [If such meat is put up on the altar, it is not removed therefrom. Why so?]

E. Because meat that has been taken out of the holy place is suitable for a high place.

F. What about the rule governing unclean meat? [If such meat is put up on the altar, it is not removed therefrom. Why so?]

G. Since meat that is unclean is subject to a remission of the prohibition affecting it in the case of an offering made in behalf of the entire community.

H. What about the rule governing the sacrificial parts of a burnt-offering that the officiating priest subjected to the intention of being burned after the proper time? [If such meat is put up on the altar, it is not removed therefrom. Why so?]

I. Since the sprinkling of the blood is effective and propitiates in making such meat refuse by reason of the improper intentionality [we leave the sacrificial portions on the altar once they have been put there].

J. What about the rule governing the sacrificial parts of a burnt-offering that the officiating priest subjected to the intention of being eaten outside of the proper place? [If such meat is put up on the altar, it is not removed therefrom. Why so?]

K. Since sacrificial meat in that class is treated as analogous to sacrificial meat that has been subjected to an improper

Analogical-Contrastive Thinking and the Problem of Dialectical Thought 59

           intentionality in respect to eating the meat outside of the proper time.

L. What about the rule governing the sacrificial parts of a burnt-offering the blood of which unfit priests have received and tossed, when such unfit persons are eligible for an act of service in behalf of the community...? [This question is not answered.]

M. [Reverting to C-E:] Now can an analogy be drawn concerning something that has been disposed of in the proper manner for something that has not been disposed of in the proper manner? [If the sacrificial parts are kept over night, they are not taken off the altar, and therefore the meat kept overnight is fit; but the meat may be kept overnight, while the sacrificial parts may not. So, too, when the Temple stood, the flesh might not be taken outside, but where there was no Temple and only high places, the case is scarcely analogous!]

N. *The Tannaite authority for this rule derives it from the augmentative sense, extending the rule, deriving from the formulation, "This is the Torah of the burnt-offering" (Lev. 6:2).* [Freedman: The verse teaches that all burnt-offerings, even with the defects catalogued here, are subject to the same rule and do not get removed from the altar once they have been put there; the arguments given cannot be sustained but still support that proposition.]

The simple order of the whole allows the answer to one question to precipitate the consequent and necessary next question. I need hardly review what our authors have made so clear through their own exposition. I cannot imagine anybody's not seeing that a sustained methodological inquiry is taking place at the very surface of discourse on the bloody rite of the Temple!

V.1 A. **The remnants of their blood did one pour out on the western base of the outer altar. If he did not place [the remnants of the blood at the stated location], he did not impair [atonement]:**

B. *What is the Scripture basis for this rule?*

C. Scripture has said, "And all the remaining blood of the bullock shall he pour out at the base of the altar of the burnt-offering which is at the door of the tent of meeting" (Lev. 4:7).

D. *That speaks of the first altar that one meets [as you enter from the door, and that is the western base].*

What needs to be said once does not have to be repeated: the work of the framers of the Talmud is sometimes thought about thinking, but always inquiry into the relations between Scripture and law (in the Mishnah, as elsewhere). The former must be done once, it serves then throughout; but the latter has to be repeated many times. It would therefore vastly misrepresent the Talmud were I to present only parts I-IV or to claim that the deep structure of discourse of parts I-IV is present throughout; that is contrary to fact. The reason is that the Talmud's authorship remains bound within the limits of the medium it has chosen for the expression of its ideas, which is the form of a commentary to the Mishnah. And that means, the Mishnah will be commented upon! Now that commentary proves quite cogent, pursuing a few and limited questions over and over again. And one of these is, we recall very well, the scriptural basis for the Mishnah's law. That question overrides any intent to expound the principles of comparison and contrast among genera, the linkage between genus and genus, let alone to set forth the deep structure of abstract thought on the nature of the series, that is, on the movement of an argument from point to point. All of that wonderful thought, shown in Part IV, now subsides, as we revert to our work. Once we have finished one job, we now undertake the same job, in the setting of another statement of the Mishnah. The competition between the wonders of sheer thought, at which our sages excel, and exegesis always is won by exegesis. These geniuses of ours were very modest men.

V.2 A. *Our rabbis have taught on Tannaite authority* [Freedman: There are five passages that deal with the sin-offering, Lev. 4: the sin-offering of the anointed priest, Lev. 4:1-12; the sin-offering of the entire congregation, Lev. 4:13-22, the sin-offering of a rule, Lev. 4:22-26, the female goat of an ordinary person, Lev. 4:27-32, and the lamb of an ordinary person, Lev. 4:32-35. The first two were offered on the inner altar, the other three on the outer. In regard to the first three, Scripture states that the residue of the blood is to be poured out "...at the base of the altar of the burnt-offering..." (Lev. 4:7, 18, 25), and in connection with the other two there is an allusion to the base of the altar without reference to "of the sin-offering." Here rabbis explain why Scripture specifies the altar of the burnt-offering in the first three cases. The first teaches that the residue is poured out at the base of the outer altar, the altar of the burnt-offering, but not at the base of the inner altar, even though the blood was sprinkled on the horns of the inner altar. The second is superfluous, and it teaches that only the outer altar had such a base, not the inner altar. The third reference intimates that the residue of the blood of all sacrifices whose blood is sprinkled on the altar of burnt-offering must be poured out at its base. Thus]:

B. "...at the base of the altar of the burnt-offering..." (Lev. 4:7) – and not at the base of the inner altar.

C. "...at the base of the altar of the burnt-offering..." (Lev. 4:18) – the inner altar has no base anyhow.

D. "...at the base of the altar of the burnt-offering..." (Lev. 4:25) – apply the laws governing the base to the altar of the burnt-offering.

E. But perhaps that is not the sense, but rather, let there be a base around the altar of the burnt-offering? [Freedman: Perhaps the

Analogical-Contrastive Thinking and the Problem of Dialectical Thought 61

verse says nothing about the residue of the blood but indicates that the two sprinklings of the blood of the burnt-offering must be made at that part of the altar that had a special base, excluding the southeastern horn, which did not have a special base.]

F. Said R. Ishmael, "The proposition can be shown to derive from an argument a fortiori: If the residue of the blood of the sin-offering, which does not make atonement, has to be poured out at the base, then the sprinkling of the blood of the burnt-offering itself, which does make atonement, surely would require the base [meaning, it must be a corner of the altar at which the horn has been provided with a base]." [Then a verse is not required to make that point, if the teaching is as proposed. Hence the proposed proof is null.]

G. Said R. Aqiba, "[Along the same lines,] the proposition can be shown to derive from an argument a fortiori: If the residue of the blood of the sin-offering, which does not make atonement and which is not presented for the purposes of atonement in any way, has to be poured out at the base, then the sprinkling of the blood of the burnt-offering itself, which does make atonement, and which is presented for the purposes of atonement, surely would require the base [meaning, it must be a corner of the altar at which the horn has been provided with a base]. So why does Scripture state, 'at the base of the altar of burnt-offering'? It is to indicate that the laws of the base should pertain to the altar of the burnt-offering."

V.3 A. A master has said, "'...at the base of the altar of the burnt-offering...' (Lev. 4:7) – and not at the base of the inner altar":

B. *Surely that clause is required to make its own point [and not to prove the derivative, "and not...," point]!*

C. That point itself derives from the language, "which is at the door of the tent of meeting" [indicating that the outer altar is what is required, so the specification "of the burnt-offering" is superfluous and serves the specified purpose].

V.4 A. [Supply: A master has said,] "'...at the base of the altar of the burnt-offering...' (Lev. 4:25) – **[51B]** apply the laws governing the base to the altar of the burnt-offering":

B. *For if it should enter your mind that the passage is to be read literally as written, then what need do I have for a verse of Scripture dealing with the residue, since pouring out the residue was an act done in the outer courtyard and not in the inner sanctum?*

C. *And if you should say that without that verse, I might have concluded that it is indeed to be reversed,* **[52A]** *with the residue of the inner offering to be poured at the outer altar and the residue of the outer altar to be performed at the inner altar, in point of fact, the inner altar had no base [so the interpretation is possible only as given].*

V.5 A. [Supply: A master has said,] "But perhaps that is not the sense, but rather, let there be a base around the altar of the burnt-offering": [Freedman: Perhaps the verse says nothing about the residue of the blood but indicates that the two sprinklings of the

		blood of the burnt-offering must be made at that part of the altar that had a special base, excluding the southeastern horn, which did not have a special base.]

B. But is it not written, "at the base of the altar of burnt-offering"? [Freedman: If the verse intimated that the sprinkling itself must be performed on that part of the altar that has a base, it could not refer to sin-offerings, the blood of which was sprinkled on all the horns of the altar, including the southeast. Hence it would have to refer to the burnt-offering alone. But in that case, Scripture should write, "at the base of the burnt-offering," which would intimate that the blood of the burnt-offering must be sprinkled over against the base. The word "altar" then becomes redundant.]

C. *If the verse stated, "at the base of the burnt-offering," I might have supposed that the sense was, on the top of the base [right up by the altar itself]. But since it is written, "at the base of the altar of burnt-offering," the meaning is, "at the top of the base."*

D. Said R. Ishmael, "What need do I have for a verse to tell me that it is to be spilled out at the top of the base? It would follow through an argument a fortiori: If the residue of the blood of the sin-offering, which does not make atonement, has to be poured out at the top of the base, then the sprinkling of the blood of the burnt-offering itself, which does make atonement, surely would require the top of the base."

E. Said R. Aqiba, "[Along the same lines,] the proposition can be shown to derive from an argument a fortiori: If the residue of the blood of the sin-offering, which does not make atonement and which is not presented for the purposes of atonement in any way, has to be poured out at the top of the base, then the sprinkling of the blood of the burnt-offering itself, which does make atonement, and which is presented for the purposes of atonement, surely would require the top of the base. So why does Scripture state, 'at the base of the altar of burnt-offering'? It is to indicate that the laws of the base should pertain to the altar of the burnt-offering."

V.6 A. *In what regard do the two authorities differ?*

B. Said R. Adda b. Ahbah, "At issue between them is whether or not the pouring out of the residue of the blood is indispensable to the rite. One authority maintains that pouring out of the residue of the blood is indispensable to the rite. The author takes the view that pouring out of the residue of the blood is not indispensable to the rite."

C. R. Pappa said, "All parties maintain that pouring out of the residue of the blood is not indispensable to the rite. But here what is at issue is whether or not the draining out of the blood of a bird that has been presented as a sin-offering is indispensable to the rite. One authority takes the view that it is, the other, that it is not, indispensable to the rite."

D. *There is a Tannaite formulation in accord with the theory of R. Pappa:*

Analogical-Contrastive Thinking and the Problem of Dialectical Thought

E. "'And all the remaining blood of the bullock [of the offering of the anointed priest] shall he pour out at the base of the altar': (Lev. 4:7) – Why does Scripture make reference to 'the bullock' [since the context makes clear that that is what is at issue]? It teaches concerning the bullock that is offered on the Day of Atonement that the blood has to be poured out at the base of the altar," the words of R. [Aqiba].

F. Said R. Ishmael, "It is an argument a fortiori [that that is the case, and a prooftext is not required]. If the blood of an offering that is not obligatory [the bullock presented by a sin-offering by the anointed priest, which is not an obligatory offering in that the man does not have to have said], presented on the inner altar, has to be poured out at the base, the blood of an offering that is obligatory, [the bullock presented on the Day of Atonement, which is required, whether or not the high priest has sinned], presented on the inner altar, surely should have to be poured out at the base!"

G. Said R. Aqiba, "If an offering that is neither obligatory nor even a matter of a mere religious duty, the blood of which is not brought into the inner sanctum [the Holy of Holies], has to be poured out onto the base of the altar, an offering that is a statutory obligation, the blood of which is taken into the inner sanctum, surely should require a base!"

H. "Now you might have supposed that the pouring out of the residue is indispensable for the rite [of the bullock on the Day of Atonement], and therefore Scripture states, 'And he shall make an end of atoning' (Lev. 16:20), meaning, all of the rites of atonement are now complete," the words of R. Ishmael.

I. [Reverting to the claim of D:] Now it is an argument a fortiori in regard to the bullock of the anointed priest, namely, if the blood of an offering that is neither obligatory nor even a matter of religious duty which is not taken to the inner altar but still has to be poured out at the base of the altar, surely the blood of an offering whether obligatory or a matter of religious duty should have to be poured out at the base of the altar!

J. Might one suppose that it is indispensable to the rite?

K. Scripture states, "And all the remaining blood of the bullock he shall pour out," and in this way Scripture turns the matter into the residual aspect of a religious duty, indicating that pouring out the residue is not indispensable to the correct carrying out of the rite.

V.7 A. *But does R. Ishmael really take the position [as Pappa has claimed] that* draining out of the blood of a bird that has been presented as a sin-offering is indispensable to the rite? And has it not been set forth as a Tannaite rule by the Tannaite authority of the household of R. Ishmael, "'And the rest of the blood shall be drained out': – what is left is to be drained out, [52B] but what is not left is not drained out"? [Freedman: All the blood may be used in sprinkling, so that nothing is left for draining, hence draining cannot be indispensable.]

B. *There is a conflict among Tannaite versions of the opinions of R. Ishmael.*

V.8 A. Said Rami bar Hama, "The following Tannaite authority takes the view that pouring out the residue of the blood is indispensable. For it has been taught on Tannaite authority":

B. "This is the law of the sin-offering...the priest who offers it for sin [having correctly carried out the rite in every detail] shall eat it" (Lev. 6:18-19) – "it" meaning, the one, the blood of which has been tossed above the red line around the altar, and not the one the blood of which was tossed below the red line around the altar.

C. Now explain [why you might have supposed that even though the blood was not properly sprinkled, the meat nonetheless still may be eaten, absent a prooftext to the contrary]!

D. It is a conclusion that can have been implied by the following verse, "and the blood of your sacrifices shall be poured out...and you shall eat the meat" (Deut. 12:27) – thereby we have learned concerning a case in which it is required to toss the blood four times, that if one has tossed the blood in a single action, he has achieved atonement.

E. Might one therefore suppose that if the blood that was supposed to be sprinkled above the red line was sprinkled below, the offering might also have achieved atonement for the donor?

F. For it is a matter of logic: There is blood that is to be tossed above the red line [a sin-offering made of a beast], and there is blood that is to be tossed below the red line [a sin-offering of a bird], so, just as the blood that is supposed to be tossed below the red line does not atone if it is tossed above, so blood that is supposed to be tossed above the red line will not atone if it is sprinkled below it.

G. Not at all. If you invoke that rule in the case of blood that is supposed to be sprinkled below the red line, it is because in the end it will not be above at all, but will you say the same of blood that is to be sprinkled above the red line, which ultimately will be located down below [in the form of the residue]? [Freedman: Hence when he sprinkles the blood below the line, he is putting it where it will eventually be located and so effects atonement.]

H. Let blood that is to be tossed on the inner altar prove the case, for it is going in the end to be brought outside [where the residue is poured out around the base of the outer altar], and yet if the blood that is to be tossed on the inner altar to begin with is tossed on the outer altar, the priest has not effected atonement.

I. Not at all, for if you raise the issue of blood to be tossed on the inner altar, that is because the rite performed on the inner altar does not complete the ritual attached to the entire liturgy [since after the blood is sprinkled on the inner altar, the residue has to be poured out at the base of the outer altar]. But can you say the same of the tossing of the blood on the upper part of the altar, in which case putting the blood on the horns completes the rite [and no further action is indispensable once the blood has been sprinkled on the horns of the altar]? Since sprinkling the blood on the horns of the altar completes the rite, if the priest sprinkled below the red line, the rite also is fit.

J. [Because of the possibility of composing such an argument,] Scripture states, "This is the law of the sin-offering...the priest who offers it for sin [having correctly carried out the rite in every detail] shall eat it" (Lev. 6:18-19) – "it" meaning, the one, the blood of which has been tossed above the red line around the altar, and not the one the blood of which was tossed below the red line around the altar.

K. *What is the meaning of the phrase, the rite performed on the inner altar does not complete the ritual attached to the entire liturgy? Surely this refers to the residue of the blood [and that proves that pouring out the residue of the blood is an indispensable part of the rite].*

L. *Said Raba to him, "If so, then you may prove the point through an argument a fortiori: If to begin with blood of an offering performed on the inner altar which is poured out on the outer altar does not make atonement, even though in the end it will be obligatory to pour out that blood on the outer altar, then as to blood that is to be sprinkled above the red line, which in the end is not subject to the obligation of being poured out below the line for the sacrifice to achieve its goal of atonement, if to begin with one sprinkled such blood below the red line, the offering should not secure atonement [Freedman: the sacrifice is invalid, and the meat may not be eaten. So why is a verse of Scripture required to prove the point? Hence the premise of this argument, that pouring out of the residue is essential, must be false.]*

M. Rather, this is the sense: It is not tossing the blood on the altar alone that completes the rite, but tossing the blood on the veil as well.

V.9 A. *Our rabbis have taught on Tannaite authority:*

B. "'And he shall make an end of atoning for the holy place and the tent of meeting and the altar' (Lev. 16:20) – if he atoned [by carrying out the rites required for atonement in other matters, e.g., the four sprinklings on the altar, the seven before the veil (Freedman)], he has completed the rite, but if he has not atoned, he has not completed the rite," the words of R. Aqiba.

C. Said to him R. Judah, "Why should we not say, 'if he made an end to the rite, he has atoned, and if not, he did not atone'? [So the rites, including the four applications, are necessary, and it is on that basis that that fact is to be demonstrated]."

D. *What is at issue between them?*

E. R. Yohanan and R. Joshua b. Levi:

F. *One said, "At issue is the correct interpretation of Scripture"* [Freedman: but not in law. Both hold that all four applications of blood are indispensable, and that pouring out the residue is not. Aqiba holds that the conclusion, atoning, illumines the beginning, make an end, so completion depends on atonement, on the four applications. Judah maintains that 'atoning' might merely refer to a single application of blood, and therefore the interpretation must be revised, and the beginning of the verse illuminates the end; only when he completely finishes the rite, having done the four applications, is atonement done.]

G. *The other said, "At issue is whether or not pouring out the residue of the blood at the base is indispensable to the rite."*

H. *Now you may draw the conclusion that it is R. Joshua b. Levi who took the position that at issue is whether or not pouring out the residue of the blood at the base is indispensable to the rite. For said R. Joshua b. Levi, "In the opinion of the one who said that pouring out the residue of the blood is an indispensable part of the rite, one must bring another bullock and begin the rite on the inner altar." [Freedman: If the residue of the blood was spilled after the four applications, another bullock must be slaughtered and its blood first sprinkled at the inner altar, and then the residue poured out at the base of the outer altar. But the priest cannot simply pour out all the blood at the base, for then it is not a residue, and it is indispensable that a residue be poured out. Thus Joshua b. Levi holds that there is a view that pouring out of the residue is indispensable.]*

I. *But does R. Yohanan not maintain this same theory of matters? And has not R. Yohanan said, "R. Nehemiah taught as a Tannaite authority in accord with the opinion of one who maintains that the pouring out of the residue of the blood is indispensable to the rite"?*

J. *Rather, you have to say, "In accord with the words of him who says...," but not, "in accord with the words of these Tannaite authorities in particular" [Aqiba and Judah], and so, too, here [in the matter of Joshua b. Levi], "In accord with the words of him who says...," but not, "in accord with the words of these Tannaite authorities in particular."*

To see the composite whole: Part IV is the important component of this astonishingly coherent piece of writing. Nos. 5-16 build on No. 4, systematically and patiently working through the entire repertoire of possibilities on the exegetical rules for deriving lessons from Scripture. The range of exegetical principles – argument a fortiori, argument based on analogy established through shared verbal choices, argument based on analogy established through other than shared verbal choices, analogy based on the congruence of other shared traits [but not verbal ones in context] – is entirely systematic, with each exegetical technique compared to all of the others. The unified and accumulative effect of the whole is demonstrated by No. 10, which appeals to foregoing materials to make its point. Obviously this beautifully articulated composition – not a mere composite – has been worked out prior to insertion here; but the relevance to our chapter's rules and interests is obvious, and we have been prepared to anticipate just such a theoretical exercise. But the chapter as a whole turns out to provide a laboratory case on that matter.

Two important facts are now clear and prepare the way for me to explain why I conceive the metapropositional issue at hand to concern the questions, when is a list a series, or, Can a list be a series? First, in its interest in finding the connection to Scripture of a rule that is set forth by the Mishnah, the chapter presents this metaproposition that encompasses the numerous specific propositions: How do we make connections between rules and their point of origin. Every time we ask, "What is the source [in Scripture] for this statement?" we find an answer that is left to stand. So one fundamental and ubiquitous metaproposition of the Bavli may be set forth in this language:

1. It is important to link laws that occur in one source to those that occur in another.
2. Among the compilations [components of "the one whole Torah of Moses, our rabbi," in later mythic language] that enjoy canonical status [in our language], the premier is Scripture.
3. So whenever we find a statement of a rule in the Mishnah and ask for its source, the implicit criterion of success will be, "the rule is founded on language of Scripture, properly construed."
4. So, consequently, the proposition implicit in numerous propositions, common to them all and holding them all together, is this: all rules cohere, and the point of origin of nearly all of them is the written part of the Torah revealed by God to Moses at Sinai.

The particular document in which the rules now circulate does not place into a hierarchy the various rules, because they all are one; but the reason they all are one is that nearly all of them find a point of origin in the written part of the Torah; and every single one of them is harmonious in principle with each of the others – once we identify the principle implicit in the cases that make up the law. Now if we asked the framers of the Mishnah their judgment upon these allegations of one of the metapropositional planks of the platform of the Bavli, they will have found surprising only our inquiry. For, while not common or characteristic of Mishnaic discourse, each of these traits can be located therein. The Mishnah's framers sometimes explicitly cite a verse of Scripture in support of the law; they occasionally undertake the exegesis of a verse of Scripture in order to discover the law; they know the distinction between rulings of the Torah and rulings of scribes, the latter standing a cut below the former; and their heirs, in undertaking vast exercises of linkage of the Mishnah to Scripture in such documents as Sifra to Leviticus and Sifré to Deuteronomy, engage in a persistent and compelling demonstration of the same metapropositional program, point by point. And yet we cannot then assign to the authorship of our chapter (and the numerous other chapters in which a principal, recurrent concern and point of generative tension is the link of the law contained in the Mishnah or other Tannaite compilations to the law contained in Scripture and its particular wording) merely the task of saying explicitly what the framers of the Mishnah occasionally said and commonly implied.

For there is a second metaproposition in our chapter, one so profound as to demand for itself priority over all other questions and answers. It addresses the issue of the nature and structure of thought. When we understand that issue, we shall see the remarkable intellectual achievement of the authorship of the Bavli's reading of Mishnah-tractate Zebahim 5:1-2. At stake in this appreciation of what they have accomplished is the demonstration that metapropositions in the Bavli are not only particular to the problem of the documentary provenance of rules – Scripture forms the basis of nearly all rules; all rules harmonize, at their foundations in abstract principles, with all other rules. The metapropositional program turns out, as I shall now show through a reprise of the pertinent propositions of the Bavli's reading of Mishnah-tractate Zebahim 5:1-2, to be so abstract as vastly to transcend rules and their generalizations and harmonies, rising to the height of principles of thought that guide the intellect in contemplation of all being and all reality.

To grasp the metapropositional program that, in my view, defines the stakes of discourse, let me specify what I conceive to be the counterpart program, pertaining to not connecting rules to Scripture, but rather, connecting principle to (consequent) principle: how thought really takes place, which is, not in a stationary pool but in a moving stream. To state the result up front: the Mishnah portrays all things at rest, a beautifully composed set in stasis, a stage on which nothing happens. The Bavli portrays all things in motion, a world of action, in which one thing leads to some other, and nothing stands still. All of this is accomplished in a shift in the received mode of thought, and the shift is set forth in the metaproposition, fully exposed, in the reading of two paragraphs of the Mishnah. We now consider what I conceive to be the counterpart program to the one that, in my view, the Bavli's sages inherited from the Mishnah and spelled out in tedious and unending particulars. To understand what is fresh and important in the Bavli's metapropositional program concerning the nature of thought, we have to call to mind what they inherited, for what they did was to impose the stamp of their own intellect upon the intellectual heritage that the Mishnah had provided for them.

To set forth the basic theory of the framers of the Mishnah on how thought takes place, which is to say, how we may understand things and know them, we must recall a simple fact. The Mishnah teaches the age-old method of scientific thought through comparison and contrast.

Analogical-Contrastive Thinking and the Problem of Dialectical Thought 69

Like things follow like rules, unlike things, the opposite rules, and the task of thought is to show what is like something else and therefore follows the rule that governs that something else; or what is unlike something else and therefore follows the opposite of the rule that governs that something else. So the Mishnah's mode of thought establishes connections between and among things and does so, as is clear, through the method of taxonomy, comparison and contrast, list-making of like things, yielding the rule that governs all items on the list.

List making places on display the data of the like and the unlike and implicitly (ordinarily, not explicitly) then conveys the rule. The Mishnah is then a book of lists, with the implicit order, the nomothetic traits of a monothetic order, dictating the ordinarily unstated general and encompassing rule. And all this why? It is in order to make a single statement, endless times over, and to repeat in a mass of tangled detail precisely the same fundamental judgment. The framers of the Mishnah appeal solely to the traits of things. List making then defines a way of proving propositions through classification, so establishing a set of shared traits that form a rule which compels us to reach a given conclusion. Probative facts derive from the classification of data, all of which point in one direction and not in another. A catalogue of facts, for example, may be so composed that, through the regularities and indicative traits of the entries, the catalogue yields a proposition. A list of parallel items all together point to a simple conclusion; the conclusion may or may not be given at the end of the catalogue, but the catalogue – by definition – is pointed. All of the catalogued facts are taken to bear self-evident connections to one another, established by those pertinent shared traits implicit in the composition of the list, therefore also bearing meaning and pointing through the weight of evidence to an inescapable conclusion. The discrete facts then join together because of some trait common to them all. This is a mode of classification of facts to lead to an identification of what the facts have in common and – it goes without saying, an explanation of their meaning.

What is at stake in the making of lists, that is, the formation of classes of things, is the comparison and contrast of one class of things with some other, yielding at the end the account of the hierarchization of all classes of things in correct sequence and grade. The following abstract shows us through the making of connections and the drawing of conclusions the propositional and essentially philosophical mind that animates the Mishnah and makes explicit what that authorship always wants to know: the relationships, in hierarchical order, between classes of things. In the following passage, drawn from

Mishnah-tractate Sanhedrin Chapter Two, the authorship wishes to say that Israel has two heads, one of state, the other of cult, the king and the high priest, respectively, and that these two offices are nearly wholly congruent with one another, with a few differences based on the particular traits of each. Broadly speaking, therefore, our exercise is one of setting forth the genus and the species. The genus is head of holy Israel. The species are king and high priest. Here are the traits in common and those not shared, and the exercise is fully exposed for what it is, an inquiry into the rules that govern, the points of regularity and order, in this minor matter, of political structure. My outline, imposed in boldface type, makes the point important in this setting. We deal with Mishnah-tractate Sanhedrin Chapter Two:

1. **The rules of the high priest: subject to the law, marital rites, conduct in bereavement**

    2:1 A. A high priest judges, and [others] judge him;
    B. gives testimony, and [others] give testimony about him;
    C. performs the rite of removing the shoe [Deut. 25:7-9], and [others] perform the rite of removing the shoe with his wife.
    D. [Others] enter levirate marriage with his wife, but he does not enter into levirate marriage,
    E. because he is prohibited to marry a widow.
    F. [If] he suffers a death [in his family], he does not follow the bier.
    G. "But when [the bearers of the bier] are not visible, he is visible; when they are visible, he is not.
    H. "And he goes with them to the city gate," the words of R. Meir.
    I. R. Judah says, "He never leaves the sanctuary,
    J. "since it says, 'Nor shall he go out of the sanctuary' (Lev. 21:12)."
    K. And when he gives comfort to others
    L. the accepted practice is for all the people to pass one after another, and the appointed [prefect of the priests] stands between him and the people.
    M. And when he receives consolation from others,
    N. all the people say to him, "Let us be your atonement."
    O. And he says to them, "May you be blessed by Heaven."
    P. And when they provide him with the funeral meal,
    Q. all the people sit on the ground, while he sits on a stool.

2. **The rules of the king: not subject to the law, marital rites, conduct in bereavement**

    2:2 A. The king does not judge, and [others] do not judge him;
    B. does not give testimony, and [others] do not give testimony about him;
    C. does not perform the rite of removing the shoe, and others do not perform the rite of removing the shoe with his wife;

Analogical-Contrastive Thinking and the Problem of Dialectical Thought 71

        D.   does not enter into levirate marriage, nor [does his brother] enter levirate marriage with his wife.
        E.   R. Judah says, "If he wanted to perform the rite of removing the shoe or to enter into levirate marriage, his memory is a blessing."
        F.   They said to him, "They pay no attention to him [if he expressed the wish to do so]."
        G.   [Others] do not marry his widow.
        H.   R. Judah says, "A king may marry the widow of a king.
        I.   "For so we find in the case of David, that he married the widow of Saul,
        J.   "For it is said, 'And I gave you your master's house and your master's wives into your embrace' (II Sam. 12:8)."

2:3   A.   [If] [the king] suffers a death in his family, he does not leave the gate of his palace.
        B.   R. Judah says, "If he wants to go out after the bier, he goes out,
        C.   "for thus we find in the case of David, that he went out after the bier of Abner,
        D.   "since it is said, 'And King David followed the bier' (2 Sam. 3:31)."
        E.   They said to him, "This action was only to appease the people."
        F.   And when they provide him with the funeral meal, all the people sit on the ground, while he sits on a couch.

3.   Special rules pertinent to the king because of his calling

2:4   A.   [The king] calls out [the army to wage] a war fought by choice on the instructions of a court of seventy-one.
        B.   He [may exercise the right to] open a road for himself, and [others] may not stop him.
        C.   The royal road has no required measure.
        D.   All the people plunder and lay before him [what they have grabbed], and he takes the first portion.
        E.   "*He should not multiply wives to himself*" (Deut. 17:17) – only eighteen.
        F.   R. Judah says, "He may have as many as he wants, so long as they *do not entice him* [to abandon the Lord (Deut. 7:4)]."
        G.   R. Simeon says, "Even if there is only one who entices him [to abandon the Lord] – lo, this one should not marry her."
        H.   If so, why is it said, "He should not multiply wives to himself"?
        I.   Even though they should be like Abigail [1 Sam. 25:3].
        J.   "*He should not multiply horses to himself*" (Deut. 17:16) – only enough for his chariot.
        K.   "*Neither shall he greatly multiply to himself silver and gold*" (Deut. 17:16) – only enough to pay his army.
        L.   "*And he writes out a scroll of the Torah for himself*" (Deut. 17:17).
        M.   When he goes to war, he takes it out with him; when he comes back, he brings it back with him; when he is in session in court, it is with him; when he is reclining, it is before him,

	N.	as it is said, *"And it shall be with him, and he shall read in it all the days of his life"* (Deut. 17:19).
2:5	A.	[Others may] not ride on his horse, sit on his throne, handle his scepter.
	B.	And [others may] not watch him while he is getting a haircut, or while he is nude, or in the bathhouse,
	C.	since it is said, *"You shall surely set him as king over you"* (Deut. 17:15) – that reverence for him will be upon you.

The subordination of Scripture to the classification scheme is self-evident. Scripture supplies facts. The traits of things – kings, high priests – dictate classification categories on their own, without Scripture's dictate.

The philosophical cast of mind is amply revealed in this essay, which in concrete terms effects a taxonomy, a study of the genus, national leader, and its two species, [1] king, [2] high priest: how are they alike, how are they not alike, and what accounts for the differences. The premise is that national leaders are alike and follow the same rule, except where they differ and follow the opposite rule from one another. But that premise also is subject to the proof effected by the survey of the data consisting of concrete rules, those systemically inert facts that here come to life for the purposes of establishing a proposition. By itself, the fact that, for example, others may not ride on his horse, bears the burden of no systemic proposition. In the context of an argument constructed for nomothetic, taxonomic purposes, the same fact is active and weighty. The whole depends upon three premises: [1] the importance of comparison and contrast, with the supposition that [2] like follows the like, and the unlike follows the opposite, rule; and [3] when we classify, we also hierarchize, which yields the argument from hierarchical classification: If this, which is the lesser, follows rule X, then that, which is the greater, surely should follow rule X. And that is the whole sum and substance of the logic of *Listenwissenschaft* as the Mishnah applies that logic in a practical way.

If I had to specify a single mode of thought that established connections between one fact and another, it is in the search for points in common and therefore also points of contrast. We seek connection between fact and fact, sentence and sentence in the subtle and balanced rhetoric of the Mishnah, by comparing and contrasting two things that are like and not alike. At the logical level, too, the Mishnah falls into the category of familiar philosophical thought. Once we seek regularities, we propose rules. What is like another thing falls under its rule, and what is not like the other falls under the opposite rule. Accordingly, as to the species of the genus, so far as they are alike,

Analogical-Contrastive Thinking and the Problem of Dialectical Thought 73

they share the same rule. So far as they are not alike, each follows a rule contrary to that governing the other. So the work of analysis is what produces connection, and therefore the drawing of conclusions derives from comparison and contrast: the *and*, the *equal*. The proposition then that forms the conclusion concerns the essential likeness of the two offices, except where they are different, but the subterranean premise is that we can explain both likeness and difference by appeal to a principle of fundamental order and unity.

To make these observations concrete, we turn to the case at hand. The important contrast comes at the outset. The high priest and king fall into a single genus, but speciation, based on traits particular to the king, then distinguishes the one from the other. Now if I further had to set forth what I conceive to form the deepest conviction at the most profound layers of thought, it is that things set in relationship always stand in that same relationship. The work of making connections and drawing conclusions produces results that are fixed and final. If we establish a connection between one set of things and another, that connection forms the end of matters – that, and not a series, by which the connection between A and B serves as a guide to a movement from C to A via B, that is, as we shall now see, the formation of not a connection but a series of things that are connected only to one another, but not to other components of the same series – which is to say, a series.

To put matters very simply, if A is like B, and B is like C, then is C like A? And if – as the received logic of the age insists! – we entertain the possibility of a series, then, and much more to the point: *Precisely what are the rules of connection that form the links of the results of comparison and contrast?*

In other words, in the aftermath of classification comes not hierarchization but movement, this thing in relationship to that, that in relationship to the other, all things in movement, nothing at rest. So, if a series is possible, then how is a series composed? That is the question answered by the Bavli, the question no one in the Mishnah asked, because the Mishnah's framers contemplated a world at rest, and the Bavli's, a world in motion.

In so stating, I have leapt over each of the necessary stages of my exposition, So let us begin from the beginning. Now that the Mishnah's position is in hand, we revert to my claim that the Bavli's own statement in the chapter under discussion concerns the nature of thought. Let us first of all review the points that are made, and the sequence in which they are set forth. We begin with the point of intersection:

1. It is important to know how to connect rules to Scripture.

2. The principles that govern the making of connections to Scripture are those that govern making connections not between words and words ("the hermeneutical principles") but rather between one thing and something else, that is, defining a genus and its species; so when we know how to compare and contrast, find what is like something else and what is different from something else, we know how to conduct the passage from rules to Scripture.
3. Exegetical rules tell us how to form classes of things in relationship to Scripture.
4. Dialectical rules tell us how to move from one class of things to another class of things.

To state matters simply: What makes a list into a series? And how are we supposed to effect that transformation – that movement? Step two then marks the point of departure, and Steps 3 and 4 denote the remarkable shift in the passage. We go not only from rule to generalization, or from case to principle. That, to be sure, takes place and forms an everywhere-present metaproposition, as the tedium of the remainder of the chapter showed us. Rather, we go from thinking about things and their connections (comparison and contrast) to thinking about thought itself. So what I have represented as the rules of dialectical thinking – not merely argument! – turn out to tell us how thought happens; the Bavli's reading of Mishnah-tractate Zebahim 5:1-2 forms a fundamental exercise of thought about thinking.

When we review the principal steps in the sustained and unfolding inquiry, we realize that, in particulars and in detail, the framers of the passage have set forth a profound essay on thought. In the terms just now given, if A=B, and B=C, then does A=C? Is a series possible? Are there limits to the extension of a series? And on what basis do we construct a series? Do the media of linkage between A and B, that is, A=B, have to be the same as those that link B to C, for C to stand in the series that A has begun? These abstract questions have to become concrete before the sense of matters will emerge. So let us now review what the chapter has already told us: the sequence of points that represent the inquiry into the making of connections, which is to say, the Bavli's metapropositional statement on the character of a series. For it is the series, first this, then that, finally the third thing, and the rules that govern the movement from this, to that, to the third thing, that defines what is the center of deep thought in the Bavli's reading of the specified Mishnah paragraphs. I cite the pertinent language, where necessary restating what has already been given in

Analogical-Contrastive Thinking and the Problem of Dialectical Thought 75

the context of the exposition of the text, but I do not then repeat all of the text. The stages in the argument of the Talmud now are identified and repeated, as marked by boldface capital letters. The argument is astonishing for its sustained quality; it moves in an inexorable course, rigorously insisting on settling one question before raising the next, and consequent one.

A. II.2 E. *That answer is satisfactory for him who takes the view that one may indeed derive a rule governing a prior subject from one that is given later on, but from the perspective of him who denies that fact, what is to be said?*

The opening question contains the entirety of what is to follow: the conviction that anterior to conclusions and debates on fixed propositions is a premise, and the premise concerns not issues but thought itself. For what is before us is not a hermeneutical principle that guides the exegesis of Scripture, the movement from a rule back to a scriptural formulation deemed to pertain. It is a rule of how to think. And the issue is explicit: Does thought flow, or does it stand still? Does it flow backward from conclusion to a conclusion already reached? In the context of the document at hand, the issue is one of arrangements of words, that is, a literary and therefore an exegetical question. That is, then, the proposition. But the metaproposition is otherwise, though that is not yet explicit.

B. II.2 J. *But this is the reason for the position of rabbis, who declare one exempt [from having to present a suspensive guilt-offering in the case of a matter of doubt regarding acts of sacrilege]: they derive a verbal analogy to a sin-offering based on the appearance of the word 'commandments' with reference to both matters.*
N. *They take the view that one may not derive from an argument by analogy established through the use of a word in common only a limited repertoire of conclusions [but once the analogy is drawn, then all of the traits of one case apply to the other].*

Here is an issue not of exegesis, therefore of hermeneutics, but of the rules of right thinking: thinking about thought. And what it concerns, as I have suggested in context, is how we establish not classes of things but linkage between and among classes of things. Let me state the centerpiece in simple words but with heavy emphasis: *Since I make connections through analogy and contrast, may I proceed to make connections beyond the limits of the original connection? And the answer is, I must proceed, because thought does not come to rest. Comparison and contrast yield connections, which then govern.*

In the language before us, once I draw an analogy, do all traits of the two classes of things that have been linked through analogy – of necessity only partial, since were the analogy entire, both classes would constitute a single class! – pertain to each class? In the present context, what we establish is the anonymous, therefore the governing rule. The norm is that once we draw an analogy, the connection established by the (mere) analogy takes over, so that we treat as analogous traits not covered by the analogy at all. The analogy establishes the connection; but then the movement of thought is such that the connection is deemed to have established a new class of things, all of them subject to one rule. The movement – the dialectic – therefore is not a mere trait of argument, "if you say this, I say that," but a trait of thought: if this is the result of step A, then step B is to be taken – out from, without regard to, the limitations of step A. Thought then is continuous, always in motion, and that metaproposition states in the most abstract terms possible the prior and generative metaproposition that, when we compare classes of things, the comparison initiates a process that transcends the limits of comparison. That is to say, again with emphasis, *we can effect a series.*

C. II.2 S. *One authority maintains that proof supplied by analogy [here: the analogy sustained by the use of "and" to join the two subjects] takes priority, and the other party maintains that the proof supplied by the demonstration of a totality of congruence among salient traits takes precedence. Rabbis prefer the latter, Aqiba the former position.*

T. *Not at all! All parties concur that proof supplied by analogy [here: the analogy sustained by the use of "and" to join the two subjects] takes priority. But rabbis in this context will say to you that the rule governing the subject treated below derives from the rule governing the subject treated above, so that the guilt-offering must be worth a least two silver sheqels. This is established so that you should not argue that the doubt cannot be more stringent than the matter of certainty, and just as where there is certainty of having committed a sin, one has to present a sin-offering that may be worth even so little as a sixth of a zuz in value, so if there is a matter of doubt, the guilt-offering worth only a sixth of a zuz would suffice.*

Once the connection is made, linking an earlier rule (in Scripture's orderly exposition) to a later one, then the connection is such that movement is not only forward but backward. We have established not a connection between one thing and something else, but a series that can encompass a third thing and a fourth thing, onward – but with, or without, formal limit. This principle of right thinking that the

Analogical-Contrastive Thinking and the Problem of Dialectical Thought 77

hypothesis of the series requires is revealed by Scripture, as is made explicit once more in the following:

D. III.2 I. ...And should you say that if Scripture had not included the matter, we should have reached the same conclusion by argument from analogy, then if that is the case, we can infer by analogy also the rule on laying on of hands...

The main point here is that, once an analogy serves, it serves everywhere an analogy can be drawn; there is no a priori that limits the power of an analogy to govern all like cases. A series is possible once the work of thought moves beyond contrast and analogy. And it is the rule of right thought that, once we have established a comparison and a contrast, that fact validates drawing conclusions on other aspects of the classes of things that have been connected through the comparison and contrast – analogical-contrastive thinking is then not static but in motion. Is the motion perpetual? Not at all, for Scripture, for its part, has the power to place limits on a series.

E. IV.2 B. If a matter was covered by an encompassing rule but then was singled out for some innovative purpose, you have not got the right to restore the matter to the rubric of the encompassing rule unless Scripture itself explicitly does so.

[That means that the encompassing rule does not apply to an item that Scripture, for its own purposes, has singled out. The upshot is that the identified item is now exceptional in some aspect, so it is no longer subject to a common rule governing all other items in context; then the limits of analogy are set by Scripture's treatment of the items of a series. It is worthwhile reviewing the pertinent example:] The series is subjected to limits, if an item in the sequence of connections that forms the series proves exceptional: this is connected to that, that to the other thing, but the other thing is other in some other way, so there the series ends.

H. *If [you claim that the purpose of the verse is as stated and not to teach that doing the rite at the north is indispensable, as originally proposed,] then Scripture should have stated only the rule governing the rite for the one healed from the skin ailment but not the earlier version of the rule.*

I. *Quite so – if we take the view that when something becomes the subject of a new law, it cannot then be covered by an encompassing rule that otherwise would apply, while the encompassing rule still can be derived from that special case. But if we take the view that when something becomes the subject of a new law, then it cannot be covered by an encompassing rule that otherwise would apply, and the encompassing rule also cannot be derived from that special* case, then the law [Lev. 7:1-10, indicating that the guilt-offering must be killed in the north] is needed for its own purpose!

J. Since Scripture has restored the matter to the rubric of the encompassing rule explicitly, that restoration has taken place.

K. Said Mar Zutra b. R. Mari to Rabina, "But why not say, when Scripture restored the matter to the rubric of the encompassing rule, that was solely in regard to having to present the blood and the sacrificial parts on the altar, since the priest is necessary to perform that rite. But as to slaughtering the animal, which does not have to be done by a priest, that does not have to be done at the northern side of the altar?"

L. [He said to him,] "If so, Scripture should say simply, 'for it is like the sin-offering.' Why say, 'or the guilt-offering, like the sin-offering'? It is to teach, let it be like other guilt-offerings [that must be slaughtered at the northern side of the altar]."

Here again, therefore, the issue is the limits of analogy, how these are determined.

F. IV.4 A. Raba said, "[The proposition that that which is derived on the basis of a verbal analogy does not in turn go and impart a lesson by means of a verbal analogy] derives from the following proof:

We go over familiar ground. Raba takes the view that a series is simply not possible. Others allege that if we connect one class of things to some other by means, for example, of a verbal analogy, then making that same connection once again, where another verbal analogy connects the second class of things to yet a third, is not correct. Scripture shows that verbal analogies do not validate the making of series, and this is shown in an explicit way:

B. "It is written, 'As is taken off from the ox of the sacrifice of peace-offerings' (Lev. 4:10) [namely, the sacrificial parts of the anointed priest's bullock brought for a sin-offering] – *now for what purpose is this detail given? That the lobe of the liver and the two kidneys are to be burned on the altar [as is the case with those of the sin-offering], that fact is specified in the body of the verse itself. But the purpose is to intimate that the burning of the lobe of the liver and the two kidneys of the he-goats brought as sin-offerings for idolatry are to be derived by analogy from the bullock of the community brought on account of an inadvertent sin. That law is not explicitly stated in the passage on the bullock that is brought for an inadvertent sin, but is derived from the rule governing the bullock of the anointed priest. 'As is taken off' is required so that it might be treated as something written in that very*

Analogical-Contrastive Thinking and the Problem of Dialectical Thought 79

> passage *[on the bullock of inadvertence, being superfluous in its own context]*, not as something derived on the basis of a verbal analogy that does not in turn go and impart a lesson by means of a verbal analogy."

To repeat my exposition of this matter: I have two items, A and B. I claim that B is like A, therefore the rule governing A applies also to B. Now I turn forward, to C. C is not analogous to A; there are no points of congruence or (in the exegetical formulation that our authors use) verbal intersection. But C is like B. It is like B because there is an analogy by reason of verbal intersection (the same word being used in reference to C and B.) The question is, may I apply to C, by reason of the verbal intersection between C and B, the lesson that I have learned in regard to B only by reason of B's similarity by reason of congruence, not verbal intersection, to A? Can a conclusion that is derived on the basis of a verbal analogy go and impart a lesson by reason of analogy to a third item? Raba now maintains that that is not the case. But the matter has gone in the other direction: a series is possible. But if a series is possible, then what limits are to be placed on the media by which a series is effected?

G. IV.5 A. Now it is a fact that that which is derived on the basis of a verbal analogy does in turn go and impart a lesson by means of a verbal analogy, *demonstrated whether in the manner of Raba or in the manner of Rabina.*

Now we revert to our basic issue: the validity of a series. Here we move into as yet unexplored ground, which is the basis for my claim that the order of problems is dictated by an interest in a systematic presentation of the rules of right thinking. We have been exposed to the case in favor of a series: once the analogy makes the connection, then all traits of the things connected are brought into relationship with all other such traits. Scripture then provides one limit to the length of a series: a series cannot be infinite. But there is another limit proposed, and it is not scriptural but substantive, in the nature of things, a trait of thought itself. Here is the point at which I find this sustained exposition of thinking about thought simply remarkable.

B. Is it the rule, however, that *that which is derived on the basis of a verbal analogy may in turn go and impart a lesson by means of an argument on the basis of congruence?* [Freedman: Thus the law stated in A is applied to B by analogy. Can that law then be applied to C because of congruence between B and C?]

We have proven one point. It bears a consequence. We go on to the consequence. The mode of thought is dialectical not only in form, but also in substance: if A, then B. If B, then what about C? It is one thing to have shown that if B is like A, then C, unlike A, is rendered comparable to B by a verbal analogy. But then may I take the next step and draw into the framework of B and C, joined by verbal analogy and assigned a common rule by B's congruent analogy to A, also D, E, F, and G, that is, other classes of things joined to C by verbal analogy – but not necessarily the same verbal analogy that has joined C to B? That indeed is the obvious next step to be taken, and it is now taken. It is taken in the simple words just now given, and the same point is now going to be made, in a systematic way, for each medium by which classes of things are formed and then connected to one another. Analogical-contrastive thinking therefore is not static but always in motion, since, once a connection is made, other connections made follow. If we make a connection between A and B on the basis of one set of shared traits, we may proceed to make a connection between C and A, via B, on the basis of traits shared by B and C but not by A and C. Not only so, but the same mode of thought extends to the media of connection. If I connect A to B by verbal analogy, I may connect B to other classes of things, for example, C, D, E, by other media of connection, for example, verbal analogy connects A to B, and an argument based on congruence connects B to C, and backward to A; and an argument a fortiori may connect C to D, and backward to A and B – series without end, or series that end only in the dictates of revelation, the ultimate arbiter of the classification and hierarchy of all things. What is truly impressive in what follows is the rigorous order by which each possibility is raised in its turn, the connections fore and aft, such that the framer of the whole not only makes his point in words, but also illustrates it in his own representation of matters: a series is not only possible, it is also compelling. So we see as we move forward, now with no need for further exposition, from H to M.

H. IV.6 A. That which is learned by a verbal analogy may in turn go and impart a rule by an argument a fortiori.
I. IV.7 A. Can that which is learned by verbal analogy in turn go and impart a rule by an analogy based on the congruence of other shared traits [but not verbal ones in context]?

Once more to review: we have now linked B to C via a verbal analogy. C stands in relationship to other classes of things, but not for the same reason that it stands in relationship to B, that is, through other than verbal analogical relationships. It forms a relationship a fortiori, for instance, with D, E, and F. If something applies to C, the lesser, it surely should apply to D, the greater. So now we want to know the permissible grounds for drawing relationships – comparisons and

Analogical-Contrastive Thinking and the Problem of Dialectical Thought 81

contrasts – of classes of things. So on what basis do we move from species to species and uncover the genera of which they form a part (if they do form a part)? Is it only verbal correspondence or intersection, as has been implicit to this point? Or are there more abstract bases for the same work of genus construction (in our language: category formation and re-formation)?

J. IV.8 A. Can a rule that is derived by analogy based on the congruence of other shared traits [but not verbal ones in context] turn around and teach a lesson through an analogy based on verbal analogy?

K. IV.9 A. Can a rule that is derived by an analogy based on the congruence of other shared traits [but not verbal ones in context] turn around and teach a lesson through an analogy based on the congruence of [other] shared traits?

L. IV.10 A. Can a rule that is derived by an analogy based on the congruence of other shared traits [but not verbal ones in context] go **and teach a lesson** through an argument a fortiori?

M. IV.10 F. If an argument deriving from an analogy based on verbal congruence, which cannot go and, by an argument based on verbal congruence, impart its rule to some other class – *as has been shown by either Raba's or Rabina's demonstration* – nonetheless can go and by an argument a fortiori impart its rule to some other class – *as has been shown by the Tannaite authority of the household of R. Ishmael* – then a rule that is derived by an argument based on analogy based on other-than-verbal congruence, which can for its part go and impart its lesson by an argument based on an analogy resting on verbal congruity which is like itself – *as has been shown by Rami bar Hama* – surely can in turn teach its lesson by an argument a fortiori to yet another case!

So at stake throughout is the question of how a series is composed: the media for the making of connections between one thing and something else (that is, one class of things and some other class of things, in such wise that the rules governing the one are shown by the analogy to govern the other as well). We want to know not only that a connection is made, but how it is made. And some maintain that if the connection is made between one thing and something else by means, for example, of a verbal analogy dictated by Scripture's wording, then a connection between that something else and a third thing must also be made in a manner consistent with the initial medium of connection, verbal analogy. It cannot be made by means of some other medium of connection. But the paramount position is otherwise: dialectics affect not only argument but thought itself, because connections are made through all media by which connections are made. We now reach the end of the matter, in a set of ultimately theoretical issues:

N. IV.11 A. Can a rule that is derived by an analogy based on the congruence of other shared traits [but not verbal ones in context] go and teach a lesson through an argument constructed by analogy based on the congruence of other shared traits among two or more classifications of things?
B. *That question must stand.*

O. IV.12 A. Can a rule derived by an argument a fortiori go and teach a rule established through analogy of verbal usage?
B. The affirmative derives from an argument a fortiori:
C. If an argument deriving from an analogy based on points of other-than-verbal congruence, which cannot go and, by an argument based on verbal congruence, impart its rule to some other class – *as has been shown by R. Pappa's demonstration* – then a rule that is derived by an argument a fortiori, which can be derived by an argument based on the shared verbal traits of two things – *as has been shown by the Tannaite authority of the house of R. Ishmael* – surely should be able to impart its rule to another classification of things by reason of an argument based on a verbal analogy!
D. *That position poses no problems to one who takes the view that R. Pappa's case has been made. But for one who takes the view that R. Pappa's case has not been made, what is to be said?*
E. *The question then must stand.*

P. IV.13 A. Can a rule that is derived by an argument a fortiori go and teach a lesson through an argument based on the congruence of other shared traits [but not verbal ones in context]?
B. The affirmative derives from an argument a fortiori:
C. If an argument deriving from an analogy based on points of other-than-verbal congruence, which cannot be derived from an argument based on verbal congruence, imparts its rule to some other class – *as has been shown by R. Yohanan's demonstration* – and can go and teach a lesson by an argument based on an analogy established through other-than-verbal traits, *as has been shown by Rami bar Hama* – a rule based on an argument a fortiori, which can be derived by an argument based on an analogy resting on verbal coincidence, surely should be able to impart its rule to another classification of things by reason of an argument based on an other-than-verbal analogy!

Q. IV.14 A. Can a rule based on an argument a fortiori turn around and teach a lesson through an argument based on an argument a fortiori?
B. Indeed so, and the affirmative derives from an argument a fortiori:
C. If an argument deriving from an analogy based on points of other-than-verbal congruence, which cannot be derived from

an argument based on verbal congruence, imparts its rule to some other class – *as has been shown by R. Yohanan's demonstration* – and can go and teach a lesson by an argument a fortiori, as we have just pointed out, then an argument that can be derived from an analogy based on verbal congruence – *as has been shown by the Tannaite authority of the household of R. Ishmael* – surely should be able to impart its rule by an argument a fortiori!

D. But would this then represent what we are talking about, namely, a rule deriving from an argument a fortiori that has been applied to another case by means of an argument a fortiori? Surely this is nothing more than a secondary derivation produced by an argument a fortiori!

E. Rather, argue in the following way:

F. Indeed so, and the affirmative derives from an argument a fortiori:

G. If an argument based on an analogy of a verbal character cannot be derived from another such argument based on an analogy between two classes of things that rests upon a verbal congruence – *in accordance with the proofs of either Raba or Rabina* – nonetheless can then go and impart its lesson by an argument a fortiori – *in accordance with the proof of the Tannaite authority of the household of R. Ishmael* – then an argument a fortiori, which can serve to transfer a lesson originally learned through an argument based upon verbal congruence, *in accordance with the proof of the Tannaite authority of the household of R. Ishmael* – surely should be able to impart its lesson to yet another classification of things through an argument a fortiori.

H. And this does represent what we are talking about, namely, a rule deriving from an argument a fortiori that has been applied to another case by means of an argument a fortiori.

R. IV.15 A. Can a rule based on an argument a fortiori turn around and teach a rule through an argument constructed on the basis of shared traits of an other-than-verbal character among two classifications of things?...

C. *But that is not so. For even if we concede that that is the case there, then still the rule derives from the act of slaughter of unconsecrated beasts* [Freedman].

S. IV.16 A. Can a rule derived by an argument based on shared traits of an other-than-verbal character shared among two classes of things then turn around and teach a lesson by an argument based on an analogy of a verbal character, an analogy not of a verbal character, an argument a fortiori, or an argument based on shared traits?

B. *Solve at least one of those problems by appeal to the following:*

C. On what account have they said that if blood of an offering is left overnight on the altar, it is fit? Because if the sacrificial parts are kept overnight on the altar, they are fit. And why if the sacrificial parts are kept overnight on the altar are they fit? Because if the meat of the offering is kept overnight on the altar it is fit. [Freedman: Thus the rule governing the sacrificial parts is derived by an appeal to an argument based on shared traits of an other-than-verbal character shared among two classes of things, and that rule in turn is applied to the case of the blood by another such argument based on shared traits of an other-than-verbal character shared among two classes of things].

D. What about the rule governing meat that is taken outside of the Temple court? [If such meat is put up on the altar, it is not removed therefrom. Why so?]

E. Because meat that has been taken out of the holy place is suitable for a high place....

M. [Reverting to C-E:] Now can an analogy be drawn concerning something that has been disposed of in the proper manner for something that has not been disposed of in the proper manner? [If the sacrificial parts are kept overnight, they are not taken off the altar, and therefore the meat kept overnight is fit; but the meat may be kept overnight, while the sacrificial parts may not. So too when the Temple stood, the flesh might not be taken outside, but where there was no Temple and only high places, the case is scarcely analogous!]

N. *The Tannaite authority for this rule derives it from the augmentative sense, extending the rule, deriving from the formulation,* "This is the Torah of the burnt-offering" (Lev. 6:2). [Freedman: The verse teaches that all burnt-offerings, even with the defects catalogued here, are subject to the same rule and do not get removed from the altar once they have been put there; the arguments given cannot be sustained but still support that proposition.]

The movement from point to point, first things first, second things in sequence, is so stunning in the precise logic of the order of issues – we must know **A** before we can contemplate asking about **B** – that only a brief review is called for.

We have shown that we may move from a class of things joined to another through analogy based on congruence, that is, from A to B, onward to other classes of things joined to the foregoing by verbal analogy or intersection, that is, from B to C and beyond. But can we then move from C, linked to B via verbal analogy, to D, linked to C, but not to A or B, by congruence, for example, comparable and shared traits of a salient order? The issue then, is may we move forward to further classes of things by moving "backward," to a principle of linkage of classes that has served to bring us to this point, in other words, reversing the course of principles of linkage? What our framers, then, want to know is a very logical question: Are there fixed rules that govern the order or sequence by which we move from one class of things to another, so that, if we propose to link classes of things, we can move only from A to B by one principle (comparison and contrast of salient traits), and from B to C by a necessarily consequent and always second principle (verbal intersection); then we may move (by this theory) from C to D only by verbal intersection but not by appeal to congruence. Why not? Because, after all, if C is linked to B only by verbal intersection but not by congruence, bearing no relationship to A at all, then how claim that D stands in a series begun at A, if it has neither verbal connection, nor, as a matter of fact, congruence to link it to anything in the series? What is clear in this reprise is that the issue is drawn systematically, beginning to end. By simply seeing the sequence of questions, we grasp the whole: the program, the method, the order, all dictated by the inner requirements of sustained inquiry into the logic of comparison and contrast, read as a dialectical problem. The upshot may be stated now in a very few words.

A list is never a list, it is always part of a series; thought moves but does not come to rest. That metaproposition comes to formal expression at the very surface of discourse in the ever-flowing movement of argument of the Talmud itself. That is why the framers of the Bavli never leave the Mishnah alone, allowing its formal perfection and its serene expositions of the classification of things to stand still, rather insisting on exploring the connections between classifications – the connections that shift and change, not the hierarchization that, for the framers of the Mishnah, satisfactorily portrays connection in some one, set way.

The metapropositional program contributed by the Bavli's framers concerns how series are made, which is to say, whether connections yield static or dynamic results, which is to say, how thought happens at the deepest layers of intellect. Now, at the end, we ask the framers of the Mishnah to address the question before us. And in answer, they give us silence. So we know that here we hear what is distinctive to, and the remarkable discovery of, the authorship of the Bavli. Since, it is clear, that discovery has taken place within the words of the Written Torah, and, since their deepest metaproposition maintained that the words of the Written Torah are the words of God to Moses, our rabbi, at Sinai – the words, not just the gist – we have to conclude with what I conceive to be the bedrock of the metapropositional program before us: the Torah teaches us not only what God said, but how God thinks. When we understand the Torah rightly, we engage in thinking about thought. And that is how we know God: through thought. So Spinoza was not so heretical after all.

Part One
THE CITY OF GOD IN JUDAISM: TRANSFORMATIONS OF THE SOCIAL ORDER FROM PHILOSOPHY TO RELIGION

4

The Philosophical Judaism of the Mishnah, Tosefta, and Tannaite Midrash Compilations

Between 200 and 400 Judaism changed from a philosophy to a religion. Defining the word Judaism in this context, which is not theological but descriptive and analytical and comparative, entails understanding a religion as a system of social order formed (whether in fact or in imagination) by the believers. That system in the nature of things always is portrayed in writing, and the problem of description and analysis concerns the reading of written evidence as testimonies to authors' imagination of the social world. The problem I address concerns the transformation, by continuator documents, of a Judaic system of the social order, one that was fully set forth in its initial document and both carried forward and vastly recast by continuator-documents. That problem therefore directs attention to systemic description, analysis, and interpretation of documentary evidence, for in my documentary history of ideas, by comparing one set of writings with another, I compare one system of a religion to another system within that same religion.

By a religious system (or "a Judaism" for the case at hand) I mean a theory of the social order that appeals for validation to supernatural authority and that comprises a worldview or philosophy, way of life or economics, and theory of the social entity or politics. These components of a theory of the social order formed under religious auspices may be represented by the words ethos, ethics, and ethnos. By (a) Judaism I mean a Judaic system, which is a cogent account of the social order, comprising a worldview, way of life, and theory of the social entity, "Israel," all together setting forth a response to a question deemed urgent and encompassing, providing an answer found self-evidently valid. The Jews' long history has witnessed the formation of a variety of such Judaic systems. In the first seven centuries of the Common Era (= A.D.) the canonical writings of one such system, the one that has predominated since that time, took shape.[1] That is the Judaic system, the transformation of which is under discussion in these lectures. I describe that system as it is attested or adumbrated by the canonical writings produced by sages bearing the title "rabbis." I read those writings as accounts of the principal parts of the structure and system of society, with special attention to what seem to me essential: way of life or ethics, and, in secular social science, economics; worldview or ethos, and, in secular language, philosophy (including science); and theory of the social entity that realizes the one and lives by the other, or ethnos.

By philosophy I mean very simply, a system of thought that, in the context of the same time and place, people generally deemed philosophers will have recognized as philosophical, with the proviso that there be no error as to the facts of the matter. The Mishnah, the first canonical writing of Judaism after the Hebrew Scriptures of ancient Israel ("the Old Testament") in important ways is to be read as philosophy in accord with the generally accepted understanding of philosophy in the time, ca. A.D. 200, and place, the Greek-speaking Near East. By philosophy both in that study and here, therefore, I mean specifically the philosophical tradition of the Greco-Roman world of the Second Sophistic, in particular, as I shall explain at length, the method of Aristotle and the proposition important to Middle Platonism. But philosophy in a generic sense demands its place, and by philosophy in general I mean disciplined, rigorous thought, in accord with rules subject to application without limit as to topic, that intelligibly produces generalizations demonstrated on the basis of correct principles of thought concerning this-worldly facts to govern or explain a variety of circumstances. A philosophy forms a cogent system of rational thought that treats diverse cases by appeal to a limited set of internally coherent generalizations. Such a system, as to method, abstract and intelligible, subject to reasoned explanation, as to topic, concerning a variety of concrete cases or problems, defines what I mean by (a) philosophy and, consequently, philosophical.[2]

---

[1]The definition of the system and the documentary evidence that permits describing it are set forth in a moment.

[2]I have further worked out in great detail an account of those passages in the entire Mishnah that are to be classified as philosophical, within the stated criterion, in my *The Philosophical Mishnah*. Volume I. *The Initial Probe*; Volume II. *The Tractates' Agenda. From Abodah Zarah to Moed Qatan*;

So I take the two sets of documents – the Mishnah and related Midrash compilations, the Talmud of the Land of Israel and associated Midrash collections – as evidence of systems to which they refer or attest, respectively, and it is the systems that I claim exhibit traits I can describe and connections – comparisons and contrasts – I can analyze and interpret. We are engaged, therefore, in an exercise in the study of category formation. What I show is two things. The first is how a continuous literary tradition – the Yerushalmi is represented as a (mere) continuation of, and commentary to, the Mishnah, and the several distinct groups of Midrash compilations are presented as (mere) commentary to Scripture – in fact attests to distinct religious systems. The second is how the categories that frame the initial system are received and dealt with in the successor system. It follows that the documentary method analyzes literary sources in such a way as to allow the description of religious systems by reference to the category formations characteristic of each, and it interprets those sources so as to carry out the comparison of the category formations of the one with those of the other.

Among the philosophers of the Greco-Roman philosophical tradition, the Mishnah's Judaic system can have been perceived as philosophical not merely in method but also in message. The Mishnah's method of hierarchical classification in important ways is like that of the natural history of Aristotle,[3] and the central component of its message, congruent to that of neo-Platonism. Specifically, the Mishnah's Judaic system sets forth in stupefying detail a version of one critical proposition of neo-Platonism, demonstrated through a standard Aristotelian method.[4] The repeated proof through the Aristotelian method of hierarchical classification demonstrates in detail that many things – done enough times, *all* things – really form a single thing, many species, a single genus, many genera, an encompassing and well-crafted, cogent whole. Every time we speciate – and the Mishnah

---

Volume III. *The Tractates' Agenda. From Nazir to Zebahim;* and Volume IV. *The Repertoire* (Atlanta, 1989: Scholars Press for Brown Judaic Studies).

[3]But a great deal of further study must show in all specificity how the Mishnah's method of hierarchical classification compares in detail with that of Aristotle. My observations are only the beginning of the matter.

[4]And I need hardly add that the very eclecticism of the philosophy of Judaism places it squarely within the philosophical mode of its time. See J. M. Dillon and A. A. Long, eds., *The Question of "Eclecticism." Studies in Later Greek Philosophy* (Berkeley and Los Angeles, 1988: University of California Press). But these are only general observations, not meant to suggest direct connection or even to imply that an explanation drawn from "what was floating in the air" seems to me to pertain; I have no explanation.

is a mass of speciated lists – we affirm that position; each successful labor of forming relationships among species, for example, making them into a genus, or identifying the hierarchy of the species, proves it again. Not only so, but when we can show that many things are really one, or that one thing yields many (the reverse and confirmation of the former), we say in a fresh way a single immutable truth, the one of this philosophy concerning the unity of all being in an orderly composition of all things within a single taxon. Accordingly, this Judaism's initial system, the Mishnah's, finds its natural place within philosophy because it appeals to the Aristotelian methods and medium of natural philosophy – classification, comparison and contrast, expressed in the forms of *Listenwissenschaft* – to register its position, which is an important one in Middle Platonism and later (close to a century after the closure of the Mishnah) would come to profound expression in Plotinus.[5]

Since I characterize the method as *Listenwissenschaft* and maintain that, in the Mishnaic form, that ancient mode of thought, in the Near East conventional from Sumerian times, in the Mishnah's version corresponds to Aristotle's method of natural philosophy, let me quickly define what I mean by that word. It is the presentation of a proposition, for example, a rule, through a catalogue of facts formed by appeal to common indicative traits. The list then is so composed that, through the recurring regularities traits of the entries, it will yield a proposition common to them all. Further still, the list will produce a generalization to items not on the list altogether, hence serving a syllogistic purpose. A list will therefore be made up of parallel items that all together point to a simple conclusion; in the Mishnah the proposed general conclusion may or may not be given at the end of the catalogue; but the catalogue – by definition – is pointed. All of the catalogued facts moreover are taken to bear self-evident connections to one another, established by those pertinent shared traits implicit in the composition of the list. They therefore also bear meaning and point through the weight of evidence to an inescapable conclusion.

Let us dwell on the philosophical classification of the Mishnah's mode of thought. The Mishnah's method of inquiry is that of natural history, corresponding point by point with that method of natural history characteristic of Aristotle. I do not claim that our sages of blessed memory read, or could have read, Aristotle or any other Greek

---

[5]That proposition, on the essential unity of the hierarchical nature of all being forms one important, generative premise of neo-Platonism, as we shall see in a moment. So we find a philosophical method used to establish a philosophical proposition. That, sum and substance, is what I claim to demonstrate.

The Philosophical Judaism of the Mishnah

philosopher. Aristotle's work on natural history, his reflections on scientific method, for example, the *Posterior Analytics*[6] – these works speak in their own language to their own problems, and the Mishnah's authorship has written in a different language about incomparable problems. But when we compare our philosophers' method with that of Aristotle, who also, as a matter of fact, set forth a system that, in part, appealed to the right ordering of things through classification by correct rules[7] the simple fact becomes inescapable. Before us are different people, talking about different things, but in the same way.

The heirs of the initial, philosophical Judaism received a system in which the subject of economics – the rational disposition of scarce resources – was utilized in order to set forth a systemic statement of fundamental importance. While making every effort to affirm the details of that statement and apply them, they in no way contributed to the theoretical work that the economics of the Mishnah can, and should, have precipitated. Consequently, their system repeated the given but made no significant use of what had been received. Instead, as we shall see later on, the heirs of the Mishnah invented what we must call a counterpart category, that is to say, a category that dealt with problems of the rational utilization of scarce resources, but not with those same scarce resources defined by the philosophical system of the Mishnah. The systemic category for the aborning religious system was not an economics, but corresponded, in the new system, to the position and role of economics in the old.

So far as a well-crafted theory of a social entity knows how and why scarce resources are assigned to, or end up in the hands of, one person or institution or class or other social organization, rather than some other, that system, in designing the social order, has worked out an economics for itself.[8] The Mishnah's system – alone among all of the

---

[6] I consulted Jonathan Barnes, *Aristotle's Posterior Analytics* (Oxford, 1975: Clarendon Press).

[7] And, as to proposition about the hierarchical ordering of all things in a single way, the unity of all being in right order, while we cannot show and surely do not know that the Mishnah's philosophers knew anything about Plato, let alone Plotinus's neo-Platonism (which came to expression only in the century after the closure of the Mishnah!), we can compare our philosophers' proposition with that of neo-Platonism. For that philosophy, as we shall see, did seek to give full and rich expression to the proposition that all things emerge from one thing, and one thing encompasses all things, and that constitutes the single proposition that animates the system as a whole.

[8] But not all systems work out an economics or require one. A system will address the rationality required for the disposition of scarce resources when, and only when, a systemic message may be set forth through the exemplification (or even specification) of that rationality. No Christianity

Judaic (and Christian) systems of late antiquity[9] – set forth as part of its systemic composition a fully-articulated economics, entirely congruent with the philosophical economics of Aristotle, answering questions concerning the definition of wealth, property, production and the means of production, ownership and control of the means of production, the determination of price and value and the like.

And that fact signifies that the Judaic system to which the Mishnah attests is philosophical not only in method and message but in its very systemic composition. The principal components of its theory of the social order, its account of the way of life of its Israel and its picture of the conduct of the public policy of its social entity – all of these in detail correspond in their basic definitions and indicative

---

developed an economics of systemic consequence prior to the medieval Christian encounter with Aristotle. And one of the marks of the Aristotelian character of the Mishnah's economics, as we see in this chapter, is its forthright utilization of economics in the formation and expression of its systemic message, and in the point-by-point replication of Aristotle's particular doctrines in the composition of that economics. I think the basic reason, as with politics, is that the Mishnah's framers took for granted their "Israel" formed not merely an ethnic group or a religious community (our terms, not theirs) but a nation living on its land; the enlandisement of their system necessitated address to the rational disposition of scarce resources, defined, as a matter of fact, as real estate; and the givenness of the nationhood of their system's social entity led them to reflect on the legitimate uses of violence. They took for granted theirs was an empowered social entity. Only in the diaspora do Judaic systems by-pass economics and politics as media for the making of the system's larger statement, even though episodic sayings on economic action (e.g., in ethics) or on politics (in a supernatural context ordinarily) do make their appearance here and there. The fundamental criterion for sorting out Judaisms must be, then, enlandised and empowered or not; all systems must fall on one side or another of that line. If the hypothesis just now suggested is sound, then no diaspora-Judaism should resort to economics or politics as principal systemic components. The shift then is not so odd, because while located in the Land of Israel, the framers had entered a period in which their Israel no longer governed within the Land, let alone overseas, and furthermore progressively was losing command of the real estate of what they called the Land of Israel to Christians, who called the same territory Palestine. The successor system's utter reversal of the conventional meanings of politics and economics forms a response, of a kind, to that worldly transformation of the Jews' economic and political circumstances. The really interesting question lies elsewhere: the Talmud of Babylonia and related writings and whether and how the system to which they attest yields the stigmata of disenlandisement and disempowerment. If it does not, then the criterion of provenance in the Land of Israel does not serve so decisively as, at the present, it seems to me to.

[9]For instance, history defined an important, systemically critical, category for Augustine, economics did not.

traits with the economics and the politics of Greco-Roman philosophy in the Aristotelian tradition. Specifically, the Mishnah's economics, in general in the theory of the rational disposition of scarce resources and of the management and increase thereof, and specifically in its definitions of wealth and ownership, production and consumption, point by point, corresponds to that of Aristotle.[10]

To be sure, sayings relevant to an economics may take shape within a religion or a philosophy, without that religion's or philosophy's setting forth an economics at all. For unsystematic opinions on this and that, for instance, episodic sayings about mercy to the poor, recommendations of right action, fairness, honesty, and the like do not by themselves add up to an economics. Indeed, one of the marks of a system's lacking an economics is the presence of merely occasional and ad hoc remarks about matters of wealth or poverty that, all together, attest to complete indifference to the systemic importance of a theory of the rational disposition of scarce resources, their preservation and increase. By contrast, when issues of the rational disposition of scarce resources are treated in a sustained and systematic, internally coherent theory that over all and in an encompassing way explains why this, not that, and defines market in relationship to ownership of the means of production, then we have a systematic account, an economics. Not only so, but, as in the case of Aristotle's economics, the economics will prove to serve the interests of the system of which it is part when it makes a statement in behalf of that larger system. Through economics, the Mishnah's system makes a critical part of its systemic statement, and this authorship found economics, and only economics, the appropriate medium for making that part of its statement.

But for antiquity only two theories of economics, Aristotle's and the Mishnah's, delivered principal parts of systemic statements. There are no other candidates for inclusion on the list of significant thinkers and system-builders to whom an account of an economics mattered in a systematic way in a systemic composition.[11] While other systems made episodic reference to topics of economic interest, Plato's for instance, and any number of other figures allude to issues of wealth, Jesus for the most important example, and in his model, a great many important figures in early Christianity, none produced a well-crafted account of the wealth, the market, exchange, money, value, the definition of the unit

---

[10] The Mishnah's politics is worked out along lines entirely congruent to those dictated by Aristotle's mode of political theory.
[11] For Plato the issue was episodic and bore no important systemic message; for Christian thinkers, economics makes its first consequential appearance in medieval times, with the renewal of Aristotelianism.

and means of production, and other basic components of an economics, let alone a composite of all those things into a coherent statement. And – more to the point – none but Aristotle's and the Mishnah's systems undertook to make a fundamental point in its discussion of topics of economic interest. But Aristotle's and the Mishnah's systems not only did so, they did so in this-worldly terms, by appeal to well-crafted philosophical principles about the character of society and politics. That is why I characterize the Mishnah's economics as philosophical, and why, furthermore, when we understand that the Mishnah sets forth an economics in the way it does rather than in some other, we see that economics forms an indicator of the philosophical character of the Mishnah as a system.[12]

The general point in common between Aristotle's and the Mishnah's economics comes first: for both systems economics formed a chapter in a larger theory of the social order. The power of economics as framed by Aristotle, the only economic theorist of antiquity worthy of the name, was to develop the relationship between the economy to society as a whole.[13] And the framers of the Mishnah did precisely that when they incorporated issues of economics at a profound theoretical level into the system of society as a whole that they proposed to construct. That is why (to paraphrase Polanyi's judgment of Aristotle) the authorship of the Mishnah will be seen as attacking the problem of man's livelihood within a system of sanctification of a holy people with a radicalism of which no later religious thinkers about utopias were capable. None has ever penetrated deeper into the material organization of man's life under the aspect of God's rule. In effect, they posed, in all its breadth, the question of the critical, indeed definitive place occupied by the economy in society under God's rule.

---

[12]My argument should be clarified here. I do not mean to suggest that all systems to be systemic require an economics; nor do I propose that any philosophical system lacking an economics is not philosophical. My task is to demonstrate that the Mishnah's is a distinctively philosophical system, and I have taken as my evidence the demonstration that its system is congruent in method and composition (and, as a matter of fact, here and in the next chapter, in doctrine as well) to a system everyone concedes to be philosophical, which is Aristotle's. So not all systems require an economics, and not all philosophies require an economics, but when the Mishnah's system presents its economics, it shows itself to be in structure congruent with Aristotle's, and, as it happens, what the Mishnah's economics says is the same that, and for the same purpose, that Aristotle's economics says. And that proves, in this context, the philosophical character of the Mishnah's system.
[13]Polanyi, "Aristotle Discovers the Economy," in Polanyi, Karl, Conrad M. Arensberg, and Harry W. Pearson, *Trade and Market in the Early Empires. Economies in History and Theory* (Glencoe, 1957: Free Press), 79.

The points in common between Aristotle's and the Mishnah's economics in detail prove no less indicative. Both Aristotle and the Mishnah presented an anachronistic system of economics. The theory of both falls into the same classification of economic theory, that of distributive economics, familiar in the Near and Middle East from Sumerian times down to, but not including, the age of Aristotle (let alone that of the Mishnah five centuries later). But market economics had been well established prior to Aristotle's time. Let me briefly explain the difference between the two, which is a fundamental indicator in classifying economics. In market economics merchants transfer goods from place to place in response to the working of the market mechanism, which is expressed in price. In distributive economics, by contrast, traders move goods from point to point in response to political commands. In market economics, merchants make the market work by calculations of profit and loss. In distributive economics, there is no risk of loss on a transaction.[14] In market economics, money forms an arbitrary measure of value, a unit of account. In distributive economics, money gives way to barter and bears only intrinsic value, as do the goods for which it is exchanged. It is understood as "something that people accept not for its inherent value in use but because of what it will buy."[15] The idea of money requires the transaction to be complete in the exchange not of goods but of coins. The alternative is the barter transaction, in which, in theory at least, the exchange takes place when goods change hands. In distributive economics money is an instrument of direct exchange between buyers and sellers, not the basic resource in the process of production and distribution that it is in market economics. Aristotle's economics is distributive for systemic reasons, the Mishnah's replicates the received principles of the economics planned by the Temple priests and set forth in the Priestly Code of the Pentateuch, Leviticus in particular. The result – fabricated or replicated principles – was the same.

Both systems – the Mishnah's and Aristotle's – in vast detail expressed the ancient distributive economics, in their theories of fixed value and conception of the distribution of scarce resources by appeal to other than the rationality of the market. The theory of money characteristic of Aristotle (but not of Plato) and of the Mishnah for instance conforms to that required by distributive economics; exchange takes place through barter, not through the abstract price-setting mechanism represented by money. Consequently, the representation of the Mishnah as a philosophical Judaism derives from not only general

---

[14]Davisson and Harper, *European Economic History*, 130.
[15]Ibid., 131.

characteristics but very specific and indicative traits held in common with the principal figure of the Greco-Roman philosophical tradition in economics.[16]

There was a common social foundation for the economic theory of both systems.[17] Both Aristotle and the Mishnah's framers deemed the fundamental unit of production to be the household, and the larger social unit, the village, composed of households, marked the limits of the social entity. The Mishnah's economic tractates, such as the Babas, on civil law, invariably refer to the householder, making him the subject of most predicates; where issues other than economics are in play, for example, in the political tractates such as Sanhedrin, the householder scarcely appears as a social actor. Not only so, but both Aristotle and the authorship of the Mishnah formed the conception of "true value," which maintained that something – an object, a piece of land – possessed a value extrinsic to the market and intrinsic to itself, such that, if a transaction varied from that imputed true value by (in the case of the Mishnah) 18 percent, the exchange was null. Not only so, but the sole definition of wealth for both Aristotle's and the Mishnah's economics was real estate, only land however small. Since land does not contract or expand, of course, the conception of an increase in value through other than a steady-state exchange of real value, "true value,"[18] between parties to a transaction lay outside of the theory of economics. Therefore all profit, classified as usury, was illegitimate and must be prevented.

---

[16] A basic point in common should be noted. Both Aristotle and the Mishnah composed economic theories that defied the economics of their own day. In each case a version of the then-anachronistic theory of distributive economics was made to bear the burden of the systemic message, while market-economics was accorded only a subordinated place within the larger theoretical structure. Market economics, coming into being in Greece in the very period – the sixth century B.C. – in which the Priestly Code was composed. Aristotle theorized about an economics entirely beyond anyone's ken and stated as principle the values of an economics (and a social system, too) long since transcended. Market economics, moreover, had been conveyed in practice to the Middle East a century and a half or so later by Alexander. By the time of the Mishnah, seven centuries after the Pentateuch was closed, market economics was well established as the economics of the world economy in which, as a matter of fact, the land of Israel and Israel, that is, the Jews of Palestine, had been fully incorporated.

[17] Though the politics of the Mishnah was disembedded from its economics, while the politics of Aristotle was embedded, so that the latter presents a political economy, the former does not.

[18] I do not claim to grasp the meaning of "true value."

The Philosophical Judaism of the Mishnah

When setting forth its view of power – the legitimate use of violence – and the disposition of power in society, the Mishnah's authorship describes matters in a manner that is fundamentally political, inventing a political structure and system integral to its plan for the social order. Israel forms a political entity, fully empowered in an entirely secular sense, just as Scripture had described matters. To political institutions of the social order, king, priest, and court or civil administration, each in its jurisdiction, is assigned the right legitimately to exercise violence here on earth, corresponding to, and shared with, the same empowerment accorded to institutions of Heaven. These institutions moreover are conceived permanently to ration and rationalize the uses of that power. The picture, of course, is this-worldly, but, not distinguishing crime from sin, it is not secular, since the same system that legitimates king, high priest, and court posits in Heaven a corresponding politics, with God and the court on high exercising jurisdiction for some crimes or sins, the king, priesthood, or court down below for others.

Among prior Judaisms only the scriptural system finally defined with the closure of the Pentateuch had set forth a politics at all. The appeal to politics in setting forth a theory of the social order of their particular "Israel" will have provoked some curiosity among, for one example, the framers of the Judaism portrayed by the Essene library uncovered at Qumran, and, for another, the framers of the Christianity of the Land of Israel in the first century. Both groups, heirs of the ancient Scriptures as much as were the framers of the Mishnah, found in politics no important component of the systemic structure they set forth. By contrast, the integration, within a systematic account of the social order, of a politics will not have surprised the great figures of Greco-Roman philosophy, Plato and Aristotle for example. That fact takes on consequence when we note that the Pentateuch simply does not prepare us to make sense of the institutions that the politics of Judaism for its part designs. The pentateuchal politics invokes priest and prophet, Aaron and Moses, but knows nothing of a tripartite government involving king, priest, and sage; nor do the royal narratives concede empowerment to the priest or sage. On the other hand, as we shall see, knowledge of the *Politics* of Aristotle and the *Republic* of Plato to the contrary gives perspective upon the politics of the Mishnah.

The Pentateuch, for its part, while definitive of the principles and details of the distributive economics of the Mishnah, contributes nothing to the Mishnah's scheme of routine government by king and high priest and sages' court. The Pentateuch's prophetic rule and constant appeal to God's immediate participation in the political process, and, in particular, in the administration of sanctions and acts of legitimate violence, by contrast falls into the category of a politics of charisma. The difference is not merely that the Pentateuchal institutions appeal to prophet and priest; it also is a difference in how the structure works as a political system. For the pentateuchal myth that serves to legitimate coercion – rule by God's prophet, in the model of Moses, governance through explicitly revealed laws that God has dictated for the occasion – plays no active and systemic role whatsoever in the formulation and presentation of the politics of Judaism. Philosophical systems use politics, by contrast, to set forth the rules and unchanging order of legitimate exercise of power, its teleology and its structure. Plato and Aristotle make no place for godly intervention on any particular occasion.

And for their part, among the types of political authority contained within the scriptural repertoire, the one that the Mishnah's philosophers reject is the prophetic and charismatic, and the one that they deem critical is the authority governing and governed by rules in an orderly, rational way. The principal political figures – king, high priest, the disciple of the sage – are carefully nurtured through learning of rules, not through cultivation of gifts of the spirit. The authority of sages in the politics of Judaism in particular does not derive from charisma, for example, revelation by God to the sage who makes a ruling in a given case, or even general access to God for the sage. So the politics of the Pentateuch – structure and system alike – in no way forms the model for the politics of the Mishnah. Hence the correct context for the classification of the Mishnah's politics must be located elsewhere than in a Judaism between the Pentateuch's and the Mishnah's, ca. 500 B.C. to A.D. 200. But what about the Greco-Roman tradition of philosophical politics?

With the pentateuchal precedent in mind, we can hardly judge as an indicator of the philosophical character of the Mishnah's politics merely the presence of a highly orderly and systematic political structure and system. Three specific traits, however, direct our attention toward the philosophical classification for the Mishnah's politics in framing a systemic composition, even though, to be sure, the parallels prove structural and general, rather than detailed and doctrinal,unlike the case with economics.

First, like the politics of Plato and Aristotle, the Mishnah's politics describes only a utopian politics, a structure and system of a fictive and a fabricated kind: intellectuals' conception of a politics. Serving the larger purpose of system construction, politics of necessity emerges as invention, for example, by Heaven or in the model of Heaven, not as a secular revision and reform of an existing system. While in the middle second-century Rome incorporated their country, which they called the Land of Israel and the Romans called Palestine, into its imperial system, denying Jews access to their capital, Jerusalem, permanently closing their cult center, its Temple, the authorship of the Mishnah described a government of a king and a high priest and an administration fully empowered to carry out the law through legitimate violence. So the two politics – the Mishnah's, the Greco-Roman tradition represented by Plato's and Aristotle's – share in common their origins in intellectuals' theoretical and imaginative life and form an instance, within that life, of the concrete realization of a larger theory of matters. In strange and odd forms, the Mishnah's politics falls into the class of the *Staatsroman*, the classification that encompasses, also, Plato's *Republic* and Aristotle's *Politics*. But, admittedly, the same may be said for the strange politics of the Pentateuch.

Second and more to the point, the Mishnah's sages stand well within the philosophical mode of political thought that begins with Aristotle, who sees politics as a fundamental component of his system when he says, "political science...legislates as to what we are to do and what we are to abstain from"; and, as to the institutionalization of power, I cannot imagine a more ample definition of the Mishnah's system's utilization of politics than that.[19] While that statement, also, applies to the Pentateuchal politics, the systemic message borne by politics within the Pentateuchal system and that carried by politics in the Mishnah's system do not correspond in any important ways. Aristotle and the philosophers of the Mishnah utilize politics to make systemic statements that correspond to one another, in that both comparison and contrast prove apt and pointed. Both spoke of an empowered social entity; both took for granted that ongoing institutions legitimately exercise governance in accord with a rationality discerned by distinguishing among those empowered to inflict sanctions. Both see politics as a medium for accomplishing systemic goals, and the goals derive from the larger purpose of the social order, to which politics is subordinated and merely instrumental.

But, third, the comparison also yields a contrast of importance. Specifically, since political analysis comes only after economic analysis and depends upon the results of that prior inquiry into a social system's disposition of scarce resources and theory of control of means of production, we have no choice but to follow up the results of the preceding chapter and compare the politics of Aristotle and the politics of the Mishnah, just as we did the economics of each system.

---

[19]Cited by R. G. Mulgan, *Aristotle's Political Theory* (Oxford: Clarendon Press, 1977), 3.

For when we know who commands the means of production, we turn to inquire about who tells whom what to do and why: who legitimately coerces others even through violence. And here the Mishnah's system decisively parts company with that of the Pentateuch and also with that of Aristotle.

As to the former, the distributive economics of the Pentateuch, in the Priestly stratum at the foundations, assigns both economic and political privilege to the same class of persons, the priesthood, effecting distributive economics and distributive politics. But that is not the way things are in the Mishnah's politics, which distinguishes the one in control of the means of production from the one control of the right legitimately to commit violence. The former, the householder, is not a political entity at all, and, dominant as the subject of most sentences in the economic tractates, he never appears in the political ones at all.

When we come to Aristotle, the point in common underlines the difference. For their part, both Aristotle and the Mishnah's philosophers give the same answer about what "person" (in our century we prefer "class" or "caste" or other more abstract and impersonal categories) forms the commanding presence in control of the means of production, the householder. For Aristotle and for the Mishnah's sages, the fundamental unit of economic thought and the generative social metaphor of their respective systems was the householder. The givens of the thought-world of the Mishnah's framers' theory of economics, embedded in a larger systemic plan, in fact correspond point by point with the economic program of Aristotle. And that statement simply does not apply to the pentateuchal politics. Accordingly, the context in which the political structure and system of the Mishnah finds its proper place is the Greco-Roman philosophical one; the differences from the pentateuchal politics, both in detail and in overall structural traits, decisively remove the Mishnah's politics from the scriptural tradition. But these same differences set the Mishnah's politics apart from Aristotle's as well.

So, as I said, that important point of difference from Aristotle is to be seen only within the context of the similarity that permits comparison and contrast. While the economics of Aristotle and the economics of Judaism commence with the consideration of the place and power of the person ("class," "caste," economic interest) in control of the means of production, the social metaphors that animate the politics of the two systems part company. Aristotle in his *Politics* is consistent in starting with that very same person ("class") when he considers issues of power, producing a distributive politics to match his distributive economics. But the Mishnah's philosophers build their politics with an altogether different set of building blocks. The simple fact is that the householder, fundamental to their economics, does not form a subject of political discourse at all and in no way constitutes a political class or caste. When the Mishnah's writers speak of economics, the subject of most active verbs is the householder; when they speak of politics, the householder never takes an active role or even appears as a differentiated political class. In this sense, the economics of the Mishnah is disembedded from its politics, and the politics from its economics. By contrast the economics and politics of Aristotle's system are deeply embedded within a larger and nurturing, wholly cogent theory of political economy.

5

The Religious Judaism of the Talmud of the Land of Israel, Genesis Rabbah, and Leviticus Rabbah

Why call the writings that followed the Mishnah, Tosefta, and its associated Midrash compilations "successors"? Because, in form, the writings of the late fourth and fifth centuries were organized and presented as commentaries on a received text, the Mishnah for the Talmud, Scripture for the Midrash compilations. So the later authorships insisted, in their own behalf, that they (merely) explained and amplified the received Torah. They imparted to their writings the form of a commentary. When these documents attached themselves to the Mishnah, on the one side, and the Hebrew Scriptures, on the other, they gave literary form to the theory that the one stood for the oral, the other, the written, revelation, or Torah, that God gave to Moses at Mount Sinai.

Specifically, the Talmud of the Land of Israel formed around thirty-nine of the Mishnah's sixty-two tractates, and Genesis Rabbah and Leviticus Rabbah (joined by Pesiqta deRab Kahana) addressed the first and third books of Moses, respectively, along with some other documents. The very act of choosing among the Mishnah's tractates only some and ignoring others, of course, represents an act of taste and judgment – hence system building through tacit statement made by acts of commission but also by silence. But, as a matter of fact, much of the Talmud as well as of the principal Midrash compilations do amplify and augment the base documents to which they are attached.[1] In choosing some passages and neglecting others, and, more to the point, in working out their own questions and their own answers, in addition to those of the Mishnah, the authorships[2] attest to a system that did more than merely extend and recast the categorical structure of the system for which the Mishnah stands. They took over the way of life, worldview, and social entity, defined in the Mishnah's system. And while they rather systematically amplified details, framed a program of exegesis around the requirements of clerks engaged in enforcing the rules of the Mishnah, they built their own system.

For at the same time they formed categories corresponding to those of the Mishnah, a politics, a philosophy, an economics. But these categories proved so utterly contrary in their structure and definition to those of the Mishnah that they presented mirror images of the received categories. The politics, philosophy, and economics of the Mishnah were joined by what we may wish to call an anti-politics, an anti-economics, and an utterly transformed mode of learning. In the hands of the later sages, the new mode of Torah study – the definition of what was at stake in studying the Torah – redefined altogether the issues of the intellect. As a matter of fact the successor system recast not the issues so much as the very stakes of philosophy or science. The reception of the Mishnah's category formations and their transformation therefore stands for the movement from a philosophical to a religious mode of thinking. For the system to which the Mishnah as a document attests is essentially philosophical in its rhetorical, logical, and topical program; the successor system, fundamental

---

[1] My estimate for the Talmud of the Land of Israel, in the tractates I probed, is that, in volume, as much as 90% of the Talmud serves to amplify passages of the Mishnah, and not much more than 10% contains intellectual initiatives that are fundamentally fresh and unrelated to anything in the Mishnah passage under discussion, see my *Talmud of the Land of Israel. XXXV. Introduction. Taxonomy* (Chicago, 1983: University of Chicago Press). Then my *Judaism in Society. The Evidence of the Yerushalmi. Toward the Natural History of a Religion* (Chicago, 1983) aims to show that even the passages that (merely) clarify words or phrases of the Mishnah in fact set forth a considerable, autonomous program of their own, cf. especially pp. 73-112. But what is clearly distinct from the Mishnah is set forth on pp. 113-254.

[2] This term is meant to take account of the collective and social character of much of the literary enterprise. Not a single authoritative book of Judaism in late antiquity bears the name of an identified author, and the literary traits of not a single piece of writing may securely be imputed to a private person. The means for gaining acceptance was anonymity, and the medium of authority lay in recapitulating collective conventions of rhetoric and logic, not to mention proposition. To speak of "authors" in this context is confusing, and hence the resort to the word at hand.

religious in these same principal and indicative traits of medium of intellect and mentality. So what happened was that the received categories – politics, philosophy, and economics, were preserved, but a set of counterpart categories developed to provide a religious response to the issues of politics, philosophy, and economics.

A system formed in theory to describe the social order by definition attends to the way of life, worldview, and definition of the social entity, that that system puts forth. But by "way of life" – economics – or "worldview" – politics – one system need not mean – or even refer to – exactly the same category of data that another system adopts for itself. It goes without saying, moreover, that we cannot claim functional equivalency, for obvious reasons as irrelevant as the judgment of relativism. The claim, "this is what functioned for this system in the way in which, in that system, that accomplished the (same) task," proves simply irrelevant. Such a claim forms an excuse, not a reason, for difference among systems, and, since what is at stake is systemic comparison, it hardly explains why one system sets forth its way of life by selecting data of one kind, while another one chooses data of a completely different order altogether, for the same purpose. Not only so, but what we seek to describe, analyze, and interpret are systems, on their own and (in the case of systems that prove continuous in their canonical express) also in relationship with one another.

So let me restate matters as I think a rigorous definition requires us to see them. A system selects its data to expose its systemic categories; defines its categories in accord with the systemic statement that it wishes to set forth; identifies the urgent question to which the systemic message compellingly responds. To understand a system, we begin with the whole and work our way inward toward the parts; the formation of categories then is governed by the system's requirements: the rationality of the whole dictates the structure of the categorical parts, and the structure of the parts then governs the selection of what fits into those categories.[3]

Now that we have seen the philosophical character of the initial system's worldview, way of life, and theory of the social entity, that is, its philosophy, economics, and politics, we ask how these same categories fared in the successor system's documentary evidence. As a matter of simple fact, while sharing the goal of presenting a theory of the social order, as to their categorical formations and structures, the initial, philosophical Judaic system and the successor system differ in a

---

[3]None of these points intersects with either relativism or functionalism; the issues are wholly other. At stake in systemic description, analysis, and interpretation, after all, ultimately is the comparative study of rationalities.

fundamental way. Stated very simply, what happened is that the successor system held up a mirror to the received categories and so redefined matters that everything was reversed. Left became right, down, up, and, as we shall see, in a very explicit transvaluation of values, power is turned into weakness, things of real value are transformed into intangibles. This transvaluation, yielding the transformation of the prior system altogether, is articulated and not left implicit; it is a specific judgment made concrete through mythic and symbolic revision by the later authorships themselves.[4] A freestanding document, received with reverence, served to precipitate the transvaluation of all of the values of that document's initial statement.

The categorical transformation that was underway, signaling the movement from philosophy to religion, comes to the surface when we ask a simple question. Precisely what do the authorships of the successor documents speaking not about the Mishnah but on their own account, mean by economics, politics, and philosophy? That is to say, to what kinds of data do they refer when they speak of scarce resources and legitimate violence, and exactly how – as to the received philosophical method – do they define correct modes of thought and expression, logic and rhetoric, and even the topical program worthy of sustained inquiry?

The components of the initial formation of categories were examined thoughtfully and carefully, paraphrased and augmented and clarified. But the received categories were not continued, not expanded, and not renewed. Preserved merely intact, as they had been handed on, the received categories hardly serve to encompass all of the points of emphasis and sustained development that characterize the successor documents – or, as a matter of fact, any of them. On the contrary, when the framers of the Yerushalmi, for one example, moved out from the exegesis of Mishnah passages, they also left behind the topics of paramount interest in the Mishnah and developed other categories altogether.[5] Here we find that, in these other categories, the framers of the successor system defined their own counterparts. These

---

[4] I underline that fact, since all that follows on the transvaluation of values through the formation of what I have invented as "counterpart categories" appeals to explicit statements, not a very general, post facto observation on my part.

[5] That fact is demonstrated in my *Talmud of the Land of Israel. A Preliminary Translation and Explanation. 35. Introduction. Taxonomy* (Chicago, 1983: The University of Chicago Press). There I show that when Mishnah exegesis is concluded, a quite separate agendum takes centerstage, the emphases of which find no counterpart in the Mishnah. That seems to me to justify the consideration of counterpart categories, such as I introduce here.

counterpart categories, moreover, redefined matters, following the main outlines of the structure of the social order manifest in the initial system. The counterpart categories set forth an account of the social order just as did the ones of the Mishnah's framers. But they defined the social order in very different terms altogether. In that redefinition we discern the transformation of the received system, and the traits of the new one fall into the classification of not philosophy but religion.

For what the successor thinkers did was not continue and expand the categorical repertoire but set forth a categorically fresh vision of the social order – a way of life, worldview, and definition of the social entity – with appropriate counterpart categories. And what is decisive is that these served as did the initial categories within the generative categorical structure definitive for all Judaic systems. So there was a category corresponding to the generative component of worldview, but it was not philosophical; another corresponding to the required component setting forth a way of life, but in the conventional and accepted definition of economics it was not an economics; and, finally, a category to define the social entity, "Israel," that any Judaic system must explain, but in the accepted sense of a politics it was not politics.

Addressing the issues ordinarily treated by the method and message of philosophy, economics, or politics, the counterpart categories nonetheless supplied for the social order a worldview, way of life, and definition of the social entity. And, as a matter of fact, the Judaism that emerged from late antiquity adopted as its categorical structure the counterpart categories we are going to define and explore and recast the Mishnah within them. The transformation of Judaism, therefore, from an account of the social order that was essentially philosophical to one that was fundamentally religious was accomplished by the system builders whose conceptions came to literary expression in the Talmud of the Land of Israel, Genesis Rabbah, Leviticus Rabbah, and Pesiqta deRab Kahana.

Exactly how was this categorical reformation accomplished? To state matters first in the most abstract way, it was done by reversing the flow of language, specifically taking the predicate of a sentence and moving it to the position of the subject, that is, commencing not from subject but from predicate. From "[1] economics is [2] the rational disposition of scarce resources," the category of way of life was rephrased into, "[2] the rational disposition of scarce resources is [1] (their, in context, systemic) economics."

As we shall see, the reverse reading therefore yields the counterpart category, defined by this sentence: *"a (any) theory of rational action with regard to scarcity..., then: is (for the system at hand) its economics."* The same procedure serves, too – *mutatis mutandis* – for discerning the later systems' politics and science or learning or philosophy. Precisely what the framers worked out as their economics, politics, and philosophy is laid out in this part of the book, and the result, the third part of this book will show, was a quite new system. This transvaluation of values, through not merely the reformation but the utter transformation of categories, set forth an essentially fresh answer to a fundamentally new urgent question. But here, the answer is the main point of interest.

Let me make more concrete this matter of the reverse definition of economics, placing the predicate as the subject. We recall the reason for my claim that the Judaism of the Mishnah presents a theory of economics. The Mishnaic system addresses the definition of rational action with regard both to the allocation of scarce resources, on the one side, and to the increase and disposition of wealth, on the other. It was a specifically philosophical economics because, in structure and in doctrine, it conformed with that of Aristotle. Now in the successor system, can we identify what is meant by scarce resources and can we define the rationality required for the disposition, in the systemic context at hand, of such resources? When we say, "a (or any) theory of rational action with regard to scarcity *is* (an) economics," we mean, any account of what is deemed scarce and therefore to require rational action as to allocation, increase, and disposition, functions to define the category that is the counterpart, in the philosophical system of the Mishnah, to economics. It answers the same question, but it utterly recasts the terms of the question.

Why have I found it necessary to invent the conception of a counterpart category? The results of Lecture Two compel a consideration of what, in the successor documents, we can consider as an economics, politics, and mode of thought and worldview. My premise is that a religious theory of the social order will be made up of an account of a way of life, worldview, and that social entity that realizes the one and explains itself by appeal to the other. In the Mishnah, as in other philosophical systems, the way of life finds definition in economics, the worldview in philosophy (both as to method and as to proposition), and the account of the social entity in a politics. But that is simply not the case in the successor documents, and what serves as way of life, worldview, and definition of the social entity in no way conforms to what had defined these same categories.

That fact is hardly surprising, for, as we have already noted, there are quite elaborate and well composed systems of the social order, fully spelling out the way of life, worldview, and definition of the social entity, in which – to concentrate on the case at hand – in the received and accepted sense of economics as a theory of the rational disposition of scarce resources, we simply have no economics at all. Augustine's design and account of the city of God, for example, introduces its own categories in response to the same requirements of definition and articulation of the social order. The history of salvation, deriving from the Christian Bible, for instance, forms the critical center, and philosophy, while profoundly influential on his thought, hardly generates the primary categorical structures. And the first twelve hundred years of Christian system builders found it entirely possible to set forth the Christian social order's way of life without defining an economics for themselves.[6]

It follows that for failing to present an economics, accounts of the social order do not define a way of life. To the contrary, the simple fact is that, when they do define a way of life in terms of scarce resources, what they mean is not what we ordinarily mean by economics. True, such systems omit all reference to, or treat as systemically inert and inconsequence, such topics as wealth and money, production and distribution, work and wage, ownership and conduct of economic entities. The entire repertoire of subjects comprising economic action in all its forms simply are lacking. But the issues of tangible wealth and materials goods do emerge – must emerge, and, it follows, the systems will have to identify for themselves something other than real wealth (real estate, capital, for instance) when they design those societies that express the respective systems' messages: urgent question, self-evidently valid answer, integrating the whole and rendering the system cogent and coherent.

But how to deal with such accounts of the social order that lack an economics or a politics or a philosophy in the familiar senses of these categories? To answer that question of method in the analysis of category formation, I have to discover and define what serves, in such a system, the task of economics in a philosophical system. To do so – as stated in abstract form just now – I propose the notion that, "[2] a (any) theory of rational action with regard to scarcity *is* [1] economics." Matters that hardly fall into the category of economic theory at all may yield points of congruency. As a matter of fact they may also validate those systemic comparisons and contrasts that permit us to trace the history of an ongoing system from its philosophical to its

---

[6]As with the sages of Judaism, so with the first important Christian economics, it was the encounter with Aristotle (and not with Scripture) that made urgent the formation of a Christianity encompassing, for the way of life of its social order, elaborate attention to the expression of theological truth in economics and rules for the Christian management and preservation of scarce resources, defined in the conventional sense of philosophical economics.

religious formulation. We know that we are right when we find, as we shall, that the authorships of the successor systems recognize and select the principal symbolic expression of a received category and turn it on its head: land becomes Torah learning, and that is made explicit, for one stunning instance. Then it is not merely my post-facto reading of one system as a reversal of a prior one that has yielded the counterpart category, but the documents themselves.

Let me now spell out why I find critical this two-directional reading – first, *"economics is* [or, encompasses] the theory of rational action with regard to scarcity," second, "a theory of rational action with regard to scarcity *is encompassed by economics."* To state matters negatively, if one system presents a conventional economics and another does not, then I cannot compare the one to the other (beyond the observation that one has, the other does not have, an economics). But – on the positive side – if I can show how one body of coherent thought in one system addresses the same question that another body of equally coherent thought takes up in the other, then the comparability – at the point of not detail but of the main beams of structure – of the two systems becomes possible. The sole undemonstrated premise of argument is that any system must explain in its account of the social order what people are to think and do and how they are to define themselves as a social entity. But in the very language, social order, are embedded these three components: society and order in both intellect and practice. So at stake is the comparison of systems.

In this context, by the comparison of systems, I mean the contrast of one rationality to another.[7] The comparison of rationalities then is made possible by the dual and reciprocal definition of [1] economics as the theory of rational action with regard to scarcity, and of [2] the theory of rational action with regard to scarcity as economics. The same is so, of course, for philosophy and politics.[8] When we understand

---

[7] I of course allude to the great conception of Max Weber in his studies of China, India, and ancient Israel. In asking why capitalism here, not there, he founded the comparative study of rationalities. Many present themselves as his successors, some with more reason than others, but, in the aggregate, I have not found a rich theoretical literature vastly to revise Weber's definition of issues. In this regard philosophy has gone far beyond the limits of theory in social science.

[8] Would I extend the matter to, let us say, medicine, technology, city planning, mathematics, the provision of a water supply, a department of defense, or any of the other diverse components of the social order and its culture, whether intellectual or institutional? At this moment, I should have to decline an invitation to descend into such unbounded relativism, for then everything is the equivalent of something, and nothing is to be defined in itself. So for the

The Religious Judaism of the Talmud of the Land of Israel

the particular rationality of the economics of – to take the case at hand – the Judaism of the Mishnah, we find the way to translate into categories of rationality that we can grasp that Judaism's to us familiar category with the to us alien and odd rationality of the Yerushalmi's counterpart, which, as we shall see, covers matters we do not conceive to fall into the rubric of economics at all but that answered the same questions to which, for us and for the philosophical economics of the Mishnah, economics attends.

That is to say, when we see that a category for an alien system and its rationality constitutes *its* economics and therefore forms a counterpart to economics as we understand that subject within our rationality, we learn how in a critical component to translate system to system. We may then make the statement, "In that system, within their rationality, that category of activity forms a component of economic theory, while in our system, within our rationality, we do not think of that category of activity as a component of economic theory at all." And this we do without assuming a posture of relativism, for example claiming that their economics, and, with it, their rationality, is pretty much the same, or as at least as valid, as ours. Framing the relativist judgment in that way, we see that it is simply not relevant to what is at stake. That kind of interpretation of matters is not pertinent to my exercise in translation and comparison carried out through the definition and examination of counterpart categories. We begin with the systemic counterpart to philosophy, then proceed to economics, and conclude with politics, following the order of Part One. Our first task is to follow the categorical formation of a new worldview generated by the received mode of thought, a worldview that fundamentally differed from the philosophical one at every point.

What philosophy kept distinct, religion joined together: that defines the transformation of Judaism from philosophy to religion. The reliable rules of sanctification – to invoke theological categories – are joined with the unpredictable event of salvation, and the routine – to call upon the classification of Max Weber – meets the spontaneous. Not to be gainsaid, the social order is made to acknowledge what, if disorderly, also is immediate and therefore necessary. History, that omnipresent but carefully ignored presence in the philosophical Judaism, in the form of not change but crisis, regains its rightful place at the systemic center.

The classification of the new system – so we shall now see – is religious and not philosophical. Precisely what I mean must be made

---

moment I leave matters at the basic components of any and all social orders, as I have identified them.

clear, since the Mishnaic system also was a religious one. But the received system was a religious system of a philosophical character, and the successor system was not of a philosophical character. What I mean by a religious system of a philosophical character is readily explained: this-worldly data are classified according to rules that apply consistently throughout, so that we may always predict with a fair degree of accuracy what will happen and why. And a philosophical system of religion then systematically demonstrates out of the data of the world order of nature and society the governance of God in nature and supernature: this world's data pointing toward God above and beyond. The God of the philosophical Judaism then sat enthroned at the apex of all things, all being hierarchically classified. Just as philosophy seeks the explanation of things, so a philosophy of religion (in the context at hand) will propose orderly explanations in accord with prevailing and cogent rules. The profoundly philosophical character of the Mishnah has already provided ample evidence of the shape, structure, and character of that philosophical system in the Judaic context. The rule-seeking character of Mishnaic discourse marks it as a philosophical system of religion. But, we shall now see, the successor system saw the world differently.

It follows that a philosophical system forms its learning inductively and syllogistically, by appeal to the neutral evidence of the rules shown to apply to all things by the observation of the order of universally accessible nature and society. A religious system frames its propositions deductively and exegetically by appeal to the privileged evidence of a corpus of truths deemed revealed by God. The difference pertains not to detail but to the fundamental facts deemed to matter. Some of those facts lie at the very surface, in the nature of the writings that express the system.

As we have now seen, these writings were not free-standing but contingent, and that in two ways. First, they served as commentaries to prior documents, the Mishnah and Scripture, for the Talmud and Midrash compilations, respectively. Second, and more consequential, the authorships insisted upon citing Scripture passages or Mishnah sentences as the centerpiece of proof, on the one side, and program of discourse, on the other. But the differences that prove indicative are not merely formal. More to the point, while the Mishnah's system is steady state and ahistorical, admitting no movement or change, the successor system of the Yerushalmi and Midrash compilations tells tales, speaks of change, accommodates and responds to historical moments. It formulates a theory of continuity within change, of the moral connections between generations, of the way in which one's deeds shape one's destiny – and that of the future as well. If what the framers of the Mishnah want more than anything else is to explain the order and structure of being, then their successors have rejected their generative concern. For what they, for their part, intensely desire to sort out is the currents and streams of time and change, as these flow toward an unknown ocean.

But these large-scale characterizations in well-crafted systems do not provide the only pertinent evidence. Details, too, deliver the message. The indicators for each type of system, as these are attested in their written testimonies, derive from the character of the rhetorical, logical, and propositional-topical traits of those writings. The shift from the philosophical to the religious modes of thought and media of expression – logical and rhetorical indicators, respectively – come to realization in the recasting of the generative categories of the system as well. These categories are transformed, and the transformation proved so thorough-going as to validate the characterization of the change as "counterpart categories." The result of the formation of such counterpart categories in the aggregate was to encompass not only the natural but also the supernatural realms of the social order.

That is how philosophical thinking gave way to religious. It sets forth the category formation that produced in place of an economics based on prime value assigned to real wealth one that now encompassed wealth of an intangible, impalpable, and supernatural order, but valued resource nonetheless. It points toward the replacement of a politics formerly serving to legitimate and hierarchize power and differentiate among sanctions by appeal to fixed principles by one that now introduced the variable of God's valuation of the victim and the anti-political conception of the illegitimacy of worldly power. This counterpart politics then formed the opposite of the Mishnah's this-worldly political system altogether. In all three ways the upshot is the same: the social system, in the theory of its framers, now extends its boundaries upward to Heaven, drawing into a whole the formerly distinct, if counterpoised, realms of Israel on earth and the Heavenly court above. So if I had to specify the fundamental difference between the philosophical and the religious versions of the social order, it would fall, quite specifically – to state with emphasis – *upon the broadening of the systemic boundaries to encompass Heaven.* The formation of counterpart categories therefore signals not a reformation of the received system but the formation of an essentially new one.

But the critical issue addressed by the new system and the central point of tension and mode of remission thereof, the exegetical focus – these remain to be identified even after we have noted the extension of systemic boundaries. And, as a matter of fact, the counterpart categories in hand themselves do not help to identify the generative problematic that defined the new system and integrated its components. For the issues I have located as the systemic economics and politics – Torah in place of land, the illegitimacy of power and the priority of the absence thereof – while present and indicative in the documentary expression of the system, assuredly do not occupy a principal position within those documents. For the successor documents' categories are not those of philosophy, on the one side, and a politics disembedded from economics, on the other.

In the nature of systemic analysis, therefore, I have brought the categories of one system to the data of another, those of the initial system to the ones of the successor system, and the result is to discover only how different are the latter from the former. So concerning the transformed Judaism of the late fourth and fifth century we now know everything but the main thing. True, since we compare the given to the new, I had no choice but to proceed as I have. But what I have done thus far is ask only *my* questions – that is, the systemic questions of philosophy and political economy or philosophical economics and politics. And these questions have been turned upon a literature that dealt with such questions essentially by dismissing them. For the upshot of the formation of counterpart categories turns out to be the destruction of the received categories, now turned on their heads and emptied of all material and palpable content, refilled then with intangibles of intellect and virtuous attitude alone. Knowing how a system has revalued value and reconstructed the sense of legitimate power by deeming legitimate only the victim and never the actor, does not tell us what the system locates at its center.

6
The Categorical Reformation of Judaism as a Religion

What the philosophical Judaism kept apart, the religious Judaism now joined together, and it is just there, at that critical joining, that we identify the key to the system: its reversal of a received point of differentiation,[1] its introduction of new points of differentiation altogether. The source of generative problems for the Mishnah's politics is simply not the same as the source that served the successor system's politics, and, systemic analysis being what it is, it is the union of what was formerly asunder that identifies for us in quite objective terms the critical point of tension, the sources of problems, the centerpiece of systemic concern throughout. Let me show how this process of reintegration was worked out in the categorical reformation under way in the Yerushalmi and related writings.

We begin with the shift from philosophy to Torah; philosophy yields accurate and rational understanding of things; knowledge of the Torah, by contrast, yields power over this world and the next, capacity to coerce to the sage's will the natural and supernatural worlds alike, on that account. The Torah is thus transformed from a philosophical enterprise of the sifting and classification of the facts of this world into a gnostic process of changing persons through knowledge. It is on that basis that in the Yerushalmi and related writings I find in the Torah the counterpart category to philosophy in the Mishnah. Now we deal with a new intellectual category: Torah, meaning, religious learning *in place of* philosophical learning. What is the difference between the

---

[1] For, after all, the problematic of the Mishnah's politics is the principle of differentiation among legitimate political agencies, first between Heaven's and humanity's, second, among the three political institutions of the Mishnah's "Israel."

one and the other? First comes appeal to revealed truth as against perceived facts of nature and their regularities, second, the conception of an other-worldly source of explanation and the development of a propositional program focused upon not nature but Scripture, not the nations in general but Israel in particular, and third, the gnosticization of knowledge in the conception that knowing works salvation.

What was to change, therefore, was not the mode of thought. What was new, rather, was the propositions to be demonstrated philosophically, and what made these propositions new was the focus of interest, on the one side, and data assembled by way of demonstrating them, on the other. From a philosophical proposition within the framework of free-standing philosophy of religion and metaphysics that, we saw, the Mishnah's system aimed to establish, we move to religious and even theological propositions within the setting of contingent exegesis of Scripture. Then how do we know that what was changing was not merely topical and propositional but *categorical* in character? The answer lies in the symbolic vocabulary that would be commonly used in the late fourth and fifth century writings but not at all, or not in the same way, in the late second century ones. When people select data not formerly taken into account and represent the data by appeal to symbols not formerly found evocative or expressive, or not utilized in the way in which they later on were used, then – so I claim – we are justified in raising questions about category formation and the development of new categories alongside, or instead, of the received ones. In the case at hand, the character of the transformation we witness is shown by the formation of a symbol serving to represent a category. And that is not a matter of subjective judgment, for we shall find right on the surface the explicit substitution of one category for another category, symbol for symbol.

To signal what is to come, we shall find the quite bald statement that, in the weighing of the comparative value of capital, which in this time and place meant land or real property, and Torah, Torah was worthwhile, and land was not – a symbolic syllogism that is explicit, concrete, repeated, and utterly fresh for the documents we consider. On the basis of that quite explicit symbolic comparison I speak of transformation – symbolic and therefore *categorical* transformation, not merely thematic shifts in emphasis or even propositional change. And that is why I hold that we witness in the successor writings the formation of a system connected with, but asymmetrical to, the initial, philosophical one. Then for the worldview of the transformed Judaism, the counterpart category to philosophy is formulated by appeal to the symbolic medium for the theological message, and it is the category, the Torah, expressed, as a matter of fact, by the symbol of Torah.[2]

Philosophy sought the generalizations that cases might yield. So too did religion (and, in due course, theology would too). But the range of generalization vastly differed. Philosophy spoke of the nature of things, while theology represented the special nature of Israel in particular. Philosophy then appealed to the traits of things, while theology to the special indicative qualities of Israel. What of the propositional program that the document sets forth? The philosophical proposition of the Mishnah demonstrated from the facts and traits of things the hierarchical order of all being, with the obvious if merely implicit proposition that God stands at the head of the social order. The religious propositions of the successor documents speak in other words of other things, having simply nothing in common with the propositional program of the Mishnah's philosophy.

If I ask the Mishnah for a verbal symbol for philosophy, the document remains dumb. Philosophy for the Mishnah serves as source of method and taxon of proposition. But the Mishnah's framers have no word for philosophy, nor for natural science, nor for learning, nor for system, nor for any of my other analytical categories.[3] Nor, despite their formidable powers of abstraction in thought and expression do they even set forth the abstract proposition concerning the hierarchical unity of being that in point of fact is their principal result. Certainly, in the Mishnah the symbol, Torah, like "Israel," serves as a taxic indicator and does not convey more than it expresses; "Torah", with or without the definite article, with or without a capital T, serves no symbolic functions; bears no symbolic valence. And there is, in the Mishnah, no other. Whatever single symbol captures the entirety of the Mishnah's message in the Mishnah's own language, it is not the symbol of Torah.[4]

---

[2]Much that is said here alludes to the results of my *Torah: From Scroll to Symbol in Formative Judaism* (Philadelphia, 1985: Fortress; second printing: Atlanta, 1989: Scholars Press for Brown Judaic Studies).

[3]And that fact has rightly impressed those who have not recognized the philosophical character of the document; there is no philological evidence that suggests knowledge of any concrete philosophical modes of thought, let alone propositions.

[4]The truth is, I can think of no single symbol that serves the entirety of the Mishnah as a medium of expressing the whole or evoking it. Surely, in tractate Avot, fifty years or so later, we may readily point to "Torah" as that symbol, referring to not a document but a status, but vividly so and not merely (as with the Mishnah) as a medium of taxonomic thought. That is to say, in tractate Avot we can point to the object, Torah, speak of words of Torah, identify the status of a person or a gesture or action within the classification of Torah, and

By contrast, if I ask the Midrash compilations associated with the Yerushalmi to express, in a single word, the medium and the message that constitute their worldview, they have that word and use it constantly, and it is the word, *Torah*. It is the Torah that conveys the generative facts of learning; it is Torah, losing its definite article, that defines the range of truth. The *Torah now defines the category, worldview.* As a symbol, the Torah no longer denotes a particular book, let alone the contents of such a book. In the Talmud of the Land of Israel and its associated writings, as a matter of fact, the Torah, with or without its definite article, and, as I said, with or without a capital t, connotes a broad range of clearly distinct categories of noun and verb, concrete fact and abstract relationship alike.[5] "Torah" stands for a kind of human being. It connotes a social status and a sort of social group. It refers to a type of social relationship. It further denotes a legal status and differentiates among legal norms. As symbolic abstraction, the word encompasses things and persons, actions and status, points of social differentiation and legal and normative standing, as well as "revealed truth." The new category, conveyed by the symbol, Torah, treated the knowledge represented by the Torah (whether scroll, contents, or act of study) as source and guarantor of salvation.

Accordingly, category denoted by the word, Torah, encompasses the centerpiece of a theory of Israel's history, on the one side, and an account of the teleology of the entire system, on the other. Torah

---

so in a single symbol speak of the whole and state the message of the whole. In the Mishnah, by contrast, I find no such symbolic centerpiece. I could make the case that the symbolic system of the Mishnah comes to expression not pictorially or visually or verbally (as with the object "Torah") but rather in what is as recurrent in the Mishnah as Torah is in tractate Avot, and that is, the deepest structures of syntax, the orderly formation of thought in well-patterned language. But if I can find in any few sentences of the Mishnah the whole of the Mishnah in its syntactic structure (and, I have claimed, also its message as well, as in my *A History of the Mishnaic Law of Purities* (Leiden, 1977: Brill) XXI. *The Redaction and Formulation of the Order of Purities in the Mishnah and Tosefta,* that does not seem to me to be the same thing as a symbol of the order of Torah or The Torah. But then, it seems fair to claim, philosophers in that context did not convey their messages through symbolic but rather through verbal discourse and argument, and the Mishnah's very philosophicality explains its failure to give us in a single way a medium for saying many things. Then, to take a step further, the formation of the counterpart category for worldview, Torah, which is religious, for philosophy, in medium and message alike, is signalled by the symbolic transaction represented by the word Torah.

[5]The basis of these statements again is in my *Torah: From Scroll to Symbol in Formative Judaism.*

indeed has ceased to constitute a specific thing or even a category or classification when stories about studying the Torah yield not a judgment as to status (that is, praise for the learned man) but promise for supernatural blessing now and salvation in time to come. And the new category, corresponding to philosophy in its mode of thought, counterpart to philosophy in its message, must be classed as a fundamentally religious category, in that knowledge now formed the medium of salvation: knowing the Torah changed the one who knows it, in a way in which, in the Mishnah and related writings, knowing the hierarchical structure and order of things, pointing toward the unity of the natural order, in no way led to the transformation of the one who knew the facts that yielded that knowledge. No wonder then, that, in the Yerushalmi, mastery of Torah transformed the man engaged in Torah learning into a supernatural figure, who could do things ordinary folk could not do.

Consideration of the transvaluation of value brings us to the successor system's counterpart category, that is, the one that in context forms the counterpart to the Mishnah's concrete, this-worldly, material and tangible definition of value in conformity with the familiar, philosophical economics.[6] We have now to ask, what, in place of the received definition of value and the economics thereof, did the new system set forth? The transformation of economics involved the redefinition of scarce and valued resources in so radical a manner that the concept of value, while remaining material in consequence and character, nonetheless took on a quite different sense altogether.[7] The counterpart category of the successor system, represented by the authorships responsible for the final composition of the Yerushalmi, Genesis Rabbah, Leviticus Rabbah, and Pesiqta deRab Kahana, concerned themselves with the same questions as did the conventional economics, presenting an economics in function and structure, but one that concerned things of value other than those identified by the initial

---

[6]which the Mishnah set forth but the successor documents did not develop.
[7]Does that fact then suggest the new system's theory of the social order set forth no economics at all? After all, there is no reason that a theory of the social order required an economics at all, since a variety of theories of the social order of the same time and place other than Aristotle's and the Mishnah's – Plato's for one, the Gospels' for another, the Essene Community at Qumran's for a third – managed to put forth a compelling theory of society lacking all sustained and systematic, systemically pertinent attention to economics at all. I insist, however, that the successor system put forth a theory of the way of life that must be characterized as an economics, not as a theology that made reference, by the way, to topics of economic interest but an economics. It was, however, one involving a different value from the ultimate value, real property, characteristic of Aristotle's and the Mishnah's economics.

system. So indeed we deal with an economics, an economics of something other than real estate.

But it was an economics just as profoundly embedded in the social order, just as deeply a political economics, just as pervasively a systemic economics, as the economics of the Mishnah and of Aristotle. Why so? Because issues such as the definition of wealth, the means of production and the meaning of control thereof, the disposition of wealth through distributive or other media, theory of money, reward for labor, and the like – all these issues found their answers in the counterpart category of economics, as much as in the received and conventional philosophical economics. The new "scarce resource" accomplished what the old did, but it was a different resource, a new currency. At stake in the category meant to address the issues of the way of life of the social entity, therefore, were precisely the same considerations as confront economics in its (to us) conventional and commonplace, philosophical sense. But since the definition of wealth changes, as we have already seen, from land to Torah, much else would be transformed on that account.

That explains why, in the formation of the counterpart category of value other than real value but in function and in social meaning value nonetheless, we witness the transformation of a system from philosophy to religion. We err profoundly if we suppose that in contrasting land to Torah and affirming that true value lies in Torah, the framers of the successor system have formulated an essentially spiritual or otherwise immaterial conception for themselves, that is, a surrogate for economics in the conventional sense. That is not what happened. What we have is an economics that answers the questions economics answers, as I said, but that has chosen a different value from real value – real estate, as we have already seen – as its definition of that scarce resource that requires a rational policy for preservation and enhancement. Land produced a living; so did Torah. Land formed the foundation of the social entity, so did Torah.

The transvaluation of value was such that an economics concerning the rational management and increase of scarce resources worked itself out in such a way as to answer, for quite different things of value from real property or from capital such as we know as value, precisely the same questions that the received economics addressed in connection with wealth of a real character: land and its produce. Systemic transformation comes to the surface in articulated symbolic change. The utter transvaluation of value finds expression in a jarring juxtaposition, an utter shift of rationality, specifically, the substitution of Torah for real estate. We recall how in a successor document (but in none prior to the fifth century compilations) Tarfon thought wealth took the form of land, while Aqiba explained to him that wealth takes the form of Torah learning. That the sense is material and concrete is explicit: land for Torah, Torah for land. Thus, to repeat the matter of how Torah serves as an explicit symbol to convey the systemic worldview, let us note the main point of the now-familiar passage:

Leviticus Rabbah

XXXIV:XVI
1. B. R. Tarfon gave to R. Aqiba six silver centenarii, saying to him, "Go, buy us a piece of land, so we can get a living from it and labor in the study of Torah together."
   C. He took the money and handed it over to scribes, Mishnah teachers, and those who study Torah.
   D. After some time R. Tarfon met him and said to him, "Did you buy the land that I mentioned to you?"
   E. He said to him, "Yes."
   F. He said to him, "Is it any good?"
   G. He said to him, "Yes."
   H. He said to him, "And do you not want to show it to me?"
   I. He took him and showed him the scribes, Mishnah teachers, and people who were studying Torah, and the Torah that they had acquired.
   J. He said to him, "Is there anyone who works for nothing? Where is the deed covering the field?"
   K. He said to him, "It is with King David, concerning whom it is written, 'He has scattered, he has given to the poor, his righteousness endures forever' (Ps. 112:9)."

The successor system has its own definitions not only for learning, symbolized by the word Torah but also for wealth, expressed in the same symbol. Accordingly, the category formation for worldview, Torah in place of philosophy, dictates, as a matter of fact, a still more striking category reformation, in which the entire matter of scarce resources is reconsidered, and a counterpart category set forth.

It follows that, while in the successor system's theory of the component of the social order represented by the way of life, we find an economics, it is an economics of scarce resources defined as something other than particular real estate. Why do I insist that these questions are economic in character? It is because they deal with the rules or theory of the rational management of scarce resources, their preservation and increase, and do so in commonplace terms of philosophical economics, for example, the control of the means of production, the definition of money and of value, the distribution of valued goods and services, whether by appeal to the market or to a theory of distributive economics, the theory of the value of labor and the like. But while the structure remained the same, the contents radically would differ, hence the transvaluation of value. It was as if a new currency were issued to replace the old, then declared of no value, capable of purchasing nothing worth having. In such an economics, there is far more than a currency reform, but rather a complete economic revolution, a new beginning, as much as a shift from socialism to capitalism. But the transvaluation, in our case, was more thoroughgoing still, since involved was the very reconsideration of the scarcity of scarce resources. Both elements then underwent transvaluation: the definition of resources of value, the rationality involved in the management of scarcity. In a word, while real estate cannot increase and by definition must always prove scarce, the value represented by Torah could expand without limit. Value could then increase indefinitely, resources that were desired and scarce be made ever more abundant, in the transformed economics of the successor system.

Philosophical politics tells who may legitimately do what to whom. When a politics wants to know who ought *not* to be doing what to whom, we find in hand the counterpart category to the received politics.[8] The received category set forth politics as the theory of legitimate violence, the counterpart category, politics as the theory of *illegitimate* violence. The received politics had been one of isolation and interiority, portraying Israel as *sui generis* and autocephalic in all ways. The portrait in the successor documents is a politics of integration among the nations; a perspective of exteriority replaces the inner-facing one of the Mishnah, which recognized no government of Israel but God's – and then essentially *ab initio*. The issues of power had found definition in questions concerning who legitimately inflicts sanctions upon whom within Israel. They now shift to give an account of who illegitimately inflicts sanctions upon ("persecutes") Israel. So the points of systemic differentiation are radically revised, and the politics of the successor system becomes not a revision of the received category but a formation that in many ways mirrors the received one: once more a counterpart category. Just as, in the definition of scarce resources, Torah study has replaced land, so now weakness forms the focus in place of strength, illegitimacy in place of legitimacy. Once more the mirror image of the received category presents the perspective of the counterpart category.

The politics of the successor system turns outward, its attention focussed upon the world in which Israel finds itself. Israel differentiated by its castes, Israel as taxic indicator – these categories

---

[8]That is, of course, as much as, in the contrast of real wealth and true value, that is to say, land and Torah learning, we identify not a revised economics but a counterpart category to the familiar economics.

no longer formed the center of exegetical attention. Instead, with Israel viewed whole, the opposite of "Israel" is now not "levite, then priest," or (in the opposite direction) "gentile," but "the nations." Israel then is one and whole vis-à-vis outsiders, who are seen as many and distinct. Israel as the victim of illegitimate violence and the nations as illegitimately empowered now defined the main-beams of the categorical structure of the successor system's politics. That fact justifies the classification of the system's politics as not a mere revision but an utter inversion, hence, as is now clear, a counterpart category. The received components – way of life, worldview, social entity – all are recast in category, not merely content, and that explains why, in regard to the definition of the social entity, the realm of empowerment, in particular, to be "Israel" now meant to be the victim of the illegitimate exercise of power. The new system then classified Israel in context and transitively, as a nation among nations, subject to the will of outsiders, not out of context and intransitively, as an autonomous and free-standing social entity.

The data given to us in the successor documents, when they speak on their own account and not in clarification of the Mishnah and related writings, shift in character. Now we find the answers to these questions: to whom is violence illegitimately done, and also, who may not legitimately inflict violence? With the move from the politics of legitimate to that of illegitimate power, the systemic interest now lies in defining not the who legitimately does what, but rather, the to whom, against whom, is power illegitimately exercised. And this movement represents not the revision of the received category, but its inversion. For thought on legitimate violence is turned on its head. A new category of empowerment is worked out alongside the old. The entity that is victim of power is at the center, rather than the entity that legitimately exercises power. That entity is now Israel *en masse*, rather than the institutions and agencies of Israel on earth, Heaven above – a very considerable shift in thought on the systemic social entity. Israel as disempowered, rather than king, high priest, and sage as Israel's media of empowerment, defines the new system's politics.

In laying claim to the status of empowerment, thought on legitimate violence now asks about the illegitimacy of violence inflicted upon social entities – which nonetheless also are conceived as political entities, rather than the legitimacy of violence inflicted by them.[9] This is as much a new mode of classification, an utterly fresh

---

[9]Israel in the successor system is not only a social entity. It also is represented as empowered to make choices and set norms and impose sanctions, hence must be deemed also a political entity.

category as the odd and unpredictable economics reconsidered in the transvaluation of value. But as that remained an economics, so in hand is still a politics. The reason is that the question we now seek to answer remains the same as before: who inflicts sanctions on whom and why? On what entities do discussions of violence focus?

It follows that we address a political question to an empowered entity. But the answer – the focus of attention within political thought – now centers upon the violence inflicted upon Israel, the nation, and differentiation now is among those who illegitimately act violently. True, when they speak of who legitimately exercises violence (in addition to Heaven, of course), sages refer to the sage. That happens to constitute a mere extension of the received system, which had assigned sages mastery of the courts, alongside the monarchy and the high priesthood. But when the successor writings tell us upon whom violence is legitimately exercised and by whom, there is a wholly new realm of thinking going on.

We recall that the Mishnah's government for Israel had comprised, on earth, a tripartite structure of high priest and a king, with administrative courts of sages alongside, ascending upward to the authority of the Temple mount. Above, and corresponding, is the court in Heaven. That court bears its jurisdiction for some actions, the earthly political institutions each exercised its jurisidiction for others, and the point of differentiation set forth the urgent and compelling systemic issue in the political component of the system, just as it did in the other components. The Talmud of the Land of Israel and its companion compilations of scriptural exegeses for their part do not even pretend that such an ordered, self-governing world existed in their time, or, for that matter, ever. They present the portrait of administration by an unstructured set of small-claims courts standing outside an appellate structure of authority, petty bureaus of administration of trivial things, over which rabbis, defined as judges, lawyers, and masters of disciples in the law, presided. At the head of it all is a patriarch, not a king, on the one side or a priest anointed for the purpose, on the other. And the patriarch is variously represented as honorable and not. So many well-composed institutions of politics now give way to a single kind of institution, and a vertical structure is set aside by a horizontal one. These institutional differences as to fact signal a deeper difference as to system.

The Mishnah's account of practical politics and that of the Yerushalmi prove discontinuous not only in structure but also in system, for the discontinuity reveals itself in the theory of empowerment. Now gentiles are deemed not only empowered but also subject to differentiation. The earlier system had concerned itself with the internal politics of (an) Israel, with politics seen as principal taxic indicator of the social order. The later politics, by contrast, turned toward the external relationships of (an) Israel located in the disorderly world of nations. So the new politics has not only inverted the issue of violence and turned its illegitimate side upward. It also has revised the systemic vision so that attention faced outward, differentiation among the outsider vis-à-vis (an) undifferentiated Israel being the result. So the successor system's definition of what is at stake in the theory of legitimate violence that forms the centerpiece of politics therefore proves wholly other.

The burden of the systemic message assigned to the component of politics remained equally heavy in the successor system. But the contents proved quite dissimilar. The Mishnah's political theory had focused upon the inner structure and composition of Israel's social order; politics served the systemic purpose of setting forth the hierarchical taxonomy of power, just as each of the other principal parts of the Mishnah's statement of the social order represented the classification and ordering of all classes of things. When, for the Mishnah's politics, we know who within Israel legitimately inflicts sanctions upon whom within Israel, the principle of differentiation yields a clear picture of the organization of Israelite society. So the role of politics in the philosophical statement of Judaism is to represent the theoretical standing of the empowered institutions, the ones that bear the political role and responsibility. As we shall now see, the task of politics in the successor system accomplished a different sort of differentiation altogether.

The systemic message now concerned an Israel lacking all capacity to effect violence, requiring an explanation of its illegitimacy. No longer an empowered nation, Israel – within the systemic writings of the late fourth and fifth century – speculates on who is the worst among the nations, what will come of Israel, when Israel will once more take charge of its own affairs. That explains why, to deliver the systemic message, it was not only the *illegitimate* exercise of power, but differentiation among the entities, institutions and persons, that illegitimately inflict violence would require attention.[10] Formerly

---

[10] The explanation for the shift deriving from the change in Israel's historical political condition begs the question. When the Mishnah was written, Israel did not govern itself through a king, high priest, and sages' court, and such a system was a complete fabrication. There never was a point in the history of Israel in the land of Israel in which such a fabrication approximated political facts. So if the initial system presented a political fantasy, we have no reason to explain its revision, or complete rejection in favor of a different system, by reason of a discovery of a change in the facts of the matter. On the contrary,

sorting out who properly inflicts which sanction upon whom, now the system's political analysis concerns both the actor, now the illegitimate one, and the victim, equally illegitimate. And that inversion brings us back to our interest in not the reformation of received categories but the formation of the counterpart ones: to what systemic purpose? The answer, for the economics of never-scarce Torah of the successor system, lies right at the surface. What about the politics of weakness?

At stake is always the social entity, for a politics – commonplace and conventional or counterpart and odd – bears the burden of definition of the social entity of the encompassing system. And here we locate the systemic message delivered by the anti-politics. The counterpart category is one that in fact rejects as beside the point what makes a politics political: the legitimate use of violence. The data that will be sought attest to the very opposite facts. For now, as a matter of fact, all violence, but God's and the sages', is illegitimate. The political entity that Israel is to form is an anti-political one, in that it defines itself not by appeal to its legitimate exercise of sanctions, but rather by its exercising no power at all. The social entity in the politics at hand is made, therefore, to affirm the status of the victim, once again a social entity for an anti-politics indeed.

The upshot is that the successor system has reconsidered not merely the contents of the received structure, but the composition of the structure itself. In place of its philosophy, we have now a new medium for the formulation of a worldview; in place of a way of life formulated as an economics, a new valuation of value, in place of an account of the social entity framed as a politics, a new conception of legitimate violence. So much for the formation of counterpart categories.

---

the sages of the successor documents had no more keen interest in empirical observation and verification than did the ones of the Mishnah and its companions. The systemic theory, that alone, accounts for the character of matters.

7

From Philosophy to Religion: Systemic Integration

In the successor system represented by the Yerushalmi and related documents, knowledge more than merely informs, it saves. And knowledge that saves is gnostic. What happens to me in Torah study in the theory of the religious successor system that does not happen to me in Torah study in the theory of the initial, philosophical system is that I am changed in my very being. This transformation of the one who knows is not alone as to knowledge and understanding (let alone mere information), nor even as to virtue and taxic status, but as to what the knower is. I become something different from, better and more holy than, what I was before I knew, and whether the complement is "the mysteries" or "the Torah [as taught by sages]" makes no material difference.

But, as a matter of fact, that conception of the Torah as transformative contains another important trait we call gnostic, which is, the power to do things I could not do before I had attained knowledge in the correct way. The marks of the transformation emerge in the supernatural power that I have by reason of my (new) knowledge, learning in the Torah. That is what I mean by the new learning and what justifies the classification of Torah learning as gnostic. For when (mere) knowledge so transforms the knower that he or she is deemed "saved," or otherwise transformed into something utterly different from the condition characteristic of the prior one marked by ignorance and by unredemption, then that knowledge may be called gnostic. For in general, by "gnostic," people mean salvific knowledge, transitive, transformative learning, joining the two quite distinct categories of intellect and personal salvation or regeneration.[1]

That jarring juxtaposition, identifying ignorance (not knowing a given fact) with the personal condition of unregeneracy, knowledge with supernatural standing and, hence, also power – that juxtaposition relates what need not, and commonly is not, correlated: the moral or existential condition of the person and the level of intellectual enlightenment of that same person. Certainly the framers of the Mishnah did not imagine that such a correlation could be made, nor did their heirs for quite some time. But in the successor system, a principal point of integration of what philosophy had deemed distinct was between knowledge and one's condition or classification as to supernatural things. Knowledge of the Torah, quite specifically, changed a person and made him (never her) simply different from what he had been before or without that same knowledge: physically weaker, but also strengthened by power that we might call magical, but that they called supernatural. Before proceeding, let me give a good example of what I mean by knowledge of Torah represented as transformative and salvific.

I can point to a story that explicitly states the proposition that the obeying the Torah, with obedience founded on one's own knowledge thereof, constitutes a source of salvation. In this story we shall see that because people observed the rules of the Torah, they expected to be saved. And if they did not observe, they accepted their punishment. So the Torah now stands for something more than revelation and life of study, and (it goes without saying) the sage now appears as a holy, not merely a learned, man. This is because his knowledge of the Torah has transformed him. Accordingly, we deal with a category of stories and sayings about the Torah entirely different from what has gone before. We find at Y. Taanit 3:8 one among numerous examples in which the symbol of the Torah and knowledge of the Torah bear salvific consequence, a claim never set forth in behalf of knowledge, let alone knowledge of the Torah, in the Mishnah:[2]

II

[A] As to Levi ben Sisi: troops came to his town. He took a scroll of the Torah and went up to the roof and said, "Lord of the ages! If a

---

[1] I of course bypass the word, Gnostic with a capital G, bearing quite specific meanings in the study of late antiquity. A variety of meanings circulate, attached to various writings. What the common adjective, gnostic, with the denotative adjective, Gnostic, have in common is that the latter falls into the class of the former: saving knowledge.

[2] Not even at M. Hag. 2:2!

From Philosophy to Religion: Systemic Integration 131

[B] single word of this scroll of the Torah has been nullified [in our town], let them come up against us, and if not, let them go their way."

[B] Forthwith people went looking for the troops but did not find them [because they had gone their way].

[C] A disciple of his did the same thing, and his hand withered, but the troops went their way.

[D] A disciple of his disciple did the same thing. His hand did not wither, but they also did not go their way.

[E] This illustrates the following apophthegm: You can't insult an idiot, and dead skin does not feel the scalpel.

What is interesting here is how taxa into which the word Torah previously fell have been absorbed and superseded in a new taxon. The Torah is an object: "He took a scroll...." It also constitutes God's revelation to Israel: "If a single word...." The outcome of the revelation is to form an ongoing way of life, embodied in the sage himself: "A disciple of his did the same thing...." The sage plays an intimate part in the supernatural event: "His hand withered...." Here the Torah is a source of salvation. How so? The Torah stands for, or constitutes, the way in which the people Israel saves itself from marauders. This straightforward sense of salvation will not have surprised the author of Deuteronomy. But in our documents, there is more to the relationship of the Torah to salvation than mere obedience to its rules.

For now we discern an approach to the mere learning of the Torah – as distinct from obedience to its rules – that promises not merely intellectual enlightenment but personal renewal or transfiguration or some other far-reaching change. And since that view presents a gnostic[3] reading of learning, in the successor system we confront a Torah, knowledge of which not merely informs or presents right rules of conduct, but which transforms, regenerates, saves.[4] In that context and

---

[3] Resorting to the adjective "Faustian" while defensible seems to me less exact.
[4] Obviously, this "gnostic" is with a small g; I in no way mean to identify the Torah of the successor Judaism with the Gnostic systems, Christian, Judaic, and pagan, of which we have knowledge in the same time and place, as well as earlier and later. My supposition is that, in any religious system, the intellectual component by the nature of the systemic setting is going to bear the same transformative and salvific valence as I show here pertained to the Torah. The counterparts in other religions, which impute to knowledge of the correct sort in the proper manner salvific power, are numerous. That seems to me to justify treating "gnostic" as a generic classification for religious knowledge. But is there religious knowledge that is not gnostic, but merely (for one example) validating or qualifying? Indeed, there is a great deal of such knowledge, and the Mishnah's conception of knowing, as set forth in the apologetic of tractate Avot, is exactly of that kind. There, as we shall see,

by these definitions, the theory of the Torah and of Torah study set forth in the successor documents promises a fully-realized transformation to those who study and therefore know the Torah. They gained not merely intellectual enlightenment but supernatural power and standing. In this context, that encompassed such salvation as would take place prior to the end of time. The new learning defined as the consequence of Torah study imputed by the Talmud of the Land of Israel, Genesis Rabbah, Leviticus Rabbah, and Pesiqta deRab Kahana – but not by the Mishnah and its companions, tractate Avot and the Tosefta – changes not merely the mind but the moral and salvific condition of the one who engages in that learning.

To the rabbis the principal salvific deed was to "study Torah," by which they meant memorizing Torah sayings by constant repetition, and, as the Talmud itself amply testifies, (for some sages) profound analytic inquiry into the meaning of those sayings. This act of "study of Torah" imparted supernatural power. For example, by repeating words of Torah, the sage could ward off the angel of death and accomplish other kinds of miracles as well. So Torah formulas served as incantations. Mastery of Torah transformed the man who engaged in Torah learning into a supernatural figure, able to do things ordinary folk could not do. In the nature of things, the category of "Torah" was vastly expanded so that the symbol of Torah, a Torah scroll, could be compared to a man of Torah, namely, a rabbi. Since what made a man into a sage or a disciple of a sage or a rabbi was studying the Torah through discipleship, what is at stake in the symbolic transfer is quite obvious. If I know the Torah, I can join in the making of the Torah, and that claim in my behalf as a sage forms solid evidence of the allegation that studying the Torah not only endows one with power but actually changes the man from what he had been into something else. He had been ordinary, now he is not merely powerful but holy.

Is Judaism in its rabbinic form then a religion of Torah? Not at all. Time and again, knowledge of the Torah forms a way-station on a path to a more distant, more central goal: attaining *zekhut*, which I have translated as "the heritage of virtue and its consequent entitlements." Torah study is one means of attaining access to that heritage, of gaining *zekhut*. There are other equally suitable means, and, not only so, but the merit gained by Torah study is no different from the merit gained

---

studying the Torah brings God's presence to join those who repeat Torah words, whether one or many. But there is no consequent claim that the Torah words' repetition has changed those who have said them, only that God has joined their study circle. And that claim is of a considerably different kind from the one we shall see in numerous stories of the correlation between knowing the Torah and supernatural power.

From Philosophy to Religion: Systemic Integration 133

by acts of supererogatory grace. Since, in the successor system, it is points of integration, not of differentiation, that guide us to the systemic problematic, we must take seriously the contingent status, the standing of a dependent variable, accorded to Torah study in such stories as the following:

Y. *Taanit* 3:11

IV
- C. There was a house that was about to collapse over there [in Babylonia], and Rab set one of his disciples in the house, until they had cleared out everything from the house. When the disciple left the house, the house collapsed.
- D. And there are those who say that it was R. Adda bar Ahwah.
- E. Sages sent and said to him, "What sort of good deeds are to your credit [that you have that much merit]?"
- F. He said to them, "In my whole life no man ever got to the synagogue in the morning before I did. I never left anybody there when I went out. I never walked four cubits without speaking words of Torah. Nor did I ever mention teachings of Torah in an inappropriate setting. I never laid out a bed and slept for a regular period of time. I never took great strides among the associates. I never called my fellow by a nickname. I never rejoiced in the embarrassment of my fellow. I never cursed my fellow when I was lying by myself in bed. I never walked over in the marketplace to someone who owed me money.
- G. "In my entire life I never lost my temper in my household."
- H. This was meant to carry out that which is stated as follows: "I will give heed to the way that is blameless. Oh when wilt thou come to me? I will walk with integrity of heart within my house" (Ps. 101:2).

What I find striking in this story is that mastery of the Torah is only one means of attaining the *zekhut* that had enabled the sage to keep the house from collapsing. And Torah study is not the primary means of attaining *zekhut*. The question at E provides the key, together with its answer at F. For what the sage did to gain such remarkable *zekhut* is not to master such-and-so many tractates of the Mishnah. It was rather acts of courtesy (*courtesia* in the Spanish sense perhaps), consideration, gentility, restraint. These produced *zekhut*, all of them acts of self-abnegation or the avoidance of power over others and the submission to the will and the requirement of self-esteem of others. Torah study is simply an item on a list of actions or attitudes that generate *zekhut*.

Here, in a moral setting, we find the politics replicated: the form of power that the system promises derives from the rejection of power that the world recognizes – legitimate violence replaced by legitimation of the absence of the power to commit violence or of the failure to commit violence. And, when we ask, whence that sort of power? The answer lies in the gaining of *zekhut* in a variety of ways, not in the acquisition of *zekhut* through the study of the Torah solely or even primarily. But, we note, the story at hand speaks of a sage in particular. He has gained *zekhut* by not acting the way sages are commonly assumed to behave but in a humble way.

In context of this story, *zekhut* then may prove a virtue dependent upon the situation of the Torah and its study, in consequence of which we should have to impute to the gnostic Torah systemic priority, indeed centrality, finding in the new learning the key to the successor system as a whole. But that is, in fact, not so. At hand is not a religious system in which the transformation of the individual through salvific knowledge provides the compelling answer to the question of personal salvation. A different question stands at center-stage, and a different answer altogether defines the dramatic tension of the theatrical globe. At stake, as we shall now see, is a public and a national question, one concerning Israel's history and destiny, to which the individual and his salvation, while important, are distinctly subordinated. Not Torah study, which may generate *zekhut*, but *zekhut* itself defines what is at issue, the generative problematic of the system, and only when we grasp the answer provided by *zekhut* shall we reach a definition of the question that precipitated the systemic construction and the formation of its categories, principal and contingent alike.[5]

The importance of the gnostic Torah in no way diminishes when we recognize the subordinate position of the Torah in the successor system. For the upshot remains systemically indicative. In unifying the distinct categories of learning and not deeds or virtue but one's personal condition in the supernatural world, the recasting of the category of the worldview from an intellectual and even a moral to a salvific and a supernatural indicator, encompassing data not formerly noted or even assembled at all, shows the successor system's novel power of integration. If Torah study changes me not only in my knowledge or even virtue but my relationship to Heaven, endowing me with the

---

[5]Until this inquiry I had always taken for granted that the center of the Judaism of the Dual Torah was located in the theory of the Torah as the critical symbol of the whole, a position conveyed by the title of my textbook, *The Way of Torah. An Introduction to Judaism* (Belmont: 1979: Wadsworth Publishing Co.). But Torah is contingent and instrumental, *zekhut* is uncontingent and the system's sole (so it appears at this moment) independent variable. And yet, it seems to me clear, the symbol of Torah does remain the center and heart of the Judaism that emerged from late antiquity. What this impression suggests to me is that in the third stage in the formation of the Judaism of the Dual Torah, attested by the Bavli and associated Midrash compilations, I should find *zekhut* a not-central, but now-contingent variable, replaced by Torah as the independent variable and court of final appeal. Whether that will be the case I cannot now predict.

supernatural power, then the system as a whole signals a union of Heaven and earth that was formerly unimagined. What I know concerns not only earth but Heaven, the power that knowledge brings governs in both realms.

Study of the Torah changed the one who studied because through it he entered into the mind of God, learning how God's mind worked when God formed the Torah, written and oral alike and (in the explicit view of Genesis Rabbah 1:1) consulted the Torah in creating the world. And there, in the intellect of God, in their judgment humanity gained access to the only means of uniting intellect with existential condition as to salvation. The Mishnah had set forth the rules that governed the natural world in relationship to Heaven. But knowledge of the Torah now joined the one world, known through nature, with the other world, the world of supernature, where, in the end, intellect merely served in the quest for salvation. Through Torah study sages claimed for themselves a place in that very process of thought that had given birth to nature; but it was a supernatural process, and knowledge of that process on its own terms would transform and, in the nature of things, save. That explains the integrative power of imputing supernatural power to learning. And, now that we realize what was at stake in the gnostic Torah, we understand the full gravity of the simple statement that the system's orbit encircled not the Torah but *zekhut*.

It must follow that *zekhut*, not Torah, in a single word defines the generative myth, the critical symbol of the successor Judaism. The signal that the gnostic Torah formed a mere component in a system that transcended Torah study and defined its structure in some way other than by appeal to the symbol and activity of the Torah comes from a simple fact. Ordinary folk, not disciples of sages, have access to *zekhut* entirely outside of study of the Torah. In stories not told about rabbis, a single remarkable deed, exemplary for its deep humanity, sufficed to win for an ordinary person the *zekhut* – "the heritage of virtue and its consequent entitlements" – that elicits the same marks of supernatural favor enjoyed by some rabbis on account of their Torah study.

Accordingly, the systemic centrality of *zekhut* in the structure, the critical importance of the heritage of virtue together with its supernatural entitlements – these emerge in a striking claim. It is framed in extreme form – another mark of the unique place of *zekhut* within the system. Even though a man was degraded, one action sufficed to win for him that heavenly glory to which rabbis in lives of Torah study aspired. The mark of the system's integration around *zekhut* lies in its insistence that all Israelites, not only sages, could gain *zekhut* for themselves (and their descendants). A single remarkable deed, exemplary for its deep humanity, sufficed to win for an ordinary person the *zekhut* that elicits supernatural favor enjoyed by some rabbis on account of their Torah study. The centrality of *zekhut* in the systemic structure, the critical importance of the heritage of virtue together with its supernatural entitlements therefore emerge in a striking claim. Even though a man was degraded, one action sufficed to win for him that heavenly glory to which rabbis in general aspired. The rabbinical storyteller whose writing we shall consider assuredly identifies with this lesson, since it is the point of his story and its climax.

In all three instances that follow, defining what the individual must do to gain *zekhut*, the point is that the deeds of the heroes of the story make them worthy of having their prayers answered, which is a mark of the working of *zekhut*. It is deeds beyond the strict requirements of the Torah, and even the limits of the law altogether, that transform the hero into a holy man, whose holiness served just like that of a sage marked as such by knowledge of the Torah. The following stories should not be understood as expressions of the mere sentimentality of the clerks concerning the lower orders, for they deny in favor of a single action of surpassing power sages' lifelong devotion to what the sages held to be the highest value, knowledge of the Torah:

Y. *Taanit* 1:4

I

F.   A certain man came before one of the relatives of R. Yannai. He said to him, "Rabbi, attain *zekhut* through me [by giving me charity]."

G.   He said to him, "And didn't your father leave you money?"

H.   He said to him, "No."

I.   He said to him, "Go and collect what your father left in deposit with others."

J.   He said to him, "I have heard concerning property my father deposited with others that it was gained by violence [so I don't want it]."

K.   He said to him, "You are worthy of praying and having your prayers answered."

The point of K, of course, is self-evidently a reference to the possession of entitlement to supernatural favor, and it is gained, we see, through deeds that the law of the Torah cannot require but must favor: what one does on one's own volition, beyond the measure of the law. Here I see the opposite of sin. A sin is what one has done by one's own volition beyond all limits of the law. So an act that generates *zekhut* for the individual is the counterpart and opposite: what one does by one's own volition that also is beyond all requirements of the law.

From Philosophy to Religion: Systemic Integration   137

L. A certain ass driver appeared before the rabbis [the context requires: in a dream] and prayed, and rain came. The rabbis sent and brought him and said to him, "What is your trade?"

M. He said to them, "I am an ass driver."

N. They said to him, "And how do you conduct your business?"

O. He said to them, "One time I rented my ass to a certain woman, and she was weeping on the way, and I said to her, 'What's with you?' and she said to me, 'The husband of that woman [me] is in prison [for debt], and I wanted to see what I can do to free him.' So I sold my ass and I gave her the proceeds, and I said to her, 'Here is your money, free your husband, but do not sin [by becoming a prostitute to raise the necessary funds].'"

P. They said to him, "You are worthy of praying and having your prayers answered."

The ass driver clearly has a powerful lien on Heaven, so that his prayers are answered, even while those of others are not. What he did to get that entitlement? He did what no law could demand: impoverished himself to save the woman from a "fate worse than death."

Q. In a dream of R. Abbahu, Mr. Pentakaka ["Five sins"] appeared, who prayed that rain would come, and it rained. R. Abbahu sent and summoned him. He said to him, "What is your trade?"

R. He said to him, "Five sins does that man [I] do every day, [for I am a pimp:] hiring whores, cleaning up the theater, bringing home their garments for washing, dancing, and performing before them."

S. He said to him, "And what sort of decent thing have you ever done?"

T. He said to him, "One day that man [I] was cleaning the theater, and a woman came and stood behind a pillar and cried. I said to her, 'What's with you?' And she said to me, 'That woman's [my] husband is in prison, and I wanted to see what I can do to free him,' so I sold my bed and cover, and I gave the proceeds to her. I said to her, 'Here is your money, free your husband, but do not sin.'"

U. He said to him, "You are worthy of praying and having your prayers answered."

Q moves us still further, since the named man has done everything sinful that one can do, and, more to the point, he does it every day. So the singularity of the act of *zekhut*, which suffices if done only one time, encompasses its power to outweigh a life of sin – again, an act of *zekhut* as the mirror-image and opposite of sin. Here again, the single act of saving a woman from a "fate worse than death" has sufficed.

V. A pious man from Kefar Imi appeared [in a dream] to the rabbis. He prayed for rain and it rained. The rabbis went up to him. His

	householders told them that he was sitting on a hill. They went out to him, saying to him, "Greetings," but he did not answer them.
W.	He was sitting and eating, and he did not say to them, "You break bread too."
X.	When he went back home, he made a bundle of faggots and put his cloak on top of the bundle [instead of on his shoulder].
Y.	When he came home, he said to his household [wife], "These rabbis are here [because] they want me to pray for rain. If I pray and it rains, it is a disgrace for them, and if not, it is a profanation of the Name of Heaven. But come, you and I will go up [to the roof] and pray. If it rains, we shall tell them, 'We are not worthy to pray and have our prayers answered.'"
Z.	They went up and prayed and it rained.
AA.	They came down to them [and asked], "Why have the rabbis troubled themselves to come here today?"
BB.	They said to him, "We wanted you to pray so that it would rain."
CC.	He said to them, "Now do you really need my prayers? Heaven already has done its miracle."
DD.	They said to him, "Why, when you were on the hill, did we say hello to you, and you did not reply?"
EE.	He said to them, "I was then doing my job. Should I then interrupt my concentration [on my work]?"
FF.	They said to him, "And why, when you sat down to eat, did you not say to us 'You break bread too'?"
GG.	He said to them, "Because I had only my small ration of bread. Why would I have invited you to eat by way of mere flattery [when I knew I could not give you anything at all]?"
HH.	They said to him, "And why when you came to go down, did you put your cloak on top of the bundle?"
II.	He said to them, "Because the cloak was not mine. It was borrowed for use at prayer. I did not want to tear it."
JJ.	They said to him, "And why, when you were on the hill, did your wife wear dirty clothes, but when you came down from the mountain, did she put on clean clothes?"
KK.	He said to them, "When I was on the hill, she put on dirty clothes, so that no one would gaze at her. But when I came home from the hill, she put on clean clothes, so that I would not gaze on any other woman."
LL.	They said to him, "It is well that you pray and have your prayers answered."

The pious man of V, finally, enjoys the recognition of the sages by reason of his lien upon Heaven, able as he is to pray and bring rain. What has so endowed him with *zekhut*? Acts of punctiliousness of a moral order: concentrating on his work, avoiding an act of dissimulation, integrity in the disposition of a borrowed object, his wife's concern not to attract other men and her equal concern to make herself attractive to her husband. None of these stories refers explicitly to *zekhut*; all of them tell us about what it means to enjoy not an entitlement by inheritance but a lien accomplished by one's own supererogatory acts of restraint.

Zekhut integrates what has been differentiated. Holding together learning, virtue, and supernatural standing, by explaining how Torah study transforms the learning man, *zekhut* further makes implausible those points of distinction between economics, and politics that bore the systemic message of the initial philosophy. Hierarchical classification, with its demonstration of the upward-reaching unity of all being, gives way to a different, and more compelling proposition: the unity of all being within the heritage of *zekhut*, to be attained equally and without differentiation in all the principal parts of the social order. The definition of *zekhut* therefore carries us to the heart of the integrating and integrated religious system of Judaism.

The word *zekhut* bears a variety of meanings, as Jastrow summarizes the data,[6] and the pertinence of each possible meaning is to be determined in context: [1] acquittal, plea in favor of the defendant; [2] doing good, blessing; [3] protecting influence of good conduct, merit; [4] advantage, privilege, benefit. The first meaning pertains solely in juridical (or metaphorically-juridical) contexts; the second represents a very general and imprecise use of the word, since a variety of other words bear the same meaning. Only the third and the fourth meanings pertain, since they are particular to this word, on the one side, and also religious, on the other. That is to say, only through using the word *zekhut* do authors of compositions and authorships of composites express the sense given at No. 3. Moreover, it will rapidly become clear, in context that No. 4 is not to be distinguished from No. 3, since "protecting influence of good conduct" when the word *zekhut* appears always yields "advantage, privilege, benefit." It follows that, for the purposes of systemic analysis, passages in which the word *zekhut* bears the sense, in Jastrow's words, of "the protecting influence of good conduct" which yields "advantage, privilege, or benefit" will tell us how the word *zekhut* functions.

My simple definition emphasizes "heritage," because the advantages or privileges conferred by *zekhut* may be inherited and also passed on; it stresses "entitlements" because advantages or privileges always, invariably result from receiving *zekhut* from ancestors or acquiring it on one's own; and I use the word "virtue" to refer to those supererogatory acts that demand a reward because they form matters of choice, the gift of the individual and his or her act of free will, an act

---

[6]Marcus Jastrow, *A Dictionary of the Targumim, The Talmud Babli and Yerushalmi, and the Midrashic Literature* (repr. New York, 1950: Pardes Publishing House), 398.

that is at the same time [1] uncompelled, for example, by the obligations imposed by the Torah, but [2] also valued by the Torah. The systemic importance of the conception of *zekhut*, we shall see in Chapter Nine, derives from its capacity to unite the generations in a heritage of entitlements; *zekhut* is fundamentally a historical category and concept, in that, like all historical systems of thought, it explains the present in terms of the past, and the future in terms of the present.

Because *zekhut* is something one may receive as an inheritance, out of the distant past, *zekhut* imposes upon the definition of the social entity, "Israel," a genealogical meaning. It furthermore imparts a distinctive character to the definitions of way of life. So the task of the political component of a theory of the social order, which is to define the social entity by appeal to empowerment, and of the economic component, which is to identify scarce resources by specification of the rationality of right management, is accomplished in a single word, which stands for a conception, a symbol, and a myth. All three components of this religious theory of the social order turn out to present specific applications, in context, for the general conception of *zekhut*. For the first source of *zekhut* derives from the definition of Israel as family; the entitlements of supernatural power deriving from virtue then care inherited from Abraham, Isaac, and Jacob. The second source is personal: the power one can gain for one's own heirs, moreover, by virtuous deeds. *Zekhut* deriving from either source is to be defined in context: what can you do if you have *zekhut*, that you cannot do if you do not have *zekhut*. and to whom can you do it. The answer to that question tells you the empowerment of *zekhut*.

Now in the nature of things, a theory of power or violence that is legitimately exercised falls into the category of a politics, and a conception of the scarce resource, defined as supernatural power that is to be rationally managed, falls into the category of an economics. That is why in the concept of *zekhut*, we find the union of economics and politics into a political economy: a theory of the whole society in its material and social relationships as expressed in institutions that permanently are given the right to impose order through real or threatened violence and in the assignment of goods and benefits, as systemically defined to be sure, through a shared rationality.

Zekhut serves, in particular, that counterpart category that speaks of not legitimate but illegitimate violence, not power but weakness. In context, time and again, we observe that *zekhut* is the power of the weak. People who through their own merit and capacity can accomplish nothing, can accomplish miracles through what others do for them in leaving a heritage of *zekhut*. And, not to miss the stunning message of the triplet of stories cited above, *zekhut* also is what the weak and excluded and despised can do that outweighs in power what the great masters of the Torah have accomplished. In the context of a system that represents Torah as supernatural, that claim of priority for *zekhut* represents a considerable transvaluation of power, as much as of value. And, by the way, *zekhut* also forms the inheritance of the disinherited: what you receive as a heritage when you have nothing in the present and have gotten nothing in the past, that scarce resource that is free and unearned but much valued. So let us dwell upon the definitive character of the transferability of *zekhut* in its formulation, *zekhut avot*, the *zekhut* handed on by the ancestors, the transitive character of the concept and its standing as a heritage of entitlements.

The systemic statement made by the usages of *zekhut* speaks of relationship, function, the interplay of humanity and God. One's store of *zekhut* derives from a relationship, that is, from one's forebears. That is one dimension of the relationships in which one stands. *Zekhut* also forms a measure of one's own relationship with Heaven, as the power of one person, but not another, to pray and so bring rain attests. What sort of relationship does *zekhut*, as the opposite of sin, then posit? It is not one of coercion, for Heaven cannot force us to do those types of deeds that yield *zekhut*, and that, story after story suggests, is the definition of a deed that generates *zekhut*: doing what we ought to do but do not have to do. But then, we cannot coerce Heaven to do what we want done either, for example, by carrying out the commandments. These are obligatory, but do not obligate Heaven.

Whence then our lien on Heaven?[7] It is through deeds of a supererogatory character – to which Heaven responds by deeds of a supererogatory character: supernatural favor to this one, who through deeds of ingratiation of the other or self-abnegation or restraint exhibits the attitude that in Heaven precipitates a counterpart attitude, hence generating *zekhut*, rather than to that one, who does not. The simple fact that rabbis cannot pray and bring rain, but a simple ass driver can, tells the whole story. The relationship measured by *zekhut* – Heaven's response by an act of uncoerced favor to a person's uncoerced gift, for example, act of gentility, restraint, or self-abnegation – contains an element of unpredictability for which appeal to the *zekhut* inherited from ancestors accounts. So while I cannot coerce heaven, I can through *zekhut* gain acts of favor from Heaven, and that is by doing what Heaven cannot require of me. Heaven then

---

[7] The answer to that question forms the bridge to the interpretation, in context, of the system as a whole: the determination of the self-evidently valid answer that the system posits – and therefore the identification of the urgent question that precipitated the formation of the system as a whole.

responds to my attitude in carrying out my duties – and more than my duties. That act of pure disinterest – giving the woman my means of livelihood – is the one that gains for me Heaven's deepest interest.

So *zekhut* forms the political economy of the religious system of the social order put forward by the Talmud of the Land of Israel, Genesis Rabbah, Leviticus Rabbah, and related writings. Here we find the power that brought about the transvaluation of value, the reversal of the meaning of power and its legitimacy. *Zekhut* expresses and accounts for the economic valuation of the scarce resource of what we should call moral authority. *Zekhut* stands for the political valorization of weakness, that which endows the weak with a power that is not only their own but their ancestors'. It enables the weak to accomplish goals through not their own power, but their very incapacity to accomplish acts of violence – a transvaluation as radical as that effected in economics. And *zekhut* holds together both the economics and the politics of this Judaism: it makes the same statement twice.

Zekhut as the power of the powerless, the riches of the disinherited, the valuation and valorization of the will of those who have no right to will. In the context of Christian Palestine, Jews found themselves on the defensive. Their ancestry called into question, their supernatural standing thrown into doubt, their future denied, they called themselves "Israel," and the land, "the Land of Israel." But what power did they possess, legitimately, if need be through violence, to assert their claim to form "Israel"? And, with the holy land passing into the hands of others, what scarce resource did they own and manage to take the place of that measure of value that now no longer was subjected to their rationality? Asserting a politics in which all violence was illegitimate, an economics in which nothing tangible, even real property in the Holy Land, had value, the system through its counterpart categories made a single, simple, and sufficient statement. But those whom Judaism knows as "our sages of blessed memory" were not the only system builders, and theirs was not the only question about the social order framed in historical and theological, rather than analytical and philosophical terms. Their contemporary, the Bishop of Hippo whom Christianity knows as Saint Augustine, set forth an account of the social order framed in the same terms and addressed to the same urgent and critical question. It is in the context of comparison that, in the end, we interpret the system that has now been described and analyzed: the Judaism transformed from a philosophy to a religion.

8

The City of God in the Conceptions of the Social Order of Our Sages of Blessed Memory and of St. Augustine

"Make his wishes yours, so that he will make your wishes his... Anyone from whom people take pleasure, God takes pleasure" (Abot 2:4). These two statements hold together the two principal elements of the conception of the relationship to God that in a single word *zekhut* conveys. Give up, please others, do not impose your will but give way to the will of the other, and Heaven will respond by giving a lien that is not coerced but evoked. By the rationality of discipline within, we have the power to form rational relationships beyond ourselves, with Heaven; and that is how the system expands the boundaries of the social order to encompass not only the natural but also the supernatural world.[1]

For it is the rationality of that relationship to God that governs the social order, defining the three components thereof: ethics, ethnos, ethos. For within that relationship we discern the model of not merely ethics but economics, not merely private morality in society but the public policy, the politics that delineates the limns of the ethnic community, and not alone the right attitude of the virtuous individual but the social philosophy of an entire nation – so the system proposes.

---

[1] I use the word "rationality" in the sense in which it is used in the thought of Max Weber: the systemic sense of what is appropriate and proper. The comparison of the rationalities of the initial and the successor systems is undertaken in the closing paragraphs. This is not, of course, an account of the concept of rationality in the thought of Weber. I believe my characterization, for the limited purpose of these remarks, is entirely accurate.

And that is the this-worldly social order that joins with Heaven, the society that is a unique and holy family, so transformed by *zekhut* inherited and *zekhut* accomplished as to transcend the world order. That ordering of humanity in society, empowered and enriched in an enchanted political economy, links private person to the public polity through the union of a common attitude: the one of renunciation that tells me how to behave at home and in the streets, and that instructs Israel how to conduct its affairs among the nations and throughout history.

Treating every deed, every gesture as capable of bringing about enchantment, the successor system imparted to the givens of everyday life – at least in their potential – remarkable power. The conviction that, by dint of special effort, I may so conduct myself as to acquire an entitlement of supernatural power turns my commonplace circumstance into an arena encompassing Heaven and earth. God responds to my – and holy Israel's – virtue, filling the gap – so to speak – about myself and about my entire family that I and we leave when we forebear, withdraw, and give up what is mine and ours: our space, my self. When I do, then God responds; my sacrifice evokes memories of Abraham's readiness to sacrifice Isaac;[2] my devotion to the other calls up from Heaven what by demanding I cannot coerce. What imparts critical mass to the conception of *zekhut*, that gaining of supernatural entitlements through the surrender of what is mine, is the recasting, in the mold and model of that virtue of surrender, of the political economy of Israel in the Land of Israel. That accounts for the definition of legitimate power in politics as only weakness, economics as the rational increase of resources that are, but need not be, scarce, valued things that are capable of infinite increase.

That not only accounts for the inversion of the received categories and their reformation into mirror images of what the philosophers had made of them. In my view it also explains why a quite fresh, deeply religious system has taken the place of a compelling and well-

---

[2] Note the fine perception of S. Levy, *Original Virtue and Other Studies*, pp. 2-3: "Some act of obedience, constituting the Ascent of man, is the origin of virtue and the cause of reward for virtue....What is the conspicuous act of obedience which, in Judaism, forms the striking contrast to Adam's act of disobedience, in Christianity? The submission of Isaac in being bound on the altar...is regarded in Jewish theology as the historic cause of the imputation of virtue to his descendants." It is not an accident, then, as we shall see, that Augustine selected as his paradigmatic historical exemplum the conflict of Cain and Abel, the city of God being inhabited by Abel and his descendants; he required a virtue pertinent to all of humanity, not to Israel alone, for his argument, so it seems to me as an outsider to the subject.

composed philosophical one. The Mishnah's God can scarcely compete with the God of the Yerushalmi and the Midrash compilations.[3] For the God of the philosophers, the apex of the hierarchy of all being as the framers of the Mishnah have positioned God, has made the rules and is shown by them to form the foundation of order. All things reach up to one thing, one thing contains within itself many things: these twin propositions of monotheism, which the philosophical system demonstrates in theory and proposes to realize in the facts of the social order, define a God who in an orderly way governs all the palpable relationships of nature as of supernature – but who finds a place, who comes to puissant expression, in not a single one of them. The God of the philosophers assures, sustains, supports, nourishes, guarantees, governs. But the way that God responds to what we do is all according to the rule. That is, after all, what natural philosophy proposes to uncover and discern, and what more elevated task can God perform than the nomothetic one accomplished in the daily creation of the world.

But God in the successor system gains what the philosophical God lacks, which is personality, active presence, pathos and empathy. The God of the religious system breaks the rules, accords an entitlement to this one, who has done some one remarkable deed, but not to that one, who has done nothing wrong and everything right. So a life in accord with the rules – even a life spent in the study of the Torah – in Heaven's view is outweighed by a single moment, a gesture that violates the norm, extending the outer limits of the rule, for instance, of virtue. And who but a God who, like us, feels, not only thinks, responds to impulse and sentiment, can be portrayed in such a way as this?

> So I sold my ass and I gave her the proceeds, and I said to her, 'Here is your money, free your husband, but do not sin [by becoming a prostitute to raise the necessary funds].'"
>
> They said to him, "You are worthy of praying and having your prayers answered."

No rule exhaustively describes a world such as this. If the God of the philosophers' Judaism makes the rules, the God of the religious Judaism breaks them. The systemic difference, of course, is readily extended outward from the personality of God: the philosophers' God thinks, the God of the religious responds, and we are in God's image, after God's likeness, not only because we through right thinking penetrate the principles of creation, but through right attitude replicate the heart of the Creator. Humanity on earth incarnates God

---

[3]My initial comments on that matter are in *The Incarnation of God: The Character of Divinity in Formative Judaism* (Philadelphia, 1988: Fortress Press).

on high, the Israelite family in particular, and, in consequence, earth and Heaven join – within.

Perhaps the first system contained within itself – as I shall argue in a moment – the flaw that, like a grain of sand in an oyster, so irritated the innards as to form a pearl. And perhaps even the philosophers, with their exquisitely ordered and balanced social world, can have made a place for God to act; but, knowing how they thought, we must imagine that like philosophers later on, they will have insisted that miracles, too, follow rules and demonstrate the presence of rules. But now, in the religious Judaism, the world now is no longer what it seems. At stake in what is remarkable is what falls beyond all power of rules either to describe or to prescribe.

What is asked of Israel and of the Israelite individual now is Godly restraint, supernatural generosity of soul that is "in our image, after our likeness": that is what sets aside all rules. And, since as a matter of simple fact, that appeal to transcend the norm defined not personal virtue but the sainthood of all Israel, living all together in the here and in the now, we must conclude that, within Israel's society, within what the Greco-Roman world will have called its *polis*, its political and social order, the bounds of earth have now extended to Heaven. In terms of another great system composed in the same time and in response to a world-historical catastrophe of the same sort, Israel on earth dwells in the city of God. And, it must follow, God dwells with Israel, in Israel: "Today, if you will it."

That insistence upon the systemic centrality of the conception of *zekhut*, with all its promise for the reshaping of value, draws our attention once more to the power of a single, essentially theological, conception to impart shape and structure to the social order. The Judaism set forth in the successor documents portrayed a social order in which, while taking full account of circumstance and historical context, individuals and nation alike controlled their own destiny. The circumstance of genealogy dictated whether or not the moral entity, whether the individual or the nation, would enjoy access to entitlements of supernatural favor without regard to the merit of either one. But, whether favored by a rich heritage of supernatural empowerment as was the nation, or deprived, by reason of one's immediate ancestors, of any lien upon Heaven, in the end both the nation and the individual had in hand the power to shape the future. How was this to be done? It was not alone by keeping the Torah, studying the Torah, dressing, eating, making a living, marrying, procreating, raising a family, burying and being buried, all in accord with those rules.

That life in conformity with the rule, obligatory but merely conventional, did not evoke the special interest of Heaven. Why should it? The rules describe the ordinary. But (in language used only in a later document) "God wants the heart," and that is not an ordinary thing. Nor was the power to bring rain or hold up a tottering house gained through a life of merely ordinary sanctity. Special favor responded to extraordinary actions, in the analogy of special disfavor, misfortune deemed to punish sin. And just as culpable sin, as distinct from mere error, requires an act of will, specifically, arrogance, so an act of extraordinary character requires an act of will. But, as mirror image of sin, the act would reveal in a concrete way an attitude of restraint, forbearance, gentility, and self-abnegation. A sinful act, provoking Heaven, was one that one did deliberately to defy Heaven. Then an act that would evoke Heaven's favor, so imposing upon Heaven a lien that Heaven freely gave, was one that, equally deliberately and concretely, displayed humility.

But the systemic focus upon the power of a single act of remarkable generosity, the surrender to the other of what is most precious to the self, whether that constituted an opinion or a possession or a feeling, in no way will have surprised the framers of the philosophical Judaism. They had laid heavy emphasis upon the power of human intentionality to settle questions of the status of interstitial persons, objects, or actions, within the larger system of hierarchical classification. So in the philosophical Judaism attitude and intentionality classified what was of doubtful status, that is to say, forming the active and motivating component of the structure and transforming the structure, a tableau of fixed and motionless figures, into a system of action and reaction. Then, in the process of transformation, we should hardly find surprising the appeal to the critical power of attitude and intentionality. For what we find in the successor system is a fundamental point of connection. What was specific before, intentionality, is now broadened and made general through extension to all aspects of one's attitude.

Now the powerful forces coalescing in intentionality gained very precise definition, and in their transformation from merely concrete cases of the taxonomic power of intentionality that worked one way here, another way there, into very broad-ranging but quite specific and prescribed attitudes, the successor system took its leave from the initial one without a real farewell. Then what is the point of departure? It is marked by the intense interest, in the religious Judaism, upon not the fixed given of normative intentionality,[4] but rather changing people, both individually and nationally, from what they were to something else. And, if the change is in a single direction, it is, nonetheless, also always personal and individual.

The change is signalled by the conception that study of the Torah not only illuminated and educated but transformed, and, moreover, so changed the disciple that he gained in supernatural standing and authority. This gnostic conception of knowledge, however, proved only a component of a larger conception of national transformation and personal regeneration, since, as we saw, Torah study produced *zekhut*, and all things depended upon the *zekhut* that a person, or the nation as a whole, possessed. Mastery of what we classify as "the system's worldview" changed a person by generating *zekhut*, that is, by so affecting the person as to inculcate attitudes that would produce remarkable actions (often: acts of omission, restraint, and forbearance) to generate *zekhut*. The change was the end, the Torah study, the medium.

But the system's worldview was not the sole, or even the principal, component that showed how the received system was transformed by the new one. The conception of *zekhut* came to the fore to integrate of the system's theory of the way of life of the social order, its economics, together with its account of the social entity of the social order, its politics. The remarkable actions – perhaps those of omission more than those of commission – that produced *zekhut* yielded an increase in the scarcest of all resources, supernatural favor, and at the same time endowed a person rich in entitlements to Heavenly intervention with that power to evoke that vastly outweighed the this-worldly power to coerce in the accomplishment of one's purpose.

This rapid account of the systemic structure and system, its inversion of the received categories and its formation of anti-categories of its own, draws our attention to the specificity of the definition of right attitude and puissant intentionality by contrast to the generality of those same matters when represented in the philosophical system of the Mishnah. We have, therefore, to ask ourselves whether the quite concrete and definition of those attitudes and correct will and proper intentionality that lead to acts that generate *zekhut* will have surprised framers of documents prior to those that attest the transformed Judaism before us. The answer is negative, and that fact

---

[4]That is, an assessment of what people will ordinarily think or propose or wish to have happen. The rule is set by that norm, not by exceptions, and on that basis, in the initial system, we are able to determine what (an ordinary person's) intentionality will dictate in a given interstitial case.

alerts us to yet another fundamental continuity between the two Judaisms.

As a matter of fact, the doctrine defining the appropriate attitude persisted pretty much unchanged from the beginning.[5] The repertoire of approved and disapproved attitude and intentionality remained constant through the half-millennium of the unfolding of the canon of Judaism from the Mishnah onward: humility, forbearance, accommodation, a spirit of conciliation. For one thing, Scripture itself is explicit that God shares and responds to the attitudes and intentionality of human beings. God cares what humanity feels – wanting love, for example – and so the conception that actions that express right attitudes of humility will evoke in Heaven a desired response will not have struck as novel the authors of the Pentateuch or the various prophetic writings, for example. The biblical record of God's feelings and God's will concerning the feelings of humanity leaves no room for doubt. What is fresh in the system before us is not the integration of the individual with the nation but the provision, for the individual, of a task and a role analogous to that of the nation.

With its interest in classifying large-scale and collective classes of things, the Mishnah's system treats matters of attitude and emotion in that same taxic context. For instance, while the Mishnah casually refers to emotions, for example, tears of joy, tears of sorrow, where feelings matter, it always is in a public and communal context. Where there is an occasion of rejoicing, one form of joy is not to be confused with some other, or one context of sorrow with another. Accordingly, marriages are not to be held on festivals (M. M.Q. 1:7). Likewise mourning is not to take place then (M. M.Q. 1:5, 3:7-9). Where emotions play a role, it is because of the affairs of the community at large, for example, rejoicing on a festival, mourning on a fast day (M. Suk. 5:1-4). Emotions are to be kept in hand, as in the case of the relatives of the executed felon (M. San. 6:6). If I had to specify the single underlying principle affecting all forms of emotion, for the Mishnah it is the profoundly philosophical attitude that attitudes and feelings must be kept under control, never fully expressed without reasoning about the appropriate context. Emotions must always lay down judgments.

We see in most of those cases in which emotions play a systemic and indicative, not merely an episodic and random, role, that the basic principle is the same. We can, and must so frame our feelings as to accord with the appropriate rule. In only one case does emotion play a

---

[5]I have demonstrated that fact in my *Vanquished Nation, Broken Spirit. The Virtues of the Heart in Formative Judaism* (New York, 1987: Cambridge University Press).

decisive role in settling an issue, and that has to do with whether or not a farmer was happy that water came upon his produce or grain. That case underlines the conclusion just now drawn. If people feel a given sentiment, it is a matter of judgement, therefore invokes the law's penalties. So in this system emotions are not treated as spontaneous, but as significant aspects of a person's judgment.

Whence then the doctrine, made so concrete and specific in the conception of *zekhut* as made systemically generative in the successor documents, that very specific attitudes, particular to persons, bear the weight of the systemic structure as a whole? It is in tractate Abot, which supplies those phrases cited at the outset to define the theology that sustains the conception of *zekhut*. Tractate Abot, conventionally attached to the Mishnah and serving as the Mishnah's advocate, turns out to form the bridge from the Mishnah to the Yerushalmi and its associated compilations of scriptural exegeses. That tractate presents the single most comprehensive account of religious affections. The reason is that, in that document above all, how we feel defines a critical aspect of virtue. The issue proves central, not peripheral. The very specific and concrete doctrine emerges fully exposed. A simple catalogue of permissible feelings comprises humility, generosity, self-abnegation, love, a spirit of conciliation of the other, and eagerness to please. A list of impermissible emotions is made up of envy, ambition, jealousy, arrogance, sticking to one's opinion, self-centeredness, a grudging spirit, vengefulness, and the like. Nothing in the wonderful stories about remarkable generosity does more than render concrete the abstract doctrine of the heart's virtue that tractate Abot sets forth.

People should aim at eliciting from others acceptance and good will and should avoid confrontation, rejection, and humiliation of the other. This they do through conciliation and giving up their own claims and rights. So both catalogues form a harmonious and uniform whole, aiming at the cultivation of the humble and malleable person, one who accepts everything and resents nothing. True, these virtues, in this tractate as in the system as a whole, derive from knowledge of what really counts, which is what God wants. But God favors those who please others. The virtues appreciated by human beings prove identical to the ones to which God responds as well. And what single virtue of the heart encompasses the rest? Restraint, the source of self-abnegation, humility, serves as the anecdote for ambition, vengefulness, and, above all, for arrogance. It is restraint of our own interest that enables us to deal generously with others, humility about ourselves that generates a liberal spirit towards others. And the correspondence of Heavenly and mortal attitudes is to be taken for granted – as is made explicit.

So the emotions prescribed in tractate Abot turn out to provide variations of a single feeling, which is the sentiment of the disciplined heart, whatever affective form it may take. And where does the heart learn its lessons, if not in relationship to God? So: "Make his wishes yours, so that he will make your wishes his" (Abot 2:4). Applied to relationships between human beings, this inner discipline of the emotional life will yield exactly those virtues of conciliation and self-abnegation, humility and generosity of spirit, that the framers of tractate Abot spell out in one example after another. Imputing to Heaven exactly those responses felt on earth, for example, "Anyone from whom people take pleasure, God takes pleasure" (Abot 3:10), makes the point at the most general level.

Then what has the successor system contributed? Two things: [1] the conception that acts of omission or commission expressing an attitude of forbearance and self-abnegation generate *zekhut* in particular; [2] the principle that *zekhut* functions in those very specific ways that the system deems critical: as the power to attest to human transformation and regeneration, affording, in place of philosophical politics and philosophical economics, that power inhering in weakness, that wealth inhering in giving up what one has, that in the end promise the attainment of our goals. In a single sentence, the path from one system to the other is in three stages: [1] the philosophical Judaism, portrayed by the Mishnah, assigns to intentionality and attitude systemic centrality; [2] tractate Abot, in presenting in general terms the rationale of the Mishnah's system, defines precisely the affective attitude and intentionality that are required; [3] the religious Judaism of the Yerushalmi and associated writings joins together the systemic centrality of attitude and intentionality with the doctrine of virtue laid out in tractate Abot.

But in joining these received elements the new system emerges as distinct from the old.[6] For when we deem the attitude of affirmation and acceptance, rather than aggression, and the intentionality of self-

---

[6]This is not to suggest that the substance of the doctrine of virtue was richly revised in the successor writings. That is not so. The transformation was systemic, not doctrinal. Emotions not taken up earlier in the pages of the Yerushalmi did not come under discussion. Principles introduced earlier enjoyed mere restatement and extensive exemplification. Some principles of proper feelings might even generate secondary developments of one kind or another. But nothing not present at the outset – in tractate Avot – drew sustained attention later on. The system proved essentially complete in the earliest statement of its main points. What then do the authors or compilers of the Yerushalmi contribute? Temper marks the ignorant person, restraint and serenity, the learned one. These are mere details.

abnegation and forbearance, to define the means for gaining *zekhut*, what we are saying is contrary and paradoxical: if you want to have, then give up, and if you want to impose your judgment, then make the judgment of the other into your own, and if you want to coerce Heaven, then evoke in Heaven attitudes of sympathy that will lead to the actions or events that you want, whether rain, whether long life, whether the salvation of Israel and its hegemony over the nations: to rule, be ruled by Heaven; to show Heaven rules, give up what you want to the other. *Zekhut* results: the lien upon Heaven, freely given by Heaven in response to one's free surrender to the will and wish of Heaven. And by means of *zekhut*, whether one's own, whether one's ancestors', the social order finds its shape and system, and the individual his or her place within its structure.

The correspondence of the individual to the nation, both capable of gaining *zekhut* in the same way, linked the deepest personal emotions to the cosmic fate and transcendent faith of that social group of which each individual formed a part. The individual Israelite's innermost feelings, the inner heart of Israel, the microcosm, correspond to the public and historic condition of the nation, of Israel, the macrocosm. In the innermost chambers of the individual's deepest feelings, the Israelite therefore lives out the public history and destiny of the people, Israel.

What precipitated deep thought upon fundamental questions of social existence was a simple fact. From the time that Christianity attained the status of a licit religion, the Jews of Palestine witnessed the formation of circumstances that had formerly been simply unimaginable: another Israel, in the same place and time, competed with them in their terms, quoting their Scriptures, explaining who they were in their own categories but in very different terms from the ones that they used. We need not explain the profundities of religious doctrine by reducing them to functions and necessities of public policy. But it is, a matter of simple fact, that the Jews in the fourth century had witnessed a drastic decline in their power to exercise legitimate violence (which is to say, violence you can make stick), as well as in their command of the real estate of Palestine that they knew as the Holy Land and its wealth. The system's stress upon matters of intentionality and attitude, subject to the governance of even the most humble of individuals, even the most insignificant of nations, exactly corresponded to the political and social requirements of the Jews' condition in that time. The transformed Judaism made of necessity a theological virtue, and, by the way, the normative condition of the social order.

The City of God in the Conceptions of the Social Order

In the fourth century, from Constantine's great victory and legitimation of Christianity in the beginning, to the Theodosian code that subordinated Jewry and limited its rights at nearly the end, Jews confronted a remarkable shift in the character of the Roman empire. The state first legalized, then established Christianity as most favored religion, and – by the end of that century – finally undertook to extirpate paganism, and, by the way, to subordinate Judaism. Therein lies the urgency of the critical question addressed by the system as a whole – if not the self-evidence of the truth of its response to that question. Dealing with world-historical change in the character of the Roman Empire consequent on the legalization of Christianity by Constantine and the establishment of Christianity as the state religion by his heirs and successors, the transformed Judaism made its statement in answer to the fundamental question confronting the social order: precisely what are we now to do?

That political question – the "do" part of the question – concerning the assessment of the legitimate use of violence in this Judaism called into doubt the legitimacy of any kind of violence at all, Jews' having none. But no less subject to reflection was that "doing" that referred to making a living, the economics of the acquisition and management of scarce resources, and, it goes without saying, the making of a life, the philosophy of rational explanation of all things in some one way. At stake, then, were the very shape and structure of the social order, reconsidered at what was, and was certainly perceived as, the critical turning.

This utter reordering of society framed a question that had to be faced and could not be readily answered.[7] It concerned the meaning and end of history, Israel's history, now that the prophetic promises were claimed by the Christian competition to have been kept in the past, leaving nothing in the future for which to hope. When, for a brief moment, in 361-3 the emperor Julian disestablished Christianity and restored paganism, proposing also to rebuild the Jews' Temple in

---

[7]And certainly had not been answered by the Mishnah's system, which treated history – composed of events in particular – as mere occasions for taxonomic inquiry: classifying this event in one way, according to one overriding rule, that event in some other, according to another rule; and neither rule bore any relationship to history. The regularization and ordering of disorderly events – counterpart to what we know as social science today – denied to history all status as the source of category-formation. I have spelled all this out in my *Messiah in Context*. *[The Foundations of Judaism. Method, Teleology, Doctrine.* (Philadelphia, 1983-1985: Fortress Press. Second printing: Lanham, 1988: University Press of America). *Studies in Judaism* Series. I-III. II. *Messiah in Context. Israel's History and Destiny in Formative Judaism]*.

Jerusalem, Christianity met the challenge and regained power. The Temple was not rebuilt, and Julian's brief reign brought in its wake a ferocious counter-revolution, with the Christian state now suppressing the institutions of paganism, and Christian men in the streets of the towns and villages taking an active role on their own as well. Julian's successors persecuted pagan philosophy. In 380 the emperor Theodosius (379-395) decreed the end of paganism:

> It is our desire that all the various nations which are subject to our clemency and moderation should continue in the profession of that religion which was delivered to the Romans by the divine Apostle Peter.

Paganism found itself subjected to penalties. The state church – a principal indicator of the Christian civilization that the West was to know – now came into being. In 381 Theodosius forbade sacrifices and closed most temples. In 391-392 a new set of penalties was imposed on paganism. And, while tolerated, Judaism, together with the Jews, suffered drastic change in their legal standing as well.

The upshot is simple. In the beginning of the fourth century Rome was pagan, in the end, Christian. In the beginning Jews in the Land of Israel administered their own affairs. In the end their institution of self-administration lost the recognition it had formerly enjoyed. In 300 the area of Palestine where Jews lived was mainly settled by Jews, hence, palpably and visibly, the Land of Israel, while in 400, the country was populated with Christian shrines.[8] In the beginning Judaism enjoyed entirely licit status, and the Jews, the protection of the state. In the end Judaism suffered abridgement of its former liberties, and the Jews of theirs. In the beginning, the Jews lived in the Land of Israel, and in some numbers. In the end they lived in Palestine.

As a matter of fact, each of the important changes in the documents first redacted at the end of the fourth century dealt with a powerful challenge presented by the triumph of Christianity in Constantine's age.[9] The first change revealed in the unfolding of the sages' canon

---

[8]Constantine and his mother had built churches and shrines all over the country, but especially in Jerusalem, so the Land of Israel received yet another name, for another important group, now becoming the Holy Land.

[9]I have spelled these matters out in *Judaism and Christianity in the Age of Constantine. Issues of the Initial Confrontation.* (Chicago, 1987: University of Chicago Press); *Midrash in Context. [The Foundations of Judaism. Method, Teleology, Doctrine* (Philadelphia, 1983-1985: Fortress Press. Second printing: Atlanta, 1988: Scholars Press for Brown Judaic Studies). *Studies in Judaism* Series. I-III. I. *Midrash in Context. Exegesis in Formative Judaism]*; and, in summary, in *Judaism in the Matrix of Christianity* (Philadelphia, 1986: Fortress Press. British edition, Edinburgh, 1988, T. & T. Collins).

pertains to the use of Scripture. The change at hand specifically is in making books out of the collection of exegeses of Scripture. That represents an innovation because the Mishnah, and the exegetical literature that served the Mishnah, did not take shape around the order of biblical passages, even when relevant, let alone the explanation of verses of Scripture. In the third, and especially, in the later fourth centuries, other writings, entering the canon, took shape around the explanation of verses of Scripture, not a set of topics. What this meant was that a second mode of organizing ideas, besides the topical mode paramount for the Mishnah, the Tosefta, the Yerushalmi (and the Bavli later on), now made its way.

The second concerned extensive consideration of the topic of the Messiah, formerly not accorded a principal place among the parts of the social system.[10] The philosophers of the Mishnah did not make use of the Messiah myth in the construction of a teleology for their system. They found it possible to present a statement of goals for their projected life of Israel which was entirely separate from appeals to history and eschatology. The appearance in the Talmuds of a messianic eschatology fully consonant with the larger characteristic of the rabbinic system – with its stress on the viewpoints and prooftexts of Scripture, its interest in what was happening to Israel, its focus upon the national-historical dimension of the life of the group – indicates that the encompassing rabbinic system stands essentially autonomous of the prior, Mishnaic system.

Third, the Mishnah had presented an ahistorical and, in the nature of things, noneschatological teleology, and did not make use of the messiah theme to express its teleology. By contrast, the Talmud not only provides an eschatological and therefore a Messiah-centered teleology for its system, its authorship also formed a theory of history and found it appropriate to compose important narratives, episodic to be sure, concerning events that, in prior systemic writings, were treated as mere taxic indicators. Now what happened counted, not only that something happened, and the details of events were to be narrated and preserved. So far as the definition of an event comprises a cultural indicator, the telling of stories about events tells us that, for the Talmud of the Land of Israel and related writings, the very formation of culture has been transformed.

No wonder, then, that the Mishnah's philosophical (therefore also social-scientific) and ahistorical Judaism, a Judaism of rules, gave way to the religious and historical (therefore also eschatological) Judaism of the Talmud of the Land of Israel, a Judaism of exceptions to

---

[10]This is worked out in *Messiah in Context*.

the rules. These important shifts show that the later system set forth a Judaism intersecting with the Mishnah's but essentially asymmetrical with it. Given the political changes of the age, with their implications for the meaning and end of history as Israel would experience it, the foci of the connected but autonomous system now directed attention to the media for salvation in the here and now, for Israel and the individual alike, and in time to come for all Israel. A single word captured the whole: *zekhut* yielded a broad variety of answers to one urgent question. It was a question encompassing society and history, now and the coming age, Israel and the nations, the social order in the here and now and the great society comprised by nature and supernature. To the question posed by the simple statement of the religious system set forth in the late fourth and fifth century documents is this: the entire social order forms one reality, in the supernatural world and in nature, in time and in eternity.

The sages who wrote the Talmud of the Land of Israel, Genesis Rabbah, Leviticus Rabbah, and Pesiqta deRab Kahana, did not stand alone in their profound reflection on how earth and Heaven intersect, and how the here and the now forms a moment in history. As it happens, at the same time and, as a matter of fact, under similar circumstances of historical crisis, another system builder was at work. When we appreciate the commonalities of the task facing each party and the dimensions that turn out to take the measure of the results of each, we realize how different people, speaking each to their own world, delivering each their own statement, turn out in the same time to answer the same question in what is, as a matter of fact, pretty much the same cosmic dimensions, and, it would turn out, with the same enduring results for the formation of Western civilization.[11]

Augustine of Hippo's life, in North Africa and Italy, (354-430) coincided with the period in which, to the east, the sages of the Land of Israel produced their Talmud in amplification of the Mishnah as well as their Midrash compilations in extension of Moses' books of Genesis and Leviticus. But he comes to mind, for comparison and contrast, not merely because of temporal coincidence. Rather, the reason is that, like the sages of Judaism, he confronted the same this-worldly circumstance, one in which the old order was coming to an end – and was acknowledged to be closing. And the changes were those of power and political. In 410 the Goths took Rome, refugees of Alaric's

---

[11] One need not exaggerate the influence of either St. Augustine or our sages of blessed memory to claim that the Christianity and the Judaism framed by each, respectively, defined norms and set the course for the two great religions of the West.

conquest fleeing to North Africa (as well, as a matter of fact, as to the Land of Israel/Palestine, as events even early in the story of Jerome in Jerusalem tell us).[12] At the very hour of his death, some decades later, Augustine's own city, Hippo, lay besieged by the Vandals. So it was at what seemed the twilight of the ancient empire of Rome that Augustine composed his account of the theology of the social order known as the *City of God*. Within his remarkable *oeuvre*, it was that work that renders of special interest here the sages' contemporary and their counterpart as a system builder.

Like the critical issue of political calamity facing sages in the aftermath of the triumph of Christianity and the failure of Julian's brief restoration of both paganism and (as to Jerusalem) Judaism, the question Augustine addressed presented a fundamental challenge to the foundations of the Christian order, coming as it did from Roman pagan aristocrats, taking refuge in North Africa.[13] What caused the fall of

---

[12] I refer to J. N. D. Kelly, *Jerome: His Life, Writings, and Controversies* (New York, 1975: Harper & Row).

[13] In no way claiming to know the scholarship on Augustine, even in the English language, I chose to rely mostly upon a single work, consulting others mostly for my own illumination. It is the up-to-date and, I think, universally respected account by Peter Brown, *Augustine of Hippo* (Berkeley and Los Angeles, 1967: University of California Press). The pertinent passage is on p. 302. All otherwise unidentified page references to follow are to this work. My modest generalizations about the intersection of the two systems on some points important to each rests, for Augustine, entirely on Brown. I found very helpful the outline of the work presented by John Neville Figgis, *The Political Aspects of S. Augustine's 'City of God'* (London, 1921: Longmans Green and Co.), 1-31, and the characterization of Augustine's thought by Herbert A. Deane, *The Political and Social Ideas of St. Augustine* (New York & London, 1963: Columbia University Press). In Deane's lucid account, anyone in search of specific doctrinal parallels between sages' system and that of Augustine will find ample evidence that there is none of consequence. As will become clear, what I find heuristically suggestive are structural and functional parallels, not points of doctrinal coincidence of any material importance. My sense is that the success of Brown's book overshadowed the important contribution of Gerald Bonner, *St. Augustine of Hippo. Life and Controversies* (London, 1963: SCM Press, Ltd.), a less dazzling, but more systematic and (it seems to me) useful presentation. A brief and clear account of the two cities is in Eugene Teselle, *Augustine the Theologian* (New York, 1970: Herder and Herder), 268-278, who outlines the variety of approaches taken to the description and interpretation of the work: polemical, apologetic; philosophy or theology of history; analysis of political ideology; source of principles of political and moral theory; and of ecclesiastical policy; and the like. The achievement of F. Van der Meer, *Augustine the Bishop. Religion and Society at the Dawn of the Middle Ages* (New York, 1961: Harper & Row). Translated by Brian Battershaw and G. R. Lamp, is not to be missed: a fine example of the narrative reading of religion by a historian of religion of one useful kind. Precisely what Augustine means by

Rome, if not the breaches in its walls made by Christianity? The first three books of *The City of God* responded, in 413, and twenty-two books in all came to a conclusion in 426: a gigantic work.[14] While *The City of God* (re)presents Christian faith "in the form of biblical history, from Genesis to Revelation,[15] just as sages present important components of their system in historical form of narrative, I see no important doctrinal points in common between the program of Israel's sages in the Land of Israel and that of the great Christian theologian and philosopher. Each party presented in an episodic way what can be represented as an orderly account of the social order,[16] each for the edification of its chosen audience; neither, I think, would have understood a line of the composition of the other, in writing or in concept. And that unbridgeable abyss makes all the more striking the

---

"the city of God" is worked out by John O'Meara, *The Charter of Christendom: The Significance of the City of God* (New York, 1961: Macmillan Co.), who says (p. 43) that "the city of God exists already in heaven and, apart from certain pilgrim men who are on their way to it while they are on this earth, in heaven only." When I speak of sages' having extended the boundaries of the social system from earth to Heaven, I mean to suggest something roughly parallel, in that, when women and men on earth conform to the Torah, they find themselves in the image and after the likeness of Heaven. The sense of the concept "history," then, is "the story of two cities," so Hardy, pp. 267ff. (cf. Edward R. Hardy, Jr., "The City of God," in Roy W. Battenhouse, *A Companion to the Study of St. Augustine* (New York, 1955: Oxford University Press), 257-286. I find the story of Israel among the nations as the equivalent, unifying and integrating conception of history in the doctrine(s) of history in the Yerushalmi and Leviticus Rabbah; this then means Israel forms the counterpart to the city of God, and I think that is the beginning of all systemic comparison in this context (and, I should suspect, in all others).

[14]Ibid., 303.

[15] John H. S. Burleigh, The City of God. A Study of St. Augustine's Philosophy. Croall Lectures, 1944 (London, 1949: Nisbet & Co. Ltd.), 153.

[16]But the two parties have in common the simple fact that the representation of their respective systems is the accomplishment of others later on, indeed, in the case of sages, much later on indeed. Note the judgment of Deane, Augustine "was not a system-builder....Virtually everything that Augustine wrote...was an occasional piece" (Herbert A. Deane, *The Political and Social Ideas of St. Augustine* (New York & London, 1963: Columbia University Press, viii). Sages' documents, it is quite obvious, do not utilize the categories for the description of the social order that I have imposed: ethos, ethics, ethnos; worldview, way of life, doctrine of the social entity. But systemic description in its nature imputes and of necessity imposes system, and that is so, whether the system is deemed social or theological in its fundamental character. I have no difficulty in defending the proposition that sages' system was in its very essence a system of society, that is, of the holy people, Israel, and the union of social and theological thought in Augustine is signalled by the very metaphors he selected for his work, in his appeal to "the city."

simple fact that, from one side of the gap to the other, the distance was slight. For each party addressed questions entirely familiar, I think, to the other, and the gross and salient traits of the system of the one in some striking ways prove symmetrical to those of the other.[17]

The relationship of the opposing cities of God and the devil, embodied in the pilgrim Church and the empirical state, presents the chief systematic problem of *The City of God*.[18] Augustine covered, in five books, "those who worshipped the gods for felicity on earth"; in five, "those who worshipped them for eternal felicity;" and twelve, the theme of the origin of "two cities, one of God, the other of the world," "their unfolding course in the part," "their ultimate destinies."[19] True, sages reconsidered the prior disinterest in history, but they did not then produce a continuous account of everything that had ever happened, and Augustine did. Nor do the two literary monuments, Augustine's and sages', bear anything in common as to form, style, sources, mode of argument, selection of audience, literary convention of any kind. Then why treat the system of sages and the systematic statement of Augustine as so connected as to warrant comparison? For the obvious reason that the authorship of Israel and

---

[17] When William Green recommended the choice of Augustine and I accepted it, the recommendation and recognition of its rightness bore a certain rationality too. Drawing a comparison with Augustine is by no means capricious, based merely on the temporal coincidence of our sages of blessed memory in the Yerushalmi and related writings and Augustine. What I think more compelling is the fact that sages inherited a Middle Platonic doctrine concerning the unity of all being and reworked it in historical-narrative terms, therefore finding in (among other concepts) the notion of *zekhut* a medium for the unification of the generations, past and present. Augustine, for his part, is everywhere described as a reworking the heritage of Platonism, drawing chiefly from Plotinus, so for instance Burleigh, p. 157. As a guess, therefore, I would venture that the principal shift in the large-scale modes of thought from the Mishnah through to the Yerushalmi along with Genesis Rabbah, Leviticus Rabbah, and Pesiqta deRab Kahana, was the movement away from Aristotelian modes of thought, such as characterized the Mishnah, to those of Middle Platonism. But not being a historian of philosophy in antiquity, I am able only to suggest that hypothesis as a subject for further inquiry. In any event one did not have to adopt the inheritance of Plato, in the formulation of Middle Platonism, Neo-Platonism, or Plotinus, to focus upon the social order as the centerpiece of philosophical, systematic thought and system building. Aristotle (much less influential in this period, to be sure) provided an equally accessible model for anyone who might wish to rethink the foundations of the polis or of the social being of Israel, the holy people, in the Land of Israel, the holy land.

[18] So Teselle, p. 270.

[19] Ibid., 303-304. Cf. also Burleigh, pp. 166ff., on Augustine's attitude toward "the concrete political structures of history."

the Christian author not only responded to the same circumstance but also framed the question deemed posed by that common circumstance in the same terms: a recasting, in historical terms, of the whole of the social order, a rethinking, in the image of Augustine, of God's city.

What then was the value of the polis, which throughout these pages I have rendered as "the social order," and exactly who lived in the city of the earth? It was "any group of people tainted by the Fall," any that failed to regard "the 'earthly' values they had created as transient and relative."[20] To this Augustine responds, "Away with all this arrogant bluffing: what, after all, are men but men!"[21] The rise of Rome is reduced, in Brown's words, "to a simple common denominator...the 'lust for domination.'" The Romans were moved by "an overweening love of praise: 'they were, therefore, "grasping for praise, open-handed with their money; honest in the pursuit of wealth, they wanted to hoard glory."'"[22] But the true glory resides not in Rome but in the city of God: "the virtues the Romans had ascribed to their heroes would be realized only in the citizens of this other city; and it is only within the walls of the Heavenly Jerusalem that Cicero's noble definition of the essence of the Roman Republic could be achieved."[23] The Judaic sages – we now realize – assuredly concurred on whence comes glory, whence shame: the one from humility, the other, pride.

The system of Augustine addresses the crisis of change with an account of history, and it is, therefore, in the same sense as is the system of the Judaic sages, a deeply historical one: "The whole course of human history...could be thought of as laden with meanings which might be seized, partially by the believer, in full by the seer."[24] So Brown: "In his *City of God*, Augustine was one of the first to sense and give monumental expression to a new form of intellectual excitement." God communicates through both words and events. Specifically, history proves the presence of a division between an earthly and a heavenly city.[25] Why do I find this historical interest pertinent to my

---

[20]Ibid., 309.
[21]Ibid., 309.
[22]Ibid., 310.
[23]Ibid., 311-312.
[24]Ibid., 317.
[25]Ibid., 319. See Burleigh, pp. 185ff., "A philosophy of history." He cites the following: "St. Augustine's De Civitate Dei...may be regarded as the first attempt to frame a complete philosophy of history....It was...a singularly unsuccessful attempt; for it contained neither philosophy nor history, but merely theology and fiction." Whether or not so of Augustine, that statement seems to me an apt description of the form of history as invented in the pages of the Talmud of the Land of Israel. My presentation of sages' thought on

picture of a Judaism's social order? Because, in Brown's words, "there is room, in Augustine's view of the past, for the consideration of whole societies...."[26] But the building block of society is relationship, and the whole of human history emerges out of the relationship of Cain and Abel, natural man after the fall, citizen of this world, against a man who built no city, "by hoping for something else...he waited upon the name of the Lord."[27] Brown says:

> Augustine treats the tension between Cain and Abel as universal, because he can explain it in terms applicable to all men. All human society...is based on a desire to share some good. Of such goods, the most deeply felt by human beings is the need for 'peace': that is, for a resolution of tensions, for an ordered control of unbalanced appetites in themselves, and of discordant wills in society...the members of the [city of earth], that is, fallen men, tend to regard their achievement of such peace in society as sufficient in itself....[28]

The city of Heaven is "the consecrated commonwealth of Israel," the city of earth, everybody else.[29] Brown's summary of Augustine's main point with slight alteration serves as epitome of sages' views:

> What was at stake, in the City of God and in Augustine's sermons, was the capacity of men to 'long' for something different, to examine the nature of their relationship with their immediate environment; above all, to establish their identity by refusing to be engulfed in the unthinking habits of their fellows.[30]

How alien can sages, concerned as they were with the possibilities of extraordinary conduct or attitude, have found Augustine's interest in establishing identity by reflection on what others deemed routine? The obvious answer justifies juxtaposing the two systems as to not only their ineluctable questions, but also their self-evidently valid answers.

---

history is in *Messiah in Context*. This matter has not played a principal role in my exposition of the successor system, because it seems to me ancillary and not categorically definitive. Burleigh describes the dominant philosophy of the age, characteristic of Augustine as well, as antihistorical. But Augustine's "Platonic Biblicism in effect brings them [history and philosophy] into the closest relation. Biblical History is Platonic idealism in time." That statement seems to me to run parallel to the characterization of the rabbinic uses of history in the form of persons and events as exemplary and cyclical, rather than unique and linear.

[26]Ibid., 320.
[27]Ibid., 320.
[28]Ibid., 322.
[29]Ibid., 322.
[30]Ibid., 322.

Two further rhetorical questions seem justified: if Augustine spoke of "resident aliens" when referring to the citizens of God's city,[31] then how difficult can sages have found interpreting the identity of their social entity, their Israel, in the same way: here now, but only because of tomorrow: the pilgrim people, *en route* to somewhere else. And why should we find surprising, as disciples of Israel's sages, a city of God permeated, as was Augustine's, by arguments for hope:[32]

> "'Lord, I have loved the beauty of Thy house.' From his gifts, which are scattered to good and bad alike in this, our most grim life, let us, with His help, try to express sufficiently what we have yet to experience."[33]

Two systems emerged from the catastrophes of the fifth century, Augustine's[34] for the Christian, sages' for the Judaic West. Constructed in the same age and in response to problems of the same character and quality, the systems bore nothing in common, except the fundamentally same messages about the correspondence of the individual's life to the social order, the centrality of relationship, the rule of God, and the response of God to what transcended all rules.

By both systems, each in its own way, God is joined to the social order because it is in relationships that society takes shape and comes to expression, and all relationships, whether between one person and another or between mortals and God, are wholly consubstantial.[35] That

---

[31]Ibid., 323
[32]Ibid., 328.
[33]Ibid., 328.
[34]Note Burleigh, p. 218: "The Fifth Century...was a period of radical historical change." But just as Augustine expressed no sense of "the end of an era," so in the pages of the documents surveyed here I find no world-historical foreboding, only an optimistic and unshakeable conviction that Israel governed by its own deeds and attitudes its own destiny every day. That seems to me the opposite of a sense that all things are changing beyond repair. I can find no more ample representation of the historical convictions of our sages of blessed memory than Burleigh's representation of Augustine's: "Rome might pass away. The protecting fostering power of her emperors might be withdrawn. But God endured. His purpose of gathering citizens into His Eternal City was not frustrated by transient circumstances. St. Augustine had no anxiety for the Empire or for civilization, even 'Christian' civilization, because he found a better security in God." It is interesting to note that Burleigh gave his lectures in 1944, responding it seems to me to the impending dissolution of the British Empire in his rereading of Augustine – and dismissing an interest in the fate of Empires as essentially beside the point for Augustine. So I think it was for our sages.
[35]Burleigh characterizes matters in this way: "He seems to have been satisfied to show...that the exposition and defence of the Christian faith necessitates a

The City of God in the Conceptions of the Social Order

is why, for Augustine, the relationship between the individuals, Cain and Abel, can convey and represent the relationships characteristic of societies or cities, and that is why, for sages, the relationships between one person and another can affect God's relationship to the village needing rain or the householder needing to shore up his shaky dwelling place.

True, we deal with the two utterly unrelated systems of the social order, fabricated by different people, talking about different things to different people, each meant to join the society of humanity (or a sector thereof) with the community of Heaven. But both formed quite systematic and well-crafted responses to one and the same deep (and in my judgment, thoroughly merited) perception of disorder, a world that has wobbled, a universe out of line. Rome fallen, home besieged, for Augustine, corresponding to the end of autonomy and the advent of another (to be sure, *soi-disant*) "Israel," for sages, called into question orders of society of very ancient foundation. And that produced a profound sense that the rules had been broken, generating that (framing matters in contemporary psychological terms) alienation that was overcome by Augustine in his way, by sages in theirs.[36]

How, in the language of Judaism as our sages formulated it, may we express the answer to the question of the times? The shaking of the foundations of the social order shows how Israel is estranged from God. The old rules have been broken, therefore the remarkable and the exceptional succeeds. What is unnatural to the human condition of pride is humility and uncertainty, acceptance and conciliation. Those attitudes for the individual, policies for the nation, violate the rule. Then let God respond to transcending rules. And when – so the system maintains – God recognizes in Israel's heart, as much as in the nation's deliberation, the proper feelings, God will respond by ending that estrangement that marks the present age. So the single word encompassing the question addressed by the entire social system of the successor-Judaism must be *alienation*. The human and shared sense of crisis – whether Augustine reflecting on the fall of Rome, or sages confronting the end of the old order – finds its response in the doctrine of

---

survey of all History, which is in its essence God's providential government of the human race" (p. 202).

[36] The basic motif of alienation, personal, cosmic, political, theological, as much as affective characterizes the two systems, because it defines the condition that provokes for each system the generative question, and because it is in the mode of reintegration that each system finds its persistent statement. True, alienation defines a purely contemporary category and forms a judgment made by us upon the circumstance or attitude of ancients. But the category does serve to specify, for our own understanding, what is at stake.

God's assessment, God's response. God enters the social order imagined by sages because God in the natural order proves insufficient, a Presence inadequate to the human situation. God must dwell in the city of humanity, and Israel in the city of God. So what in secular terms we see as a historical crisis or in psychological terms as one of alienation, in religious terms we have to identify as a caesura in the bounds of eternity. The psychological theology of the system joins the human condition to the fate of the nation and the world – and links the whole to the broken heart of God.

And yet that theological observation about the incarnate God of Judaism does not point us toward the systemic center, which within my definitions of what a system is must be social and explain the order of things here and now. For in the end, a religious theory of the social order describes earth, not Heaven.[37] It simply begs the question to claim that the system in the end attended to the condition of God's heart, rather than humanity's mundane existence. For a religious system is not a theological one, and questions about the way of life, worldview, and social entity, admittedly bearing theological implications or even making theological statements, in the end find their answers in the reconstruction of the here and now. So I have not identified the central tension and the generative problematic, nor have I specified the self-evident answer to that question that the system, in every sentence and all details means to settle. It is for identifying that generative problematic of the religious Judaism of the fifth century that the comparison between the Judaism of our sages of blessed memory and the Christianity of Augustine in his *City of God* proves particularly pertinent.

To state matters very simply, as we now realize, Augustine's personal circumstance and that of our sages correspond, so do Augustine's central question and the fundamental preoccupation of our sages. Augustine's *City of God* and the Talmud of the Land of Israel took shape in times that were changing, and both systemic statements accommodated questions of history. But we see the answer, therefore the question, when we realize that, as a matter of fact, both did so in the same way.

Specifically, Augustine, bringing to fruition the tradition of Christian historical thought commencing with Eusebius, provided for Christianity a theory of history that placed into the right perspective the events of the day. And our sages did the same, first of all affirming that events required recognition, second, then providing a theory of

---

[37]To be sure, earth in the model of Heaven, or, as we might prefer, Heaven in the model of earth.

events that acknowledged their meaning, that is, their historicity, but that also subordinated history to considerations of eternity. The generative problematic of the successor system concerned history: vast changes in the political circumstance of Israel, perceived mutations in the tissue of social relationship, clearly an interest in revising the plain meaning of ordinary words: value, power, learning. And the systemic answer for its part addressed questions of long-term continuity, framed in genealogical terms for the now-genealogically defined Israel: the past lives in us, and the system explains in very precise and specific terms just how that takes place, which is through the medium of inherited entitlement or attained entitlement. The medium was indeed the same. The message carried by *zekhut* counseled performance of actions of renunciation, in the hope that Heaven would respond. Power was weakness, value was knowledge, and knowledge was power: all things formed within the Torah.

But if that was the message by way of answer to the historical question of change and crisis, then how had the question of history come to be formulated? It was, of course, precisely what events should be deemed to constitute history, what changes matter, and what are we to do. The answer – our sages' and Augustine's alike – was that only certain happenings are eventful, bear consequence, require attention. And they are eventful because they form paradigms, Cain and Abel for Augustine, Israel's patriarchs and matriarchs for our sages.[38] Then what has happened to history as made by the barbarians at Rome and Hippo, the Byzantine Christians at Tiberias and Sepphoris? It has ceased to matter, because what happened at Rome, what happened at Tiberias, is no happening at all, but a mere happenstance. The upshot is not that history follows rules, so we can predict what will be, not at all.

Augustine did not claim to know what would happen tomorrow morning, and our sages interpreted events but did not claim to shape them, except through the Torah. The upshot is that what is going on really may be set aside in favor of what is really happening, and the story that is history has already been told in (for Augustine) the Bible and (for our sages) the Torah. But, then, that is no longer history at all, but merely, a past made into an eternal present. So, if I may specify what I conceive to be the systemic answer, it is, there are some things

---

[38]But while I think they are primary, as the formation of Genesis Rabbah at this time indicates, they are not alone; Israel at Sinai, David on the throne, and other historical moments serve as well. It is a mere impression, not a demonstrable fact, that the patriarchs and matriarchs provide the primary paradigm.

that matter, many that do not, and the few that matter echo from eternity to eternity, speaking in that voice, the voice of God, that is the voice of silence, still and small.

The systemic question, urgent and immediate and critical, not merely chronic, then, concerned vast historical change, comprising chains of events. The answer was that, in an exact sense, "event" has no meaning at all. Other than historical modes of organizing existence governed, and history in the ordinary sense did not form one of them. Without the social construction of history, there also is no need for the identification of events, that is, individual and unique happenings that bear consequence, since, within the system and structure of the successor Judaism, history forms no taxon, being replaced by *zekhut*, a historical category that was – we now realize – in the deepest sense antihistorical. So, it must follow, no happening is unique, and, on its own, no event bears consequence.

Neither Augustine nor our sages produced narrative history; both, rather, wrote reflections *on* history, a very different matter. For neither did narrative history, ordinarily a sustained paraphrastic chronicle, serve as a medium for organizing and explaining perceived experience. True, both referred to events in the past, but these were not strung together in a continuing account. They were cited because they were exemplary, not because they were unique. These events then were identified out of the unlimited agenda of the past as what mattered, and these occasions of consequence, as distinct from undifferentiated and unperceived happenings were meant to explain the things that mattered in the chaos of the everyday.

In responding as they did to what we conceive to be historical events of unparalleled weight, Augustine and our sages took positions that, from our perspective, prove remarkably contemporary. For we now understand that all histories are the creation of an eternal present, that is, those moments in which histories are defined and distinguished, in which events are identified and assigned consequence, and in which sequences of events, "this particular thing happened here *and therefore...,*" are strung together, pearls on a string, to form ornaments of intellect. Fully recognizing that history is one of the grand fabrications of the human intellect, facts not discovered but invented, explanations that themselves form cultural indicators of how things are in the here and now, we may appreciate as far more than merely instrumental and necessary the systemic responses to the urgent questions addressed in common by our sages and by Augustine.

The City of God in the Conceptions of the Social Order 167

Shall we then represent the successor Judaism as a historical religion,[39] in that it appeals for its worldview to not myth about gods in heaven but the history of Israel upon earth – interpreted in relationship to the acts of God in heaven to be sure? And shall we characterize that Judaism as a religion that appeals to history, that is, to events, defined in the ordinary way, important happenings, for its source of testing and establishing truth? I think not. That Judaism identifies an event through its own cognitive processes. Just as the canon that recapitulates the system, so events – things that happen given consequence – recapitulate the system. Just as the system speaks in detail through the canon, so too through its repertoire of events granted recognition the system delivers its message. But just as the canon is not the system, so the recognition of events does not classify the system as historical.

This brings me directly to the final question of systemic description: what exactly does the successor Judaism mean by events? To answer that question succinctly is simple. In the canonical literature of the successor Judaism, events find their place, within the science of learning of *Listenwissenschaft* that characterizes this literature, along with sorts of things that, for our part, we should not characterize as events at all. Events have no autonomous standing; events are not unique, each unto itself; events have no probative value on their own. Events form cases, along with a variety of other cases, making up lists of things that, in common, point to or prove one thing. Not only so, but among the taxonomic structure at hand, events do not make up their own list at all, for what is truly eventful generates *zekhut*. It is the act of *zekhut* that unites past and present, and it is the act that gains *zekhut* that makes history for tomorrow.

Events of other kinds, even those that seem to make an enormous, and awful, difference in Israel's condition, will appear on the same list as persons, places, things. And the contrary lists – very often in the form of stories as we have seen – tell us events that in and of themselves change biography (the life and fate of an ass driver) and make history. That means that events other than those that gain *zekhut* not only have no autonomous standing on their own, but also that events constitute no species even within a genus of a historical order. For persons, places, and things in our way of thinking do not belong on the same list as events; they are not of the same order. Within the logic of our own minds, we cannot classify the city, Paris, within the same genus as the event, the declaration of the rights of man, for instance, nor is Sinai or Jerusalem of the same order of things as the Torah or the

---

[39] I leave for Augustine scholarship the counterpart question on him.

Temple, respectively. But in the logic of the Judaism before us, Jerusalem stands for sanctity and for Temple; it is of precisely the same taxic order.

What then shall we make of a list that encompasses within the same taxic composition events and things? Answering that question shows us how our sages sort out what matters from what does not, and events, by themselves, do not form a taxon and on their own bear no means and therefore do not matter. For one such list made up of events, persons, and places, is as follows: [1] Israel at the Sea; [2] the ministering angels; [3] the tent of meeting; [4] the eternal house [= the Temple]; [5] Sinai. That mixes an event (Israel redeemed at the Sea), a category of sensate being (angels), a location (tent of meeting, Temple), and then Sinai, which can stand for a variety of things but in context stands for the Torah. In such a list an event may or may not stand for a value or a proposition, but it does not enjoy autonomous standing; the list is not defined by the eventfulness of events and their meaning, the compilation of matters of a single genus or even a single species (tent of meeting, eternal house, are the same species here). The notion of event as autonomous, even unique, is quite absent in this taxonomy. And once events lose their autonomy, that process of selection gets under way that transforms one event into history bearing meaning and sets aside as inconsequential in the exact sense all other events.

Since this point is systemically so fundamental, let me give the case of another such list, which moves from events to other matters altogether, finding the whole subject to the same metaphor, hence homogenized. First come the events that took place at these places or with these persons: Egypt, the Sea, Marah, Massah and Meribah, Horeb, the wilderness, the spies in the Land, Shittim, for Achan/Joshua and the conquest of the Land. Now that mixture of places and names clearly intends to focus on particular things that happened, and hence, were the list to which I refer to conclude at this point, we could define an event for the successor Judaism as a happening that bore consequence, taught a lesson or exemplified a truth, in the present case, an event matters because it the mixture of rebellion and obedience. But there would then be no doubt that "event" formed a genus unto itself, and that a proper list could not encompass both events, defined conventionally as we should, and also other matters altogether.

But the literary culture at hand, this textual community proceeds, in the same literary context, to the following items: [1] the Ten Commandments; [2] the show-fringes and phylacteries; [3] the *Shema* and the Prayer; [4] the tabernacle and the cloud of the Presence of God in the world to come. Why we invoke, as our candidates for the

The City of God in the Conceptions of the Social Order

metaphor at hand, the Ten Commandments, show-fringes and phylacteries, recitation of the *Shema* and the Prayer, the tabernacle and the cloud of the Presence of God, and the mezuzah, seems to me clear from the very catalogue. These reach their climax in the analogy between the home and the tabernacle, the embrace of God and the Presence of God. So the whole is meant to list those things that draw the Israelite near God and make the Israelite cleave to God. And to this massive catalogue, events are not only exemplary – which historians can concede without difficulty – but also subordinated.

They belong on the same list as actions, things, persons, places, because they form an order of being that is not to be differentiated between events (including things that stand for events) and other cultural artifacts altogether. A happening is no different from an object, in which case "event" serves no better, and no worse, than a hero, a gesture or action, recitation of a given formula, or a particular locale, to establish a truth. It is contingent, subordinate, instrumental.[40] And why find that fact surprising, since all history comes to us in writing, and it is the culture that dictates how writing is to take place; that is why history can only paraphrase the affirmations of a system, and that is why events recapitulate in acute and concrete ways the system that classifies one thing that happens as event, but another thing is not only not an event but is not classified at all. In the present instance, an event is not at all eventful; it is merely a fact that forms part of the evidence for what is, and what is eventful is not an occasion at all, but a condition, an attitude, a perspective and a viewpoint. Then, it is clear, events are subordinated to the formation of attitudes, perspectives, viewpoints – the formative artifacts of not history in the conventional sense but culture in the framework of Sahlin's generalization, "history is culturally ordered, differently so in different societies, according to meaningful schemes of things."[41]

Events not only do not form a taxon, they also do not present a vast corpus of candidates for inclusion into some other taxon. Among the candidates, events that are selected by our documents are few indeed. They commonly encompass Israel at the Sea and at Sinai, the destruction of the first Temple, the destruction of the second Temple, events as defined by the actions of some holy men such as Abraham, Isaac, and Jacob (treated not for what they did but for who they were),

---

[40] I can think of no more apt illustration of Geertz's interesting judgment: "an event is a unique actualization of a general phenomenon, a contingent realization of the cultural pattern." But my principal master in the present matter is Sahlin, cited in the next note.

[41] See his *Islands of History* (Chicago, 1985: University of Chicago Press).

Daniel, Mishael, Hananiah, and Azariah, and the like. It follows that the restricted repertoire of candidates for taxonomic study encompasses remarkably few events, remarkably few for a literary culture that is commonly described as quintessentially historical!

Then what taxic indicator dictates which happenings will be deemed events and which not? What are listed throughout are not data of nature or history but of theology: The issue of history is one of relationship, just as with Augustine. Specifically, God's relationship with Israel, expressed in such facts as the three events, the first two in the past, the third in the future, namely, the three redemptions of Israel, the three patriarchs, and holy persons, actions, events, what-have-you – these are facts that are assembled and grouped. What we have is a kind of recombinant theology given narrative form through tales presented individually but not in a sustained narrative. This recombinant theology through history is accomplished when the framer ("the theologian") selects from a restricted repertoire a few items for combination. What we have is a kind of subtle restatement, through an infinite range of possibilities, of the combinations and recombinations of a few essentially simple facts (data).

The net effect, then, is to exclude, rather than to include: the world is left outside. The key to systemic interpretation lies in the exegesis of that exegetical process that governs selection: what is included, what is excluded. In this context I find important Jonathan Z. Smith's statement:

> An almost limitless horizon of possibilities that are at hand...is arbitrarily reduced...to a set of basic elements....Then a most intense ingenuity is exercised to overcome the reduction...to introduce interest and variety. This ingenuity is usually accompanied by a complex set of rules.[42]

If we know the complex set of rules in play here, we also would understand the system that makes this document not merely an expression of piety but a statement of a theological structure: orderly, well composed and proportioned, internally coherent and cogent throughout.

The canonical, therefore anything but random, standing of events forms a brief chapter in the exegesis of a canon. That observation draws us back to Smith, who observes:

> The radical and arbitrary reduction represented by the notion of canon and the ingenuity represented by the rule-governed exegetical enterprise to apply the canon to every dimension of human life is that

---

[42]"Sacred Persistence: Towards a Redescription of Canon," in William Scott Green, ed., *Approaches to Ancient Judaism* (1978), 1:11-28. Quotation: p. 15.

most characteristic, persistent, and obsessive religious activity....The task of application as well as the judgment of the relative adequacy of particular applications to a community's life situation remains the indigenous theologian's task; but the study of the process, particularly the study of comparative systematics and exegesis, ought to be a major preoccupation of the historian of religions.[43]

Smith speaks of religion as an "enterprise of exegetical totalization," and he further identifies with the word "canon" precisely what we have identified as the substrate and structure of the list. If I had to define an event in this canonical context, I should have to call it merely another theological thing: something to be manipulated, combined in one way or in another, along with other theological things.

In insisting that the successor system remains connected to the initial one, I have until now left open the identification of the joining threads of thought. But now I scarcely need to elaborate. The systems are connected because the successor system sustains the generative mode of thought of the initial one, which was list-making. But now the lists derive from data supplied by Scripture (as with the bulk of Augustine's historical events of paradigmatic consequence), rather than by nature. Now as before, list-making is accomplished within a restricted repertoire of items that can serve on lists; the list-making then presents interesting combinations of an essentially small number of candidates for the exercise. But then, when making lists, one can do pretty much anything with the items that are combined; the taxic indicators are unlimited, but the data studied, severely limited. So the systems connect because the successor system in mode of thought and medium of expression has recapitulated the initial system.

The radical shift in category formation, the utterly fresh systemic composition and construction – these turn out to carry forward received modes of thought. So far as the two systems may both be called Judaisms, and so far as these Judaisms so join as to form one ongoing Judaism, continuity is in not message but method. The history of religion is the exegesis of exegesis, and, for the case before us, the transformation of Judaism likewise tells two stories. The one portrays successive and essentially distinct, free-standing systems. The other narrates that enduring process that sustains and unites and nourishes – and, therefore, also defines.

---

[43]Ibid., p. 18.

Part Two
ETERNITY AND HISTORY IN JUDAISM:
COMPARATIVE STUDIES

9

How is "Eternity" To Be Understood in the Theology of Judaism? An Exercise in Comparative Theology[*]

We take for granted we may compare not only religions but also theologies, for example, the theology of Judaism and the theology of Christianity. And that premise of learning must be affirmed, if we are to hope to understand religions or theologies, since if we study only one religion, we understand no religion. But how we are to conduct comparison and contrast is not equivalently clear. For to begin with, the problem of category formation intervenes.

The modes of discourse and the categories that serve one religion for its theological system and expression may not make possible comparison – at least, ready comparison – with those of some other. To illustrate that simple point, let us consider the comparison of the surely ubiquitous conception of "eternity" in Judaism with an appropriate counterpart in Christianity. The very first step – identifying data suitable for comparison, defining a shared category for the comparative enterprise – proves more difficult to take than people commonly recognize. The canonical books of Judaism, to which we turn for the definition of theological categories and doctrines, for one thing, rarely set forth ideas in the form of abstractions and generalizations, with the result that understanding any generative theological categories requires the philological exegesis of texts. In the case of the Judaic canon, the pertinent texts are the those of the Torah, written and oral. When we turn to the written Torah, which the West knows as the Old Testament, and to the Oral Torah, which Judaism assembles out of the

---

[*]This paper began as an address to a conference at Institut de philosophie, arts et sciences humaines, Université de Tours, France, on October 19, 1990.

Mishnah, the two Talmuds, the Midrash compilations of the formative age, our work only begins. For we have also to determine for ourselves what words, in the canonical writings, stand for, or refer us to, the counterpart category that our Christian and Greek philosophical heritage has conferred upon us. When, as we shall see, we ask ourselves about how the classical theology of Judaism conceives of "eternity," we therefore engage in a prior inquiry into what we mean by "eternity" and how in the Judaic canon's substrate of theology we may locate the counterpart language for that meaning. Not only so, but we have further to find out in what context thought takes place on the category, "eternity": when and why is discourse on eternity precipitated in the canonical theology of Judaism? And when not?

When we understand how "eternity" is conceived within the theology of Judaism, what we learn concerns not "eternity" but the theology of Judaism – and we learn, also that the philosophical and theological world of the West that defines "eternity" in the way that it does likewise appeals to what is not a universal, but only a native category. In medieval terms, what we set forth in the framework of a realistic composition turns out to form a nominalist construct: an episode in a culture, not a universal in a philosophy everywhere pertaining.

Like all abstractions, "eternity" with its counterpart and opposite, "time," proves to be a category distinctively native to the philosophical system that deems the matter constitutive. Neither "time" nor "eternity" in fact defines a generative category in the canonical documents of the oral Torah, upon which I shall focus. These standing by themselves are invariably contingent, instrumental, never autonomous and taxonomic. "Time" may be holy or profane, but then the native categories are the sacred and the ordinary, and "time," like a variety of categories that in other systems of thought prove independent variables, turns out to be dependent and merely acted upon. The constitutive categories, "holy," "ordinary," utilize a variety of data, including the passage of time, to register whatever it is that they wish to say. And, since, by definition, the same is so of "eternity," the counterpart, complement, and opposite of time, it is clear that our task – how do people deliver their message concerning "eternity," when does the question of "eternity" arise, and how are we to define what they conceived when they spoke of "eternity" – that task proves somewhat more complicated than a mere lexical inquiry would suggest.

When we attempt to find, in some other setting, the right vocabulary to guide us to those canonical writings of Judaism in which the category proves definitive, we note how what we put forward as abstract, general, universal in its power to classify and define, turns out the opposite. The categories, "eternity" and "time," emerge as not ubiquitous structures of systems of thought put forth here and there and everywhere: universal categories. Rather, we see them as concrete, specific, and entirely particular to the writings that (as a matter of fact) imagine the category to be self-evident and universal. That paradox of our Christian and Hellenistic heritage of philosophical thinking, justly proud of its capacity to make something general and susceptible to sustained analysis out of anything particular and distinctive to a given cultural and intellectual circumstance, disconcerts. And well it should, since much of Western philosophy has turned out to incapacitate us in our encounter with the thought of other worlds, besides our own, and even of different worlds within our own.

If I had then to specify those traits that characterize "eternity" when we use the category in general, I should identify these as necessary: age without end; age without change; time beyond time as we know it; time past time that is authentic and meaningful, perfect because unchanging; the age of perfection in which truth flourishes and true life is lived. Then the counterpart, complement, and opposite, "time," must be an age that will end; an age that is differentiated and subject to change; time that is awaiting for meaning to emerge, significance to be established. Then the contrast is between the inauthentic and meaningless age, and the authentic and meaningful one; the age that is differentiated, changing, and contingent and the age that is undifferentiated (hence, beyond time), permanent (beyond change), and absolute. The proposed contrast is hardly subjective, since any dictionary, in any Western language, is likely to give for eternal the synonyms of unceasing, unending, lasting, permanent, perpetual, undying, as against ephemeral, evanescent, momentary, passing, temporary, transient – and so forth.

If this definition of the conception of eternity and time prove acceptable, then we shall find reason to wonder whether, in the theology of the Judaism of the Dual Torah in particular, there is a conception of "eternity" in contrast to "time" that corresponds in any important way to the meanings and usages of the categories, "eternity" and "time" that characterize Western philosophical and theological thought. What we shall see, in a single important case, is that when, in Western thought, particularly Christian theological thought, we have a right to expect to find "eternity" as an age that is beyond differentiation, in the Judaic theology adumbrated by a critical canonical document of the Dual Torah, the Mishnah, "eternity" proves differentiated just as much as is "time." But then that must mean, as we understand "eternity," there is no eternity in Judaism.

Having shaded over from the canon of the Judaism of the Dual Torah to a single canonical document, the Mishnah, I have to ask for a definition of "eternity" deriving from a Christian writing of a roughly contemporary period and type. The Mishnah speaks of concrete things, so the Christian counterpart must be of not a philosophical and abstract but a specific and concrete character. Among many candidates, one in which I find important reflection on the nature of the "age to come" or "eternity" is the Revelation to John. And since the Mishnah reached closure at ca. A.D. 200, drawing on materials that took shape over the preceding hundred years or so, I turn to the Revelation to John, for it is generally assigned to the end of the first century. There we find a vision of the coming age, the end of time as it is known. Here we find a fair point of intersection, for, as we shall see in a moment, both the Mishnah's and John of Patmos's treatment of "eternity" appeals for the media of thought and expression to highly mythic and pictorial language. Here is the vision of eternity:

> A new heaven and a new earth, for the first heaven and the first earth had passed away...behold the dwelling of God is with men. He shall dwell with them, and they shall be his people, and God himself will be with them; he will wipe away every tear from their eyes, and death shall be no more, neither shall there be mourning nor crying nor pain any more, for the former things have passed away (Revelation 21:1-4).

Now the great philosophical theologians of Christianity in antiquity will have framed their doctrine of eternity in the language of abstraction and generalization that they spoke so fluently; but they will have found their doctrine of eternity in terms entirely congruent to this vision, with its stress on the permanence of eternity, on the radical shift from now to then, from here to there. And, we see, when we find a vision and a doctrine of eternity, what precipitates discourse is deep thought on the nature of now in light of what is coming: time and eternity, death and life beyond, an utter change in the nature of being. Very rapidly we shall observe that, were the great philosophical theologians of Judaism, when they came along in the Middle Ages, to have framed in their language of abstraction and generalization what we shall find in the Mishnah, they would have had reason to formulate doctrines of not eternity but the social order. But in making such an observation I have moved ahead of my argument.

Let me ask, first of all, what in imagination of the authors of the Mishnah will precipitate discourse on issues of eternity, life after death, and the world to come? The answer is not life after death and eternity, but the social order of Israel, the holy people. That is to say, when the political structure and system that the Mishnah sets forth proposes to express the theory of its teleology, it does so by recourse to the language eternity and the world to come and life after death; its account of the theory of power over the nation, Israel, appeals in the end to the conception of an entire nation outliving the grave. The set, eternity/time, defines not a free-standing but a contingent category. What is independent, autonomous, and generative is the category, Israel, the holy people. Then eternity will be conceived as a variable, and it serves discourse, where and when it does, solely in relationship to – not time but – Israel. And "Israel" forms a category different in not species but genus: Israel is a social and a political entity, eternity/time are temporal/historical categories. If in the Christian discourse undertaken by John of Patmos, eternity/time form a category that is an independent variable – and the contrast between now and then forms the sub-structure and foundation of that writing, in Judaism these constitute not an independent variable at all, and, therefore, they form a category of a different classification of categories altogether, species of a genus, not *sui generis* at all. And the counterpart category – one that in this system, Judaism, is free-standing and independent and *sui generis* – is Israel (and its counterpart, the gentiles).

It follows, as we shall now see, that in Judaism, eternity is conceived as a dependent variable, dependent wholly in relationship to the independent variable, Israel/nations. And that calls into question whether Judaism in its classical statement sets forth a conception of eternity in the way that Christianity and philosophy in their classical statements set forth a conception of eternity. For, as I have now underlined, how can we compare a category that defines with one that is defined, or one that is autonomous with one that is subordinate? In Judaism the category, eternity, forms a subordinated detail of a political structure, not a temporal grid. And that simple, but fundamental fact, makes us wonder whether, in Judaism, there is a conception of eternity that can correspond with that of philosophy and Christianity, since what is subordinate also will prove differentiated, impermanent, and not absolute but relative. But if by "eternity" we mean what is permanent, absolute, enduring, authentic, whole and complete, then in Judaism there is something else than eternity that will meet the definition of eternity, that is, that exhibits those indicative traits that, as a matter of fact, make eternity "eternal."

This is stated very simply in the opening lines of the protracted account of who gets, and who does not get, a share in the world to come. The importance of the passage requires us to consider it in full detail. The passage has as its topic eternity: life of the world to come. And it forms, as a matter of fact, also the single most important political statement in the Mishnah; and it is quintessentially a political statement, about the state of the people, Israel, and about the state that they create, complete with the program of sanctions, spelled out in

Mishnah-tractate Sanhedrin, of which the following comes as the climactic formulation:[1]

Mishnah-tractate Sanhedrin 10:1A-B

A.   All Israelites have a share in the world to come,
B.   as it is said, *Your people also shall be all righteous, they shall inherit the land forever; the branch of my planting, the work of my hands, that I may be glorified* (Isa. 60:21).

The prooftext at B bears a definition of the world to come, with its reference to [1] the land, to [2] permanent possession of the land, to [3] Israel's possession of the land as God's doing. Here then is the world to come: locativity attained at the end, the fulfillment of a utopian politics in some one place. True, that one place is not of this world at all. It finds its boundaries not in space but in time and space joined in union with God. It constitutes life eternal in the land of Israel under God's protection. But, as we see, this offers a vision of eternity that is, as a matter of fact, deeply political in its essence. For the system's teleology speaks of a political entity, this people forming a nation, that is, "Israel," with its system of penalties and sanctions, that is, its politics, located in a particular place, the "land," and a permanent possession of enduring life in that community, that "people" that is "your people" and "righteous." True, too, the principle is static, not dynamic. No matter what happens now or in the short term, and without regard to who does or does not do what is expected, all Israel has a share in that coming world. Clearly, we have here a politics of eternity, not a politics of time at all. But that judgment is rapidly given nuance, and, with the nuance, the politics of eternity looks suspiciously worldly: there is change, impermanence, and things prove remarkably relative.

In eternity everybody will get that "world to come" that is comprised by none other than the "Israel" of the here and now. What makes the statement a doctrine of eternity? Well, first of all, the introduction of life without death, that is, life beyond death: eternal life. Israelites then – beyond time, hence by definition, in eternity – will never die and (by way of definition) they will always possess the sanctified territory in which God does God's planting. No wonder that – in the law of the Mishnah – death at the hands of the earthly court or extirpation by the Heavenly court prove ephemeral; everybody, that is, every Israelite, will live forever pretty much in the place and

---

[1] I have dealt with this matter more systematically in my *Rabbinic Political Theory: Religion and Politics in the Mishnah* (Chicago, 1991: University of Chicago Press).

in the manner of the present, except that all will be righteous, none will die, and God will secure the society and state of that unending present coming in the indeterminate future.

Some actions permanently exclude a person from ongoing existence, from life beyond the grave:

M. 10:1C-G

C. And these are the ones who have no portion in the world to come:
D. (1) He who says the resurrection of the dead is a teaching which does not derive from the Torah, (2) and the Torah does not come from Heaven; and (3) an Epicurean.
E. R. Aqiba says, "Also, he who reads in heretical books,
F. "and he who whispers over a wound and says, *I will put none of the diseases upon you which I have put on the Egyptians, for I am the Lord who heals you* (Ex. 15:26)."
G. Abba Saul says. "Also: he who pronounces the divine Name as it is spelled out."

Clearly, the true mortal sins comprise doctrinal violations directed against God. These include, for example, denying the resurrection of the dead as a teaching of the Torah. Such a denial effectively denies the world to come – and what one denies one cannot have. As for denying that the Torah comes from God, practicing the sin of Epicureanism, reading heretical books, using God's name in healing, or expressing God's ineffable name, these form mere concretizations of the same species of sin. Unlike sins or crimes committed against other human beings – or even against the law of the Torah and the social order – these sins or crimes directly and immediately engage God. They misuse God's name, deny God's Torah, and above all and first of all, reject the view that God has provided life as the permanent condition of creation. Why should my utterances in these matters make so profound a difference, overriding all other crimes or sins? Because in misusing God's name and in denying the Torah, the Israelite places his or her will over the will of God in an explicit and articulated way.

The various forms of blasphemy that provoke political penalties that happen to take place in eternity but can take place in time – that is, whether from Heaven or on earth – deny that the human being is like God – if the Torah does not teach that the human being gets "the world to come," which is to say, lives beyond the grave, then the Torah does not represent the human being as like God, who lives forever. These two notions unite into a single sanction: denying eternal life for the human being means rejecting the image of God as it defines human beings, and, species of the same genus of crime and sin, misusing the name or the image of God provokes the same odious penalty. What motivates the politics is the issue of death or life. And eternity then forms a motivation for politics, at the service of the social order.

No wonder, then, that those who have no access to "the world to come," in this context, in light of the definitive prooftext, to eternal life beyond the grave, require specification. Kings and commoners, prophets and ordinary people, all are listed, with their crimes or sins alongside. The kings are those who caused Israel to sin. Then come entire political entities, complete communities, "the generation of the flood," "the generation of Babel," "the men of Sodom." These are gentiles, but not individuals. They are political entities, and what these have in common is that as entire communities, they form counterparts to Israel as a whole nation.[2] They rebelled against God, so they lost eternal life. Then come individual Israelites, too.[3]

Which Israelites lose the world to come? The counterpart to rejecting God is rejecting the Land. In light of the definitive prooftext with which we began, that hardly presents a surprise. The spies who rejected the land have lost their portion in the world to come. So, too, have the generation of the wilderness, which did not believe and trust. Clearly, then, the counterpart to the kings who made Israel sin and the gentiles who warred against God, are the Israelites who rejected the Land, on the one side, or who rejected God, on the other.

M. 10:2

A. Three kings and four ordinary folk have no portion in the world to come.
B. Three kings: Jeroboam, Ahab, and Manasseh.
C. R. Judah says, "Manasseh has a portion in the world to come,
D. 'since it is said, *And he prayed to him and he was entreated of him and heard his supplication and brought him again to Jerusalem into his kingdom* (II Chron. 33:13)."
E. They said to him, "To his kingdom he brought him back, but to the life of the world to come he did not bring him back."
F. Four ordinary folk: Balaam, Doeg, Ahitophel, and Gahazi.

---

[2]Gentiles considered as individuals, not part of political entities, do not come under consideration. The sins or crimes that deny a person the world to come all pertain to beliefs or actions of Israelites (as M. 10:1D1, 2, and E make clear). The ethnic venue of "Epicurean" is not so self-evident as the others; I take it the sense is that it is an Israelite who maintains Epicurean beliefs or attitudes. The context surely requires that view.
[3]Once more it seems to me that Israelites are treated as persons whose individual actions bear consequence, while gentiles are not.

M. 10:3

I
- A. The generation of the flood has no share in the world to come,
- B. and they shall not stand in the judgment,
- C. since it is written, *My spirit shall not judge with man forever* (Gen. 6:3) –
- D. neither judgment not spirit.

II
- E. The generation of the dispersion has no share in the world to come,
- F. since it is said, *So the Lord scattered them abroad from up there upon the face of the whole earth* (Gen. 11:8).
- G. *So the Lord scattered them abroad* – in this world.
- H. *And the Lord scattered them from there* – in the world to come.

III
- I. The men of Sodom have no portion in the world to come,
- J. since it is said, *Now the men of Sodom were wicked and sinners against the Lord exceedingly* (Gen. 13:13) –
- K. *Wicked* – in this world,
- L. *And sinners* – in the world to come.
- M. But they will stand in judgment.
- N. R. Nehemiah says, "Both these and those will not stand in judgment,
- O. "for it is said, *Therefore the wicked shall not stand in judgment, not sinners in the congregation of the righteous* (Ps. 1:5) –
- P. "*Therefore the wicked shall not stand in judgment* – this refers to the generation of the flood.
- Q. "*Nor sinners in the congregation of the righteous* – this refers to the men of Sodom."
- R. They said to him, "They will not stand in the congregation of the righteous, but they will stand in the congregation of the sinners."

IV
- S. The spies have no portion in the world to come,
- T. as it is said, *Even those men who brought up an evil report of the land died by the plague before the Lord* (Num. 14:37) –
- U. *Died* – in this world.
- V. *By the plague* – in the world to come.

V
- W. (1) "The generation of the wilderness has no portion in the world to come and will not stand in judgment,

X.	"for it is written, *In this wilderness they shall be consumed and there they shall die* (Num. 14:25)," the words of R. Aqiba.
Y.	R. Eliezer says, "Concerning them it says, *Gather my saints together to me, those that have made a covenant with me by sacrifice* (Ps. 50:5)."
Z.	(2) "The party of Korah is not destined to rise up,
AA.	"for it is written, *And the earth closed upon them* – in this world.
BB.	"*And they perished from among the assembly* – in the world to come," the words of R. Aqiba.
CC.	And R. Eliezer says, "Concerning them it says, *The Lord kills and resurrects, brings down to Sheol and beings up again* (I Sam. 2:6)."
DD.	(3) "The ten tribes are not destined to return,
EE.	"since it is said, *And he cast them into another land, as on this day* (Deut. 29:28). Just as the day passes and does not return, so they have gone their way and will not return," the words of R. Aqiba.
FF.	R. Eliezer says, "Just as this day is dark and then grows light, so the ten tribes for whom it now is dark – thus in the future it is destined to grow light for them."

From historical, we turn to contemporary political entities, communities acting all together in such a way as to lose their eternal life. What follows identifies a city, that is, a political entity, that has no portion in the world to come. It explains how collective punishment is applied.

Mishnah-tractate Sanhedrin 10:4

A.	The townsfolk of an apostate town have no portion in the world to come,
B.	as it is said, *Certain base fellows have gone out from the midst of thee and have drawn away the inhabitants of their city* (Deut. 13:14).
C.	And they are not put to death unless (1) those who misled the [town] come from that same town and from that same tribe,
D.	and unless (2) the majority is misled,
E.	and unless (3) men did the misleading.
F.	[If] (1) women or children misled them,
G.	or if (2) a minority of the town was misled,
H.	or if (3) those who misled the town came from outside of it,
I.	lo, they are treated as individuals [and not as a whole town],
J.	and they [thus] require [testimony against them] by two witnesses, and a statement of warning, for each and every one of them.
K.	This rule is more strict for individuals than for the community:

L.	for individuals are put to death by stoning.
M.	Therefore their property is saved.
N.	But the community is put to death by the sword,
O.	Therefore their property is lost.

The city as a whole is penalized, as was Sodom, when it conforms to the stated conditions. The importance for the larger argument is self-evident.[4]

As if to underline the proposition that what people do together dictates their fate, we end with the apostate town. That is as it should be, since we began with an account of those convictions and actions that constitute examples of apostasy. Here we conclude with the sanction inflicted upon an entire community by the nation at large. And that, too, is as it should be, since political sanctions preserve the public order that secures for the nation now and in time to come ("the world to come") ongoing life.

Not surprisingly, the penalty for the apostate group is to be gathered together and killed together, to be subjected to that one form of the death penalty that does not right the relationship with God. Only as individuals can we correct that relationship. This penalty, then, extinguishes for all time the political entity that has ultimately and finally denied God. There is a certain exact justice in such a sanction: one loses what one has denied. But it is a terrible justice indeed, imposing upon the system as a whole responsibility for matters, private as much as public, that the human being rightly or wrongly settles for himself or herself. Freedom to affirm is also liberty to perish.

As we review the catalogue of those who have lost life beyond the grave, we notice a curious disjuncture between the initial catalogue and the illustrative materials. Our account of who has no share in the world to come begins with those who commit crimes or sins against God. Such crimes or sins are individual, since they concern matters of conviction, on the one side, and misappropriation of divine power by the individual, on the other. But the account goes on to deal with kings and ordinary folk as public figures. Its kings are those who made Israel sin; its ordinary folk are false prophets, again, persons who have access to legitimate power and who have misused it. And then, as if to underline the utterly public and shared political sanction at hand, the catalog provides a series of gentile, then Israelite, political entities that are denied eternal life. This means that a share in the world to come is something one gains, or loses, as part of an entire community,

---

[4]The remainder of the passage is given in *The Social Study of Judaism*, Chapter Eight.

and that the condition of the public interest dictates the fate of the private person. Entire generations of gentiles, groups, and an entire generation of Israelites form such entities.

So the political entity, Israel, will endure forever: *eternity is relative to Israel.* That political entity, Israel, moreover is made up of persons who will never really die, in that, in the world to come, they will live forever. What is changeless is not time beyond time; there, as we know, there is promised a series of great events indeed, culminating after all in the last judgment. What is changeless, permanent, absolute, is Israel; the nations form the opposite, being ephemeral, transient, contingent. And as to time and eternity, these, as we have seen, take on importance in relationship to what is permanent and authentic and unchanging, which is Israel. To answer how "eternity" is conceived in the theology of the Judaism of the Dual Torah, I may then say very simply: *People individually did not want to die, and collectively wanted to stay right where they were and do pretty much what they then were doing. So, as we saw in those simple, but definitive words, "life in the world to come" means life in the Land, secured by God, living and not dying.*[5]

The theological system of this Judaism, viewed as a whole, is meant to secure that here-and-now of life in the Land, the life of the people sustained by the Land, the life beyond death for individuals and for nation alike. And that teleological and eschatological vision forms not only the goal of politics but also the explanation and justification for the most violent media available to the political entity, which is denial of life. None then can miss the appropriate quality of the passion and its complement, the pathos, of the political theology that defines eternity: eternity is for Israel to live forever, or if merited, to lose life forever. Forever – eternity – is a strange thing, therefore, taking on meaning and consequence, for the theology of Judaism, solely within the social order. Can John of Patmos, with his vision of "a new heaven and a new earth" have concurred? In detail, of course, no. But in mode of thought and argument, in uniting this "new

---

[5]In his *Jewish Symbols in the Greco-Roman Period,* Erwin R. Goodenough underlined the passion for eternal life contained within the symbols used by Jewish artists for synagogues and cemeteries. Here in the depths of the Mishnah, in its politics for Israel, I find the same source of passion, in a context never considered by Goodenough, since these literary evidences fell (quite properly) outside of his range of analysis. That the results converge is suggestive. In my *Symbol and Theology in Judaism* (Minneapolis, 1991: Fortress Press) I have dealt at greater length with the same problem of convergence and divergence of the symbolic vocabulary of Judaic canonical writings and of synagogues and burial places.

heaven and new earth" with a radical change in the social order, I think he will have found much to affirm, and modes of thought entirely congruent with his own. Whether or not the great philosophical and Christian theological statements of eternity found in John of Patmos a suitable model, either for language of discourse or for categories of thought, is not for me to say. But when the Judaic counterparts in medieval theology spoke of eternal Israel, they paraphrased the Mishnah language before us – and went on to other things.

So to conclude, when we address to alien cultures and their languages categories that we deem self-evidently valid in *every* context and circumstance, we turn out to ask for a word in some other language to serve for what we mean in ours, only to discover that that other language has no word that fits. And since the limits of my language form the limits of my world, we discover at each further stage in asking how that alien culture defines and interprets a category deemed normal by our own the full intransigeance of categories, those of the other culture and also those of our own. The labor of comparison and contrast begins when we realize that categories so natural to our own conception scarcely retain their self-evidence in cultures other than our own. How is "eternity" to be understood in the theology of Judaism? It is by realizing that so far as we understand "eternity" in the context of Western thought, both philosophical and theological, "eternity" simply is not conceived at all within the theology of Judaism. As with so many other things, so with "eternity," we now see, the theology of Judaism means simply to speak of different things to different people altogether. That is, the category "eternity" in Judaism simply does not correspond to the category "eternity" in Western philosophical and Christian theological thought at all, but functions in a different way, refers to other things, and bears its own meaning and significance. So, as I said at the outset, when we understand how "eternity" is conceived within the theology of Judaism, what we learn concerns not "eternity" but the theology of Judaism.

10

History in Judaism Reconsidered

The writing of history – narrative of things that have happened, propositions deriving from events, their order and significance – provides one reliable guide to the course of the history of Judaism. Whether or not people wrote history at all, and if they did, the purpose they imputed to events and their sequence differentiate one Judaism – a Judaic system comprising a worldview, way of life, and account of the social entity, "Israel" – from another. Some Judaisms have set forth elaborate accounts of history, others have treated events as episodic and anecdotal and merely exemplary, drawing no large pictures of connected events and making slight effort to derive meaning and religious truth from those connections. The differentiation of one Judaism from another, therefore, may play off the indicative trait supplied by the religious and theological uses of history that define one Judaism but not some other. Since all Judaisms (by definition) appeal to the Hebrew Scriptures of ancient Israel (also known as "the Old Testament," "the Written Torah," "Tanakh"), that work of differentiation and classification, moreover, gains perspective against a shared reference point among them all. And because the ancient Scriptures themselves present their systemic statement through a remarkable, sustained historical narrative, with a beginning, a middle, and an end, and since such books as Genesis, Exodus, Numbers, Deuteronomy-Joshua-Judges-Samuel-Kings, as well as the whole of the prophetic writings, insist on the priority of events, viewed as connected and probative, history forms a native category of the first Judaic system, the pentateuchal one.

That fact makes all the more surprising the formation, in centuries beyond the closure of the Pentateuch by Ezra in ca. 450 B.C., of Judaisms that found in historical thinking no hermeneutic, in historical events no heuristic challenge, and in the large view of the message and meaning of history no materials of theological consequence, let alone of probative value. In the pages of this anthology, a variety of papers underline the fact that history served as a source of mere "hagiography with footnotes," as a source of paradigms, not differentiated and singular events. The character of the Judaism that nurtured medieval and early modern thought on history and history writing explains why that fact indeed is not at all surprising. And when, in modern times, modern Jewish historiography emerged, that development signalled a new Judaism aborning – connected to, but essentially not continuous with, the ahistorical Judaism of the Dual Torah that reached its authoritative statement in the Talmud of Babylonia and that shaped the anti-historical thinking of its continuator systems, the Judaisms that flourished, paramount, from then to nearly the present day and that continue to occupy the center stage of Judaism even now.

So while the Judaism of the Dual Torah makes ample use of the Old Testament in its account of itself, in the end, the canon of the Dual Torah – written and oral, encompassing the two Talmuds and various Midrash compilations – appealed to events but produced very little history. In the writings of the Judaism of the Dual Torah there is no counterpart, for example, to Eusebius, none to Augustine. We should expect that the canon of heirs to the deuteronomic historians would encompass narrative history, but it does not. We should expect to find therein accounts of events of not only times past but also the present explained by the past, but we do not. We should go in search of the description of one-time, unique happenings – events in the conventional sense – but, if we did, we should return disappointed. The result will be quite opposite. When we read matters properly, we shall find out how to read. For the archaeology of texts uncovers abstract structure in the identification and explication of the concrete event.

If we ask ourselves, then, how the invention of history within the pentateuchal Judaic system served the larger systemic interests of the Judaism that of the Dual Torah, the answer is by no means the one we should anticipate. Specifically, while that Judaism utilized events, it produced no history, and the precise character of the Judaic utilization of history requires definition. The answer, not surprisingly, is that history served at the altar of theology – and, as a matter of fact, did not take a principal part in that service. We see that fact with great clarity when we ask ourselves what exactly does Judaism mean by "events"? For, until our own time, "events" formed the raw material of history, the source of probative evidence of propositions, the pattern that, all together and all at once, pointed to that truth that history proved. When, therefore, we can say how the Judaism of the canon of the Dual Torah defined and utilized events, we shall have a clear picture of the theological uses to which, in Judaism, history was put. That in turn will explain not only why that Judaism produced no history, but also how history served the theological interests of an a-historical and essentially anti-historical Judaic system.

To answer that question succinctly is simple. When we know how Judaism *classifies* events, we shall have the answer to the question of defining events – a perfectly routine procedure in the natural history of ideas. So, too, when we know how Judaism *utilizes* events, assessing with accuracy, and on the basis of a vast and characteristic kind of writing, the heuristic value, the probative standing, of events, we once again shall have our answer.

In the canonical literature of the Judaism of the Dual Torah, formed between the second and the seventh centuries and authoritative to this day, events find their place, within the science of learning of *Listenwissenschaft* that characterizes this literature, along with sorts of things that, for our part, we should not characterize as events at all. It follows that the Judaism of the canon in no way appeals to history as a sequence of ordered events, yielding a clear truth and meaning, in the way, for instance, that history in the deuteronomic sequence of Deuteronomy, Joshua, Judges, Samuel, and Kings forms a sequence of events that comprise history. In canonical Judaism, by contrast, events have no autonomous standing; events are not unique, each unto itself; events have no probative value on their own; and events are not to be strung together as explanations for how things are. In this writing, philosophical and scientific, rather than (in the aggregate) historical and theological, events form cases, along with a variety of other cases, making up lists of things that, in common, point to or prove one thing.

Not only so, but events do not make up their own list at all. That is to say, just as in the canon of Judaism of the Dual Torah is not a single piece of writing of sustained narrative, something we might call history as Josephus (as portrayed here by Shaye J. D. Cohen) or the Deuteronomists wrote history, so we have only episodically and then unsustainedly the representation of events as merely exemplary, never probative by reason of connection and sequence and order. Events therefore do not form components of an independent variable, and history constitutes no independent variable. Events will appear on – form components of – the same list as persons, places, things. That means that events not only have no autonomous standing on their own, but also that events constitute no species even within a genus, the historical order. For persons, places, and things in our way of thinking do not belong on the same list as events; they are not of the same order. Within the logic of our own minds, we cannot classify the city, Paris, within the same genus as the event, the declaration of the rights of man, for instance, nor is Sinai of the same order of things as the Torah.

These are facts that are assembled and grouped; in Song of Songs Rabbah the result is not propositional at all, or, if propositional, then essentially the repetition of familiar propositions through unfamiliar data. What we have is a kind of recombinant theology, in which the framer ("the theologian") selects from a restricted repertoire a few items for combination, sometimes to make a point (for example, the contrast of obedient and disobedient Israel we saw just now), sometimes not. What is set on display justifies the display: putting this familiar fact together with that familiar fact in an unfamiliar combination constitutes what is new and important in the list; the consequent conclusion one is supposed to draw, the proposition or rule that emerges – these are rarely articulated and never important.

True, the list in Song of Songs Rabbah may comprise a rule, or it may substantiate a proposition or validate a claim; but more often than not, the effect of making the list is to show how various items share a single taxic indicator, which is to say, the purpose of the list is to make the list. The making of connections among ordinarily unconnected things is then one outcome of *Listenwissenschaft*. What is engaging is the very variety of things that, on one list or another, can be joined together – a list for its own sake. What we have is a kind of subtle restatement, through an infinite range of possibilities, of the combinations and recombinations of a few essentially simple facts (data). It is as though a magician tossed a set of sticks this way and that, interpreting the diverse combinations of a fixed set of objects. The propositions that emerge are not the main point; the combinations are.

That seems to me an important fact, for it tells me that the culture at hand has defined for itself a repertoire of persons and events and conceptions (for example, Torah study), holy persons, holy deeds, holy institutions, presented candidates for inclusion in the repertoire, which, while restricted and not terribly long, made possible a scarcely limited variety of lists of things with like taxic indicators. That is to say, since the same items occur over and over again, but there is no pattern to how they recur. By a pattern I mean that items of the repertoire may appear in numerous constructions or not; they may keep company with only a fixed number of other items, or they may not. Most things can appear in a composition with most other things. Being interchangeable, they help prove a point, but they do not themselves define the proposition to be proved: they are subordinate, contingent, merely relevant. They are not paramount, autonomous, determinative and generative.

The upshot is simple. List making is accomplished within a restricted repertoire of items that can serve on lists; the list making then presents interesting combinations of an essentially small number of candidates for the exercise. But then, when making lists, one can do pretty much anything with the items that are combined; the taxic indicators are unlimited, but the data studied, severely limited. And that fact returns us to our starting point, the observations on history as a cultural artifact that form the premise for the study of history within the archaeology of knowledge. In fact, in Judaism history serves the theological sciences and therefore cannot be said to constitute history in any ordinary sense at all; but that is a trivial and obvious observation. More to the point, history, in the form of events, contributes to a rather odd way of conducting theological science.

For history constitutes one among a variety of theological data – names, places, events, actions deemed to bear theological weight and to affect attitude and action. The play is worked out by a reprise of available materials, composed in some fresh and interesting combination. When three or more such theological "things" – whether person, whether event, whether action, whether attitude – are combined, they form a theological structure, and, viewed all together, all of the theological "things" in a given document constitute the components of the entire theological structure that the document affords. The propositions portrayed visually, through metaphors of sight, or dramatically, through metaphors of action and relationship, or in attitude and emotion, through metaphors that convey or provoke feeling and sentiment, when translated into language prove familiar and commonplace. The work of the theologian in this context is not to say something new or even persuasive, for the former is unthinkable by definition, the latter unnecessary in context. It is rather to display theological "things" in a fresh and interesting way, to accomplish a fresh exegesis of the canon of theological "things."

The combinations and recombinations defined for us by our document form events into facts, sharing the paramount taxic indicators of a variety of other facts, comprising a theological structure within a larger theological structure: a reworking of canonical materials. An event is therefore reduced to a "thing," losing all taxic autonomy, requiring no distinct indicator of an intrinsic order. It is simply something else to utilize in composing facts into knowledge; the event does not explain, it does not define, indeed, it does not even exist within its own framework at all. Judaism by "an event" means, in a very exact sense, nothing in particular. It is a component in a culture that combines and recombines facts into structures of its own design, an aspect of a culture that comes to full expression in recombinant theology.

Events then form a problem of exegesis, in which, from what a culture defines as a consequential happening, we find our way back to the system and structure that that culture means to form. The work before us will teach us, in the case of Judaism, how from the study of what are defined as events to describe the process of interrogation that has produced the result we see before us, this particular plausibility structure that has persuaded holy Israel, from then to now (as indeed all the Israels that revere the Song of Songs have been persuaded), to read the erotic as the best, the only way to express precisely who is God in relationship to Israel, and who is Israel in relationship to God. The theology of this Judaism – that is to say, our account of the worldview that comes to expression within this literary culture and textual community – will take shape within the exegesis of that exegesis.

The upshot is that in an exact sense, "event" has no meaning at all in Judaism, since Judaism forms culture through other than historical modes of organizing existence. That is why the Judaism of the Dual Torah produced no historical writing. Without the social construction of history, there also is no need for the identification of events, that is, individual and unique happenings that bear consequence, since, within the system and structure of Judaism, history forms no taxon, assuredly not the paramount one, and, it must follow, no happening is unique, and, on its own, no event bears consequence. These statements rest upon modes of the analysis of history as the fabrication of culture, including a religious culture, and require us to review the recent formation of thought on history as culturally ordered, and on the event as "contingent realization of the cultural pattern," for it is only in that context that we may make sense, also, of the representation of both history and its raw materials, events, in Judaism in its definitive canon.

The history that Judaism invented therefore differs radically from the history that, in general, people assume ancient Judaism, in the pages of the Hebrew Scriptures for instance, invoked. History served the cause of theological truth, but it was never the source of theological truth. The Torah set forth the truth; history, if truth be told, was not needed to prove any element of the truth that the Torah revealed. History was subordinate, not probative; at best exemplary, but never normative. That conception of history draws us far from the contemporary one. For some time now in the West we have called upon history to serve as arbiter of truth, history as mediator of sensibility and source of explanation. But before its own entry into the Western intellect, in the nineteenth and twentieth centuries, Judaism knew nothing of that other use of history, so different from its own.

Indeed, these honored roles in the court of intellect came to history only in the formative centuries of our own civilization. We should,

History in Judaism Reconsidered

after all, have to trace the path back to the Protestant Reformation, with its insistence on the priority of historical fact, deriving from a mythic age of perfection, in dictating the legitimacy of social reality in the present moment. Renewed in the romantic reentry into historical discourse, this same preference for history as a medium of organizing the everyday and explaining it characterized the formation of the historical sciences in the nineteenth century: history proves, history teaches, the verdict of history, the lessons of history – these and other accepted formulations bear the single message. Cutting through the detritus and sediment of the long centuries of increment and accumulation, therefore appealing not to *Listenwissenschaft*, but to a different, more autonomous kind of judgment altogether, for the logic of their discourse, the Reformation theologians and the nineteenth century German historians who were their secular continuators identified history, the record of what happened (in this case) in Scripture, as the instrument for the validation of reform. Reform then would accomplish the renewal of times past, times perfect, appealing therefore to the court of appeal formed by history. Describing "Judaism" as a historical religion therefore classifies what was philosophical as historical, a religion that sought the rules of the social order in regularity as one that appealed to the singular and the extraordinary. But history is of more than one kind, in religion as much as in the life of intellect, and the kind of history that Judaism invented in the fourth century and carried on from then to the nineteenth finds more in common with modes of thought familiar to us today, in the social scientific reconsideration of the meaning of historical knowledge, than with the Protestant theological appeal to history as a source of validation of reform, as the source of Reformation.

Turning toward the future, we do well to reflect on the subordination of history by Judaism in light of the current recognition that history forms a discourse of contemporary taste and judgment, events become eventful only because we make them so, and, in all, history is culturally ordered, and events are defined and identified as statements of an intensely contemporary perception. It follows, we now understand, that all histories are the creation of an eternal present, that is, those moments in which histories are defined and distinguished, in which events are identified and assigned consequence, and in which sequences of events, "this particular thing happened here and therefore...," are strung together, pearls on a string, to form ornaments of intellect. And, with that understanding well in hand, fully recognizing that history is one of the grand fabrications of the human intellect, facts not discovered but invented, explanations that themselves form cultural indicators of how things are in the here and now, we find ourselves no longer historians of ideas of history, or analysts of the history of culture, let alone practitioners of the dread narrative history that makes of historical writing a work of elegant imagination. We find ourselves, rather, archaeologists, working from the surface, that is known, through the detritus of the unknown, in quest of a material understanding of a reality that is not known but for its artifacts, not susceptible of explanation and understanding except in categories and terms that are defined by those same artifacts. And that quest is, we all recognize, not a very smooth one.

Today we understand that events in particular, and history in general, form cultural indicators. Accomplishing the analysis of events for what they teach us about the culture that identifies a given happening as eventful, neglecting some other as inconsequential or routine, is important. In the vast canon of the two Talmuds and the Midrash compilations that took shape in late antiquity, the first seven centuries A.D., under the title, the Oral Torah, history was invented within Judaism for the distinctive purposes of Judaism: it was not a general thing, and was never meant to be. That labor of rewriting and recasting of one thing in light of something else that produced the Judaism of the Dual Torah forms a rich set of cases in cultural transformation, in the determination, by a system, of its own past, in the identification, within a system, of its own resources. For, after all, while a system speaks through its canon, and while theologians commonly read the canon to describe the system, in point of fact it is the canon that recapitulates the system, the system that speaks, in detail to be sure, through the canon. History forms part of not the system but merely the canon. So the writing of history defines a critical category for the study of the history of Judaic religions systems – Judaisms. Not only so, but since, as we noted at the outset, the generative and principal Judaic system, the pentateuchal one, makes its statement wholly within the idiom of historiography, we may say that history defines a native category of Judaism. When we have produced so contradictory a result – history as a native category of the initial Judaic system, history as essentially irrelevant to the dominant Judaic system that rests, if asymmetrically, upon that initial system – we have reached the threshold of a new century of research. We have come as far as we can within the received episteme.

Part Three
THE THEOLOGICAL INITIATIVE

11

Re-presenting the Torah: Sifra's Rehabilitation of Taxonomic Logic and the Judaic Conception of How through the Torah We Enter The Mind of God

A profound exercise on the nature of Torah – God's revelation to humanity through Israel, Sifra engages in a two-pronged argument. On the one side, the authorship of Sifra calls into question the exercise of rule making through classification of like and contrast with the unlike, characteristic of the Mishnah's mode of thought. While, as a matter of fact, Sifra's authorship demonstrates that *Listenwissenschaft* is a self-evidently valid mode of demonstrating the truth of propositions the reason is that *the* source of the correct classification of things is Scripture and only Scripture. Without Scripture's intervention into the taxonomy of the world, we should have no knowledge at all of which things fall into which classifications and therefore are governed by which rules. How all of this leads us into a profound reconsideration of the nature of Torah – revelation – becomes clear only at the end.

Let us begin with a sustained example of the right way of doing things. Appropriately, what the opening composition of Sifra shows is the contrast between relying on Scripture's classification, and the traits imputed by Scripture to the taxa it identifies, and appealing to categories not defined and endowed with indicative traits by Scripture.

I. The Affirmation of *Listenwissenschaft*, Rightly Carried Out:

I:I
1. A. "The Lord called [to Moses] and spoke [to him from the tent of meeting, saying, 'Speak to the Israelite people and say to them']" (Lev. 1:1):
   B. He gave priority to the calling over the speaking.
   C. That is in line with the usage of Scripture.
   D. Here there is an act of speaking, and in connection with the encounter at the bush [Ex. 3:4: "God called to him out of the bush, 'Moses, Moses'"], there is an act of speaking.
   E. Just as in the latter occasion, the act of calling is given priority over the act of speaking [even though the actual word, "speaking" does not occur, it is implicit in the framing of the verse], so here, with respect to the act of speaking, the the act of calling is given priority over the act of speaking.
2. A. No [you cannot generalize on the basis of that case,] for if you invoke the case of the act of speaking at the bush, which is the first in the sequence of acts of speech [on which account, there had to be a call prior to entry into discourse],
   B. will you say the same of the act of speech in the tent of meeting, which assuredly is not the first in a sequence of acts of speech [so there was no need for a preliminary entry into discourse through a call]?
   C. The act of speech at Mount Sinai (Ex. 19:3) will prove to the contrary, for it is assuredly not the first in a sequence of acts of speech, yet, in that case, there was an act of calling prior to the act of speech.
3. A. No, [the exception proves nothing,] for if you invoke in evidence the act of speech at Mount Sinai, which pertained to all the Israelites, will you represent it as parallel to the act of speech in the tent of meeting, which is not pertinent to all Israel?
   B. Lo, you may sort matters out by appeal to comparison and contrast, specifically:
   C. The act of speech at the bush, which is the first of the acts of speech, is not of the same classification as the act of speech at Sinai, which is not the first act of speech.
   D. And the act of speech at Sinai, which is addressed to all Israel, is not in the same classification as the act of speech at the bush, which is not addressed to all Israel.
4. A. What they have in common, however, is that both of them are acts of speech, deriving from the mouth of the Holy One, addressed to Moses, in which case, the act of calling comes prior to the act of speech,
   B. so that, by way of generalization, we may maintain that every act of speech which comes from the mouth of the Holy One to Moses will be preceded by an act of calling.
5. A. Now if what the several occasions have in common is that all involve an act of speech, accompanied by fire, from the mouth of the Holy One, addressed to Moses, so that the act of calling was

Re-presenting the Torah

                given priority over the act of speaking, then in every case in which there is an act of speech, involving fire, from the mouth of the Holy One, addressed to Moses, should involve an act of calling prior to the act of speech.

     B.   But then an exception is presented by the act of speech at the tent of meeting, in which there was no fire.

     C.   [That is why it was necessary for Scripture on this occasion to state explicitly,] "The Lord called [to Moses and spoke to him from the tent of meeting, saying, 'Speak to the Israelite people and say to them']" (Lev. 1:1).

     D.   That explicit statement shows that, on the occasion at hand, priority was given to the act of calling over the act of speaking.

I:II

1.   A.   ["The Lord called to Moses and spoke to him from the tent of meeting, saying, 'Speak to the Israelite people and say to them'" (Lev. 1:1)]: Might one suppose that the act of calling applied only to this act of speaking alone?

     B.   And how on the basis of Scripture do we know that on the occasion of all acts of speaking that are mentioned in the Torah, [there was a prior act of calling]?

     C.   Scripture specifies, "from the tent of meeting,"

     D.   which bears the sense that on every occasion on which it was an act of speaking from the tent of meeting, there was an act of calling prior to the act of speaking.

2.   A.   Might one suppose that there was an act of calling only prior to the acts of speech alone?

     B.   How on the basis of Scripture do I know that the same practice accompanied acts of saying and also acts of commanding?

     C.   Said R. Simeon, "Scripture says not only, '...spoke,...,' but '...and he spoke,' [with the inclusion of the *and*] meant to encompass also acts of telling and also acts of commanding."

The exercise of generalization addresses the character of God's meeting with Moses. The point of special interest is the comparison of the meeting at the bush and the meeting at the tent of meeting. And at stake is asking whether all acts of God's calling and talking with, or speaking to, the prophet are the same, or whether some of these acts are of a different classification from others. In point of fact, we are able to come to a generalization, worked out at I:I.5.A. And that permits us to explain why there is a different usage at Lev. 1:1 from what characterizes parallel cases. I:II.1-2 proceeds to generalize from the case at hand to other usages entirely, a very satisfying conclusion to the whole. I separate I:II from I:I because had I:I ended at 5, it could have stood complete and on its own, and therefore I see I:II as a brief appendix. The interest for my argument should not be missed. We seek generalizations, governing rules, that are supposed to emerge by the comparison and contrast of categories or of classifications. The way to do this is to follow the usage of Scripture, that alone. And the right way of doing things is illustrated. The first lesson in Sifra's rehabilitation of taxonomic logic is then clear. Scripture provides reliable taxa and dictates the indicative characteristics of those taxa. The next step in the argument is to maintain that Scripture alone can set forth the proper names of things: classifications and their hierarchical order.

II. Scripture as the Sole Source of Valid Classification of Species

How then do we appeal to Scripture to designate the operative classifications? Here is a simple example of the alternative mode of classification, one that does not appeal to the traits of things but to the utilization of names by Scripture. What we see is how by naming things in one way, rather than in another, Scripture orders all things, classifying and, in the nature of things, also hierarchizing them.

VII:V
1. A. "...and Aaron's sons the priests shall present the blood and throw the blood [round about against the altar that is at the door of the tent of meeting]":
   B. Why does Scripture make use of the word "blood" twice [instead of using a pronoun]?
   C. [It is for the following purpose:] How on the basis of Scripture do you know that if blood deriving from one burnt-offering was confused with blood deriving from another burnt-offering, blood deriving from one burnt-offering with blood deriving from a beast that has been substituted therefore, blood deriving from a burnt-offering with blood deriving from an unconsecrated beast, the mixture should nonetheless be presented?
   D. It is because Scripture makes use of the word "blood" twice [instead of using a pronoun].
2. A. Is it possible to suppose that while if blood deriving from beasts in the specified classifications, it is to be presented, for the simple reason that if the several beasts while alive had been confused with one another, they might be offered up,
   B. but how do we know that even if the blood of a burnt-offering were confused with that of a beast killed as a guilt-offering, [it is to be offered up]?
   C. I shall concede the case of the mixture of the blood of a burnt-offering confused with that of a beast killed as a guilt-offering, it is to be presented, for both this one and that one fall into the classification of Most Holy Things.
   D. But how do I know that if the blood of a burnt-offering were confused with the blood of a beast slaughtered in the classification of peace-offerings or of a thanksgiving-offering, [it is to be presented]?
   E. I shall concede the case of the mixture of the blood of a burnt-offering confused with that of a beast slaughtered in the classification of peace-offerings or of a thanksgiving-offering, [it is

Re-presenting the Torah

F. to be presented], because the beasts in both classifications produce blood that has to be sprinkled four times.

F. But how do I know that if the blood of a burnt-offering were confused with the blood of a beast slaughtered in the classification of a firstling or a beast that was counted as tenth or of a beast designated as a passover, [it is to be presented]?

G. I shall concede the case of the mixture of the blood of a burnt-offering confused with that of a beast slaughtered in the classification of firstling or a beast that was counted as tenth or of a beast designated as a passover, [it is to be presented], because Scripture uses the word "blood" two times.

H. Then while I may make that concession, might I also suppose that if the blood of a burnt-offering was confused with the blood of beasts that had suffered an invalidation, it also may be offered up?

I. Scripture says, "...its blood," [thus excluding such a case].

J. Then I shall concede the case of a mixture of the blood of a valid burnt-offering with the blood of beasts that had suffered an invalidation, which blood is not valid to be presented at all.

K. But how do I know that if such blood were mixed with the blood deriving from beasts set aside as sin-offerings to be offered on the inner altar, [it is not to be offered up]?

L. I can concede that the blood of a burnt-offering that has been mixed with the blood deriving from beasts set aside as sin-offerings to be offered on the inner altar is not to be offered up, for the one is offered on the inner altar, and the other on the outer altar [the burnt-offering brought as a freewill-offering, under discussion here, is slaughtered at the altar "...that is at the door of the tent of meeting," not at the inner altar].

M. But how do I know that even if the blood of a burnt-offering was confused with the blood of sin-offerings that are to be slaughtered at the outer altar, it is not to be offered up?

N. Scripture says, "...its blood," [thus excluding such a case].

In place of the rejecting of arguments resting on classifying species into a common genus, we now demonstrate how classification really is to be carried on. It is through the imposition upon data of the categories dictated by Scripture: Scripture's use of language. That is the force of this powerful exercise. No. 1 sets the stage, simply pointing out that the use of the word "blood" twice encompasses a case in which blood in two distinct classifications is somehow confused in the process of the conduct of the cult. In such a case it is quite proper to pour out the mixture of blood deriving from distinct sources, for example, beasts that have served different, but comparable purposes. We then systemically work out the limits of that rule, showing how comparability works, then pointing to cases in which comparability is set aside. Throughout the exposition, at the crucial point we invoke the formulation of Scripture, subordinating logic or in our instance the process of classification of like species to the dictation of Scripture. I cannot imagine a more successful demonstration of what the framers wish to say.

Now what about the Mishnah? In the following component of the composition, we see how the framers encompass the Mishnah's pertinent paragraph within their larger statement. This is integral to the program of the document as a whole, namely, the demonstration not merely that rules of the Mishnah derive from Scripture, which was accomplished in more than the way taken here, but also that the correct location of the Mishnah's rules is in the united Dual Torah set forth as The Torah.

VII:VIII
1. A. ["...and Aaron's sons the priests shall present the blood and throw the blood round about against the altar that is at the door of the tent of meeting":]
   B. "...the blood...against the altar...":
   C. but the one who tosses the blood is not standing against the altar, [but on the pavement]. [The rule for the disposition of the blood of a beast in the classification of a sin-offering is different. In that case the one who tosses the blood goes up to the altar to sprinkle the blood on the corners of the altar.]
2. A. Another rule: "...the blood...against the altar...":
   B. even though there is no valid meat [deriving from that offering. That is, if the meat got lost or was made unclean, nonetheless the blood is tossed on the altar. The operative criterion is the validity of the blood.]
   C. How then shall interpret the verse [which equates the blood and the meat, hence if the one is invalidated, the other should also not be acceptable,] "And you shall offer your burnt-offerings, the flesh and the blood" (Deut. 12:27)?
   D. Scripture joins the flesh to the blood. Just as blood is offered by being tossed on the altar, so flesh is offered by being tossed on the altar.
   E. Might one think that one tosses the flesh but neatly piles up the meat on the altar?
   F. Scripture says, "And the priest shall arrange them" Lev. 1:12), meaning, he tosses and arranges them, but he does not toss them and pile them up on the altar [T. Zeb. 4:2: Eliezer].

No. 1 supplies an important clarification and also eliminates the classification of all acts of tossing the blood in a single genus, by maintaining that some acts of tossing the blood require remaining down below, others require the priests' ascending up the ramp and standing at the corner of the altar. No. 2 simply tacks on a fragment of a discussion of the base verse in another context altogether. That it hardly belongs is shown by the simple fact that the issue important at No. 2 is not raised anywhere in the present exposition. But the motive in including the passage of the Mishnah is self-evident.

III. The Reason for Scripture's Unique Power of Classification: The Possibility of Polythetic Classification

From this simple account of the paramount position of Scripture in the labor of classification, let us turn to the specific way in which, because of Scripture's provision of taxa, we are able to undertake the science of *Listenwissenschaft*, including hierarchical classification, in the right way. What can we do because we appeal to Scripture, which we cannot do if we do not rely on Scripture? It is to establish the possibility of polythetic classification. We can appeal to shared traits of otherwise distinct taxa and so transform species into a common genus for a given purpose. Only Scripture makes that initiative feasible, so our authorship maintains. What is at stake? It is the possibility of doing precisely what the framers of the Mishnah wish to do. That is to join together masses of diverse data into a single, encompassing statement, to show the rule that inheres in diverse cases.

In what follows, we shall see an enormous, coherent, and beautifully articulated exercise in the comparison and contrast of many things of a single genus. The whole holds together, because Scripture makes possible the statement of all things within a single rule. That is, as we have noted, precisely what the framers of the Mishnah proposed to accomplish. Our authorship maintains that only by appeal to The Torah is this fete of learning possible. If, then, we wish to understand all things all together and all at once under a single encompassing rule, we had best revert to The Torah, with its account of the rightful names, positions, and order, imputed to all things.

XXII:I
1.   A.   [With reference to M. Men. 5:5:] There are those [offerings which require bringing near but do not require waving, waving but not bringing near, waving and bringing near, neither waving nor bringing near: These are offerings which require bringing near but do not require waving: the meal-offering of fine flour and the meal-offering prepared in the baking pan and the meal-offering prepared in the frying pan, and the meal-offering of cakes and the meal-offering of wafers, and the meal-offering of priests, and the meal-offering of an anointed priest, and the meal-offering of gentiles, and the meal-offering of women, and the meal-offering of a sinner. R. Simeon says, "The meal-offering of priests and of the anointed priest – bringing near does not apply to them, because the taking of a handful does not apply to them. And whatever is not subject to the taking of

a handful is not subject to bringing near,"] [Scripture] says, "When you present to the Lord a meal-offering that is made in any of these ways, it shall be brought [to the priest who shall take it up to the altar]":
B. What requires bringing near is only the handful alone. How do I know that I should encompass under the rule of bringing near the meal-offering?
C. Scripture says explicitly, "meal-offering."
D. How do I know that I should encompass all meal-offerings?
E. Scripture says, using the accusative particle, "the meal-offering."

2. A. I might propose that what requires bringing near is solely the meal-offering brought as a freewill-offering.
B. How do I know that the rule encompasses an obligatory meal-offering?
C. It is a matter of logic.
D. Bringing a meal-offering as a freewill-offering and bringing a meal-offering as a matter of obligation form a single classification. Just as a meal-offering presented as a freewill-offering requires bringing near, so the same rule applies to a meal-offering of a sinner [brought as a matter of obligation], which should likewise require bringing near.
E. No, if you have stated that rule governing bringing near in the case of a freewill-offering, on which oil and frankincense have to be added. will you say the same of the meal-offering of a sinner (Lev. 5:11), which does not require oil and frankincense?
F. The meal-offering brought by a wife accused of adultery will prove to the contrary, for it does not require oil and frankincense, but it does require bringing near [as is stated explicitly at Num. 5:15].
G. No, if you have applied the requirement of bringing near to the meal-offering brought by a wife accused of adultery, which also requires waving, will you say the same of the meal-offering of a sinner, which does not have to be waved?
H. Lo, you must therefore reason by appeal to a polythetic analogy [in which not all traits pertain to all components of the category, but some traits apply to them all in common]:
I. the meal-offering brought as a freewill-offering, which requires oil and frankincense, does not in all respects conform to the traits of the meal-offering of a wife accused of adultery, which does not require oil and frank incense, and the meal-offering of the wife accused of adultery, which requires waving, does not in all respects conform to the traits of a meal-offering brought as a freewill-offering, which does not require waving.
J. But what they have in common is that they are alike in requiring the taking up of a handful and they are also alike in that they require bringing near.
K. I shall then introduce into the same classification the meal-offering of a sinner, which is equivalent to them as to the matter of the taking up of a handful, and also should be equivalent to them as to the requirement of being drawn near.
L. But might one not argue that the trait that all have in common is that all of them may be brought equally by a rich and a poor

person and require drawing near, which then excludes from the common classification the meal-offering of a sinner, which does not conform to the rule that it may be brought equally by a rich and a poor person, [but may be brought only by a poor person,] and such an offering also should not require being brought near!
M. [The fact that the polythetic classification yields indeterminate results means failure once more, and, accordingly,] Scripture states, "meal-offering,"
N. with this meaning: all the same are the meal-offering brought as a freewill-offering and the meal-offering of a sinner, both this and that require being brought near.

The elegant exercise draws together the various types of meal-offerings and shows that they cannot form a classification of either a monothetic or a polythetic character. Consequently, Scripture must be invoked to supply the proof for the classification of the discrete items. The important language is at H-J: these differ from those, and those from these, but what they have in common is.... Then we demonstrate, with our appeal to Scripture, the sole valid source of polythetic classification, M. And this is constant throughout Sifra.

The power of taxonomic logic is to draw together all manner of data and to set them into relationship with one another. And, in that context, the strength of argument of our authorship is manifest: the capacity to demonstrate how diverse things relate through points in common, so long as the commonalities derive from a valid source. And that leads us to the central and fundamental premise of all: Scripture, its picture of the classifications of nature and supernature, its account of the rightful names and order of all things, is the sole source for that encompassing and generalizing principle that permits scientific inquiry into the governing laws to take place.

Does the Mishnah's authorship know the principle of polythetic taxonomy? Indeed it does, as a mere glance at the opening pericopes of Mishnah-tractate Baba Qama Chapters One and following tells us: "The distinctive feature of the ox is not the same as that of the crop-destroying beast, nor is the indicative feature of the crop-destroying beast the same as that of the ox; nor is that of either of these, which are animate, the same as that of fire, which is inanimate, nor is the indicative trait of any of these, who ordinarily go out and do damage, the same as that of the pit, which does not go out and do damage. What they have in common is that they may cause injury and you are responsible to take responsibility for them, and if one of them caused injury, whoever is responsible pays restitution by handing over land of the highest quality that he has," so M. B.Q. 1:1. Polythetic taxonomy presents no surprises to the framer of the cited passage. Not only so, but a glance at the exegesis of this passage supplied in the successor writings will reassure us that the framers of the Mishnah surely have made reference, in defining the indicative traits of the taxa under discussion, to Scripture. Where our authorship will take issue with that of the Mishnah is in those cases, and they are exceedingly numerous, in which the Mishnah's authorship effects its taxonomy, and, consequently, its hierarchical classification, without reference to the dictates of Scripture. In our authorship's view, that is never a reliable procedure. To borrow language that originally served another debate altogether: at stake is the principle, systematically advanced by Sifra, of proof *sola Scriptura*.

IV. Sifra's Theory of Torah and Revelation: The Rehabilitation of Taxonomic Logic within the Re-presentation of The Torah

In consequence of Scripture's provision of valid taxa, we can, of course, proceed to invoke and utilize precisely that logic of hierarchical classification that the framers of the Mishnah employed. Here is a full statement of the consequence of adopting Scripture's categories. We find the appeal to comparison and contrast time and again, and at no point do we distinguish one category from another in such wise as to make comparison no longer logical. Let us now examine specific illustrations of the right way of pursuing that same taxonomic logic of hierarchical classification that the Mishnah's framers have carried out in the wrong way. Our first example allows us to see an unimpeded flow of classification: this is like that, therefore this falls under the rule of that, pure and simple.

CCIX:I
1. A. ["If a man lies with a beast, he shall be put to death, and you shall kill the beast. If a woman approaches any beast and lies with it, you shall kill the woman and the beast; they shall be put to death, their blood is upon them" (Lev. 20:13-16).]
   B. "If a man":
   C. excluding a minor.
   D. "lies with a beast":
   E. whether large or small.
2. A. "he shall be put to death":
   B. through stoning.
   C. You say that it is through stoning. But perhaps it is some another of the modes of execution decreed by the Torah.
   D. Scripture says, "and you shall kill the beast."
   E. Here we find reference to "killing," and elsewhere likewise we find the same ["If a woman approaches any beast and lies with it, you shall kill the woman and the beast; they shall be put to death, their blood is upon them"].
   F. Just as elsewhere "killing" involves stoning [as is proven presently], so here too, "killing" involves stoning.

Re-presenting the Torah

3. A. We thereby derive the penalty for one who commits sexual relations upon a beast. Whence do we find the penalty for serving as the passive partner in sexual relations with a beast?
   B. Scripture says, "Whoever lies with a beast will surely die" (Ex. 22:18).
   C. Since [in the context of the present verse] it cannot speak of one who commits sexual relations upon a beast, interpret it to provide an admonition against serving as the passive partner in sexual relations with a beast.
4. A. We have derived the penalty for both the active and the passive partner to sexual relations with a beast.
   B. Whence then the admonition?
   C. Scripture says, "And you shall not lie with any beast and defile yourself with it, [neither shall any woman give herself to a beast to lie with it; it is perversion]" (Lev. 18:23).
   D. We thereby derive the admonition for the active partner. Whence the admonition for the passive partner?
   E. "Scripture says, 'No Israelite man may be a cult prostitute' (Deut. 23:18).
   F. "And further: 'And there were also cult prostitutes in the land' (1 Kgs. 14:24)," the words of R. Ishmael.
   G. R. Aqiba says, "It is not necessary to derive proof from those passages. Lo, Scripture says, 'And you shall not lie with any beast [and defile yourself with it],' you shall not lie as passive partner."
5. A. "If a woman approaches any beast and lies with it, you shall kill the woman and the beast; they shall be put to death, [their blood is upon them]":
   B. You maintain that it is through stoning, but perhaps it is through any one of the other forms of inflicting the death penalty that the Torah specifies?
   C. Scripture says, "his blood is upon him,"
   D. and elsewhere we find the same language, "their blood is on their head" (Lev. 20:27).
   E. Just as that usage elsewhere refers to inflicting the death penalty through stoning, so the same language here involves stoning.
6. A. We thereby have derived the penalty. Whence the admonition?
   B. Scripture says, "Neither shall any woman give herself to a beast to lie with it; it is perversion" (Lev. 18:23).

The predictable materials, Nos. 1-6, go through the necessary motions. What is important is the givenness of the classifications. This demonstrates beyond doubt that our authorship accepts the principles of *Listenwissenschaft,* with like following the rule of like, unlike following the opposite of that rule. Once categories are defined, no one will call into question the basic logic of comparison and contrast in a system of hierarchization.

V. Silence and the Articulated Critique of the Mishnah's Logic: When Sifra's Authorship Does and Does Not Demolish the Logic of Comparison and Contrast

While setting forth its critique of the Mishnah's utilization of the logic of comparison and contrast in hierarchical classification, the authorship of Sifra is careful not to criticize the Mishnah. Its position favors restating the Mishnah within the context of Scripture, not rejecting the conclusions of the Mishnah, let alone its authority. Consequently, when we find a critique of applied reason divorced from Scripture, we rarely uncover an explicit critique of the Mishnah, and when we find a citation of the Mishnah, we rarely uncover linkage to the ubiquitous principle that Scripture forms the source of all classification and hierarchy. In the following passage we see how our authorship treats the Mishnah when it wishes to cite passage of the Mishnah and also to set into the correct relationship categories of things that the Mishnah sets forth.

XXI:I
1. A. "If your offering is a meal-offering on a griddle, [it shall be of choice flour with oil mixed in, unleavened. Break it into bits and pour oil on it; it is a meal-offering:]"
   B. This teaches that the offering requires the use of a utensil [for its preparation and presentation].
2. A. Reference is made twice to the word "your offering." ["If your offering is a meal-offering on a griddle, it shall be of choice flour with oil mixed in, unleavened. Break it into bits and pour oil on it; it is a meal-offering. If your offering is a meal-offering in a pan, it shall be made of choice flour in oil."] This serves to establish an analogy.
   B. Here "your offering" forms the basis for a classification. Just as 'your offering" here involves adding oil and saturating the meal with oil, so "your offering," used later invokes the requirement of adding oil and saturating the meal with oil.
   C. And, further, just as the classification of "your offering" noted below involves putting on oil in a utensil prior to the preparation of the offering, so "your offering" in the present instance also involves putting on oil in a utensil prior to the preparation of the offering.

Here the classification of two species into a single genus does succeed, so No. 2, with both species subject to the same rule. No objection is raised.

XXI:II
1. A. "...choice flour with oil mixed in":
   B. This teaches that one mixes the oil into the fine flour. [M. Men. 6:3A-B: All meal-offerings prepared in a utensil (baking pan or frying pan) require three applications of oil:

Re-presenting the Torah

            pouring oil into the utensil, stirring the meal into the oil, and then again putting oil into the utensil.]
- C. Rabbi says, "And as to the loaves [baked in an oven, one stirs them with oil (M. Men. 6:3C)] ["In the case of loaves, they stir oil into them...as it is said, 'Loaves mixed with oil'" (Lev. 7:12) (T. Men. 8:7B-C)]."
- D. They said to him, "But in connection with the cakes that accompany the thank-offering, is it not said, 'Flour mixed with oil' (Lev. 23:13)" (T. Tos. 8:7C)]?
- E. "And it is possible to stir in only with flour. [B. Men. 75a: It was not possible to mingle the cakes with oil but only the flour.]
- F. How does one do this? One puts oil into the flour and stirs it in, then oil into a utensil and prepares it, and stirs it, and mixes [the flour] with oil. [Tosefta's version: "How does one do this? He puts oil into the utensil and fries it. Then he puts oil into the flour and stirs it and breaks it up. And he then pours oil on it as one pours oil on pounded beans" (T. Men. 8:5C-D)].
- G. Rabbi says, "One puts oil into a utensil and prepares it, and stirs it, and then mixes the flour with oil, and then goes and pours oil on it."

All I see here is a reworking of the language we find, also, in the Mishnah and the Tosefta. I see no motif of critique of the Mishnah for its omission of prooftexts. Perhaps it is implicit or tacit; but, if so, in it I find no stakes at all. Our authorship knows that the Mishnah contains the Torah, and that is why, I maintain, it has undertaken the work it presents to us here.

XXI:III

1.
   - A. "unleavened":
   - B. Might one suppose that this is merely the desirable way of doing the deed [but still, optional]?
   - C. Scripture says, "...it will be...,"
   - D. meaning that it is a firmly-established requirement of the rite.
2.
   - A. "Break it into bits":
   - B. Might one suppose that that means into two pieces?
   - C. Scripture says, "bits."
3.
   - A. Might one suppose one should turn it into crumbs?
   - B. Scripture says, "...it...."
   - C. It is to be broken into pieces, but the pieces are not to be broken into pieces.
4.
   - A. As to the meal-offering of an Israelite, one folds it one into two, then two into four parts, and divides it at each fold. As to the meal-offering of priests, one folds it one into two, then two into four parts, but does not divide it. As to the meal-offering of the anointed priest, one did not fold it up. R. Simeon says, "The meal-offering of priests and the meal-offering of an anointed priest are not subject to the requirement of breaking up, because they are not subject to the taking of a handful, and anything which is not subject to

the taking of a handful is not subject to breaking up" [M. Men. 6:4B-G].

The systematic exegesis leads to a restatement of the Mishnah's rule in the Mishnah's language. But of course the point important to the Mishnah, which is the definition of the rule of breaking up in accord with the hierarchization of the castes, is utterly outside the frame of reference.

XXI:IV
1.   A.   "Break it into bits and pour oil on it; it is a meal-offering":
      B.   This serves to extend the rule of breaking up to all meal-offerings.
      C.   Might one suppose that that same rule extends also to the two loaves and the show bread?
      D.   Scripture says, "it...."
      E.   How come you encompass all meal-offerings but exclude the two loaves and the show bread?
      F.   After Scripture has used inclusionary language, it has then made an exclusion.
      G.   Just as these are distinguished in that part of the offering is placed on the altar fires, so excluded are the two loaves of bread and the show bread, none of which is put on the altar fire [but all of which is given to the priests to eat].
2.   A.   "Break it into bits and pour oil on it; it is a meal-offering":
      B.   This serves to extend the rule of pouring oil on the offering to all meal-offerings.
      C.   Might one suppose that that rule extends also to a meal-offering that is baked?
      D.   Scripture says, "on it."
      E.   I shall then exclude the loaves, but not the wafers?
      F.   Scripture says, "it is [a meal-offering]," [encompassing wafers under the rule of applying oil].

The clarification introduces other forms of meal-offering and speciates them.

XXI:V
1.   A.   "If your offering is a meal-offering in a pan, it shall be made of choice flour in oil":
      B.   What is the difference between a baking pan and a frying pan? "The frying pan has a cover, and the baking pan has no cover," the words of R. Yosé the Galilean. R. Hananiah b. Gamaliel says, "A frying pan is deep, and what is cooked in it is spongy, and a baking pan is flat, and what is cooked in it is hard" [M. Men. 5:8C-E].
2.   A.   "...it shall be made of choice flour in oil":
      B.   This teaches that preparing this meal-offering requires putting oil in a utensil prior to preparing the flour.

Re-presenting the Torah

Once more we simply review the Mishnah's clarification of Scripture, now represented the Mishnah as merely a secondary amplification of what Scripture says.

The laconic passage at hands contains an important fact. When the Mishnah is cited by our authorship, it will be presented as part of the factual substrate of the Torah. When the logic operative throughout the Mishnah is subjected to criticism, the language of the Mishnah will rarely, if ever, be cited in context. The operative language in dealing with the critique of the applied logic of *Listenwissenschaft* as represented by the framers of the Mishnah ordinarily is, "is it not a matter of logic?" Then the sorts of arguments against taxonomy pursued outside of the framework of Scripture's classifications will follow. When, by contrast, the authorship of Sifra wishes to introduce into the context it has already established a verbatim passage of the Mishnah, it will ordinarily, though not always, use, *mikan amru*, which, in context, means, "in this connection [sages] have said." It is a simple fact that when the intent is to demolish improper reasoning, the Mishnah's rules in the Mishnah's language rarely, if ever, occur. When the authorship of Sifra wishes to incorporate paragraphs of the Mishnah into their re-presentation of The Torah, they will do so either without fanfare, as in the passage at hand, or by the neutral joining language "in this connection [sages] have said."

VI. *The Torah* as a Proper Noun and the Rehabilitation of Hierarchical Classification

The authorship of Sifra never called into question the self-evident validity of taxonomic logic. Its critique is addressed only to how the Mishnah's framers identify the origins of, and delineate, taxa. But that critique proves fundamental to the case that that authorship proposed to make. For, intending to demonstrate that *The Torah* was a proper noun, and that everything that was valid came to expression in the single, cogent statement of The Torah, the authorship at hand identified the fundamental issue. It is the debate over the way we know things. In insisting, in agreement with the framers of the Mishnah, that there are not only cases but also rules, not only species but also genera, the authorship of Sifra also made its case in behalf of the case for The Torah as a proper noun. This carries us to the theological foundation for Sifra's authorship's sustained critique of applied reason.

VII. Sifra's Theology of Revelation

In appealing to the principle, for taxonomy, of *sola Scriptura*, I mean to set forth what I conceive really to be at stake. It is the character of The Torah and what it is, in The Torah, the thing that we wish to discern. And the answer to that question requires theological, not merely literary and philosophical, reflection on our part. For I maintain that in their delineation of correct hierarchical logic, our authorship uncovered, within The Torah (hence by definition, written and oral components of The Torah alike) an adumbration of the working of the mind of God. That is because the premise of all discourse is that The Torah was written by God and dictated by God to Moses at Sinai. And that will in the end explain why our authorship for its part has entered into The Torah long passages of not merely clarification but active intrusion, making itself a component of the interlocutorial process. To what end we know: it was to unite the Dual Torah. But on what basis? To answer this question let me start once again from the very beginning: the place of Sifra in its canonical context.

VIII. The Singularity of Sifra

The authorship of Sifra stands all by itself in the canon of the Judaism of the Dual Torah. Its reading of Scripture and uses of Scripture, put together in the way in which Sifra presents its statement of Scripture and the Mishnah within the context of Scripture, enjoy virtually unique standing. True, in formal terms, Sifra falls into the standard classification of verse-by-verse commentary to a book of the Written Torah. In general, in making midrash compilations, redactors would gather materials of Scripture exegesis and organize them in the order of appearance of verses of Scripture or of the unfolding of a story in Scripture. At the outset, people adhered to the exegetical and redactional pattern already established by the Yerushalmi's verse by verse or sentence by sentence reading set forth for the Mishnah. That is to say, they followed the order of verses of a biblical book, just as the framers of the Yerushalmi followed the order of Mishnah sentences of a given tractate. They undertook to explain words or phrases, imposing upon Scripture that set of values they regarded as self-evident and factual, the values of sages' worldview and way of life. The same modes of exegesis and organization – that is, the same logoi and topoi – that determined the content of self-evident comment in self-evident order on the Mishnah also dictated what would be done on Scripture. So the original work of collecting and arranging the compilations of exegeses of Scripture followed the patterns set in collecting and arranging exegeses of the Mishnah. Just as the Talmud, which is Mishnah exegesis, treats the Mishnah, so the earliest collections of scriptural exegesis treat Scripture. My thesis, as is clear, may be expressed as a simple formula of relationship:

Talmud	*Exegetical Collection*
Mishnah	Scripture

But while Genesis Rabbah on Genesis is to be compared to a Talmud tractate devoted to a particular tractate of the Mishnah on that tractate, Sifra on Leviticus bears slight resemblance to a Talmud tractate's treatment of a tractate of the Mishnah.

While it is the fact that Genesis Rabbah is composed of units of discourse as cogent, in their way, as the ones in the Talmud of the Land of Israel, we should look in vain in the Talmud of the Land of Israel for a tractate that, instead of commenting on a Mishnah tractate, undertakes essentially to rewrite large tracts of it. For when we pass the, admittedly considerable, passages in which words or phrases are amplified, what do we find in Sifra? It is a series of discursive essays, such as we have now examined at length, in which profound reflection on the nature of probative logic is expressed in examples and cases. While the units of discourse of Genesis Rabbah fall into precisely the same taxonomical categories as those of the Talmud of the Land of Israel, the paramount classification of units of discourse in our document surely do not.

That is not to suggest we find in the two Talmuds no counterpart to the critique of applied reason that we have examined with such admiration. It is to state as mere fact that the two Talmuds, and certainly not the Bavli, in no way undertake the deconstruction and recomposition of a Mishnah tractate in the way in which our authorship has taken apart and then put back together in a different way the book of Leviticus. The Mishnah in the Bavli always retains its paramount and autonomous position, dictating the program of discourse throughout those passages in which the Mishnah is at issue; Scripture fills the rest. Neither Talmud, and certainly not the Bavli, proposes to rewrite the Mishnah tractate in the way in which our authorship restates, within the setting of Scripture, the language and propositions of the Mishnah; and none pretends to penetrate into the deep structure of probative logic in the way in which our authorship has accomplished its purpose.

To appreciate the singular position attained for themselves by our authorship, we do well to reflect on the contrary position defined for themselves by the framers of midrash compilations for Scripture, represented by Genesis Rabbah. Their work, in the main, was dictated for them by the program of Mishnah exegesis worked out in the two Talmuds, particularly in the first of the two. Let me explain. What the masters of biblical exegesis did in Genesis in the compilation, Genesis Rabbah, was what the masters of Mishnaic exegesis did in whatever Mishnah tractate they chose for study. It follows that the compiling of the first collection of biblical exegesis falls into the same intellectual framework as the Talmud of the Land of Israel, whether this was before, at the same time as, or in the aftermath of the composition of the Yerushalmi. Like the Yerushalmi, Genesis Rabbah emerges in two distinct literary stages: first, people worked out its components; second, people arranged them. These may well have been the same people at much the same time, but the literary work divides into separate and distinct stages. First came writing compositions expressive of complex ideas, framed in sophisticated ways. Second came selecting and arranging these units of discourse into the composition now before us. As I said, the taxonomical framework suitable for all units of discourse of the Yerushalmi moves, without significant variation or revision, to encompass and categorize the materials of the earliest composition of scriptural exegesis, Genesis Rabbah. This fact I demonstrated in *Midrash in Context* (Philadelphia, 1984; second printing: Atlanta, 1988: Scholars Press for Brown Judaic Studies).

Let me make this more concrete. The framer of an exegetical unit of discourse in the Yerushalmi ordinarily would do one of two things: first, a phrase-by-phrase exegesis of the Mishnah; second, amplification of the meaning of a passage of the Mishnah. So a Talmudic sage confronting the Mishnah had the choice of explaining the meaning of a particular passage or expanding upon the meaning, or the overall theme, of a particular passage. The same was so for scriptural verses. True, in dealing with Scripture a sage might systematically interpret one thing in terms of something else, a verse of Scripture in light of an autonomous set of considerations not explicit in Scripture but (in his mind) absolutely critical to its full meaning. But that is still not much more than the exegesis of the passage at hand for a given purpose, established a priori. That is an exercise fully familiar to the framers of the units of discourse of the Talmud in their confrontation with the Mishnah.

To move on to the taxonomical categories for a scriptural book, these are four, of which the first two are closely related and the fourth of slight consequence. The first category encompasses close exegesis of Scripture, by which I mean a word-for-word or phrase-by-phrase interpretation of a passage. In such an activity, the framer of a discrete

Re-presenting the Torah

composition will wish to read and explain a verse or a few words of a verse of the Scripture at hand, pure and simple. This is a commonplace in Sifra as well. The second category, no less exegetical than the first, is made up of units of discourse in which the components of the verse are treated as part of a larger statement of meaning rather than as a set of individual phrases, stichs requiring attention one by one. Accordingly, in this taxon we deal with wide-ranging discourse about the meaning of a particular passage, hence an effort to amplify what is said in a verse. I cannot find a dozen instances of this kind of discourse in Sifra.

Nor is there a parallel in Sifra to the useful third taxon of the other midrash compilations, which encompasses units of discourse in which the theme of a particular passage defines a very wide-ranging exercise. In this discussion the cited passage itself is unimportant. It is the theme that is definitive. Accordingly, in this third type we take up a unit of discourse in which the composer of the passage wishes to expand on a particular problem, (merely) illustrated in the cited passage. The problem, rather than the cited passage, defines the limits and direction of discourse. The passage at hand falls away, having provided a mere pretext for the real point of concern. The fourth and final taxon, also deriving from the Yerushalmi, takes in units of discourse shaped around a given topic but not intended to constitute cogent and tightly framed discourse on said topic. These units of discourse then constitute topical anthologies rather than carefully composed essays. In place of these last three taxa, as we now recognize full well, comes the preoccupation with the Mishnah and the problem of the Mishnah.

The taxonomic structure just now described derives from the categories inductively discovered for the Yerushalmi, and it serves for other midrash compilations, but not for Sifra. The upshot is that types of units of discourse that we find in the Yerushalmi and the ones that comprise Genesis Rabbah fall into precisely the same categories and only into those categories. Taxonomically, all that changes from Genesis Rabbah and the compilations like it to the Yerushalmi (or vice versa) is the document subjected to exegesis (as well, of course, as what is said about it). Because the modes of thought and discourse turn out to exhibit precisely the same definitive traits and only those traits, they sustain a remarkably monothetic taxonomy. Third, that is why I propose the simple equation: The Yerushalmi is to the Mishnah as compilations of exegesis are to Scripture. But none of this is the case for Sifra.

IX. The Parsimonious Proper Noun and the Capacious Common Noun

We have concentrated upon Sifra's authorship's brilliant critique of applied reason. Its rehabilitation of the available system of reason was accomplished in such a way as to reopen the entire question of the definition of the Torah. By returning to Scripture as the source for taxa, by appealing to Scripture, and Scripture alone, as the criterion for like and unlike, and by then restating the whole of Scripture, for the book of Leviticus, to encompass words not in the original, Written Torah but only in the other, Oral Torah, that authorship exhibited remarkable imagination. Certainly, by any intellectual criterion, their solution to the problem of the Mishnah exhibited the wit and daring that merely laying things out side by side, exegesis of Scripture, exegesis of the Mishnah, such as had been done in the Bavli, scarcely adumbrated.

Two solutions to the problem of the Mishnah competed, at least in logic and intellect. A brief review at the end places into context the conclusion of the study as a whole. The one, we recall, transformed the word *torah* into a common noun, denoting many things, above all, status and classification. A teaching, book, or person might enter the status of *torah* or the classification of *torah*. That left ample space for actions, persons, books, and a broad range of categories of entities, so that *torah* might serve as an adjective as much as a common noun, for example, a Torah teaching, a Torah community, and the like. While, therefore, the Torah remained the scroll that contained the Pentateuch, a variety of other meanings broadened the sense of *torah*. In consequence, from the Mishnah onward, the canon of Judaism called *torah* or *the Torah* found ample space for endless candidates for inclusion. The other solution preserved the limited sense of the word *torah*, referring always and only to The Torah, that is to say, the Pentateuch. But then this other approach reread The Torah, the Written Torah, and found space for a variety of fresh candidates for inclusion. This was accomplished through a vast restatement of The Torah, a new and extraordinarily widened statement of what was encompassed within the Torah.

X. How the Torah Leads Us into the Mind of God

It is one thing to absorb the Torah, oral and written, into a single sustained and systematic statement, as did the authors of the Talmud of Babylonia. But it is quite another to join in the processes of thought, the right way of thinking, that sustain the Torah. The authorship of Sifra proposed to regain access to the modes of thought that guided the formation of the Torah, oral and written alike: comparison and contrast in this way, not in that, identification of categories in one manner, not in another. Since those were the modes of thought that, in our authorship's conception, dictated the structure of intellect upon which the Torah, the united Torah, rested, a simple conclusion is the sole possible one. Now to answer the question of the basis on which our authorship represented itself as participants in, and interlocutors of, The Torah, such that they were prepared to re-present, that is to say, simply rewrite (and therefore, themselves write) The Torah.

In their analysis of the deepest structures of intellect of the Torah, the authorship of Sifra supposed to enter into the mind of God, showing how God's mind worked when God formed the Torah, written and oral alike. And there, in the intellect of God, in their judgment humanity gained access to the only means of uniting the Torah, because that is where the Torah originated. But in discerning how God's mind worked, the intellectuals who created Sifra claimed for themselves a place in that very process of thought that had given birth to The Torah. Our authorship could rewrite the Torah because, knowing how The Torah originally was written, they too could write (though not reveal) The Torah.

12

The Role of Scripture in the Torah: Is Judaism a "Biblical Religion"?

I. Writing with Scripture in Judaism and Christianity

Judaism inherits and makes its own the Hebrew Scriptures of ancient Israel, just as does Christianity. And just as Christianity rereads the entire heritage of ancient Israel in the light of "the resurrection of Jesus Christ," so Judaism understands the Hebrew Scriptures as only one part, the written one, of "the one whole Torah of Moses, our rabbi." So the Old Testament forms no model for a single piece of writing in the rabbinic canon, by contrast to the situation in the library found at Qumran, where imitation of the scriptural psalms and other writings proved common. But what does that simple fact mean when we wish to understand the role of the Scriptures of ancient Israel in Judaism? While the writings of ancient Israel, which Judaism knows as "the Written Torah," formed a principal component of the Torah, these writings were both differentiated but also made into an integral part of a single autonomous statement of a determinate logic and cogency. So Judaism is not a "biblical religion," but the Torah of Judaism encompasses the Hebrew Scriptures of ancient Israel – a very different thing. That fact explains why the Old Testament provided no model for writers within the framework of rabbinic Judaism.

The received Scriptures formed an instrumentality for the expression of a writing bearing its own integrity and cogency, appealing to its own conventions of intelligibility, and, above all, making its own points. Any notion therefore that the authorships of Judaism proposed a systematic exegesis of Scripture conducted in terms of the original or historical program of Scripture, or appealed to Scripture for validation or vindication of doctrine or practice perceived as independent of

Scripture, distorts the character of the discourse of Judaism.[1] Scripture formed part of the Torah. The authorships of Judaism, particularly in late antiquity, also participated in the discourse and statement of the Torah. They did not write *about* Scripture, they wrote *with* Scripture, for Scripture supplied the syntax and grammar of their thought, hence, "writing with Scripture." But then, Judaism cannot be classified as "a biblical religion," because Judaism – the Torah – utilized the Hebrew Scriptures (which in context means "the Bible") for whatever purposes authors formed on their own. The conception that Judaism continues and paraphrases and restates the original message of the Hebrew Scriptures derives from narrowly apologetic motives and is no more defensible than the Christian-theological claim that forms its counterpart and comes to expression in the titles of the parts of the Bible, Old Testament, New Testament.

The Judaism of the Dual Torah, oral and written, which people ordinarily mean when they speak of "Judaism," commonly makes its appearance as a "biblical religion." That is to say, people ordinarily take for granted that that Judaism (like all other Judaisms) appeals for validation to the Hebrew Scriptures or Old Testament. Consequently, we tend to compare Judaism to Christianity, regarding both of them, each in its own way, as biblical: appealing to Scripture, whether the Written Torah (Judaism) or the Old Testament (Christianity). But when we adopt such a perspective upon the two great religions of the European West and its overseas diaspora in the Western hemisphere, we treat as distinct and independent what for both religions forms part of an integrated whole. That is to say, we see Scripture (Written Torah, Old Testament) not as part of an integral revelation, in which each part illuminates all others (Oral Torah,

---

[1]That is the argument of Daniel Boyarin, for one very current example, in his *Intertextuality and the Reading of Midrash* (Indiana Studies in Biblical Literature. Bloomington & Indianapolis: Indiana University Press, 1990). The apologetic point of the work is clear: "What in the Bible's text might have motivated this gloss on this verse?" He states at the end (p. 128), "Midrash is best understood as a continuation of the literary activity which engendered the Scriptures themselves." This sounds suspiciously like the familiar claim that Midrash says what Scripture really means, and that *is* the theology of some Orthodox Judaisms. In this book the literary critical frosting covers a stale but kosher cake. When we read Boyarin's analysis of passage after passage, we know pretty much what we knew before we read his analysis. The publisher's blurb holds: "the best, most cogent and intelligent attempt to date to apply insights from modern literary criticism to the interpretation of midrash." But Indiana University Press appears to have forgotten its own publication of a far more original and compelling work, José Faur, *Golden Doves with Silver Dots* (Bloomington: Indiana University Press, 1986).

New Testament). Rather, we address one part on its own, ignoring the perspective of faith altogether. But if we read the Written Torah/Old Testament distinct from the Oral Torah/New Testament, what we do is deny the fundamental conviction of the faith of Judaism or Christianity.

We do just that when we describe as exegetical ("midrashic") the relationship of the Oral to the Written Torah or the New to the Old Testament. That is to say, we deem one document to be essentially autonomous of the other, then establishing its relationship to the other through processes of rereading and reinterpretation. On that basis we develop the conception that the original scriptures (again: Written Torah/Old Testament) enjoy an existence independent of the faith and the synagogue or church that preserve them. These original scriptures bear an autonomous meaning, determined by the criteria of initial context and historical circumstance, and that meaning stands in judgment, so to speak, upon the meanings imputed to these scriptures by the Judaism of the Dual Torah or by the Christianity of the Bible, Old and New Testaments alike. Viewed historically, the collection of writings we know as the Hebrew Scriptures or Old Testament obviously bear meaning determined by the original setting and intent of authors or authorships (individual, collective writers).

But that meaning never made a profound impact, prior to the nineteenth century, upon the reception and reading of the Israelite Scriptures. What did make its mark was the uses of those Scriptures for the makers of the Judaism of the Dual Torah, on the one side, and the Christianity we now know as Orthodox: the Christianity of the Bible, Old and New Testaments, on the other. And what mattered to those system-builders concerned the revelation of God as they received it: the Torah of Moses, our rabbi, for the Judaism of the Dual Torah, the person of Jesus Christ, God incarnate, for Christianity. To those protean conceptions, Scripture served, as did all else, as testimony and testament. It formed part of a larger, wholly cogent statement. It served important purposes in the formation and expression of that statement. But it constituted a subordinated and merely instrumental entity, not the court of last appeal and final judgment, not the ultimate source of truth and validation, except – of course – after the fact. The fact found expression in the figure of the sage, in the model of Moses, our rabbi, or in the person, as the Church received him, of Christ Jesus.

People commonly suppose that when Judaic or Christian authorships turned to Israelite Scripture, it was in search of prooftexts. The relationship was exegetical or eisegetical. The representation of either religion as forming an essentially exegetical relationship to Israelite writings, however, vastly distorts the nature of that religion.

When Judaic and Christian authorships proposed to compose their statements, they of course appealed to Scripture. But it was an appeal to serve a purpose defined not by Scripture but by the faith – the Judaic or Christian system – under construction and subject to articulation. Scripture formed a dictionary, providing a vast range of permissible usages of intelligible words. Scripture did not dictate the sentences that would be composed through the words found in that (limited) dictionary. Much as painters paint with a palette of colors, authorships wrote with Scripture. The paint is not the picture. Matthew's Gospel of Jesus is not (merely) a reprise of Isaiah. But the picture cannot be painted without the pigments on the palette, and Matthew's Gospel cannot have been created without the verses of Isaiah and other prophetic passages that provided Matthew's framework for the Gospel story of Jesus Christ. And when the Church in its first three centuries framed its Scriptures, – as everybody knows – it received the Israelite writings because of the Church's reading of those writings. It spoke through those writings. It appealed to their facts. It responded, in the formation of its imagination and metaphoric reality, to those writings. Its life and being were nourished by those writings. But the Church came first, then the Scriptures, and, ultimately, the Bible, Old and New Testaments forming one complete and wholly harmonious, seamless statement and document. And so it was with the Judaism of the Dual Torah, in its framework and within its inner logic and discipline.

What follows from these propositions is clear. If we wish to understand the place and power of the Israelite Scriptures in the Judaism of the Dual Torah and in the writings of nascent Christianity, we must begin by freeing ourselves of one conception and exploring the implications of another. The negative is this: we must abandon any notion of a perceived distinction between the Oral and the Written Torahs, or between the New and Old Testaments. The positive is that we must see the two Torahs as the one whole Torah of Moses, our rabbi. We must see the two Testaments as "the Bible." The negative: we cannot take for granted that the appearance of a verse of the Israelite Scriptures in a rabbinic composition or a New Testament writing serves a single, determinate purpose, for example, as a "prooftext," as a source of vindication or validation for a statement a later author wishes to prove. The positive: we have to undertake an inductive inquiry into the uses and authority of the received scriptures of ancient Israel, allowing diverse documents to provide, each its own indication of where and how the inherited, authoritative writings serve the purposes of an author or authorship.

The founders of Judaism engaged in dialogue with the Scriptures of ancient Israel. They turned to Scripture not for prooftexts, let alone for pretexts, to say whatever they wanted, anyhow, to say. They used Scripture as an artist uses the colors on the palette, expressing ideas through and with Scripture as the artists paints with those colors and no others. This reading of the ways in which the Judaic sages read Scripture insists on two propositions. Sages created within a limited and well-defined vocabulary of thought, contrary to the conception that these same sages engaged in an essentially indeterminate and unlimited process of thought. They appealed to Scripture not merely for prooftexts as part of an apologia but for a far more original and sustained mode of discourse. Verses of Scripture served not merely to prove but to instruct. Israelite Scripture constituted not merely a source of validation but a powerful instrument of profound inquiry.

It follows that the category, "prooftexts," does not correspond to the role and authority of Scripture in the Torah. It is supposed that people settled questions by discovering a verse to demonstrate what they wished to say, with the further implication, within Judaic and Christian apologetics of the present century, of an original and determinate meaning of a Scripture, perceived as complete and autonomous, that validates, historically, the claim of the faith. That second premise, of course, imputes conceptions discovered only in modern times. We all recognize, of course, that ancient Israel no more testified to the Oral Torah, now written down in the Mishnah and later rabbinic writings, than it did to Jesus as the Christ. In both cases, religious circles within Israel of later antiquity reread the entire past in the light of their own conscience and convictions. They took for granted that the Torah and the contents of their conscience and convictions coalesced. Hence the conception that Scripture formed a court of last appeal, an authoritative criterion established out of a completed past, contradicts the situation of intellect and faith in which the authorships of the Judaism at hand endured. True, the Written Torah formed a distinct and always distinguished corpus of writing.[2]

---

[2] The distinction between the authority of Scripture and the authority of scribes, for example, forms a commonplace. But that distinction did not bear the sense that has commonly been assigned to it, that the Written Torah and the Oral Torah constituted distinct entities, separated from one another by centuries. The Judaism of the Dual Torah reached the firm conclusion that the two media in which the Torah was received accomplished the formulation and transmission of one whole Torah. Accordingly, the relationship between the Torah that derived from one medium, the written, and the Torah that derived from another medium, the oral, requires close analysis. That relationship

II. Defining a "Biblical Religion"

While the framers of Judaism as we know it received as divinely revealed ancient Israel's literary heritage, they picked and chose as they wished what would serve the purposes of the larger system they undertook to build. Since the Judaism at hand first reached literary expression in the Mishnah, a document in which Scripture plays a subordinate role, the founders of that Judaism clearly made no pretense at tying up to scriptural prooftexts or at expressing in the form of scriptural commentary the main ideas they wished to set out. Accordingly, Judaism rests only asymmetrically upon the foundations of the Hebrew Scriptures, and Judaism is not alone or mainly "the religion of the Old Testament."

Since Judaism is not "the religion of the Old Testament," we cannot take for granted or treat as predictable or predetermined the entry of the Hebrew Scriptures into the system of Judaism at hand. That is why we must ask exactly how the Scriptures did enter the framework of Judaism. In what way, when, and where, in the unfolding of the canon of Judaism, were they absorbed and recast, and how did they find the distinctive role they were to play from late antiquity onward? That question points toward the larger issue, namely, the place and use of Scripture in the Judaism of the Dual Torah. Once we realize that "Scripture" in the Judaism of the Dual Torah formed (merely) one component of the Torah, everything changes. Scripture loses its autonomous standing and its paramount authority and becomes one more medium for God's revealing the Torah to Israel. And other writings enter the status of that same revelation. When that shift takes place – as it does for Judaism as well as for Christianity, each within its own logic – then what of the Written Torah/Old Testament? That is what is at stake in the recognition that authorships of ancient Judaism wrote with Scripture and proposed the result to form part of the Torah.

When the Judaism of the Dual Torah had defined its matrix of myth and rite – a system of worldview and way of life focused on a particular social group – then that Judaism attained its independent voice, its inner structure and logic. At that moment – but only then – Scripture for its part also would assume its position as source of truth and proof for all (autonomously framed, independently reached) propositions. In the nature of things Scripture could form a focus of discourse only when discourse itself had expressed determinants autonomous of both the Mishnah and also Scripture – determinants, or

---

cannot be imputed on the basis of a misunderstanding of the weight and implications of the distinction between the two media.

propositions prior to all else. To revert to the operative myth, it is only when the Torah had reached full expression as an autonomous entity of logic that the (mere) components of Torah – Scripture, the Mishnah, and associated writings alike – found their proper place and proportion.

Let me take as my example the character of Scripture in the Midrash compilation, Leviticus Rabbah.[3] In Leviticus Rabbah we see how statements become intelligible not contingently, that is, on the strength of an established text, but *a priori*, that is, on the basis of a deeper logic of meaning, an independent principle of rhetorical intelligibility. The reason we say so is simple. Leviticus Rabbah is topical, not exegetical. Each of its thirty-seven *parashiyyot* pursues its given topic and develops points relevant to that topic. It is logical, in that (to repeat) discourse appeals to an underlying principle of composition and intelligibility, and that logic inheres in what is said. Logic is what joins one sentence to the next and forms the whole into paragraphs of meaning, intelligible propositions, each with its place and sense in a still larger, accessible system. Because of logic one mind connects to another, public discourse becomes possible, debate on issues of general intelligibility takes place, and an anthology of statements about a single subject becomes a composition of theorems about that subject. Accordingly, with Leviticus Rabbah rabbis take up the problem of saying what they wish to say not in an exegetical, but in a syllogistic and freely discursive logic and rhetoric.

To appreciate what was new, let us rapidly review the prior pattern of how people wrote both with and without Scripture. To seek, through biblical exegesis, to link the Mishnah to Scripture, detail by detail, represented a well-trodden and firmly-packed path. Sifra, an exegetical study of Leviticus as rabbis read the document, shows what could be done.[4] The exegetes there cite a passage of the Mishnah

---

[3]See my studies of Leviticus Rabbah in the following three monographs: *Judaism and Scripture: The Evidence of Leviticus Rabbah* (Chicago, 1986: University of Chicago Press); *The Integrity of Leviticus Rabbah. The Problem of the Autonomy of a Rabbinic Document* (Chico, 1985: Scholars Press for Brown Judaic Studies); *Comparative Midrash: The Plan and Program of Genesis Rabbah and Leviticus Rabbah* (Atlanta, 1986: Scholars Press for Brown Judaic Studies).

[4]*Sifra. An Analytical Translation* (Atlanta, 1988: Scholars Press for Brown Judaic Studies). I. *Introduction* and *Vayyiqra Dibura Denedabah* and *Vayiqqra Dibura Dehobah; Sifra. An Analytical Translation* (Atlanta, 1988: Scholars Press for Brown Judaic Studies). II. *Sav, Shemini, Tazria, Negaim, Mesora,* and *Zabim; Sifra. An Analytical Translation* (Atlanta, 1988: Scholars Press for Brown Judaic Studies). III. *Aharé Mot, Qedoshim, Emor, Behar,* and *Behuqotai;* and the two monographs based on that analytical translation,

verbatim and show that only through Scriptural exegesis, not through the processes of reason, can we reach the correct law. Scripture exegesis by rabbis also was a commonplace, as Genesis Rabbah indicates. Leviticus Rabbah was the first major rabbinic composition to propose to make topical and discursive statements, not episodically, as in Sifré to Deuteronomy, but systematically and in a disciplined framework. Not merely a phrase-by-phrase or verse-by-verse exegesis of a document, whether the Mishnah or a book of Scripture itself, Leviticus Rabbah takes a new road.

The framers of that composition undertook to offer propositions, declarative sentences (so to speak), in which, not through the exegesis of verses of Scripture in the order of Scripture but through an order dictated by their own sense of the logic of syllogistic composition, they would say what they had in mind. To begin with, they laid down their own topical program, related to, but essentially autonomous of, that of the book of Leviticus. Second, in expressing their ideas on these topics, they never undertook simply to cite a verse of Scripture and then to claim that that verse states precisely what they had in mind to begin with. Accordingly, through rather distinctive modes of expression, the framers said what they wished to say in their own way – just as had the authors of the Mishnah itself. True, in so doing, the composers of Leviticus Rabbah treated Scripture as had their predecessors. That is to say, to them as to those who had gone before, Scripture provided a rich treasury of facts.

III. Writing with Scripture in a Biblical Religion

How, very concretely, do the framers of Leviticus Rabbah accomplish that "writing with Scripture" of which we have spoken? The paramount and dominant exegetical construction in Leviticus Rabbah is the base-verse/intersecting-verse exegesis. In this construction, a verse of Leviticus is cited (hence: base verse), and another verse, from such books as Job, Proverbs, Qohelet, or Psalms, is then cited (hence: intersecting verse). The latter, not the former, is subjected to detailed and systematic exegesis. But the exegetical exercise ends up by leading the intersecting verse back to the base verse and reading the latter in terms of the former. In such an exercise, what in fact do we do? We read one thing in terms of something else. To begin with, it is the base verse in terms of the intersecting verse. But it also is

---

Uniting the Dual Torah: Sifra and the Problem of the Mishnah (Cambridge and New York, 1989: Cambridge University Press), and *Sifra in Perspective: The Documentary Comparison of the Midrashim of Ancient Judaism* (Atlanta, 1988: Scholars Press for Brown Judaic Studies).

the intersecting verse in other terms as well – a multiple layered construction of analogy and parable. The intersecting verse's elements always turn out to stand for, to signify, to speak of, something other than that to which they openly refer. If water stands for Torah, the skin disease for evil speech, the reference to something for some other thing entirely, then the mode of thought at hand is simple. One thing symbolizes another, speaks not of itself but of some other thing entirely.

How shall we describe this mode of thought? It seems to me we may call it an as-if way of seeing things. That is to say, it is as if a common object or symbol really represented an uncommon one. Nothing says what it means. Everything important speaks metonymically, elliptically, parabolically, symbolically. All statements carry deeper meaning, which inheres in other statements altogether. The profound sense, then, of the base verse emerges only through restatement within and through the intersecting verse – as if the base verse spoke of things that, on the surface, we do not see at all. Accordingly, if we ask the single prevalent literary construction to testify to the prevailing frame of mind, its message is that things are never what they seem. All things demand interpretation. Interpretation begins in the search for analogy, for that to which the thing is likened, hence the deep sense in which all exegesis at hand is parabolic. It is a quest for that for which the thing in its deepest structure stands.

Exegesis as we know it in Leviticus Rabbah (and not only there, since in the context of this article, Leviticus Rabbah is meant only as exemplary) consists in an exercise in analogical thinking – something is like something else, stands for, evokes, or symbolizes that which is quite outside itself. It may be the opposite of something else, in which case it conforms to the exact opposite of the rules that govern that something else. The reasoning is analogical or it is contrastive, and the fundamental logic is taxonomic. The taxonomy rests on those comparisons and contrasts we should call, as we said, metonymic and parabolic. In that case what lies on the surface misleads. What lies beneath or beyond the surface – there is the true reality, the world of truth and meaning. To revert to the issue of taxonomy, the tracts that allow classification serve only for that purpose. They signify nothing more than that something more.

How shall we characterize people who see things this way? They constitute the opposite of ones who call a thing as it is. Self-evidently, they have become accustomed to perceiving more – or less – than is at hand. Perhaps that is a natural mode of thought for the Jews of this period (and not then alone), so long used to calling themselves God's first love, yet now seeing others with greater worldly reason claiming that same advantaged relationship. Not in mind only, but still more, in the politics of the world, the people that remembered its origins along with the very creation of the world and founding of humanity, that recalled how it alone served, and serves, the one and only God, for more than three hundred years had confronted a quite different existence. The radical disjuncture between the way things were and the way Scripture said things were supposed to be – and in actuality would some day become – surely imposed an unbearable tension. It was one thing for the slave born to slavery to endure. It was another for the free man sold into slavery to accept that same condition. The vanquished people, the nation that had lost its city and its temple, that had, moreover, produced another nation from its midst to take over its Scripture and much else could not bear too much reality. That defeated people will then have found refuge in a mode of thought that trained vision to see other things otherwise than as the eyes perceived them. Among the diverse ways by which the weak and subordinated accommodate to their circumstance, the one of iron-willed pretense in life is most likely to yield the mode of thought at hand: things never are, because they cannot be, what they seem.

IV. The Role of Scripture: Paradigm of Renewal and Reconstruction

Everyone has always known that Jews read Scripture. Every system of Judaism has done so. But why did they do so? What place did Scripture take in the larger systems of reality presented by various Judaisms? Why one part of Scripture rather than some other, and why read it in one way rather than another? These questions do not find ready answers in the mere observation that Jews read Scripture and construct Judaisms out of it. Nor is that observation one of a predictable and necessary pattern, since some of the documents of the rabbinic canon did not focus upon Scripture or even find it necessary to quote Scripture a great deal. The Mishnah, Tosefta, and important units of discourse of both Talmuds, for example, did not express their ideas in the way in which people who "read Scripture" ought to. They make use of Scripture sparingly, only with restraint adducing proofs for propositions even when these are based upon scriptural statements. So the paramount and dominant place accorded to Scripture in Leviticus Rabbah and documents like it cannot pass without comment and explanation.

Exactly what can we say for the position of Scripture in this composition in particular, and what did Scripture contribute? We ask first about the use of Scripture in the mode of thought at hand: where, why, and how did Scripture find its central place in the minds of

The Role of Scripture in the Torah

people who thought in the way in which the framers of our document did? The answer is that Scripture contributed that other world that underlay this one. From Scripture came that other set of realities to be discovered in the ordinary affairs of the day. Scripture defined the inner being, the mythic life, that sustained Israel. The world is to be confronted as if things are not as they seem, because it is Scripture that tells us how things always are – not one time, in the past only, not one time, in the future only, but now and always. So the key to the system is what happens to, and through, Scripture. The lock that is opened is the deciphering of the code by which people were guided in their denial of one thing and recognition and affirmation of the presence of some other. It was not general, therefore mere lunacy, but specific, therefore culture.

To spell this out: the mode of thought pertained to a particular set of ideas. People did not engage ubiquitously and individually in an ongoing pretense that things always had to be other than they seemed. Had they done so, the Jewish nation would have disintegrated into a collectivity of pure insanity. The insistence on the as-if character of reality collectively focused upon one, and only one, alternative existence. All parties (so far as we know) entered into and shared that same and single interior universe. It was the one framed by Scripture. What happens in Leviticus Rabbah (and, self-evidently, in other documents of the same sort)? Reading one thing in terms of something else, the builders of the document systematically adopted for themselves the reality of the Scripture, its history and doctrines. They transformed that history from a sequence of one-time events, leading from one place to some other, into an ever-present mythic world. No longer was there one Moses, one David, one set of happenings of a distinctive and never-to-be-repeated character. Now whatever happens, of which the thinkers propose to take account, must enter and be absorbed into that established and ubiquitous pattern and structure founded in Scripture. It is not that biblical history repeats itself. Rather, biblical history no longer constitutes history as a story of things that happened once, long ago, and pointed to some one moment in the future. Rather it becomes an account of things that happen every day – hence, an ever-present mythic world, as we said.

A rapid glance at the work of the authorships of Leviticus Rabbah or Sifré to Deuteronomy (or any of their fellows) tells us that Scripture supplies the document with its structure, its content, its facts, its everything. But a deeper analysis also demonstrates that Scripture never provides the document with that structure, contents, and facts, that it now exhibits. Everything is reshaped and reframed. Whence the paradox? Scripture as a whole does not dictate the order of discourse, let alone its character. Just as the Talmudic authors destroyed the wholeness of the Mishnah and chose to take up its bits and pieces, so the exegetical writers did the same to Scripture. In our document they chose in Leviticus itself a verse here, a phrase there. These then presented the pretext for propositional discourse commonly quite out of phase with the cited passage. Verses that are quoted ordinarily shift from the meanings they convey to the implications they contain, speaking – as we have made clear – about something, anything, other than what they seem to be saying.

So the as-if frame of mind brought to Scripture brings renewal to Scripture, seeing everything with fresh eyes. And the result of the new vision was a re-imagining of the social world envisioned by the document at hand, we mean, the everyday world of Israel in its Land in that difficult time. For what the sages now proposed was a reconstruction of existence along the lines of the ancient design of Scripture as they read it. What that meant was that, from a sequence of one-time and linear events, everything that happened was turned into a repetition of known and already experienced paradigms, hence, once more, a mythic being. The source and core of the myth, of course, derive from Scripture – Scripture reread, renewed, reconstructed along with the society that revered Scripture.

So, to summarize, the mode of thought that dictated the issues and the logic of the document, telling the thinkers to see one thing in terms of something else, addressed Scripture in particular and collectively. And thinking as they did, the framers of the document saw Scripture in a new way, just as they saw their own circumstance afresh, rejecting their world in favor of Scripture's, reliving Scripture's world in their own terms. That, incidentally, is why they did not write history, an account of what was happening and what it meant. It was not that they did not recognize or appreciate important changes and trends reshaping their nation's life. They could not deny that reality. In their apocalyptic reading of the dietary and leprosy laws, they made explicit their close encounter with the history of the world as they knew it. But they had another mode of responding to history. It was to treat history as if it were already known and readily understood. Whatever happened had already happened. How so? Scripture dictated the contents of history, laying forth the structures of time, the rules that prevailed and were made known in events. Self-evidently, these same thinkers projected into Scripture's day the realities of their own, turning Moses and David into rabbis, for example. But that is how people think in that mythic, enchanted world in which, to begin with, reality blends with dream, and hope projects onto future and past alike how people want things to be.

The upshot is that the mode of thought revealed by the literary construction under discussion constitutes a rather specific expression of a far more general and prevailing way of seeing things. The literary form in concrete ways says that the entirety of the biblical narrative speaks to each circumstance, that the system of Scripture as a whole not only governs, but comes prior to, any concrete circumstance of that same Scripture. Everything in Scripture is relevant everywhere else in Scripture. It must follow, the Torah (to use the mythic language of the system at hand) defines reality under all specific circumstances. Obviously we did not have to come to the specific literary traits of the document at hand to discover those prevailing characteristics of contemporary and later documents of the rabbinic canon. True, every exercise in referring one biblical passage to another expands the range of discourse to encompass much beyond the original referent. But that is a commonplace in the exegesis of Scripture, familiar wherever midrash exegesis was undertaken, in no way particular to rabbinic writings.

V. Writing with Scripture and Rewriting Scripture

Scripture proves paramount on the surface, but subordinated in the deep structure of the logic of Leviticus Rabbah and the other Midrash compilations. Why so? Because Scripture enjoys no autonomous standing, for example, as the sole source of facts. It does not dictate the order of discussion. It does not (by itself) determine the topics to be taken up, since its verses, cited one by one in sequence, do not tell us how matters will proceed. Scripture, moreover, does not allow us to predict what proposition a given set of verses will yield. On the contrary, because of the insistence that one verse be read in light of another, one theme in light of another, augmentative one, Leviticus Rabbah (and the related writings) prohibits us from predicting at the outset, merely by reading a given verse of Scripture, the way in which a given theme will be worked out or the way in which a given proposition will impart a message through said theme.

What does it mean, then, to write with Scripture? The order of Scripture does not govern the sequence of discourse, the themes of Scripture do not tell us what themes will be taken up, the propositions of Scripture about its stated themes, what Scripture says, in its context, about a given topic, do not define the propositions of Leviticus Rabbah about that topic. The upshot is simple. Scripture contributes everything and nothing. It provides the decoration, the facts, much language. But whence the heart and soul and spirit? Where the matrix, where source? The editors, doing the work of selection, making their points through juxtaposition of things not otherwise brought into contact with one another – they are the ones who speak throughout. True, the voice is the voice of Scripture. But the hand is the hand of the collectivity of the sages, who are authors speaking through Scripture. If, moreover, Scripture contributes facts, so too do the ones who state those ineluctable truths that are expressed in parables, and so too do the ones who tell stories, also exemplifying truths, about great heroes and villains. No less, of course, but, in standing, also no more than these, Scripture makes its contribution along with other sources of social truth.

Greek science focused upon physics. Then the laws of Israel's salvation serve as the physics of the sages. But Greek science derived facts and built theorems on the basis of other sources besides physics; the philosophers also, after all, studied ethnography, ethics, politics, and history. For the sages at hand, along these same lines, parables, exemplary tales, and completed paragraphs of thought deriving from other sources (not to exclude the Mishnah, Tosefta, Sifra, Genesis Rabbah and such literary compositions that had been made ready for the Talmud of the Land of Israel) – these too make their contribution of data subject to analysis. All of these sources of truth, all together, were directed toward the discovery of philosophical laws for the understanding of Israel's life, now and in the age to come.

Standing paramount and dominant, Scripture contributed everything but the main point. That point comes to us from the framers of Midrash compilations such as Leviticus Rabbah – from them alone. So far as Leviticus Rabbah transcends the book of Leviticus – and that means, in the whole of its being – the document speaks for the framers, conveys their message, pursues their discourse, makes the points they wished to make. For they are the ones who made of Leviticus, the book, Leviticus Rabbah, that greater Leviticus, the document that spoke of sanctification but, in its augmented version at hand, meant salvation. As closely related to the book of Leviticus as the New Testament is to the Old, Leviticus Rabbah delivers the message of the philosophers of Israel's history.

We have emphasized that Leviticus Rabbah carries a message of its own, which finds a place within, and refers to, a larger system. The method of thought and mode of argument act out a denial of one reality in favor of the affirmation of another. That dual process of pretense at the exegetical level evokes the deeper pretense of the mode of thought of the larger system, and, at the deepest layer, the pretense that fed Israel's soul and sustained it. Just as one thing evokes some other, so does the rabbinic system overall turn into aspects of myth and actions of deep symbolic consequence what to the untutored eye were commonplace

The Role of Scripture in the Torah

deeds and neutral transactions. So too the wretched nation really enjoyed God's special love.

Now what are the commonplace traits of Scripture in this other, new context altogether?

1. Scripture, for one thing, forms a timeless present, with the affairs of the present day read back into the past and the past into the present, with singular events absorbed into Scripture's paradigms.
2. Scripture is read whole and atomistically. Everything speaks to everything else, but only one thing speaks at a time.
3. Scripture is read as an account of a seamless world, encompassing present and past alike, and Scripture is read atemporally and ahistorically.

All of these things surprise no one; they have been recognized for a very long time. What is new here is the claim to explain why these things are so, we mean, the logic of the composition that prevails, also, when Scripture comes to hand.

1. Scripture is read whole, because the framers pursue issues of thought that demand all data pertain to all times and all contexts. The authors are philosophers, looking for rules and their verification. Scripture tells stories, to be sure. But these exemplify facts of social life and national destiny: the laws of Israel's life.
2. Scripture is read atomistically, just as is the Mishnah, because each of its components constitutes a social fact, ever relevant to the society of which it forms a part, with that society everywhere uniform.
3. Scripture is read as a source of facts pertinent to historical and contemporary issues alike, because the issues at hand when worked out will indicate the prevailing laws, the rules that apply everywhere, all the time, to everyone of Israel.

Accordingly, there is no way for Scripture to be read except as a source of facts about that ongoing reality that forms the focus and the center of discourse, the life of the unique social entity, Israel. But the simple logic conveyed by the parable also contributes its offering of facts. The simple truth conveyed by the tale of the great man, the exemplary event of the rabbinic sage, the memorable miracle – these too serve as well as facts of Scripture. The several truths therefore stand alongside and at the same level as the truths of Scripture, which is not the sole source of rules or cases. The facts of Scripture stand no higher than those of the parable, on the one side, or of the tale of the sage, on the other. Why not? Because to philosophers and scientists, facts are facts, whatever their origin or point of application.

What we have in the Torah's use of Scripture, therefore, is the result of the mode of thought not of prophets or historians, but of philosophers and scientists. The framers propose not to lay down, but to discover, rules governing Israel's life. We state with necessary emphasis: as we find the rules of nature by identifying and classifying facts of natural life, so we find rules of society by identifying and classifying the facts of Israel's social life. In both modes of inquiry we make sense of things by bringing together like specimens and finding out whether they form a species, then bringing together like species and finding out whether they form a genus – in all, classifying data and identifying the rules that make possible the classification.

That sort of thinking lies at the deepest level of list-making, which is work of offering a proposition and facts (for social rules) as much as a genus and its species (for rules of nature). Once discovered, the social rules of Israel's national life of course yield explicit statements, such as that God hates the arrogant and loves the humble. The readily assembled syllogism follows: if one is arrogant, God will hate him, and if he is humble, God will love him. The logical status of these statements, in context, is as secure and unassailable as the logical status of statements about physics, ethics, or politics, as these emerge in philosophical thought. What differentiates the statements is not their logical status – as sound, scientific philosophy – but only their subject matter, on the one side, and distinctive rhetoric, on the other.

So rabbinic writings are anything but an exegetical exercise. We err if we are taken in by the powerful rhetoric of our documents, which resort so ubiquitously to the citation of biblical verses and, more important, to the construction, out of diverse verses, of a point transcendent of the cited verses. At hand is not a canon comprising exegetical compositions at all, nor even verses of Scripture read as a corpus of prooftexts. We have, rather, statements that stand by themselves, each document formed in its own terms and separate from Scripture, and that makes it points only secondarily, along the way, by evoking verses of Scripture to express and exemplify those same points. We miss the main point if we posit that Scripture plays a definitive or even central role in providing the program and agenda for the framers of Leviticus Rabbah. Their program is wholly their own. But of course Scripture then serves their purposes very well indeed.

So, too, their style is their own. Scripture merely contributes to an aesthetic that is at once pleasing and powerful for people who know Scripture pretty much by heart. But in context the aesthetic too is original. The constant invocation of scriptural verses compares with the place of the classics in the speech and writing of gentlefolk of an earlier age, in which the mark of elegance was perpetual allusion to classical writers. No Christian author of the age would have found alien the aesthetic at hand. So while the constant introduction of verses of Scripture provides the wherewithal of speech, these verses serve only as do the colors of the painter. The painter cannot paint without the oils. But the colors do not make the painting. The painter does. As original and astonishing as is the aesthetic of the Mishnah, the theory of persuasive rhetoric governing Leviticus Rabbah produces a still more amazing result.

VI. A Fond Farewell to the Notion of [1] Judaism as a (Mere) Paraphrase of the Hebrew Scriptures and of [2] Scripture as (Mere) Source of (Mere) Prooftexts

We may say that (again by way of example) Leviticus Rabbah provides an exegesis of the book of Leviticus just as much as the school of Matthew provides an exegesis of passages cited in the book of Isaiah. Yet, we must reiterate at the end, Leviticus serves as something other than a source of prooftexts. It is not that at all. And that is the important fact we mean to prove. What is new in Leviticus Rabbah's encounter with Scripture emerges – and that document stands for others in the canon of the Judaism of the Dual Torah – when we realize that, for former Israelite writers, Scriptures do serve principally as a source of prooftexts. That certainly is the case for the school of Matthew, for one thing, and also for the Essene writers whose library survived at Qumran, for another. The task of Scripture for the authors of the Tosefta, Sifra, Genesis Rabbah, and the Talmud of the Land of Israel emerged out of a single need. That need was to found the creations of the new age upon the authority of the old. Thus the exegetical work consequent upon the Mishnah demanded a turning to Scripture. From that necessary and predictable meeting, exegetical work on Scripture itself got under way, with the results so self-evident in most of the exegetical compositions on most of the Pentateuch, including Leviticus, accomplished in the third and fourth centuries. None of this in fact defined how Scripture would reach its right and proper place in the Judaism of the Talmuds and exegetical compositions. It was Leviticus Rabbah that set the pattern, and its pattern would predominate for a very long time. The operative rules would be these:

1. From Leviticus Rabbah onward, Scripture would conform to paradigms framed essentially independent of Scripture.
2. From then onward, Scripture was made to yield paradigms applicable beyond the limits of Scripture.

In these two complementary statements we summarize the entire argument concerning the uses of Scripture in the Torah of formative

Judaism. The heart of the matter lies in laying forth the rules of life – of Israel's life and salvation. These rules derive from the facts of history, as much as the rules of the Mishnah derive from the facts of society (and, in context, the rules of philosophy derive from the facts of nature). Scripture then never stands all by itself. Its exalted position at the center of all discourse proves contingent, never absolute. That negative result of course bears an entirely affirmative complement. Judaism is not the religion of the Old Testament because Judaism is Judaism. Scripture enters Judaism because Judaism is the religion of "the one whole Torah of Moses, our rabbi," and part of that Torah is the written part, Scripture. But that whole Torah, viewed whole, is this: God's revelation of the rules of life: creation, society, history alike.

Obviously, every Judaism would be in some way a scriptural religion. But the sort of scriptural religion a given kind of Judaism would reveal is not to be predicted on the foundations of traits of Scripture in particular. One kind of Judaism laid its distinctive emphasis upon a linear history of Israel, in a sequence of unique, one-time events, all together yielding a pattern of revealed truth, from creation, through revelation, to redemption. That kind of Judaism then would read Scripture for signs of the times and turn Scripture into a resource for apocalyptic speculation. A kind of Judaism interested not in one-time events of history but in all-time rules of society, governing for all time, such as the kind at hand, would read Scripture philosophically and not historically. That is, Scripture would yield a corpus of facts conforming to rules. Scripture would provide a source of paradigms, the opposite of one-time events.

True enough, many kinds of Judaism would found their definitive propositions in Scripture and build upon them. But while all of Scripture was revealed and authoritative, for each construction of a system of Judaism only some passages of Scripture would prove to be relevant. Just as the framers of the Mishnah came to Scripture with a program of questions and inquiries framed essentially among themselves, one which turned out to be highly selective, so did their successors who made up Leviticus Rabbah and its companions. What they brought was a mode of thought, a deeply philosophical and scientific quest, and an acute problem of history and society. In their search for the rules of Israel's life and salvation, they found answer not in the one-time events of history but in paradigmatic facts, social laws of salvation. It was in the mind and imagination of the already philosophical authors of the Rabbah-Midrash compilations that Scripture came to serve – as did nature, as did everyday life and its parables, all together – to reveal laws everywhere and always valid.

Part Four

REPRISES AND REPLIES:
ISSUES OF METHOD

13

Judaism in the Matrix of Christianity Reconsidered

Judaism as it flourished in the West was born in the encounter with Christianity in the definition in which it defined the civilization of the West, and that same Judaism lost its power to persuade Jews of its self-evident truth when Christianity did. *Judaism in the Matrix of Christianity* (Philadelphia, 1986: Fortress Press. British edition, Edinburgh, 1988: T. & T. Collins) formed part of work of mine that proposes to contribute to the study of religion a theory on the impact of political change on theological ideas. At issue is how in particular ideas relate to the political circumstances of the people who hold those ideas. Religion as a fact of politics constitutes a principal force in the shaping of society and imagination alike, while politics for its part profoundly affects the conditions of religious belief and behavior. So I want to know how a stunning shift in the political circumstance of a religion affected that religion's thought about perennial questions. In fact, I have dealt with two moments of fundamental and radical change, one at the beginning, treated here in part, and also in *Judaism and Christianity in the Age of Constantine. Issues of the Initial Confrontation* (Chicago, 1987: University of Chicago Press); the other moment at the end of the history of a religious system, treated in my *Death and Birth of Judaism. The Impact of Christianity, Secularism, and the Holocaust on Jewish Faith* (New York, 1987: Basic Books).

Clearly, I regard religion as a social fact, not merely as a set of beliefs on questions viewed in an abstract and ahistorical setting. Hence I do not analyze religious questions alone or mainly as problems of the interplay of received prooftexts and internal logic. Rather, I want to know the relationship between religious ideas and the circumstances, in particular in politics, of the society that holds them.

So I treat the human being as a political animal and religion, too, as something people do together. Not only so, but – to continue the idiom just now used – a Judaism is something Jews do not by themselves but in the context of a larger world, in the West, Jews "do Judaism" among Christians "doing Christianity" – and in response to that circumstance and setting. Historians of Judaism take as dogma the view that Christianity never made any difference to Judaism (and more than did Islam, a totally distinct set of problems). Faith of a "people that dwells apart" (these historians hold) Judaism went its splendid, solitary way, exploring paths untouched by Christians. Christianity (the theory goes) was born in the matrix of Judaism, but Judaism, from then to now, officially ignored the new "daughter" religion and followed its majestic course in aristocratic isolation. Since, moreover, Judaism (in any form) is supposed always to have ignored, and never to have been affected by, Christianity in any form, (the implicit argument), the future security of the faith of Judaism requires continuing this same policy, pretending that Christianity simply never made, and does not now make, any difference at all to Israel, the Jewish people.

I have emphasized I see no such thing as Judaism but only Judaisms. Surely that allegation contradicts the common sense view that "Judaism" differs from "Christianity." The search for a useful metaphor draws us back to human life. The several Judaic (or Christian, or Buddhist, or Islamic) systems form a family, with certain traits in common. But the family is made up of individuals, each with her or his biography. And, when it comes to families, we live and die pretty much alone, one by one. So it has been, and so it is, with Judaisms (Christianities, Buddhisms, Islams). Each forms both part of a family, with clear filiation, but, as it is born, lives, and dies, also and essentially a singular system to itself. That singular system possesses its own identity, each one with its distinctive definition, its way of life, its worldview, its address to (in the case of a Judaism) an Israel of its own designation (even the whole of Israel, the Jewish people, though that is ordinarily a matter of disbelieved rhetoric). Each demands study not in categories defined by its own claims of continuity, but in those defined by its own distinctive and characteristic choices. For a system takes shape and then makes choices – in that order. The choices, the selections out of the received materials of Judaisms – these come after the fact. The fact is formed by the (prior, fully formed) system: its points of stress, its values, above all, the problems that system has chosen for itself and has determined to solve (and has very commonly solved).

Judaism in the Matrix of Christianity *Reconsidered*

What forms the fact is what the earliest generations of the new Judaism find self-evident, the truths that demand no articulation, no defense, no argument. What is self-evident forms the system and defines its generative exegetical principles. And if I want to know what people find self-evident, I have to uncover the questions they confront and cannot evade. These questions will dictate the program of inquiry, the answers to which then follow after the fact. If I know what issues of social existence predominate, I can also uncover the point – the circumstance – of origin of a Judaism. To be sure, no one claims to know the source of urgent questions: whether political, whether cultural, whether formed within the received condition of the faith, whether framed by forces outside. Debates on such issues of beginnings rarely yield consensus. The reason is simple. In the end no one is present at the beginning, so we have no information to settle any important questions. We work our way back from the known to the unknown. But all we wish to know is whether what we trace is old and continuous, as its apologists invariably claim, or essentially new and creative, a testimony to human will and human power and human intellect, as I maintain it is: a new Judaism, for a new circumstance.

The birth of the Judaism under discussion here took place in the year 312, the year of Constantine's vision at the Milvian Bridge of a cross and the words, "By this sign you will conquer." That same Judaism died – ceased to impress nearly all Jews as self-evidently true in the year 1789, with the American Constitution and the French Revolution, which for the first time established in the West a politics distinct from Christianity. With Constantine Christianity became the definitive power in the politics of the West, and with the American Constitution and the French Revolution Christianity began its journey out of the political arena. The Judaism that took shape in the fourth century, attested by documents brought to closure in the fifth, responded to that Christianity and flourished, in Israel, the Jewish people, so long as the West was Christian. That same Judaism died – meaning, ceased to impress Israel, the Jewish people, as self-evidently true – when the Christian definition of Western civilization entered into competition with other systems of thought. The Judaism of the Dual Torah responded to a political question, and the Judaisms of the nineteenth and twentieth centuries addressed political change, and, finally, crisis and catastrophe.

Political change therefore takes the critical role in shaping theological discourse. Specifically, the Judaism that took shape in the fourth century, in response to the political triumph of Christianity in the Roman Empire, governed the mind and imagination of Israel in Christendom for the next fifteen hundred years. The reason, I hold, is that that Judaism, for Israel, dealt effectively with the urgent issues deriving from the world defined by regnant Christianity. Received for that long epoch as self-evidently true, that same Judaism began to strike some Jews as not at all self-evident at that point, and in those places, at which Christianity (in one version or another) lost control of the politics of the West. When Christianity no longer governed the political life and therefore also the symbolic transactions of the West, the Judaism that had taken shape in response to triumphant Christianity and had so long and so successfully sustained the life of Israel, the Jewish people, confronted skeptical questioning among people now standing essentially outside of its system of truths beyond all argument. That is why I say Judaism was born in 312 and died in 1789. But of course there is more to it than that. New Judaisms took shape, dealing with other agenda of urgent questions and answering those questions in ways self-evidently right for those who believed. Each of these Judaisms claimed to continue in linear succession the Judaism that had flourished for so long, to develop in an incremental succession and so to connect, through the long past, to Sinai. So we deal not only with the death of one Judaism but with the birth of several others. Here we deal, in all with eight, one I call "the Judaism of the Dual Torah," that is, the one that took shape in the fourth century, and seven others, as we shall see.

Why does the fourth century mark so critical an era in the history of Judaism? Because that was when the Judaism that would flourish in the West came to full definition and expression – and so did the Christianity that would define the civilization of the West for nineteen hundred years. The fourth century therefore marked the beginning, in a terrible union of cobra and mongoose, of the two great religious traditions of the West, unequal in numbers but well-matched in intellectual resources, Christianity and Judaism. Jews had to sort out the issues defined by the triumph of Christianity as well as their own disappointment of the same age. And, through the sages, they succeeded in doing so.

The Judaism that would thrive, that is, the Judaic system of the Dual Torah, came to expression in the matrix of Christianity. Before that time, the Christian and Judaic thinkers had not accomplished the feat of framing a single program for debate. Judaic sages had earlier talked about their issues to their audience, Christian theologians had for three centuries pursued their arguments on their distinctive agenda. The former had long pretended the latter did not exist. Afterward the principal intellectual structures of a distinctive Judaism – the definition of the teleology, method, and doctrine of that Judaism – reached definition and ample articulation. Each of these components of the system, as I shall show in Chapter One, met head-on and in a fundamental way the challenge of politically-regnant Christianity. The Judaic answers to the Christian *défi*, for believing Israel remained valid as a matter of self-evidence so long as Christianity dictated the politics in which the confrontation of Judaism and Christianity would take place. That, sum and substance, is the argument of *Judaism in the Matrix of Christianity* and its principal companions, *Judaism and Christianity in the Age of Constantine* and *Death and Birth of Judaism*. A Judaism of a particular sort was born in the matrix of Christianity, died with the death of the kind of Christian world into which it has been born, and, in the West, produced new Judaisms in response to the new worlds, Christian and other, in which Israel, the Jewish people, made its life. Not only so, but the Judaisms born since the death of Judaism constitute wonderful new inventions, discontinuous in all but their own perception of themselves with all that had gone before, hence, the death and birth of Judaism(s).

The special language in use here now requires definition, first, "system" and "religious system," second, "Judaism." A religious system comprises a worldview, explaining who people are, where they come from, what they must do, a way of life, expressing in concrete deeds that worldview and linking the life of the individual to the polity, and a particular social group, in the case of a Judaic system, an "Israel," to whom the worldview and way of life refer. A Judaic system, or simply, a Judaism, therefore comprises a worldview, a way of life, and a group of Jews who hold the one and live by the other. When we speak of the birth of a Judaism, therefore, we point to the time and circumstance in which a given worldview, way of life, and social group coalesced in a definitive way. How do we discern that moment of coalescence? We look for the resort to a striking and also distinctive symbol, something that expresses the whole all together and all at once. For the symbol – whether visual or verbal, whether in gesture or in song or in dance or in – even – the definition of the role of woman – will capture the whole and proclaim its special message: its way of life, its worldview, its definition of who is Israel.

Through the history of the Jewish people, diverse Judaisms have won the allegiance of groups of Jews here and there, each system specifying the things it regards as urgent both in belief and in behavior. All systems in common allege that they represent the true and authentic Judaism, or Torah, or will of God for Israel, and that their devotees are Israel. Each ordinarily situates itself in a single historical line – hence, a linear history – from the entirety of the past. Commonly a Judaism sees itself as the natural outgrowth, the increment of time and change. These traits of historical or even supernatural origin characterize nearly all Judaisms. How then do we know one Judaism from another? When we can identify the the principal symbol to which a given system on its own appeals, we realize that we have a wholly distinct and distinctive system in prospect.

Let me give an example of how a symbol denotes a Judaism. The Judaism of the priests, represented by the Priestly Code in Leviticus Chapters One through Fifteen and various other priestly writings in the Five Books of Moses, for example, Genesis 1:1-2:4, regarded the altar as critical in the union of the natural and the supernatural world, the sanctification of Israel through the priestly caste as central, and the holy way of life as something corresponding to the deepest structure of Creation. If I had to make up a symbol for the priestly caste, I should choose the priestly ephod – or a bleeding lamb. The Judaism of the Yahwist, represented, for example, by stories of the formation of Israel in Genesis and Exodus, regarded God's grace for Israel, the people, as the centerpiece. Its symbol? We know the symbol: Solomon in all his glory. The Judaism of the Deuteronomic historians, authors of Deuteronomy, Joshua, Judges, Samuel, and Kings as we now have them, who completed their work after the destruction of the Temple and the exile of the Jews from the Land of Israel in 586 B[efore] [the] C[ommon] E[ra] [= B.C.], laid stress on the contract between Israel and God. Keeping that contract assured prosperity, and violating it explained disaster, such as Israel then endured. The symbol of the covenant? The Torah as made up then, or the restored Temple. And, again, if we asked the Essenes of the Dead Sea Community whose library was discovered at Qumran about their Judaism, it would exhibit its own points of stress and concern. Its symbol? A table for a meal eaten by holy Israel (all that the group recognized as Israel) in a state of cultic sanctification as specified in Leviticus. Each symbol conveys the distinctive character, the different and separate system, of its Judaism. Rightly read, no symbol serves any system but its own. Seen all together, the symbols add up to a set of Judaisms: a whole family of religions, bearing polythetic definition of points of commonality, that alone.

I have now to define that particular Judaic system. Let me first explain what is unique in the symbolic system of the Judaism of the Dual Torah. It is not appeal to "the Torah," in general. Far from it. The Torah of Moses clearly occupied a critical place in all systems of Judaism from the closure of the Torah book, the Pentateuch, in the time of Ezra onward. But in late antiquity, for one group alone the book developed into an abstract and encompassing symbol. Specifically, in the Judaism that took shape in the formative age, the first seven centuries C.E. but reached its characteristic symbolic expression only at the end of the fourth century, everything was contained in that one thing. How so? When we speak of *torah*, in rabbinical literature of late antiquity, we no longer denote a particular book, on the one side, or the contents of such a book, on the other. Instead, we connote a broad range of clearly distinct categories of noun and verb, concrete fact and abstract relationship alike. "Torah" stands for a kind of human being. It connotes a social status and a sort of social group. It refers to a type of social relationship. It further denotes a legal status and differentiates among legal norms. As symbolic abstraction, the word encompasses things and persons, actions and status, points of social differentiation and legal and normative standing, as well as "revealed truth." In all, the main points of insistence of the whole of Israel's life and history come to full symbolic expression in that single word. If people wanted to explain how they would be saved, they would use the word Torah. If they wished to sort out their parlous relationships with gentiles, they would use the word Torah. Torah stood for salvation and accounted for Israel's this-worldly condition and the hope, for both individual and national alike, of life in the world to come. For the kind of Judaism under discussion, therefore, the word Torah stood for everything. The Torah symbolized the whole, at once and entire. When, therefore, we wish to describe the unfolding of the definitive doctrine of Judaism in its formative period, the first exercise consists in paying close attention to the meanings imputed to a single word.

The Judaism of the Dual Torah came to full expression in the writings of the sages of the Land of Israel ("the Holy Land," "Palestine") of the later fourth and fifth centuries and takes a position separate from all of the prior Judaisms, as well as those that would follow in modern times. What distinguishes the Judaism at hand is its doctrine of the dual media by which God's will for Israel, contained in the Torah revealed at Sinai, came down from ancient times. Specifically, this Judaism maintains, when God revealed the Torah at Sinai, God transmitted the Torah in two media, one in writing, now contained in the Written Torah (which the Christian world calls "the Old Testament." The other medium by which the Torah reached Israel was through memory, that is, the other Torah was transmitted orally and memorized by great prophets, then sages, down to the time of the sages of the age themselves.

This other, orally formulated and orally transmitted Torah – this memorized Torah – derives from this Judaism and no other. Where do we find the substance of the memorized Torah? The second component of God's revelation to Moses at Sinai, "the Oral Torah," now in writing is presented by the Mishnah, a philosophical law code closed at about the year 200 C[ommon] E[ra] [= A.D.]. Further documents that fall into classification of (Oral) Torah include the Tosefta, a collection of supplements to the Mishnah's laws, further, a commentary to the Mishnah accomplished in the Land of Israel called the Talmud of the Land of Israel, of about the year 400, a second such commentary, done in the Jewish communities of Babylonia and called the Talmud of Babylonia, of about the year 600, as well as commentaries to the Written Torah by the sages of the age, such as Sifra, to Leviticus, Sifré to Numbers, another Sifré, this one to Deuteronomy, Genesis Rabbah, Leviticus Rabbah, and the like. All of these other documents, but especially the Mishnah and its two great Talmuds, contain the teachings of sages in late antiquity, from the first through the sixth centuries of the Common Era. All together they form that other, that Oral Torah, that God revealed to Moses at Sinai.

That is the Judaism that reached its first formulation in writing some time in the late fourth or early fifth century of the Common Era. It is only in the Talmud of the Land of Israel, ca. A.D. 400, and its closely allied documents, Genesis Rabbah and Leviticus Rabbah, that that Judaism's principal and indicative doctrines, symbols, and beliefs are fully exposed. That is to say, the first full statement of that Judaism of the Dual Torah is contained in the Talmud of the Land of Israel, with complementary materials in other documents of the same age, namely, the end of that critical century which began with Constantine's declaring Christianity licit, then favored religion, and which ended with the Roman Empire's declaring Christianity the religion of the state. Precisely how the Judaism of the Dual Torah responded to the crisis at hand is explored, in part, in the pages of *Judaism in the Matrix of Christianity*.

Because of a political event that Israel could not ignore and the Church deemed probative, discourse between Judaism and Christianity would find different people talking to different people about some of the same things. For the prior three hundred years, these people had not debated a common issue, and for the next fourteen hundred years they would not do so again. The reason for the shift and the particular topics at hand? First, a common politics, and, second, common premises about the importance of politics, that is, history, premises deriving from common Scriptures. Why, then, the beginnings of the shift at the end of the eighteenth century? Because a new politics presented to Israel, the Jewish people, a new set of questions, and, by the way, called into question the self-evident truth of the enduring answers to the questions of the old agenda.

Judaism as it flourished in the Christian West was born in the age of Constantine, and that Judaism died in the beginning of the American experiment, when, in 1789, an other-than-Christian politics began with the American Constitution and the French Revolution. Constantine inaugurated the politics in which Christianity defined the civilization of the West, the American Constitution and the French Revolution brought to a conclusion the age in which a politically-paramount Christianity set the norm for the West.

What challenge emerged because the emperor of Rome adopted Christianity? To begin with, Jews had not anticipated that the new religion, Christianity, would amount to much. Christians now maintained that their faith in Jesus as Christ, Messiah and God incarnate, found full vindication. They pointed to passages in the Hebrew Scriptures that, in their view, had now come to fulfillment. They declared themselves heirs of ancient Israel and denied to the Jews the long-standing position of God's first and chosen love. So at issue in the Christians' success in imperial politics we find profoundly theological questions: (1) does history now vindicate Christianity? (2) was and is Jesus the Messiah? (3) who, in light of events, is "Israel" and who is not? The foundations of the Judaic system and structure were shaken.

Why, specifically, did the advent of Christian rule in the Roman Empire make so profound an impact as to produce a Judaism? A move of the empire from reverence for Zeus to adoration of Mithra meant nothing. To Jews paganism was what it was, lacking all differentiation. Christianity was something else. Why? *Because it was like Judaism.* In terms of our explanation, Christians caimed that theirs was a Judaism – in fact, *the* Judaism – now fulfilled in Christ. Christians read the Torah and claimed to declare its meaning. They furthermore alleged, like Israel, that they alone worshipped the one true God. And they challenged Israel's claim to know that God – and even to be Israel, continuator of the Israel of the promises and grace of ancient Scripture. Accordingly, for their part, Israel's sages cannot have avoided the issue of the place, within the Torah's messianic pattern, of the remarkable turn in world history represented by the triumph of Christianity. Since the Christians celebrated confirmation of their faith in Christ's Messiahship and Jews were hardly prepared to concur, it falls surely within known patterns for us to suppose that Constantine's conversion would have been identified with some dark moment to prefigure the dawning of the messianic age. The importance of the age of Constantine in the history of Judaism therefore derives from a simple fact.

At that time through the fourth and into the fifth century, important Judaic documents, particularly the Talmud of the Land of Israel, brought to a conclusion around ca. A.D. 400, Genesis Rabbah, a systematic expansion of the story of Creation in line with Israel's later history, and Leviticus Rabbah, a search for the laws of history and society undertaken in passages of the book of Leviticus, were completed. These writings undertook to deal with agenda defined by the political triumph of Christianity. These questions for Jews? First, the meaning of history, second, the coming of the Messiah, third, the definition of who is Israel. The triumph of Christianity called all three, for Israel, into question. Christian thinkers for their part reflected on issues presented by the political revolution in the status of Christianity. Issues of the interpretation of history from creation to the present, the restatement of the challenge and claim of Christ the King as Messiah against the continuing expectation of Israel that the Messiah is yet to come, and the definition of who is Israel – these made their appearance in Judaic and Christian writings of the day. Issues of Judaism as laid forth in documents redacted in the fourth and early fifth century exhibit remarkable congruence to the contours of the intellectual program presented by Christian thinkers. So (as I shall spell out at Chapter One) in the period at hand, in political conditions that would persist in the West, Judaic sages and Christian theologians addressed precisely the same questions, questions critical to the self-understanding of Israel, the Jewish people. That fact in my view accounts for the success of the Judaism at hand – its self-evident truth for Israel, the Jewish people – in the long centuries in which that Judaic system defined the way of life and the worldview of the Jewish people: Judaism.

But what about the first century? Did the events of that age in Christianity make no difference to Judaism? Indeed not. We begin the story of the Christian impact on Judaism in the fourth, not the first, Christian century because that is when Christianity as it would shape the West began. Why for Judaism begin at that same time? Because, as I shall show in Chapter One, it was in the age of Constantine, specifically, when, at the end of that age, the Talmud of the Land of Israel and associated writings, dated from ca. 400-450, came forth, that the Judaism that would flourish in the West reached initial formulation. Then that worldview and way of life focused on a political theory of Israel, the Jewish people, we know as Judaism reached its first clear and complete canonical expression. And that Judaism admirably responded to the political conditions defined by the Christian West and served Jewry as a self-evidently true corpus of doctrines and deeds so long as Israel, the Jewish people, lived under those political conditions that Constantine's conversion inaugurated.

So, once more, we see that the Judaism that thrived responded to a political circumstance defined by Christianity. Why, then, end the period of the self-evidence of the Judaism of the Dual Torah, which took shape in the time of Constantine? Because as a matter of fact, when other than Christian politics prevailed, then new Judaisms came to expression,. The established Judaism of the West for large sectors of the Jewish people lost its standing as self-evident truth, a set of compelling statements of how things really are. Responding to political change with the "deChristianization" of politics, first in Western, later in Eastern Europe as well, Jews put forth other Judaisms, some continuing, with important changes, the established system, others constituting altogether discontinuous Judaic systems.

The Judaic and Christian systems of the first century prepared their respective groups for worlds that would never exist. The Judaism of the day addressed a self-governing people, secure within its own political institutions, and the Christianity that emerged never envisioned a Christian state. In the fourth century the two systems traded places, the one prepared for politics lost its political system, the one unprepared inherited the world. In many ways, therefore, the fourth century marks the point of intersection of trajectories of the history of the two groups of religious systems, Judaic and Christian. For Judaism and Christianity in late antiquity present histories that mirror one another. When Christianity began, Judaism was the dominant tradition in the Holy Land and framed its ideas within a political framework until the early fifth century. Christianity there was subordinate and from the beginning had to work out against the background of what to begin with was a politically definitive Judaism. So Judaism in its principal expressions produced deep thought on political issues. But Christianity, never anticipating that it would inherit an empire and rule the world, scarcely made itself ready for its coming political power. The roles reversed themselves when the politically well-framed Judaism lost all access to an effective polity, while a politically mute Christianity entered onto responsibilities scarcely imagined a decade before they came into being.

From the time of Constantine onward, therefore matters reversed themselves. Now Christianity predominated, expressing its ideas in political and institutional terms. Judaism, by contrast, had lost its political foundations and faced the task of working out its self-understanding in terms of a world defined by Christianity, now everywhere triumphant and in charge of politics. The important shift came in the early fourth century. That we must call the West's first century. Why? Because the fourth century was when the West began in the union of Christian religion and Roman rule. As I shall explain, it also was when the Judaism that thrived in the West reached the definition it was to exhibit for the next fifteen centuries.

When, therefore, under Constantine the religious systems of Christianity became licit, then favored, and finally dominant in the government of the Roman empire, Christians confronted a world for which nothing had prepared them. But they did not choose to complain. For the political triumph of Christ, now ruler of the world in dimensions wholly unimagined, brought its own lessons. All of human history required fresh consideration, from the first Adam to the last. The writings of churches now asked to be sorted out, so that the canon, Old and New, might correspond to the standing and clarity of the new Christian situation. So, too, one powerful symbol, that selected by Constantine for his army and the one by which he won, the cross, took a position of dominance and declared its distinctive message of a Christianity in charge of things. Symbol, canon, systemic teleology – all three responded to the unprecedented and hitherto not-to-be-predicted circumstance of Christ on the throne of the nations.

Just beyond the end of that century of surprises, in the year 429, Israel in the Land of Israel lost its institution of autonomous government. The Jews of the land of Israel then confronted a situation without precedent. That year marked the end of the patriarchal government that had ruled the Jews of the Land of Israel for the preceding three centuries. It was the end of their political entity, their instrument of self-administration and government in their own land. Tracing its roots back for centuries and claiming to originate in the family of David, the Jewish government, that of the patriarch, had succeeded the regime of the priests in the Temple and the kings, first allies, then agents, of Rome on their throne. Israel's tradition of government, of course, went back to Sinai. No one had ever imagined that the Jews would define their lives other than together, as a people, a political society, with collective authority and shared destiny and a public interest. The revelation of Sinai addressed a nation, the Torah gave laws to be kept and enforced, and, as is clear, Israel found definition in comparison to other nations. It would have rulers, subject to God's authority to be sure, and it would have a king now, and a King-Messiah at the end of time.

So the fourth century brought a hitherto unimagined circumstance: an Israel lacking the authority to rule itself under its own government, even the ethnic and patriarchal one that had held things together on the other side of the end of long centuries of priestly rule in the Temple and royal rule in Jerusalem. In effect the two systems had from the first century to the eve of the fourth prepared for worlds that neither would inhabit, the one for the status of governed, not governor, the other for the opposite. Christianity in politics would define not the fringes but the very fabric of society and culture. Judaism out of politics altogether would find its power in the donated obedience of people in no way to be coerced, except from within or from on high. Whatever "Christianity" and "Judaism" would choose as their definition beyond the time of turning, therefore, would constitute mediating systems, with the task, for the systems to emerge, of responding to a new world out of an inappropriate old. The Judaism that would take shape beyond the fourth century, beginning in writings generally thought to have come to closure at the end of that momentous age, would use writings produced in one religious ecological system to address a quite different one, and so too would the Christianity that would rule, both in its Western and in its Eastern expressions.

The confrontation (there never was a dialogue) between Christianity in all its forms and Judaism in the form imparted by sages continued for centuries because the conditions that to begin with precipitated it, specifically the rise to political dominance of Christianity and the subordination of Judaism, remained constant for fifteen hundred years. It seems to me self-evident, therefore, that – so far as ideas bearing political implications matter in bonding a group – the success among the people of Israel in Europe, Western and Eastern alike, of the Judaism defined in the fourth century writings of the sages of the Land of Israel derives from the power and persuasive effect of the ideas of that Judaism. Coming to the surface in the writings of the age, that Judaism therefore secured for despairing Israel a long future of hope and confident endurance.

And with what outcome? A stunning success for that society for which, to begin with, sages, and, in sages' view, God, cared so deeply: eternal Israel after the flesh. For Israel did endure in the Christian West, enjoying the secure conviction of constituting that Israel after the flesh to which the Torah continued to speak. How do we know sages' Judaism won? Because when, in turn, Islam gained its victory, Christianity throughout the Middle East and North Africa gave way. But sages' Judaism in those same vast territories retained the loyalty and conviction of the people of the Torah. The cross would rule only where the crescent and its sword did not. But the Torah of Sinai everywhere and always sanctified Israel in time and promised secure salvation for eternity. So Israel believed and so does Israel believe today. But we have moved ahead of our story. For to show that events in the fourth century made a vast difference, producing a Judaism quite distinct from the one that had gone before even within the sages' circles, I have to characterize the shape of the Judaism of the sages prior to the point, in the fourth century, at which important documents clearly did take into account the challenge of Christianity. Otherwise we shall not realize what is fresh in the fourth century writings of sages, and we shall then miss how profound a response to the Christian challenge they formulated for Israel, the Jewish people.

Two groups of intellectuals – Judaic sages, Christian theologians – in the fourth century argued about the same matters. These concerned the meaning of history, the identification of the Messiah, and the definition of who is Israel. They appealed to the same facts (those supplied by Scripture), and employed essentially the same mode of argument (historical facts indicate social laws that reveal God's plan and purpose for society). How come? In both cases two facts account for Judaic sages' and Christian theologians' sharing such a common program.

First is the inherited and shared Scripture of ancient Israel, and, second is the political cataclysm represented by the advent of the age of Constantine. The Christianization of the Roman Empire in the fourth century and the entry of Christianity into the world of politics and government in that same age defined the issues confronting both parties. Scripture told both parties that political change mattered. The events of the day demonstrably affected Christians' conceptions of the meaning and end of history, vindicating their belief in Jesus as Christ, validating their claim to form the community of the saved, therefore (for some) "Israel." And those same facts demanded from sages a vivid and (for Israel, at any rate) persuasive reponse.

True, we do not know that in the books they produced at the end of the fourth century, the Talmud of the Land of Israel, Genesis Rabbah and Leviticus Rabbah, Israel's sages said what they said specifically because they had to meet the Christian challenge. Nor can we demonstrate that Jews for fifteen hundred years found self-evidently true the system of the sages because that system dealt with the political and intellectual challenge of Christianity. All we have is what the people said, in documents they edited, at that time. On the basis of the topics with which they dealt, we may compose a point-by-point response to the same concerns that shaped the Christians' agenda. That then is the fact: there really was an encounter, a confrontation, a kind of argument, upon the foundations of shared premises and a common core of facts agreed upon by both parties: not a dialogue but at least an argument.

Why did the Judaic system shaped at that time persist with such power in Israel, the Jewish people? Because for fifteen hundred years Jews continued to resort to address the same perennially urgent questions and respond with the same arguments about who they were and where they were headed and why they should do what God wanted of them, which was to be who they were and to travel on the road of life on which they journeyed. The same symbols, the same myth (in the sense of truth told in the form of a tale), the same books enjoyed consistent attention for so long as (to continue the metaphor) the Judaic road passed through Christendom. Christianity, in its diverse forms, preserved the power of the Judaic system at hand, because the questions the system answered retained their force and immediacy: Christians kept asking them. When the Judaic road crossed frontiers into other territory entirely, then, as we shall see, people turned to new maps – or groped their way with none but their own sensibility. For the questions the received system satisfactorily answered no longer pressed on peoples' minds, and new questions demanded attention. So the system lost its centrality (it of course never died and I believe never will die), and new Judaic systems competed for attention – and for a time won.

What exactly was the specific challenge of triumphant Christianity to Judaism? To state matters simply, with the triumph of Christianity through Constantine and his successors in the West. Christianity's explicit claims, now validated in world-shaking events of the age, demanded a reply. The sages of the Talmud provided it. At those very specific points at which the Christian challenge met head-on old Israel's worldview, sages' doctrines responded. What did Israel's sages have to present as the Torah's answer to the cross? It was the Torah. This took three forms. The Torah was defined in the doctrine, first, of the status, as oral and memorized revelation, of the Mishnah, and, by implication, of other rabbinical writings. The Torah, moreover, was presented as the encompassing symbol of Israel's salvation. The Torah, finally, was embodied in the person of the Messiah who, of course, would be a rabbi. The Torah in all three modes confronted the cross, with its doctrine of the triumphant Christ, Messiah and king, ruler now of earth as of heaven.

So how exactly did the Judaic system exposed in the later fourth century writings deal with the Christian challenge? The symbolic system of Christianity, with Christ triumphant, with the cross as the now-regnant symbol, with the canon of Christianity now defined and recognized as authoritative, called forth from the sages of the Land of Israel a symbolic system strikingly responsive to the crisis. The Messiah served, for example, to explain the purpose of the Judaic way of life: keep the rules of the Torah as sages teach them, and the Messiah will come. So the coming of the Messiah set as the teleology of the system of Judaism as sages defined that system. The symbol of the Torah expanded to encompass the whole of human existence as the system laid forth the limns of that existence. So the distinctive Judaic way of life derived, the system taught, from God's will. What about the importance of the doctrine that when God revealed the Torah to Moses at Sinai, it was in two media, written (the Hebrew Scriptures) and oral (the teaching of the sages, beginning with the Mishnah)? The canon of Sinai is thereby broadened to take account of the entirety of the sages' teachings, as much as of the Written Torah everyone acknowledged as authoritative. So the doctrine of the Dual Torah told the Jews that their sages understood God's will, and the others did not. The challenge was met. How so? Jesus, now King-Messiah, is not what the Christians say. God will yet send Israel's Messiah – when Israel does what has to be done to hasten the day. And what Israel must do is keep the faith with the holy way of life taught as Torah – God's revelation – by the sages at hand. The Torah stood as the principal symbol – that and not the cross.

Did the sages say these things in order to answer the challenge of Christianity? We shall never know, as I pointed out. No one can claim that they did. What we cannot show we do not know. We cannot speculate on motive, since we have no evidence by which to test our speculation. All we can do is point to the contrast between the sages' system as revealed in writings closed in the later second and third century, in particular the Mishnah and its closely allied documents, and the system that emerged in the writings of the later fourth and fifth centuries. The contrast tells the tale.

We now come to the specific issues treated in these pages. Let us now ask precisely how the Christianization of Rome affected the formation of the Judaism of the Dual Torah – and how it did not. The answer derives from the political facts that changed and those that did not change when Constantine became Christian. When Rome became Christian, and when Christianity became first licit, then established, and finally triumphant, the condition of Israel changed in some ways but not in others. What remained the same? The politics and social context of a defeated nation. Israel in the Land of Israel/Palestine/the Holy Land had long ago lost its major war as an autonomous political unit of the Roman Empire. In the year 70 the Romans had conquered the capital and destroyed the Temple there. In 132, a war broke out with the evident expectation that after three generations, God would call an end to the punishment, as God had done in the time of the destruction of the first Temple, in 586, and its restoration, some "seventy years" later. But that is not what happened. Israel again suffered defeat, this time worse than before. Jerusalem now transformed into a forbidden city to Jews, the Temple now in permanent ruins, Israel, the Jewish people, took up the task of finding an accommodation with enduring defeat. So whether Rome accepted pagan or Christian rule had no bearing on the fundamental fact of Israel's life: a beaten nation.

Then what changed? The circumstance and context of the religious system of Judaism. The political situation of Israel did not change. The political situation of Christianity did – and therefore, also, of Judaism. How so? Israelites in the Land of Israel persisted as a subject people. That is what they had been, that is what they remained. But Judaism now confronted a world in which its principal components – hermeneutic, teleology, symbol – confronted an effective challenge in the corresponding components of the now-triumphant faith in Christ. The Judaism that emerged dealt with that challenge in a way particular to Christianity. The doctrines that assumed central significance, those concerning the Messiah, on the one side, and the character of God's revelation in the Torah to Moses at Sinai, on the other, took up questions addressed to Judaism by Christianity and only by Christianity. So what changed changed because of the distinctive claims of Christianity, and what remained intact out of the antecedent heritage endured because Israel cointinued as a subjugated people, to the condition of which the prior heritage had already proved its congruence.

Now, as we know, the Hebrew Scriptures, the Written Torah, in Christian view demanded a reading as the Old Testament, predicting the New. Why? Because history now proved that Scripture's prophetic promises of a King-Messiah to begin with had pointed toward Jesus, now Christ enthroned. Concomitantly, the teleology of the Israelite system of old, focused as it was on the coming of the Messiah, now found confirmation and realization in the rule of Jesus, again, Christ enthroned. And the symbol of the whole – hermeneutics, teleology alike – rose in heaven's heights: the cross that had triumphed at the Milvian Bridge. No wonder, then, that the critical components of the prior system of Judaism now came under sharp revision. To be concrete, let me specify the changes I think indicative.

1. The Written Torah found completion in the oral one. So Judaism's extra-scriptural traditions found legitimacy.
2. The system as a whole now was made to point toward an eschatological teleology, to be realized in the coming of the Mishnah when Israel's condition, defined by the one whole Torah of Sinai, itself warranted. And, it would necessarily follow,
3. the symbol of the Torah would expand to encompass the teleology and hermeneutic at hand. Salvation comes from the Torah, not the cross.

So point by point, the principles of the Judaism turn out in the fresh reading of the Talmud of the Land of Israel, coming to closure at the end of the fourth century, to respond point by point to the particular challenge of the principal event of that century. So the fourth century marked the first century of Judaism as it would flourish in the West. It further indicated the first century of Christianity as Christianity enthroned would define and govern the civilization of the West.

If, now, we inquire into exactly what in fact sages did at that time, – meaning, what books did they write and what did they say in them that they had not said earlier? – the answer is clear. They composed the Talmud of the Land of Israel as we know it. They collected exegeses of Scripture and made them into systematic and sustained accounts of, initially, the meaning of the Pentateuch (assuming dates in these centuries, late third through early fifth, for Sifra, the two Sifrés, Genesis Rabbah and Leviticus Rabbah). Let us dwell on this matter of composing collections of exegeses of the Hebrew Scriptures, something that, in the Christian world, contemporaries worked out as well. When we recall what Christians had to say to Israel, we may find entirely reasonable the view that compiling scriptural exegeses constituted part of a Jewish apologetic response. For one Christian message had been that Israel "after the flesh" had distorted and continually misunderstood the meaning of what had been its own Scripture. Failing to read the Old Testament in the light of the New, the prophetic promises in the perspective of Christ's fulfillment of those promises, Israel "after the flesh" had lost access to God's revelation to Moses at Sinai. If we were to propose a suitably powerful, yet appropriately proud, response, it would have two qualities. First, it would supply a complete account of what Scripture had meant, and always must mean, as Israel read it. Second, it would do so in such a way as not to dignify the position of the other side with the grace of an explicit reply at all.

The compilations of exegeses and the Talmud of the Land of Israel accomplished at this time assuredly take up the challenge of restating the meaning of the Torah revealed by God to Moses at Mount Sinai. This the sages did in a systematic and thorough way. At the same time, if the charges of the other side precipitated the work of compilation and composition, the consequent collections in no way suggest so. The issues of the documents are made always to emerge from the inner life not even of Israel in general, but of the sages' estate in particular. Scripture was thoroughly rabbinized, as earlier it had been Christianized. None of this suggests the other side had won a response for itself. Only the net effect – a complete picture of the whole, as Israel must perceive the whole of revelation – suggests the extraordinary utility for apologetics, outside as much as inside the faith, served by these same compilations.

It follows, I think, that the changes at the surface, in articulated doctrines of teleology, hermeneutics, and symbolism, respond to changes in the political condition of Israel as well as in the religious foundations of the politics of the day. Paganism had presented a different and simpler problem to sages. Christianity's explicit claims, validated in world-shaking events of the age, demanded a reply. The sages of the Talmud of the Land of Israel provided it. So it is at those very specific points at which the Christian challenge met head-on old Israel's worldview that sages' doctrines change from what they had been. What did Israel have to present to the cross? The Torah, in the doctrine, first, of the status, as oral and memorized revelation, of the Mishnah, and, by implication, of other rabbinical writings. The Torah, moreover, in the encompassing symbol of Israel's salvation. The Torah, finally, in the person of the Messiah who, of course, would be a rabbi. The Torah in all three modes confronted the cross, with its doctrine of the triumphant Christ, Messiah and king, ruler now of earth as of heaven. So what changed? Those components of sages' worldview that now stood in direct confrontation with counterparts on the Christian side. What remained the same? Doctrines governing fundamental categories of Israel's social life to which the triumph of Christianity made no material difference.

What, in fact, can we say about sages' Judaism before the crisis of Constantine's age? We see the shape and structure of a Judaism not framed in response to the crisis of Christianity, a Judaism without Christianity. That Judaism, for one thing, will not have a richly developed doctrine of the Messiah. For another, it will work out issues of sanctification, rather than those of salvation made urgent by Christian emphasis on that category. The Mishnah, a philosophical law code brought to closure at about the year 200, shows us a Judaism framed not in response to issues urgent because of Christianity. The document responded to issues of the destruction of the Temple and the subsequent defeat in the failed war for the restoration. The two issues that defined the setting of the Mishnah, therefore its concerns, were, first, the destruction of the Temple in 70, and second, the defeat of Bar Kokhba in 135. The former set in motion expectations of redemption three generations later, just as had happened in the time of the destruction of the first Temple in 586 B.C.E. and the return three generations to Zion. But the catastrophe of Bar Kokhba's war discredited a picture of the salvation of Israel that had enjoyed prominence for nearly seven hundred years. For it was clear that whatever would happen, what would not occur is what had happened before. So Israel found itself cut off from the moorings of many centuries' endurance.

When in the aftermath of the destruction in A.D. 70 and the still more disheartening defeat of 135, sages worked out a Judaism without a Temple and a cult, they produced in the Mishnah a system of sanctification focused on the holiness of the priesthood, the cultic festivals, the Temple and its sacrifices, as well as on the rules for protecting that holiness from levitical uncleanness – four of the six divisions of the Mishnah on a single theme. When, in the aftermath of the conversion of the Roman Empire to Christianity and the triumph of Christianity in the generation beyond Julian "the apostate," sages worked out in the pages of the Talmud of the Land of Israel and in the exegetical compilations of the age a Judaism intersecting with the Mishnah's but essentially asymmetrical with it, it was a system for salvation, focused on the salvific power of the sanctification of the holy people. Judaism as a whole, with its equal emphases on sanctification in the hear and now and salvation at the end of time, would come to full and classic expression only in the Talmud of Babylonia, two hundred years beyond the Talmud of the Land of Israel. But the first of the two Talmuds set the compass and locked it into place.

If Christianity presented an urgent problem to the sages behind the Mishnah, for example given systemic prominence to a given category rather than some other, we cannot point to a single line of the document that says so. As we shall see later on, the figure of the Messiah – to take a stunning example – in no way provided the sages of the Mishnah with an appropriate way of explaining the purpose and goal of their system, its teleology. That teleology appealing to the end of history with the coming of the Messiah came to predominate only in the Talmud of the Land of Israel and in sages' documents beyond. What issues then proved paramount in a Judaism utterly out of relationship to Christianity in any form? We turn back to the Mishnah to find out.

The system portrayed in the Mishnah emerged in a world in which there was no Christianity. What points do we not find?

First, we find in the Mishnah no explicit and systematic theory of scriptural authority. We now know how much stress the Judaism in confrontation with Christianity laid on Scripture, with important commentaries produced in the age of Constantine. What the framers of the Mishnah did not find necessary was a doctrine of the authority of Scripture. Nor did they undertake a systematic exegetical effort at the linking of the principal document, the Mishnah, to Scripture. Why not? Because the authors saw no need. Christianity made pressing the question of the standing and status of the Mishnah in relationship to Scripture, claiming that the Mishnah was man-made and a forgery of God's will, which was contained only in Scripture. Then the doctrine of the Dual Torah, explaining the origin and authority of the Mishnah, came to full expression.

Second, we look in vain for a teleology focused on the coming of the Messiah as the end and purpose of the system as a whole. The Mishnah's teleology in no way invokes an eschatological dimension at all. This Judaism for a world in which Christianity played no considerable role – took slight interest in the Messiah and presented a teleology lacking all eschatological, therefore messianic focus. I shall spell this out presently.

Third, the same Judaism laid no considerable stress on the symbol of the Torah, though, of course, the Torah as a scroll, as a matter of status, and as revelation of God's will at Sinai, enjoyed prominence. And so sages produced a document, the Mishnah, so independent of Scripture that, when the authors wished to say what Scripture said, they chose to do so in their own words and in their own way. Whatever the intent of the Mishnah's authors, therefore, it clearly did not encompass explaining to a competing Israel, heirs of the same Scriptures of Sinai, just what authority validated the document, and how the document related to Scripture.

So when we listen to the silences of the Mishnah, as much as to its points of stress, we hear a single message. It is a message of a Judaism that answered a single encompassing question concerning the enduring sanctification of Israel, the people, the land, the way of life. What, in the aftermath of the destruction of the holy place and holy cult, remained of the sanctity of the holy caste, the priesthood, the holy land, and, above all, the holy people and its holy way of life? The answer: sanctity persists, indelibly, in *Israel, the people*, in its way of life, in its land, in its priesthood, in its food, in its mode of sustaining life, in its manner of procreating and so sustaining the nation. That holiness would endure. And the Mishnah then laid out the structures of sanctification: what does it mean to live a holy life. But that answer found itself absorbed, in time to come, within a successor system, with its own points of stress and emphasis. That successor system, both continuous and asymmetrical with the Mishnah, would take over the Mishnah and turn it into the one whole Torah of Moses, our rabbi, that became Judaism. The indicative marks? First, the central symbol of Torah as sages' teaching and, second, the figure of Messiah as sage.

As I explained at the outset, every detail of the religious system at hand exhibits essentially the same point of insistence, captured in the simple notion of the Torah as the generative symbol, the total, exhaustive expression of the system as a whole. That is why the definitive ritual of the Judaism under study consisted in studying the Torah as the generative symbol, the total, exhaustive expression of the system as a whole. That is why the definitive myth explained that one who studied Torah would become holy, like Moses "our rabbi," and like God, in whose image humanity was made and whose Torah provided the plan and the model for what God wanted of a humanity created in his image.

The clerks who knew and applied its law had to explain the standing of that law, meaning its relationship to the law of the Torah. But the Mishnah provided no account of itself. Unlike biblical law codes, the Mishnah begins with no myth of its own origin. It ends with no doxology. Discourse commences in the middle of things and ends abruptly. What follows from such laconic mumbling is that the exact status of the document required definition entirely outside the framework of the document itself. The framers of the Mishnah gave no hint of the nature of their book, so the Mishnah reached the political world of Israel without a trace of self-conscious explanation or any theory of validation.

The one thing that is clear, alas, is negative. The framers of the Mishnah nowhere claim, implicitly or explicitly, that what they have written forms part of the Torah, enjoys the status of God's revelation to Moses at Sinai, or even systematically carries forward secondary exposition and application of what Moses wrote down in the wilderness. Later on, I think two hundred years beyond the closure of the Mishnah, the need to explain the standing and origin of the Mishnah led some to posit two things. First, God's revelation of the Torah at Sinai encompassed the Mishnah as much as Scripture. Second, the Mishnah was handed on through oral formulation and oral transmission from Sinai to the framers of the document as we have it.

These twin explanations for the status of the Mishnah first surfaced in the Talmud of the Land of Israel, which contains clear allusions to the Dual Torah, one part in writing, the other, oral, and now in the Mishnah. That doctrine contains an ample response to those who questioned the standing and authority of both the Mishnah and the sages who applied the Mishnah in the Jewish government.

But for the two hundred years prior to the Talmud of the Land of Israel, that is, through the span of time in which the Judaic sages scarcely accorded recognition to Christianity and its challenge, that apologia for the Mishnah did not come to articulation. So once more we see the shape of Judaic doctrine framed outside of the intense exchange with Christianity. As for the Mishnah itself, its Judaism without Christianity contains not a hint that anyone has heard any such tale. The earliest apologists for the Mishnah knew nothing of the fully realized myth of the Dual Torah of Sinai. They never referred to the Mishnah as something out there, nor did they speak of the document as autonomous and complete. Only the two Talmuds, beginning with the Talmud of the Land of Israel, ca. A.D. 400, reveal that conception – alongside their mythic explanation of where the document came from and why it should be obeyed. So the first of the two Talmud's marks the change.

Still, the absence of even an implicit claim demands explanation. For when ancient Jews wanted to gain for their writings the status of revelation, of torah, or at least to link what they thought to what the Torah had said, they could do one of four things. They could sign the name of a holy man of old, for instance, Adam, Enoch, Ezra. They could imitate the Hebrew style of Scripture. They could claim that God had spoken to them. They could, at the very least, cite a verse of Scripture and impute to the cited passage their own opinion. These four methods – pseudepigraphy, stylistic imitation (hence, forgery), claim of direct revelation from God, and eisegesis – found no favor with the Mishnah's framers. To the contrary, they signed no name to their book. Their Hebrew was new in its syntax and morphology, completely unlike that of the Mosaic writings of the Pentateuch. They never claimed that God had anything to do with their opinions. They rarely cited a verse of Scripture as authority. It follows that, whatever the authors of the Mishnah said about their document, the implicit character of the book tells us that they did not claim God had dictated or even approved what they had to say. Why not? The framers simply ignored all the validating conventions of the world in which they lived. And, as I said, they failed to make explicit use of any others.

So the issue is clearly drawn. It is not whether we find in the Mishnah exaggerated claims about the priority of the disciple of a sage. We do find such claims. The issue is whether we find in the Mishnah the vivid assertion that whatever the sage has on the authority of his master in fact goes back to Sinai. We seek a definitive view that what the sage says falls into the classification of Torah, just as what Scripture says constitutes Torah from God to Moses. That is what distinguishes wisdom from the Torah as it emerges in the context of rabbinic Judaism. To state the outcome in advance: we do not find the Torah in the Mishnah, and the Mishnah is not part of the Torah.

About a generation after the formation of the Mishnah, around 250, a distinct tractate came to closure, called the Sayings of the Fathers, in Hebrew, Pirqé Abot. That tractate contained an elaborate set of sayings assigned to sages from Moses and Joshua to names occurring even in the Mishnah itself. This formed the first apologetic for the Mishnah. How so? In tractate Abot, Torah as status is instrumental. The figure of the sage, his ideals and conduct, forms the goal, focus and center. And the sage appears in the Mishnah and supplies the authority for the Mishnah. So the Mishnah is taught by sages, and what sages teach is Torah, and, it follows, the Mishnah is Torah – too. That is the syllogism of Abot. Let me unpack it.

Abot regards study of the Torah as what a sage does. The substance of the Torah to be studied is what a sage says. That is so whether or not the saying relates to scriptural revelation. The content of the sayings attributed to sages endows those sayings with status as part of the Torah of Sinai. In tractate Abot, the sages usually do not quote verses of Scripture and explain them, nor do they speak in God's name. Yet, it is clear, sages talk Torah. What follows? It is this: if a sage says something, what he says is Torah. More accurately, what he says falls into the classification of Torah. Accordingly, as I said, Abot treats Torah learning as symptomatic, an indicator of the status of the sage, hence, as I said, as merely instrumental. But then the Mishnah, which is taught by sages, forms part of the Torah, for sages teach it! But the tractate at hand does not say so explicitly, and the doctrine of a Dual Torah scarcely emerges. Only at the end of the fourth century, in the Talmud of the Land of Israel, will we find clear evidence that people were speculating about a Dual Torah, or, at least, teachings transmitted orally and in memory, as against teachings transmitted in writing.

So once more we come to the end of the fourth century, specifically, to the Talmud of the Land of Israel. As we shall now see, it is there in particular that the doctrine of the Dual Torah emerges for the first time in the unfolding canonical writings of the Judaism at hand. The Mishnah is held in the Talmud of the Land of Israel to be equivalent to Scripture (Y. Hor. 3:5). But the Mishnah is not called Torah or part of the Torah. Still, once the Mishnah entered the status of Scripture, it would take but a short step to a theory of the Mishnah as part of the revelation at Sinai – hence, Oral Torah. In the first Talmud we find the first glimmerings of an effort to theorize in general, not merely in detail, about how specific teachings of Mishnah relate to specific teachings of Scripture. The citing of scriptural prooftexts for Mishnah propositions, after all, would not have caused much surprise to the framers of the Mishnah; they themselves included such passages, though not often.

A particular abstract from the Talmud of the Land of Israel now demands attention. It will show us in a concrete way precisely the doctrine at hand. While the passage below does not make use of the language, Torah-in-writing and Torah-by-memory, it does refer to "the written" and "the oral." I believe myself fully justified in supplying the word Torah in square brackets. It makes the additional point that everything comes from Moses at Sinai. So the fully articulated theory of two Torahs (not merely one Torah in two forms) does not reach final expression in this passage. But short of explicit allusion to Torah-in-writing and Torah-by-memory, which (so far as I am able to discern) we find mainly in the Talmud of Babylonia, the ultimate theory of Torah of formative Judaism is at hand in what follows.

Y. *Hagigah* 1:7

V

- D. R. Zeirah in the name of R. Eleazar: "'Were I to write for him my laws by ten thousands, they would be regarded as a strange thing' (Hos. 8:12). Now is the greater part of the Torah written down? [Surely not. The oral part is much greater.] But more abundant are the matters which are derived by exegesis from the Written [Torah] than those derived by exegesis from the Oral [Torah]."
- E. And is that so?
- F. But more cherished are those matters which rest upon the written [Torah] than those which rest upon the Oral [Torah]....
- J. R. Haggai in the name of R. Samuel bar Nahman, "Some teachings were handed on orally, and some things were handed on in writing, and we do not know which of them is the more precious. But on the basis of that which is written, 'And the Lord said to Moses, Write these words; in accordance with these words I have made a covenant with you and with Israel' (Ex. 34:27), [we conclude] that the ones which are handed on orally are the more precious."
- K. R. Yohanan and R. Yudan b. R. Simeon – One said, "If you have kept what is preserved orally and also kept what is in writing, I shall make a covenant with you, and if not, I shall not make a covenant with you."
- L. The other said, "If you have kept what is preserved orally and you have kept what is preserved in writing, you shall receive a reward, and if not, you shall not receive a reward."

Here we have absolutely explicit evidence that people believed part of the Torah had been preserved not in writing but orally. Linking that part to the Mishnah remains a matter of implication. But it surely comes fairly close to the surface, when we are told that the Mishnah contains Torah traditions revealed at Sinai. From that view it requires only a small step to the allegation that the Mishnah is part of the Torah, the oral part. So – treating this story as a small part of the evidence on the issue in the Talmud of the Land of Israel – we conclude that the age of Constantine marks the point at which the Mishnah takes up its position as part of the Torah.

As we shall now see, because of the fresh definition of the Torah, all things received a new definition as well. From our viewpoint the most important transformation affected the Messiah, who, learned in the Torah, would be a sage, just as David in the rabbis' writings took his place in the sages' academy and taught Torah. As for Christians it was in Christ God made flesh, so the framers of the system of Judaism at hand found in the Torah that image of God to which Israel should aspire, and to which the sage in fact conformed. None of this had any bearing on the relationship with Christianity. But one thing did come to make a difference: the status of the Mishnah, on the one side, the standing of the sage, on the other. The one enjoyed the status of the Jews' law code, but it found no place in the Scripture that the Christians revered in common with the Jews. The other enjoyed authority and standing in Jewry, but on what basis? That question demanded an answer as part of the legitimation of the Judaism that flourished side by side with Christianity, the Judaism that invoked not only Scripture, which Christians acknowledged, but the writings of sages, which Christians did not recognize as God's will.

When constructing a systematic account of Judaism – that is, the worldview and way of life for Israel presented in the Mishnah – the philosophers of the Mishnah did not make use of the Messiah myth in the construction of a teleology for their system. They found it possible to present a statement of goals for their projected life of Israel which was entirely separate from appeals to history and eschatology. Since they certainly knew, and even alluded to, long-standing and widely held convictions on eschatological subjects, beginning with those in Scripture, the framers thereby testified that, knowing the larger repertoire, they made choices different from others before and after them. Their document accurately and ubiquitously expresses these choices, both affirmative and negative.

The appearance of a messianic eschatology fully consonant with the larger characteristic of the rabbinic system – with its stress on the viewpoints and prooftexts of Scripture, its interest in what was happening to Israel, its focus upon the national-historical dimension of the life of the group – indicates that the encompassing rabbinic system stands essentially autonomous of the prior, Mishnaic system. True, what had gone before was absorbed and fully assimilated. But the rabbinic system first appearing in the Talmud of the Land of Israel, is different in the aggregate from the Mishnaic system. It represents more, however, than a negative response to its predecessor. The rabbinic system of the two Talmuds, emerging in the first of the two at the end of the fourth century, took over the fundamental convictions of the Mishnaic worldview about the importance of Israel's constructing for itself a life beyond time. The rabbinic system then transformed the Messiah myth in its totality into an essentially ahistorical force. If people wanted to reach the end of time, they had to rise above time, that is, history, and stand off at the side of great movements of political and military character.

That is the message of the Messiah myth as it reaches full exposure in the rabbinic system of the two Talmuds. At its foundation it is precisely the message of teleology without eschatology expressed by the Mishnah and its associated documents. Accordingly, we cannot claim that the rabbinic or talmudic system in this regard constitutes a reaction against the Mishnaic one. We must conclude, quite to the contrary, that in the Talmuds and their associated documents we see the restatement in classical mythic form of the ontological convictions that had informed the minds of the second-century philosophers. The new medium contained the old and enduring message: Israel must turn away from time and change, submit to whatever happens, so as to win for itself the only government worth having, that is, God's rule, accomplished through God's anointed agent, the Messiah.

Within the Judaism born in the centuries after 70, the distinct traditions of priest, sage, and messianist, were joined in a new way. In the person of the sage, that is, rabbi, holy man, Torah incarnate, avatar and model of the son of David, rabbinic Judaism found its hero and symbol. So the diverse varieties of Judaic piety present in Israel before 70 came to be bonded over the next several centuries in a wholly unprecedented way, with each party to the union imposing its logic upon the other constituents of the whole. The ancient categories remained. But they were so profoundly revised and transformed that nothing was preserved intact. Through the person and figure of the rabbi, the whole burden of Israel's heritage was taken up, renewed, and handed on from late antiquity to the present day.

The character of the Israelite Scriptures, with their emphasis upon historical narrative as a mode of theological explanation, leads us to expect all Judaisms to evolve as eschatological in their definition of their goals. We should therefore anticipate all Judaisms will be deeply messianic religions, since the eschatological focus in the nature of things draws in its wake some sort of messianic doctrine, at least, among Judaisms (and all the more so Christianities). With all prescribed actions pointed toward the coming of the Messiah at the end of time, and all interest focused upon answering the historical-salvific questions ("how long?"), the Judaism of the Dual Torah presents no surprises. Its liturgy evokes historical events to prefigure salvation; prayers of petition repeatedly turn to the speedy coming of the Messiah; and the experience of worship invariably leaves the devotee expectant and hopeful.

Yet, for a brief moment, the Mishnah – again seen as our "sages' Judaism without Christianity" – presented a Judaism in which history did not define the main framework of teleology. In the Mishnah, therefore, the issue of teleology took a form other than the familiar eschatological one and – as I shall explain presently – historical events were absorbed into an ahistorical system through their trivialization within encompassing, ahistorical taxonomic structures. In the kind of Judaism in this document, Messiahs to be sure played a part. But these were mere "anointed men," for example, a priest of a certain classification, an "anointed priest," and they had no distinctive historical role. The figures in the classification of anointed undertook a task quite different from that assigned to Jesus by the framers of the Gospels. As is clear, they were merely a species of priest, falling into one classification rather than another.

So let us ask the Mishnah its answers to the questions at hand: What of the Messiah? When will he come? To whom, in Israel, will he come? And what must, or can, we do while we wait to hasten his coming? If we now reframe these questions and divest them of their mythic cloak, we ask about the Mishnah's theory of the history and destiny of Israel and the purpose of the Mishnah's own system in relationship to Israel's present and end: the implicit teleology of the philosophical law at hand. Answering these questions out of the resources of the Mishnah is not possible. The Mishnah presents no large view of history. It contains no reflection whatever on the nature and meaning of the destruction of the Temple in 70, an event which surfaces only in connection with some changes in the law explained as resulting from the end of the cult. The Mishnah pays no attention to the matter of the end time. The word "salvation" is rare, "sanctification" commonplace. More strikingly, the framers of the Mishnah are virtually silent on the teleology of the system; they never tell us why we should do what the Mishnah tells us, let alone explain what will happen if we do. Incidents in the Mishnah are preserved either as narrative settings for the statement of the law, or, occasionally, as precedents. Historical events are classified and turned into entries on lists. But incidents in any case come few and far between. True, events do make an impact. But it always is for the Mishnah's own purpose and within its own taxonomic system and rule-seeking mode of thought. To be sure, the framers of the Mishnah may also have had a theory of the Messiah and of the meaning of Israel's history and destiny. But they kept it hidden, and their document manages to provide an immense account of Israel's life without explicitly telling us about such matters.

The Messiah in the Mishnah does not stand at the forefront of the framers' consciousness. The issues encapsulated in the myth and person of the Messiah are scarcely addressed. The framers of the Mishnah do not resort to speculation about the Messiah as a historical-supernatural figure. So far as that kind of speculation provides the vehicle for reflection on salvific issues, or in mythic terms, narratives on the meaning of history and the destiny of Israel, we cannot say that the Mishnah's philosophers take up those encompassing categories of being: Where are we heading? What can we do about it? That does not mean questions found urgent in the aftermath of the destruction of the Temple and the disaster of Bar Kokhba failed to attract the attention of the Mishnah's sages. But they treated history in a different way, offering their own answers to its questions. To these we now turn. Indeed, given the stress, in the Judaisms of the nineteenth and twentieth century, on history as the source of proof-texts for Jewish belief, we had best examine with some care the view of history defined at the beginning.

For one of the stunning differences between the Judaism of the Dual Torah and the Judaisms of the nineteenth and twentieth century lies in the resort, by the latter, to proofs from "historical facts." To the framers of the Mishnah and the Talmud of the Land of Israel (as well as the other writings of the age), historical facts by themselves proved nothing and added up to nothing. Claims to continue the Judaism of the Dual Torah resting on appeals to history and to the laws of history misunderstand how the received Judaism understood history and disposed of its laws.

By "history" I mean not merely events, but how events serve to teach lessons, reveal patterns, tell us what we must do and what will happen to us tomorrow. But what lessons, in that sense, can history teach? In that context, some events contain richer lessons than others; the destruction of the Temple of Jerusalem teaches more than a crop failure, being kidnapped into slavery more than stubbing one's toe. Furthermore, lessons taught by events – "history" in the didactic sense – follow a progression from trivial and private to consequential and public. The framers of the Mishnah refer to very few events, treating those they do mention with a focus quite separate from the unfolding events themselves. They rarely create narratives; historical events do not supply organizing categories or taxonomic classifications. We find no tractate devoted to the destruction of the Temple, no complete chapter detailing the events of Bar Kokhba nor even a sustained celebration of the events of the sages' own historical lives. When things that have happened are mentioned, it is neither to narrate nor to interpret and draw lessons from the events. It is either to illustrate a point of law or to pose a problem of the law – always *en passant*, never in a pointed way.

How then does the Mishnah treat historical events? The Mishnah absorbs into its encompassing system all events, small and large. With them the sages accomplish what they accomplish in everything else: a vast labor of taxonomy, an immense construction of the order and rules governing the classification of everything on earth and in heaven. The disruptive character of history – one-time events of ineluctable significance – scarcely impresses these philosophers. They find no difficulty in showing that what appears unique and beyond classification has in fact happened before and so falls within the range of trustworthy rules and known procedures. Once history's components, one-time events, lose their distinctiveness, then history as a didactic intellectual construct, as a source of lessons and rules, also loses all pertinence. History becomes cyclical, an exercise in the reenactment of what was at the beginning – or is coming at the end.

So lessons and rules come from sorting things out and classifying them, hence deriving from the procedures and modes of thought of the philosopher or the social scientist seeking regularity. To this labor of taxonomy, the historian's way of selecting data and arranging them into patterns of meaning to teach lessons proves inconsequential. One-time events are not important. The world is composed of nature and supernature. The laws that count are those to be discovered in heaven and, in heaven's creation and counterpart, on earth. Keep those laws and things will work out. Break them, and the result is predictable: calamity of whatever sort will supervene in accordance with the rules. But just because it is predictable, a catastrophic happening testifies to what has always been and must always be, in accordance with reliable rules and within categories already discovered and well explained. That is why the lawyer-philosophers of the mid second century produced the Mishnah – to explain how things are. Within the framework of well-classified rules, there could be Messiahs, but no single Messiah.

If the end of time and the coming of the Messiah do not serve to explain, for the Mishnah's system, why people should do what the Mishnah says, then what alternative teleology does the Mishnah's first apologetic, Abot, provide? Only when we appreciate the clear answers given in that document of ca. 250, shall we grasp how remarkable is the shift, which took place in later documents of the rabbinic canon, to a messianic framing of the issues of the Torah's ultimate purpose and value. Let us see how the framers of Abot, in the aftermath of the creation of the Mishnah, explain the purpose and goal of the Mishnah: an ahistorical, non-messianic teleology. Whatever teleology the Mishnah as such would ever acquire would derive from Abot, which presents statements to express the ethos and ethic of the Mishnah, and so provides a kind of theory.

Abot agreed with the Mishnah's other sixty-two tractates: history proved no more important here than it had been before. With scarcely a word about history and no account of events at all, Abot manages to provide an ample account of how the Torah – written and oral, thus in later eyes, Scripture and Mishnah – came down to its own day. Accordingly, the passage of time as such plays no role in the explanation of the origins of the document, nor is the Mishnah presented as eschatological. Occurrences of great weight ("history") are never invoked. How then does the tractate tell the story of Torah, narrate the history of God's revelation to Israel, encompassing both Scripture and Mishnah? The answer is that Abot's framers manage to do their work of explanation without telling a story or invoking history at all. They pursue a different way of answering the same question, by exploiting a nonhistorical mode of thought and method of legitimation. And that is the main point: teleology serves the purpose of legitimation, and hence is accomplished in ways other than explaining how things originated or assuming that historical fact explains anything.

Disorderly historical events entered the system of the Mishnah and found their place within the larger framework of the Mishnah's orderly world. But to claim that the Mishnah's framers merely ignored what was happening would be incorrect. They worked out their own way of dealing with historical events, the disruptive power of which they not only conceded but freely recognized. Further, the Mishnah's authors did not intend to compose a history book or a work of prophecy or apocalypse. Even if they had wanted to narrate the course of events, they could hardly have done so through the medium of the Mishnah. Yet the Mishnah presents its philosophy in full awareness of the issues of historical calamity confronting the Jewish nation. So far as the philosophy of the document confronts the totality of Israel's existence, the Mishnah by definition also presents a philosophy of history. So much for Judaism framed in majestic indifference to the "daughter" religion, Christianity. Historical questions, asking about the meaning of large-scale patterns of events, each standing in line as a unique happening, bearing a heavy burden of meaning, scarcely demand attention.

The Mishnah's subordination of historical events contradicts the emphasis of a thousand years of Israelite thought. The biblical histories, the ancient prophets, the apocalyptic visionaries all had testified that events themselves were important. Events carried the message of the living God. Events constituted history, pointed toward, and so explained, Israel's destiny. An essentially ahistorical system of timeless sanctification, worked out through construction of an eternal rhythm which centered on the movement of the moon and stars and seasons, represented a life chosen by few outside of the priesthood. Furthermore, the pretense that what happens matters less than what is testified against palpable and memorable reality. Israel had suffered enormous loss of life. The Talmud of the Land of Israel takes these events seriously and treats them as unique and remarkable. The memories proved real. The hopes evoked by the Mishnah's promise of sanctification of a world in static perfection did not. For they had to compete with the grief of an entire century of mourning.

That brings us to the doctrines that reached expression in writings at the end of the fourth century. The most important change is the shift in historical thinking adumbrated in the pages of the Talmud of the Land of Israel, a shift from focus upon the Temple and its supernatural history to close attention to the people Israel and its natural, this-worldly history. Once Israel, holy Israel, had come to form the counterpart to the Temple and its supernatural life, that other history – Israel's – would stand at the center of things. Accordingly, a new sort of memorable event came to the fore in the Talmud of the Land of Israel. Let me give this new history appropriate emphasis: *it was the story of Israel's suffering, remembrance of that suffering, on the one side, and an effort to explain events of such tragedy, on the other.*

So a composite "history" constructed out of the Talmud of the Land of Israel's units of discourse which were pertinent to consequential events would contain long chapters on what happened to Israel, the Jewish people, and not only, or mainly, what had earlier occurred in the Temple. The components of the historical theory of Israel's sufferings were manifold. First and foremost, history taught moral lessons. Historical events entered into the construction of a teleology for the Talmud of the Land of Israel's system of Judaism as a whole. What the law demanded reflected the consequences of wrongful action on the part of Israel. So, again, Israel's own deeds defined the events of history. Rome's role, like Assyria's and Babylonia's, depended upon Israel's provoking divine wrath as it was executed by the great empire. Israel had to learn the lesson of its history to also take command of its own destiny.

But this notion of determining one's own destiny should not be misunderstood. The framers of the Talmud of the Land of Israel were not telling the Jews to please God by doing commandments in order that they should thereby gain control of their own destiny. To the contrary, the paradox of the Talmud of the Land of Israel's system lies in the fact that Israel can free itself of control by other nations only by humbly agreeing to accept God's rule. The nations – Rome, in the present instance – rest on one side of the balance, while God rests on the other. Israel must then choose between them. There is no such thing for Israel as freedom from both God and the nations, total autonomy and

Judaism in the Matrix of Christianity *Reconsidered*

independence. There is only a choice of masters, a ruler on earth or a ruler in heaven.

With propositions such as these, the framers of the Mishnah will certainly have concurred. And why not? For the fundamental affirmations of the Mishnah about the centrality of Israel's perfection in stasis – sanctification – readily prove congruent to the attitudes at hand. Once the Messiah's coming had become dependent upon Israel's condition – hence, Israel's sanctification – and not upon Israel's actions in historical time aimed at bringing salvation, then the Mishnah's system will have imposed its fundamental and definitive character upon the Messiah myth. An eschatological teleology framed through that myth then would prove wholly appropriate to the method of the larger system of the Mishnah. The Messiah then enters the system in the Talmud of the Land of Israel, but he does so as a sage. And what characterizes the true Messiah is his message: submission to God's will. There is nothing to do, but Israel has a task of being: becoming holy. The mark of sanctification? Submission to God's will as revealed in the Torah.

How shall we know that the Messiah doctrine I have outlined is paramount? It is by asking, what makes a Messiah a false Messiah? In this Talmud, it is not his claim to save Israel, but his claim to save Israel without the help of God. The meaning of the true Messiah is Israel's total submission, through the Messiah's gentle rule, to God's yoke and service. So God is not to be manipulated through Israel's humoring of heaven in rite and cult. The notion of keeping the commandments so as to please heaven and get God to do what Israel wants is totally incongruent to the text at hand. Keeping the commandments as a mark of submission, loyalty, humility before God is the rabbinic system of salvation. So Israel does not "save itself." Israel never controls its own destiny, either on earth or in heaven. The only choice is whether to place one's fate into the hands of cruel, deceitful men, or to trust in the living God of mercy and love. We shall now see how this critical position is spelled out in the setting of discourse about the Messiah in the Talmud of the Land of Israel.

Bar Kokhba, above all, exemplifies arrogance against God. He lost the war because of that arrogance. In particular, he ignored the authority of sages:

Y. *Taanit* 4:5

X

J. Said R. Yohanan, "Upon orders of Caesar Hadrian, they killed eight hundred thousand in Betar."

K. Said R. Yohanan, "There were eighty thousand pairs of trumpeteers surrounding Betar. Each one was in charge of a

	number of troops. Ben Kozeba was there and he had two hundred thousand troops who, as a sign of loyalty, had cut off their little fingers.
L.	"Sages sent word to him, 'How long are you going to turn Israel into a maimed people.
M.	"He said to them, 'How otherwise is it possible to test them?'
N.	"They replied to him, 'Whoever cannot uproot a cedar of Lebanon while riding on his horse will not be inscribed on your military rolls.'
O.	"So there were two hundred thousand who qualified in one way, and another two hundred thousand who qualified in another way."
P.	When he would go forth to battle, he would say, "Lord of the world! Do not help and do not hinder us! 'Hast thou not rejected us, O God? Thou dost not go forth, O God, with our armies'" (Ps. 60:10).
Q.	Three and a half years did Hadrian besiege Betar.
R.	R. Eleazar of Modiin would sit on sackcloth and ashes and pray every day, saying "Lord of the ages! Do not judge in accord with strict judgment this day! Do not judge in accord with strict judgment this day!"
S.	Hadrian wanted to go to him. A Samaritan said to him, "Do not go to him until I see what he is doing, and so hand over the city [of Betar] to you. [Make peace ...for you.]"
T.	He got into the city through a drain pipe. He went and found R. Eleazar of Modiin standing and praying. He pretended to whisper something in his ear.
U.	The townspeople say [the Samaritan] do this and brought him to Ben Kozeba. They told him, "We saw this man having dealings with your friend."
V.	[Bar Kokhba] said to him, "What did you say to him, and what did he say to you?"
W.	He said to [the Samaritan], "If I tell you, then the king will kill me, and if I do not tell you, then you will kill me. It is better that the king kill me, and not you.
X.	"[Eleazar] said to me, 'I should hand over my city.' ['I shall make peace ....']"
Y.	He turned to R. Eleazar of Modiin. He said to him, "What did this Samaritan say to you?"
Z.	He replied, "Nothing."
AA.	He said to him, "What did you say to him?"
BB.	He said to him, "Nothing."
CC.	[Ben Kozeba] gave [Eleazar] one good kick and killed him.
DD.	Forthwith an echo came forth and proclaimed the following verse:
EE.	"Woe to my worthless shepherd, who deserts the flock! May the sword smite his arm and his right eye! Let his arm be wholly withered, his right eye utterly blinded! (Zech. 11:17).
FF.	"You have murdered R. Eleazar of Modiin, the right arm of all Israel, and their right eye. Therefore may the right arm of that man wither, may his right eye be utterly blinded!"
GG.	Forthwith Betar was taken, and Ben Kozeba was killed.

We notice two complementary themes. First, Bar Kokhba treats heaven with arrogance, asking God merely to keep out of the way. Second, he treats an especially revered sage with a parallel arrogance. The sage had the power to preserve Israel. Bar Kokhba destroyed Israel's one protection. The result was inevitable. The Messiah, the centerpiece of salvation history and hero of the tale, emerged as a critical figure. The historical theory of this Talmud of the Land of Israel passage is stated very simply. In their view Israel had to choose between wars, either the war fought by Bar Kokhba or the "war for Torah." "Why had they been punished? It was because of the weight of the war, for they had not wanted to engage in the struggles over the meaning of the Torah." Those struggles, which were ritual arguments about ritual matters, promised the only victory worth winning. Then Israel's history would be written in terms of wars over the meaning of the Torah and the decision of the law.

Gentile kings are boastful; Israelite kings are humble. So, in all, the Messiah myth deals with a very concrete and limited consideration of the national life and character. The theory of Israel's history and destiny as it was expressed within that myth interprets matters in terms of a single criterion. What others within the Israelite world had done or in the future would do with the conviction that, at the end of time, God would send a (or the) Messiah to "save" Israel, it was a single idea for the sages of the Mishnah and the Talmuds and collections of scriptural exegesis. And that conception stands at the center of their system; it shapes and is shaped by their system. In context, the Messiah expresses the system's meaning and so makes it work.

True, the skins are new, but the wine is very old. For while we speak of sages and learning, the message is the familiar one. It is Israel's history that works out and expresses Israel's relationship with God. The critical dimension of Israel's life, therefore, is salvation, the definitive trait, a movement in time from now to then. It follows that the paramount and organizing category is history and its lessons. In the Talmud of the Land of Israel we witness, among the Mishnah's heirs, a striking reversion to biblical convictions about the centrality of history in the definition of Israel's reality. The heavy weight of prophecy, apocalyptic, and biblical historiography, with their emphasis upon salvation and on history as the indicator of Israel's salvation, stood against the Mishnah's quite separate thesis of what truly mattered. What, from their viewpoint, demanded description and analysis and required interpretation? It was the category of sanctification, for eternity. The true issue framed by history and apocalypse was how to move toward the foreordained end of salvation, how to act in time to reach salvation at the end of time. The Mishnah's teleology beyond time and its capacity to posit an eschatology without a place for a historical Mishnah take a position beyond that of the entire antecedent sacred literature of Israel. Only one strand, the priestly one, had ever taken so extreme a position on the centrality of sanctification and the peripheral nature of salvation. Wisdom had stood in between, with its own concerns, drawing attention both to what happened and to what endured. But to Wisdom what finally mattered was not nature or supernature, but rather abiding relationships in historical time.

So at the end of the fourth century the system emerges from the Talmud of the Land of Israel complete, each of its parts stating precisely the same message as is revealed in the whole. The issue of the Messiah and the meaning of Israel's history framed through the Messiah myth convey in their terms precisely the same position that we find everywhere else in all other symbolic components of the rabbinic system and canon. The heart of the matter then is Israel's subservience to God's will, as expressed in the Torah and embodied in the teachings and lives of the great sages. When Israel fully accepts God's rule, then the Messiah will come. Until Israel subjects itself to God's rule, the Jews will be subjugated to pagan domination. Since the condition of Israel governs, Israel itself holds the key to its own redemption. But this it can achieve only by throwing away the key!

The paradox must be crystal clear: Israel acts to redeem itself through the opposite of self-determination, namely, by subjugating itself to God. Israel's power lies in its negation of power. Its destiny lies in giving up all pretense at deciding its own destiny. So weakness is the ultimate strength, forbearance the final act of self-assertion, passive resignation the sure step toward liberation. (The parallel is the crucified Christ.) Israel's freedom is engraved on the tablets of the commandments of God: to be free is freely to obey. That is not the meaning associated with these words in the minds of others who, like the sages of the rabbinical canon, declared their view of what Israel must do to secure the coming of the Messiah.

It remains to ask a simple question: why the shift from the symbolic expression of the Mishnah's teleology in non-eschatological terms, such as we find in tractate Abot, to the profoundly eschatological formulation of the symbol emerging in the Talmud of the Land of Israel. In my judgment the issue of the political triumph of Christ in the Roman Empire made ineluctable the confrontation with the Messiah question. For at issue is not what sages said. As I have emphasized, I do not think they said a great deal that had not been stated in non-eschatological, non-messianic terms, by their predecessors. At issue is the mode of symbolic expression selected to convey that enduring message. If I had to explain to despairing Jews what had happened with the Christian takeover of the roman Empire, I do not see how I could avoid confronting the question of the Messiah. Specifically, if not this one, why not? The answer I see before us: because the Messiah is not going to be a king but a sage. And the kings of the gentiles do not qualify for they are arrogant. The counterpart, the sages of Israel, will qualify, through humility and conciliation and acceptance of God's will. So the upshot is a simple and strikingly relevant message: "do not despair but hope, do not rebel but accept and humbly submit, do not mistake the present for the end, which, even now, we may attain by fulfilling, by embodying the Torah."

Sages therefore presented remarkably pertinent doctrines in documents closed at the end of the first Christian century of the West. These encompassed an explanation of the authority of the Dual Torah taught by sages, an account of the meaning of Scripture as sages read it, and a clear statement on the now-urgent Messiah question. Not only so, but in their writings, sages composed a position on issues defined by Christian theologians in the same way, worked out through the same arguments, on the foundation of the same body of facts. These shared issues concerned the meaning of history, the character and identity of the Messiah, and the definition of Israel. In all, therefore, we find a systematic confrontation on a program confronting both parties for a single reason. And that reason? The political revolution accomplished by Constantine's Christian continuators.

The fact that Judaic sages conceived doctrines on a program of issues shared with Christianity would shape the future history of the Judaism formed by those sages. For as Christianity continued to harp on the same points, as it did, the Judaic party to the dispute for centuries to come could refer to the generative symbols and determinative myths of the sages' Judaism, which, to begin with dealt with these very issues. The Christian challenge, delivered through instruments of state and society, demanded a Judaic response, one involving not merely manipulation of power but exercise of intellect. Jews, continuing as a distinct society, took to heart the negative message of Christianity – "the Messiah has already come, you have no hope in the future, you are not Israel anyhow, and history proves we are right." Sages produced responses to these questions, with doctrines of the meaning of history, of the conditions in which the Messiah will come to Israel, and of the definition of Israel. The sages' Judaism's symbolic system, with its stress on Torah, the eschatological teleology of that system, with stress on the Messiah-sage coming to obedient Israel, the insistence on the equivalence of Israel and Rome, Jacob and Esau, with Esau penultimate and Israel at the end of time – these constituted in Israel powerful responses to the Christian question.

In a profound sense, therefore, the Judaism that reached canonical expression in the late fourth century succeeded in Israel because it dealt in a strikingly relevant way with both the issues and the politics of the Christian world within which Jews lived. The issues carried intellectual weight, the politics imparted to those issues urgency and power. Because of politics the issues demanded attention. Had the doctrines focused on matters not at issue at all, and had the points of direct confrontation not elicited response within Judaism, then the Judaism at hand would have proved itself simply irrelevant and died of the attrition of sheer disinterest. We know that that is the fact, for when we deal with a world that confronted Israel, the Jewish people, with other challenges enjoying self-evident urgency, the Judaism of the sages lost in large sectors of Israel its standing as self-evidently true and right.

Specifically, when we come to the world no longer defined by Christian politics and culture in any form, we deal with precisely a situation in which the inherited Judaism ceased to address urgent questions, and new compositions of symbols and systems of ideas, invented in some measure out of the received writings of ancient times to be sure, would emerge to do so. The Judaism of the canon of the later fourth century and beyond, therefore, flourished when the world to which it spoke found persuasive not the answers alone, but the very questions deemed paramount and pressing. And that Judaism ceased to speak to Jews when its message proved incongruent to the questions Jews found they had to answer. The critical issue, therefore, was congruence to circumstance – rather than truth or self-evidence of answers – and circumstance, to begin with, found salient traits in the conditions of politics: people acting together in an organized way.

14

The Talmud of Babylonia System or Tradition? A Reprise of Seven Monographs

The Talmud of Babylonia, also known as the Bavli, is a vast, anonymous writing, which has served for the community of Judaism as the principal and authoritative statement of canonical theology and law. Reaching closure by the end of the seventh century, on the eve of the birth of Islam, the document together with its commentaries, codes of its laws, and compilations of ad hoc decisions ("responsa"), defined Judaism. The importance of the Bavli as the foundation document of a complex and various set of societies, located in Asia, Europe, Africa, and North and South America, cannot be overstated. Anyone interested in media for the representation, in words, of the entirety of the social order – indeed, of a theory of world order extended from here to eternity – will find in the Talmud of Babylonia an important example of writing for a utopian constitution. The anonymity of the writing, its use of two languages, its form as a commentary to a prior document, and the ubiquity of its never-identified "voice" – these paramount traits make analysis of the document exceedingly difficult. And yet, if we want to know how language serves to set forth a vision of the social order, we shall have to find out how such a foundation document is composed. For in investigating the components and the composition of the writing, we may hope to follow the passage of a vision of society from the imagination of intellectuals to the practical and concrete formulation of writers.

One fundamental problem that requires closest attention is whether a document of this kind derives from a long agglutinative process, as the sediment of the ages accumulates into a hard tradition, or whether heirs of diverse materials reshape and restate the whole in a single formulation of their own. What is at stake in solving that problem is knowledge of how foundation-documents emerge: over time, through tradition, or all at once, through the intellection of some few persons working together in one specific context? If the former, then in the formative history of the writing, we trace what we may rightly call tradition – a historical study. If the latter, then in the analytical deconstruction and reconstitution of the tradition the framers set before us a single cogent vision, formulated into words at some one moment, a system, whole and complete – a philosophical study. In a series of seven monographs, I have examined the literary traits of the Bavli with decisive results in favor of the hypothesis that the Bavli forms not the outcome of a long sedimentary tradition, but the statement of its own framers (whether we call them compilers, authors, editors, or an authorship does not matter). Since colleagues in other fields, though interested in the methodological issues and substantive results, may find tedious the close reading of these seven books, I briefly summarize in this reprise the principal components of a large-scale and sustained research project that has come to conclusion.

Before setting forth the main results, I have to make reference to my work of (re)translating the Bavli,[1] which was required before any

---

[1] I refer to the following:
The Talmud of Babylonia. An American Translation (Chico, 1984-1985: Scholars Press for Brown Judaic Studies).

I.	*Tractate Berakhot.*
VI.	*Tractate Sukkah.*
XVII.	*Tractate Sotah.*
XXIII.A.	*Tractate Sanhedrin. Chapters I-III.*
XXIII.B.	*Tractate Sanhedrin. Chapters IV-VIII.*
XXIII.C.	*Tractate Sanhedrin. Chapters IX-XI.*
XXXII.	*Tractate Arakhin.*

The Talmud of Babylonia. An American Translation (Atlanta, 1990: Scholars Press for Brown Judaic Studies).

XXI.A.	*Tractate Baba Mesia. Introduction. Chapters One and Two.*
XXI.B.	*Tractate Baba Mesia. Chapters Three and Four.*
XXI.C.	*Tractate Baba Mesia. Chapters Five and Six.*
XXI.D.	*Tractate Bava Mesia. Chapters Seven through Ten.*
XXV.A.	*Tractate Abodah Zarah. Chapters One and Two.*
XXV.B.	*Tractate Abodah Zarah. Chapters Three, Four, and Five.*
XXXI.A.	*Tractate Bekhorot. Chapters One through Four.*
XXXI.B.	*Tractate Bekhorot. Chapters Five through Nine.*
XXXIII.	*Tractate Temurah.*
XXXIV.	*Tractate Keritot.*
XXXVI.A.	*Tractate Niddah. Chapters One through Three.*
XXXVI.B.	*Tractate Niddah. Chapters Four through Ten.*

The Talmud of Babylonia: System or Tradition?

analytical inquiry could commence. The reason is that the main problem in analyzing a sample of the Talmud of Babylonia is presented by the run-on character of the writing. Visually, what we see whether in the original languages or in English or German, Spanish or French or Italian, or any of the other languages into which the document has been translated whole or in part, simply are long columns of undifferentiated words, the sole division between a set of sentences drawn from the Mishnah and (ordinarily) much longer and more elaborate discussion of those sentences. Substantively, what we quickly perceive is that a passage of the Bavli moves far beyond the limits of Mishnah commentary, and that movement twists and turns, so that a vast amount of information will be introduced that is only tangentially relevant to the starting point in the Mishnah. Before any picture of the rules of composition of the document can emerge, we have to devise a method of identifying a whole unit of thought – beginning to end – and differentiating among its parts. This is not merely a formal problem, readily solved, as I had solved it two decades ago, by marking off chapters, paragraphs, and sentences (to draw on the metaphor of contemporary division).[2] It is a problem of a very substantial order. The reason is that the Bavli on the surface appears to be run-on, and many have found the writing to be not only confusing but confused, the result of a stream of consciousness, not propositional, not crafted and purposive at all.

The run-on and meandering quality of a Talmudic discussion is difficult to analyze as a single, cogent composition, and therefore impossible to classify as the work of showing how the Bavli's one voice

---

The Talmud of Babylonia. An American Translation (Atlanta, 1991: Scholars Press for Brown Judaic Studies).

XXVIII.A.	*Tractate Zebahim.*	*Chapters One through Three.*
XXVIII.B.	*Tractate Zebahim.*	*Chapters Four through Seven.*
XXVIII.C.	*Tractate Zebahim.*	*Chapters Eight through Ten.*
XXIX.A.	*Tractate Menahot.*	*Chapters One through Three.*
XXIX.B.	*Tractate Menahot.*	*Chapters Four through Seven.*
XXIX.C.	*Tractate Menahot.*	*Chapters Eight through Thirteen.*

[2] I published my results, in the context of the analysis of the Mishnah's division of purities, in *A History of the Mishnaic Law of Purities* (Leiden, 1977: Brill). XXI. *The Redaction and Formulation of the Order of Purities in the Mishnah and Tosefta.* There I showed how "chapter, subdivision of a chapter, a paragraph, and a sentence" (marked in my reference system by a capital Roman numeral, a Roman numeral in small letters, an Arabic numeral, and a capital letter serve as metaphors for "completed unit of systematic exposition, subunit of exposition, formation of the smallest whole units of thought into a cogent statement, and the smallest whole units of thought," respectively, would do its work.

speaks, until we realize a simple fact. The Talmud of Babylonia in contemporary terms would be presented heavy with footnotes and appendices. That is, in our mode of setting forth our ideas and the documentation for them, we include in our text the main points of proposition, evidence, and argument; we relegate to footnotes the sources upon which we draw; we place in appendices substantial bodies of secondary material, relevant to the main body of our text only tangentially, yet required for a full presentation of what we wish to say. The authorship of the Talmud of Babylonia accomplishes, within the technical limitations that governed its formulation of its proposition, evidence, and argument, what we work out through footnotes and appendices. Much of the materials subordinated to the proposition, evidence, and argument, derives from finished pieces of writing, worked out for use in a document we do not now have (and cannot even imagine!), now providing useful, if not essential, documentation for the document that we do have. Accordingly, my retranslation, for analytical purposes, made possible the work that is described here.

1. *The Bavli and its Sources: The Question of Tradition in the Case of Tractate Sukkah.* Atlanta, 1987: Scholars Press for Brown Judaic Studies.

Having worked out [1] the description of texts, read one by one, in such works as my *Judaism: The Evidence of the Mishnah, The Integrity of Leviticus Rabbah,* and parallel studies,[3] to [2] the analysis of those same texts seen in relationship to one another, that is, to comparison and contrast among a set of documents, hence to connection, as in *Judaism: The Classical Statement. The Evidence of the Bavli,* on the relationship of the Yerushalmi and the Bavli, *Comparative Midrash: The Plan and Program of Genesis Rabbah and Leviticus Rabbah* and *From Tradition to Imitation: The Plan and Program of Pesiqta deRab Kahana and Pesiqta Rabbati,*[4] I here proceeded to [3] the interpretation

---

[3]*Judaism. The Evidence of the Mishnah* (Chicago, 1981: University of Chicago Press. Paperback edition: 1984. Second printing, 1985. Third printing, 1986. Second edition, augmented: Atlanta, 1987: Scholars Press for Brown Judaic Studies); *The Integrity of Leviticus Rabbah. The Problem of the Autonomy of a Rabbinic Document* (Chico, 1985: Scholars Press for Brown Judaic Studies).

[4]*Judaism: The Classical Statement. The Evidence of the Bavli* (Chicago, 1986: University of Chicago Press); *Comparative Midrash: The Plan and Program of Genesis Rabbah and Leviticus Rabbah* (Atlanta, 1986: Scholars Press for Brown Judaic Studies). *From Tradition to Imitation. The Plan and Program of Pesiqta deRab Kahana and Pesiqta Rabbati* (Atlanta, 1987: Scholars Press for Brown Judaic Studies). [With a fresh translation of Pesiqta Rabbati *Pisqaot* 1-5, 15];

of texts under the aspect of continuity. When we describe the relationships between two documents or among three or more, we know what a given group of editors or authorities has contributed on its own, and also how that authorship restated or reworked what it received from a prior group. The authorship of a document that stands in a relationship of connection to prior writings will make use of their materials essentially in its own way. The authorship of a document that works in essential continuity with prior writings will cite and quote and refine those received writings but will ordinarily not undertake a fundamentally original statement of its own framed in terms of its own and on a set of issues defined separately from the received writings or formulations. In this monograph, for Bavli-tractate Sukkah, I showed that the Bavli proves connected with earlier documents and also with some received sayings not written down in a systematic way in prior compilations. But the connections appear episodic and haphazard, not systematic, except in respect to the Mishnah. The Bavli cannot be shown systematically and generally to continue the program and inquiry of predecessors. The Bavli contains ample selections from available writings. The authorship of the Bavli leaves no doubt that it makes extensive use of extant materials, sayings and stories. But in the Bavli we deal with an authorship of amazingly independent mind, working independently and in an essentially original way on materials on which others have handed on a quite persuasive and cogent statement. Tosefta on the one side, Scripture and a heritage of conventional reading thereof on the other – neither has defined the program of our document or determined the terms in which it would make its statement, though both, in a subordinated position and in a paltry limited measure, are given some sort of a say. The Bavli is connected to a variety of prior writings but continuous with none of them.

2. *Making the Classics in Judaism: The Three Stages of Literary Formation*. Atlanta, 1990: Scholars Press for Brown Judaic Studies.

Two questions in the framing of a theory of the history of the anonymous literature of formative Judaism form the program of this book. The first is, what is the correct starting point of analysis of a document and its formative history? The second is, what are the

---

Note also *Canon and Connection: Intertextuality in Judaism* (Lanham, 1986: University Press of America). *Studies in Judaism* Series, and *Midrash as Literature: The Primacy of Documentary Discourse* (Lanham, 1987: University Press of America). *Studies in Judaism* Series; and *Midrash as Literature: The Primacy of Documentary Discourse* (Lanham, 1987: University Press of America). *Studies in Judaism* Series.

principal results of starting from that designated point of entry? I test the hypothesis that the discrete sayings (lemmas) form the correct point of entry and show, through the formation and testing of a null hypothesis, that that hypothesis is false. We cannot begin work in the assumption that the building block of documents is the smallest whole unit of thought, the lemma, nor can we proceed in the premise that a lemma traverses the boundaries of various documents and is unaffected by the journey. The opposite premise is that we start our work with the traits of documents as a whole, rather than with the traits of the lemmas of which documents are (supposedly) composed. Since, in a variety of books, I had set forth the documentary hypothesis for the analysis of the rabbinic literature of late antiquity,[5] I turned immediately to the exploration of the second of the two possibilities. How shall we proceed, if we take as our point of entry the character and conditions of the document of integrity, seen whole? Once I have demonstrated beyond any doubt that a rabbinic text is a well-crafted text and not merely a compilation of this and that, and further specified in acute detail precisely the aesthetic, formal, and logical program followed by each of those texts, I am able to move to the logical next step. That is to show that in the background of the documents that we have is writing of three types: [1] writing that is not shaped by documentary requirements, [2] writing that is not shaped by the documentary requirements of the compilations we now have, and also [3] writing that is entirely formed within the rules of the documents that now present that writing. These then are the three kinds of writing that form, also, the three stages in the formation of the classics of Judaism. Which kind of writing dictates the character of a document? In the work that followed, I demonstrated that it is writing of the third type; authors, compilers, or editors formed a theory of what they wished to do in their particular compilation, and then they picked and chose out of the heritage of prior writings, reproducing verbatim what they had received, revising as they wished, or something in between – the whole a process of selection. This hypothesis, deriving from the present work, derived from *The Bavli and its Sources* and dictated the problem of *Tradition as Selectivity* and also *The Bavli That Might Have Been*.

---

[5]For the Talmud of the Land of Israel, also known as the Yerushalmi, for example, in *The Talmud of the Land of Israel. A Preliminary Translation and Explanation* (Chicago: University of Chicago Press: 1983). XXXV. *Introduction. Taxonomy;* and *Judaism in Society: The Evidence of the Yerushalmi. Toward the Natural History of a Religion* (Chicago, 1983: University of Chicago Press. Second printing, with a new preface: Atlanta, 1991: Scholars Press for South Florida Studies in the History of Judaism).

3. *Tradition as Selectivity: Scripture, Mishnah, Tosefta, and Midrash in the Talmud of Babylonia. The Case of Tractate Arakhin.* Atlanta, 1990: Scholars Press for South Florida Studies in the History of Judaism.

The specific research problem of this book is how the Bavli (the Talmud of Babylonia), as exemplified in one tractate, relates to its sources, by which I mean, materials it shares with other and (by definition) earlier-redacted documents. In this instance what I want to know is how Bavli Arakhin deals with the topic and facts set forth at [1] Lev. 27:1-7, 16-25, the prior reading of [2] Sifra to those verses, [3] the received version of those same facts set forth by [3] Mishnah-tractate Arakhin, and the exegesis of Mishnah-tractate Arakhin by [4] Tosefta Arakhin. What is at stake is an account of just how "traditional" the Bavli is. The question that defines the problem is how the Bavli has formed of available writings (redacted in documents now in hand) a single, cogent, and coherent statement presented by the Bavli's authorship as summary and authoritative: a canonical statement on a given subject. In what ways does a Bavli tractate frame such a (theologically canonical) statement out of what (as attested in extant writings) its authorship has in hand? In the exercise of which the present work is a continuation, *The Bavli and its Sources*, the prior source was the Talmud of the Land of Israel. The prior sources in this book are the Tosefta and Sifra. In both monographs my question is whether and how – in concrete, literary terms – a document makes its part of such a traditional statement, speaking, for its particular subject, in behalf of the entirety of the antecedent writings of the Judaic system at hand and standing in a relationship of continuity – not merely connection – with other such writings. The answer to that question will tell me how a traditional writing is formulated. If the question has no answer, and in the Bavli it does not, then it must follow that the Bavli is a document that has been framed through a process of not tradition but selection. And that is how I see the Bavli. Here, therefore, we inquire into the standing of a Bavli tractate as testimony on its subject within the larger continuous system of which it is reputed to form a principal part. What we want to know about that testimony, therefore, is how the Bavli relates to prior documents. The reason is that we want to know whether or not the Bavli constitutes a statement of a set of such antecedent sources, therefore a step in an unfolding tradition, so Judaism constitutes a traditional religion, the result of a long sedimentary process. As is clear, the alternative and complementary issue is whether or not the Bavli makes its own statement and hence inaugurates a "new tradition" altogether. In these pages I drew to a conclusion my work on the relationship between the Bavli and prior writing, both formed into completed documents (Yerushalmi, Sifra) and also not contained in closed compilations now available to us. In *The Bavli and its Sources* I had shown that earlier authorships – represented by the Talmud of the Land of Israel – wished to investigate in the Mishnah the points they wished to prove by reference to verses of Scripture important in our tractate – these have little or nothing in common with the points of special concern systematically worked out by the authorship of the Bavli. The Bavli's authorship at ca. 600 approaches Mishnah exegesis with a program distinct from that of the Yerushalmi's authorship of ca. 400, and the Bavli's authorship reads a critical verse of Scripture within a set of considerations entirely separate from those of interest to the authorships of Leviticus Rabbah and Pesiqta deRab Kahana of ca. 450 and 500. Any notion that the Bavli's authorship has taken as its principal task the restatement of received ideas on the Mishnah topics and Scripture verses at hand derives no support to speak of from the sample we shall examine. The same result, for Arakhin, emerged in this monograph.

4. *Language as Taxonomy. The Rules for Using Hebrew and Aramaic in the Babylonian Talmud.* **Atlanta, 1990: Scholars Press for South Florida Studies in the History of Judaism.**

Another, and separate, route of inquiry was defined by the linguistic traits of the Bavli, which differ from those of all other writings in the rabbinic canon of late antiquity except for the Yerushalmi. These traits support the claim that the Bavli explicitly recognizes the availability, and authority, of received writings or documents or traditions and the Bavli's authors distinguish their own contribution from what they have received – a case, in contemporary literary critical jargon, of not intertextuality but intratextuality. Not only by routinely and ubiquitously using such language as "as it is said," or "as it is written," did the authorities of the Talmud of Babylonia separate their statements from those of Scripture. Also by their choice of the very language in which they would express what they wished to say on their own account they differentiated themselves from their antecedents. When it came to citations from prior, nonscriptural authorities, they used one formation of the Hebrew language, specifically, Middle, or Mishnaic, Hebrew; when it came to the conduct of their own analytical process, they used one formation of the Aramaic language, Eastern or Talmudic Aramaic. They never alluded to authoritative facts, they always cited them in so many words; but the indication of citation – in a writing in which the modern sigla of

The Talmud of Babylonia: System or Tradition?

quotation marks and footnotes were simply unavailable – came to expression in the choice of language. The Bavli is in one language, not two, and that language is Aramaic. The infrastructure of the document, its entire repertoire of editorial conventions and sigla, are in Aramaic. When a saying is assigned to a named authority, the saying may be in Hebrew or in Aramaic, and the same named authority may be given sayings in both languages – even within the same sentence. But the editorial and conceptual infrastructure of the document comes to expression only in Aramaic, and when no name is attached to a statement, that statement is always in Aramaic, unless it forms part of a larger, autonomous Hebrew composition, cited by, or parachuted down into, "the Talmud." The Talmud speaks in a single voice, forms a unitary discourse, beginning, middle, and end, and constitutes one wholly coherent and cogent document, everywhere asking questions drawn from a single determinate and limited repertoire of intellectual initiatives – and always framing those questions, pursuing those inquiries, in Aramaic. Then where and why do the framers of this writing utilize the Hebrew language? Specifically, what signal is given, what purpose is served by the bi- or multi-lingualism of the Talmud, what do we know without further ado, when we are given a composition or a component of a composition in Hebrew, and what is the implicit meaning of making a statement in Aramaic? The answer is that the choice of language signals a taxonomic meaning. If we know which language is used, we also know where we stand in the expression of thought, and the very language in which a statement is made therefore forms part of the method of thought and even the message of discourse of the document. What is said in Hebrew is represented as authoritative and formulates a normative thought or rule. What is said in Aramaic is analytical and commonly signals an argument and formulates a process of inquiry and criticism. That is how language serves a taxonomic purpose: Hebrew is the language of the result, Aramaic, of the way by which the result is achieved; Hebrew is the formulation of the decision, Aramaic, of the work of deliberation. Each language serves to classify what is said in that language, and we always know where we stand, in a given process of thought and the exposition of thought, by reference to the language that is used at that particular place in the sustained discourse to which we are witness.

5. *The Bavli That Might Have Been: The Tosefta's Theory of Mishnah Commentary Compared with that of the Babylonian Talmud.* Atlanta, 1990: Scholars Press for South Florida Studies in the History of Judaism.

Yet a third kind of inquiry seemed to me called for, one that compared two or more documents' authorships' approach to the same problem. Since the Bavli is set forth as a commentary to the Mishnah, I decided to compare the Bavli's authorships' definition of their work with the Tosefta's counterparts' framing of the same task. For the Tosefta forms a commentary to the Mishnah, and so too does the Talmud of Babylonia or the Bavli. The latter document differs from the former in its conception of what is to be done with the Mishnah. By comparing the Tosefta's with the Bavli's treatment of the Mishnah, I show not only that the Bavli's approach to Mishnah commentary differs from the Tosefta's (which is hardly surprising), *but that the differences in the aggregate are uniform and predictable.* I prove beyond doubt, on the basis of a substantial sample, the fact that the comparison yields a fixed and coherent set of contrasts. So what? It follows, in my way of thinking, that, as I demonstrated to be the case for the Tosefta's authorship in my *The Tosefta: Its Structure and its Sources*,[6] so, too, the Bavli's authorship referred to a coherent and cogent program of exegetical principles when they turned to the Mishnah. That is why I attach such weight to the fact that the differences between the two documents – like those between the Bavli and the prior, and available, Yerushalmi, dealt with in *The Bavli and its Sources,* are fixed and predictable. When we compare one document's reading of the original source to the other document's reading of that same source, therefore, we are able to show by the persistence of a fixed set of differences that the latter document is a well-crafted and thoughtfully composed statement, not a mere compilation of this and that: a composition, not a compilation. Since the Bavli is commonly represented as a mere conglomeration of whatever people happened to have received – a sedimentary piece of writing, not a planned and considered one, the result of many centuries of accumulation, not the work of a generation or two of thoughtful writers – these results provide a detailed argument against one proposition and in favor of another. What is important therefore is not only difference, but a pattern of difference: the Bavli's framers differ in their theory of Mishnah commentary from the Tosefta's framers, and the differences are consistent throughout. In the contrast between the

---

[6](Atlanta, 1986: Scholars Press for Brown Judaic Studies).

Tosefta and the Talmud of Babylonia, the Talmud of Babylonia emerges as a well-crafted and highly purposive document, and certainly not a mere compilation of this-and-that, the result of centuries of the accumulation, in a haphazard way, of the detritus of various schools or opinions. Any sample of the Talmud that we take presents itself as exceedingly carefully and well crafted, a sustained and cogent inquiry. Scarcely a single line is out of place; not a sentence in the entire passage sustains the view of a document that is an agglutinative compilation. Ordinarily, for example, at any given passage of the Bavli, we begin with the clarification of the Mishnah paragraph, turn then to the examination of the principles of law implicit in the Mishnah paragraph, and then broaden the discussion to introduce what I called analogies from case to law and law to case. These are the three stages of our discussion. It would be very easy to outline a given Talmudic discussion, beginning to end, and to produce a reasoned account of the position and order of every completed composition and the ordering of the several compositions into a composite.

6. *The Rules of Composition of the Talmud of Babylonia. The Cogency of the Bavli's Composite.* Atlanta, 1991: Scholars Press for South Florida Studies in the History of Judaism.

The Bavli's authors of compositions and framers of composites followed not only rules of language, but also laws of composition. These laws told them how to formulate their thought within a limited and determinate repertoire of rhetorical patterns and further dictated what issues must come first, which ones may be treated later, in the exposition of their ideas. These rules may be discerned only when we define the units of complete discourse that were to be composed. In this work I show that the composite of several distinct compositions formed the unit of complete discourse, and that, when the framer of a large-scale passage of the Bavli referred to rules of language and laws of composition that would govern his work, his goal was to put together in correct form and sequential order a set of composites. The rules of composition then governed composing composites. Here I show that all authors found guidance in the same limited repertoire of rules of composition. Not only so, but a fixed order of discourse – a composition of one sort, A, always comes prior to a composite of another type, B. A simple logic instructed framers of composites, who sometimes also were authors of compositions, and who sometimes drew upon available compositions in the making of their cogent composites. When we understand that logic, which accounts for what for a very long time has impressed students of the Talmud as the document's run-on, formless, and meandering character, we see the writing as cogent and well crafted, always addressing a point that, within the hegemony of this logic, and not some other, was deemed closely linked to what had gone before and what was to follow. And on that basis we perceive as entirely of a piece, cogent and coherent, large-scale constructions, not brief compositions of a few lines, which therefore become subject to classification whole and complete. So the work of uncovering the laws of composition involve our identifying the entirety of a piece of coherent writing and classifying that writing – not pulling out of context and classifying only the compositions that, in some measure, form constituents of a larger whole. Were we to classify only the compositions, we should gain some knowledge of types of writing accomplished by authors, but none concerning types of writing that comprise our Talmud. Why insist that a composite – and not the several compositions that may find their redactional location within a given composite – forms the basic building block of thought, and the irreducible minimum of discourse, of the Bavli? The reason is that only when we grasp how a variety of materials, some of them already completed compositions, are drawn together into a single sustained and comprehensive statement, shall we understand the work of the compiler. The Bavli is a work of purposive compilation, and when we understand the rules of composition in the twin sense – the writing of compositions, the formation of composites – we shall have a clear picture of what the framers of the Bavli did. By contrast, if we knew only the rules that dictated the writing of the distinct compositions that the framers utilized, we should know only how the parts took shape, but not how the whole, served by those parts, found its coherence and cogency. The importance of recognizing that some pieces of writing were composed to serve the purposes of the formation of a particular document in which they occur, others to serve the purposes of some other document than one we now have, and still others to serve the purposes of a document that we now cannot even imagine, in the present context then is clear. The results of this work – demonstrating the cogency of the Bavli's composite – prepared the way for this final chapter in a six-year study.

7. *The Bavli's One Voice: Types and Forms of Analytical Discourse and their Fixed Order of Appearance.* Atlanta, 1991: Scholars Press for South Florida Studies in the History of Judaism.

This monograph provides a final solution to the Bavli problem framed in narrowly literary terms: who speaks through the Bavli? Is it the voice of the penultimate and ultimate authorship, or does the document resonate with the voices of a variety of authors and authorships? Here I demonstrate through analysis of eleven tractates and classifying more than three thousand composites that the Bavli throughout speaks in a single and singular voice. It is single because it is a voice that expresses the same limited set of notes everywhere. It is singular because these notes are arranged in one and the same way throughout. The Bavli's one voice, sounding through all tractates, is the voice of exegetes of the Mishnah. The document is organized around the Mishnah, and that is not a merely formal, but a substantive order. At every point, if the framers have chosen a passage of Mishnah exegesis, that passage will stand at the head of all further discussion. Every turning point brings the editors back to the Mishnah, always read in its own order and sequence. So the Bavli's voice speaks in a single way about some few things, and that is the upshot of this sustained inquiry. It follows that well-crafted and orderly rules governed the character of the sustained discourse that the writing in the Bavli sets forth. All framers of composites and editors of sequences of composites found guidance in the same limited repertoire of rules of analytical rhetoric: some few questions or procedures, directed always toward one and the same prior writing. Not only so, but a fixed order of discourse dictated that a composition of one sort, A, always comes prior to a composite of another type, B. A simple logic instructed framers of composites, who sometimes also were authors of compositions, and who sometimes drew upon available compositions in the making of their cogent composites. So we have now to see the Bavli as entirely of a piece, cogent and coherent, made up of well-composed large-scale constructions.

The Bavli's one voice utilizes only a few, well-modulated tones: a scale of not many notes. When we classify more than three thousand composites, spread over eleven tractates, we find that nearly 90% of the whole comprises Mishnah commentary of various kinds; not only so, but the variety of the types of Mishnah commentary is limited, as a review of the representation of Temurah in detail, and of the ten tractates of our sample in brief characterization, has shown. Cogent composites are further devoted to Scripture or to topics of a moral or theological character not closely tied to the exegesis of verses of Scripture; these form in the aggregate approximately 10% of the whole number of composites, but, of tractates to begin with not concerned with scriptural or theological topics (in our sample these are Sanhedrin and Berakhot), they make up scarcely 3 percent of the whole. So the Bavli has one voice, and it is the voice of a person or persons who propose to speak about one document and to do so in some few ways. Let me spell out precisely what I mean. The results of the survey of eleven tractates and classification of all of the composites of each one of them yields firm and one-sided results. First, we are able to classify all composites in three principal categories: [1] exegesis and amplification of the law of the Mishnah; [2] exegesis and exposition of verses of, or topics in, Scripture; [3] free-standing composites devoted to topics other than those defined by the Mishnah or Scripture. That means that my initial proposal of a taxonomic system left no lacunae. Second, with the classification in place, we see that much more than four-fifths of all composites of the Bavli address the Mishnah and systematically expound that document. These composites are subject to sub-classification in two ways: Mishnah exegesis and speculation and abstract theorizing about the implications of the Mishnah's statements. The former type of composite, further, is to be classified in a few and simple taxa, for example, composites organized around [1] clarification of the statements of the Mishnah, [2] identification of the authority behind an anonymous statement in the Mishnah, [3] scriptural foundation for the Mishnah's rules; [4] citation and not seldom systematic exposition of the Tosefta's amplification of the Mishnah. That means that most of the Bavli is a systematic exposition of the Mishnah. Third, the other fifth (or less) of a given tractate will comprise composites that take shape around [1] Scripture or [2] themes or topics of a generally theological or moral character. Distinguishing the latter from the former, of course, is merely formal; very often a scriptural topic will be set forth in a theological or moral framework, and very seldom does a composite on a topic omit all reference to the amplification of a verse or topic of Scripture. The proportion of a given tractate devoted to other-than-Mishnah exegesis and amplification is generally not more than 10 percent. My figure is distorted by the special problems of tractates Sanhedrin and Berakhot, and, in the former, Chapter Eleven in particular.

These two tractates prove anomalous for the categories I have invented because both of them contain important components that are devoted to begin with to scriptural or theological topics. Tractate Sanhedrin Chapter Eleven, for example, lists various scriptural figures in catalogues of those who do, or do not, inherit the world to come; it further specifies certain doctrines that define the norms of the community of Israel that inherits the world to come. It will therefore prove quite natural that numerous composites will attend to scriptural or theological topics. Tractate Berakhot addresses matters of prayer and other forms of virtue, with the same consequence. In the analysis that follows, therefore, I calculate the averages of proportions of various types of composites both with and without these anomalous tractates. The upshot is that a rather inconsequential proportion of most tractates, and a small proportion of the whole, of the Bavli, is

The Talmud of Babylonia: System or Tradition?

devoted to the systematic exposition of either verses of Scripture or topics of a theological or moral character. Seen in the aggregate, the proportions of the eleven tractates devoted solely to Mishnah exegesis average 83 percent. If we omit reference to the two clearly anomalous tractates, Berakhot and Sanhedrin, the proportion of Mishnah exegesis rises to 89.5 percent. If, then, we combine exegesis of the Mishnah and exegesis of the broader implications of the Mishnah's law – and in the process of classification, it was not always easy to keep these items apart in a consistent way – we see a still more striking result. More than 86 percent of the whole of our tractates is devoted to the exegesis of the Mishnah and the amplification of the implications of its law; without the anomalous tractates, the proportion is close to 94–95 percent.

So the Talmud speaks through one voice, that voice of logic that with vast assurance reaches into our own minds and by asking the logical and urgent next question tells us what we should be thinking. Fixing our attention upon the Mishnah, the Talmud's rhetoric seduces us into joining its analytical inquiry, always raising precisely the question that should trouble us (and that would trouble us if we knew all of the pertinent details as well as the Talmud does). In this final monograph I have now demonstrated beyond a shadow of a doubt that the Bavli speaks about the Mishnah in essentially a single voice, about fundamentally few things. Its mode of speech as much as of thought is uniform throughout. Diverse topics produce slight differentiation in modes of analysis. The same sorts of questions phrased in the same rhetoric – a moving, or dialectical, argument, composed of questions and answers – turn out to pertain equally well to every subject and problem. The Talmud's discourse forms a closed system, in which people say the same thing about everything. The fact that the Talmud speaks in a single voice supplies striking evidence (1) that the Talmud does speak in particular for the age in which its units of discourse took shape, and (2) that that work was done toward the end of that long period of Mishnah reception that began at the end of the second century and came to an end at the conclusion of the sixth century.

It follows that the whole – the composites of discourse as we know them, the sequence of composites as we have them – was put together at the end. At that point everything was in hand, so available for arrangement in accordance with a principle other than chronology, and in a rhetoric common to all sayings. That other principle will then have determined the arrangement, drawing in its wake resort to a single monotonous voice: "the Talmud." The principle is logical exposition, that is to say, the analysis and dissection of a problem into its conceptual components. The dialectic of argument is framed not by considerations of the chronological sequence in which sayings were said but by attention to the requirements of reasonable exposition of the problem. That is what governs. If there is a single governing method, then what can we expect to learn about the single, repeated message? The evidence before us indicates that the purpose of the Talmud is to clarify and amplify selected passages of the Mishnah. We may say very simply that the Mishnah is about life, and the Talmud is about the Mishnah. That is to say, while the Mishnah records rules governing the conduct of the holy life of Israel, the holy people, the Talmud concerns itself with the details of the Mishnah. The one is descriptive and free-standing, the other analytical and contingent. Were there no Mishnah, there would be no Talmud. But what is the message of the method, which is to insist upon the Mishnah's near monopoly over serious discourse? To begin with, the very character of the Talmud tells us the sages' view of the Mishnah. The Mishnah presented itself to them as constitutive, the text of ultimate concern. So, in our instance, the Mishnah speaks of a quarrel over a coat, the Talmud, of the Mishnah's provision of an oath as a means of settling the quarrel in a fair way: substance transformed into process. What the framers of the Bavli wished to say about the Mishnah will guide us toward the definition of the message of their method, but it will not tell us what that message was, or why it was important. A long process of close study of texts is required to guide us toward the center of matters.

The upshot of the long series of studies that conclude here is simple. We may speak about "the Talmud," its voice, its purposes, its mode of constructing a view of the Israelite world. The reason is that, when we claim "the Talmud" speaks, we replicate both the main lines of chronology and the literary character of the document. These point toward the formation of the bulk of materials – its units of discourse – in a process lasting (to take a guess) about half a century, prior to the ultimate arrangement of these units of discourse around passages of the Mishnah and the closure and redaction of the whole into the document we now know. What comes next? Well, now that we know that the Bavli is a document of remarkable integrity, repeatedly insisting upon the harmony of the parts within a whole and unitary structure of belief and behavior, we want to know what the Bavli says: the one thing that is repeated in regard to many things. Dismantling ("deconstructing") its components and identifying them, perhaps even describing the kinds of compilations that the authors of those components can have had in mind in writing their compositions – these activities of literary criticism yield no insight into the religious system that guided the document's framers. But the Talmud of Babylonia recapitulates, in grand and acute detail, a religious system, and the generative problematic of that writing directs our attention not to the aesthetics of writing as literature, but to the religion of writing as a document of faith in the formation of the social order. So we have now to turn to the message of the method of the Bavli: what the Bavli's one voice always wishes to convey.

It remains to state only that now in progress, is [8] *The Bavli's One Statement. The Metapropositional Program of Babylonian Talmud Tractate Zebahim Chapters One, Two, and Five, and of Babylonian Talmud Tractate Niddah Chapter One*, and this will be followed by [9] *The Message of the Method of the Talmud of Babylonia. The Metapropositional Program of Babylonian Talmud Tractates Erubin, Yebamot, Qiddushin, Gittin, Baba Qamma, Baba Batra, Zebahim, and Menahot.*

15

Translating Rabbinic Documents: The Importance of an Analytical Reference System

In making my translations of the canon of the Judaism of the Dual Torah – Mishnah, Tosefta, two Talmuds, various Midrash compilations – I supply to the canonical writings a systematic and uniform reference system, corresponding, in the Bible, to the use of numbers for chapters and verses, for example, Gen. 1:12. Because of the failure of all prior translators as well as editors of critical versions of the received classics to provide a reference system, I found it necessary to retranslate all canonical writings of the Judaism of the Dual Torah that already had been presented in English, as well as to translate for the first time those many documents that were not in English. The reason, as I shall show here, is simply that no analytical work of any kind is possible without a reference system that identifies the parts of a large passage. Not only so, but in a bilingual document, readers must be told what language the original authors used. But until very recently, no translation differentiated one language from the other. Since, it is clear, colleagues engaged in the same work of translation of rabbinic canonical writings do not yet grasp why an analytical reference system of some kind is required, recent works in German and Spanish,[1] for instance, at best

---

[1]Spanish, for one example: *Midrás Exodo Rabbah I*, by Luis-Fernando Girón Blanc. Biblioteca Midrásica, 8 (Valencia, Spain: Institución San Jerónimo, 1989). 190 pp. But the critical Hebrew text, of Exodus Rabbah used by the Spanish translation, that of A. Shinan, also has no analytical reference system that anyone can use. Not one [!] German "scientific" translation – Wewers's translation of the Talmud of the Land of Israel, for example – has recognized the requirement of a reference system to make possible further study of the translated documents, with the result that all we have in German is the contents of the Hebrew, but not the

numbering paragraphs, but, ordinarily, not doing even that, I propose to show what is at stake in a very simple exercise.

The problem goes beyond translation. No Hebrew language reprinting of the Talmud has ever made possible any sort of large-scale analytical work at all. Not only so, but I do not believe that any Hebrew edition, for example, a critical text, at which Israeli colleagues think they excel, attends to that minimum task. Giving page and line references hardly suffices, since these supply no signals, let alone visual evidence, on what is before us. Not only so, but – perhaps it was deemed more "authentic" because "traditional" – every current translation into various European languages fails to provide even the most minimal sigla, for example, indications of the smallest whole units of thought, sentences, paragraphs, completed expositions of a single idea, components of larger presentations of propositions, and the like – nothing, except page and line references (if that). No wonder the Bavli (among all writings) is (mis)represented as utterly confused, a hodgepodge of this and that, when, in fact, it is an orderly and well-disciplined construction. Accordingly, the whole of rabbinic literature has had to be retranslated in such a way as to indicate the individual components of a composition, for example, sentences, paragraphs, chapters or completed whole presentations of propositions. I have accomplished most of that task, out of an interest in not philology, let alone text criticism, but history of religion.

Only if the reader first meets an undifferentiated text, merely translated fairly literally, but in no way re-presented within the extant technology by which we organize information in a purposive manner, will the necessity of a differentiated text become self-evident. That is why, in what follows, I first present, without comment, a sizable abstract, marking each sentence off from the others only for the purpose of allowing the reader some sort of minimal access to what is said. I do not differentiate between Hebrew and Aramaic, and I do not include any signals on how a given sentence relates to what has gone before or to what is to follow. So I omit the signals that I have devised to ease the

---

construction or indications of the composition. Analytical scholarship on these documents is possible only within my, or some counterpart, reference system. Translators may maintain that analysis is not part of their work. But as soon as we who translate supply periods, commas, and quotation marks, we state what we conceive to be the elements of construction and composition. Then why not mark the sentences, one by one, so people can refer to them? And why not say what we conceive the "chapters" to be as well? I have done nothing more "radical" than was done by the printers who originally presented the Bible in printed form and added chapter and verse numbers. But, as is clear, I have had to do this work for the entirety of rabbinical literature of late antiquity.

reader's progress through the document, that is, not highlighting what the intended audience automatically will have grasped from shifts in language and other signals, articulated or implicit, in the flow of language. To facilitate some minimal intelligibility, to be sure, I do include quotation marks; many of the "modern, scientific" translations do not give even that mark.

Then, immediately afterward, I re-represent the entire passage, this time showing it as a differentiated set of citations and quotations from various sources (now, the passages of the Mishnah and Tosefta will be in boldface type). By giving Hebrew in plain type and Aramaic in italics, further, I differentiate the two languages and thus draw upon the signals that language choice delivers. I also display in indentation – further and further to the right-hand column, as an item glosses a gloss, or provides an appendix to a gloss, or footnotes a footnote – what I conceive to be the secondary or subordinated discussions. As to the body of the materials, I differentiate what I conceive to be the smallest whole units of thought ("sentences") paragraph by paragraph, marking each with a letter for ready reference. I then identify what I conceive to be complete propositional formulations ("paragraphs") by marking a set of lettered "sentences" with Arabic numerals. Finally, I mark what I maintain are fully and exhaustively presented composites of propositions ("chapters") by a Roman number. Working from the whole to the parts, I move from a complete statement through the components of that statement to the smallest whole units of thought of which that statement is comprised.[2] A variety of issues is at stake in providing such an analytical reference system, inclusive of the signification of secondary and tertiary discourses by progressive indentation. In the present context, my discussion will then show how in presenting a vast corpus of material, and in fully providing the apparatus of information, not only the main points of proposition, evidence, and argument, the framers have followed a few simple rules, which a sensitive reader will have grasped after only minimal study.

Presenting the opening Mishnah paragraph and following Babylonian Talmud tractate Abodah Zarah, folios 2A-3B, I first offer the whole, differentiated only by periods, sentence by sentence. All translations of all documents of rabbinic literature except for mine, wherever and whenever made, will follow this format (a glance at the

---

[2] I invented this reference system originally for my translation of the Mishnah, explaining its terms and categories, in *A History of the Mishnaic Law of Purities* (Leiden, 1977: Brill). XXI. *The Redaction and Formulation of the Order of Purities in the Mishnah and Tosefta*, which, to my knowledge, received not a single review.

fine translation published by Soncino Press, London, will validate my claim on how translations represent the original of these pages):

> **Mishnah:** Before the festivals of gentiles for three days it is forbidden to do business with them, to lend anything to them or to borrow anything from them, to lend money to them or to borrow money from them, to repay them or to be repaid by them. R. Judah says, "They accept repayment from them, because it is distressing to him." They said to him, "Even though it is distressing to him now, he will be happy about it later."
> **Gemara:** Rab and Samuel [in dealing with the reading of the key-word of the Mishnah, translated festival, the letters of which are 'aleph daled, rather than 'ayin daled, which means, calamity]: one repeated the formulation of the Mishnah as, "their festivals." And the other repeated the formulation of the Mishnah as "their calamities." The one who repeated the formulation of the Mishnah as "their festivals" made no mistake, and the one who repeated the formulation of the Mishnah as "their calamities" made no mistake. For it is written, "For the day of their calamity is at hand" (Deut. 32:15). The one who repeated the formulation of the Mishnah as "their festivals" made no mistake, for it is written, "Let them bring their testimonies that they may be justified" (Isa. 43:9). And as to the position of him who repeats the formulation of the Mishnah as "their festivals," on what account does he not repeat the formulation of the Mishnah to yield, "their calamities"? He will say to you, "'Calamity' is preferable [as the word choice when speaking of idolatry]." And as to the position of him who repeats the formulation of the Mishnah as "their calamities," on what account does he not repeat the formulation of the Mishnah to yield "their festivals"? He will say to you, "What causes the calamity that befalls them if not their testimony, so testimony is preferable!" And as to the verse, "Let them bring their testimonies that they may be justified" (Isa. 43:9), is this written with reference to gentiles? Lo, it is written in regard to Israel. For said R. Joshua b. Levi, "All of the religious duties that Israelites carry out in this world come and give testimony in their behalf in the world to come: 'Let them bring their witnesses that they may be justified' (Isa. 43:9), that is, Israel; 'and let them hear and say, It is truth' (Isa. 43:9) – this refers to gentiles." Rather, said R. Huna b. R. Joshua, "He who formulates the Mishnah to refer to their calamities derives the reading from this verse: 'They that fashion a graven image are all of them vanity,

and their delectable things shall not profit, and their own witnesses see not nor know' (Isa. 44:9)." As to the exposition [of the verse,"They that fashion a graven image are all of them vanity, and their delectable things shall not profit, and their own witnesses see not nor know" (Isa. 44:9)]: "In the age to come the Holy One, blessed be He, will bring a scroll of the Torah and hold it in his bosom and say, 'Let him who has kept himself busy with it come and take his reward.' Then all the gentiles will crowd together: 'All of the nations are gathered together' (Isa. 43:9). The Holy One, blessed be He, will say to them, 'Do not crowd together before me in a mob. But let each nation enter together with [2B] its scribes, 'and let the peoples be gathered together' (Isa. 43:9), and the word 'people' means 'kingdom': 'and one kingdom shall be stronger than the other' (Gen. 25:23)." But can there be a mob scene before the Holy One, blessed be He? Rather, it is so that from their perspective they not form a mob, so that they will be able to hear what he says to them. "The kingdom of Rome comes in first." How come? Because they are the most important. How do we know on the basis of Scripture they are the most important? Because it is written, "And he shall devour the whole earth and shall tread it down and break it into pieces" (Gen. 25:23), and said R. Yohanan, "This Rome is answerable, for its definition [of matters] has gone forth to the entire world. [Mishcon: 'This refers to Rome, whose power is known to the whole world.']" And how do we know that the one who is most important comes in first? It is in accord with that which R. Hisda said. For said R. Hisda, "When the king and the community [await judgment], the king enters in first for judgment: 'That he maintain the case of his servant [Solomon] and [then] the cause of his people Israel' (1 Kgs. 8:59)." And how come? If you wish, I shall say it is not appropriate to keep the king sitting outside. And if you wish, I shall say that [the king is allowed to plea his case] before the anger of the Holy One is aroused." "The Holy One, blessed be He, will say to them, 'How have you defined your chief occupation?' They will say before him, 'Lord of the world, a vast number of marketplaces have we set up, a vast number of bathhouses we have made, a vast amount of silver and gold have we accumulated. And all of these things we have done only in behalf of Israel, so that they may define as their chief occupation the study of the Torah.' The Holy One, blessed be He, will say to them, 'You complete idiots! Whatever you have done has been for your own convenience. You have set up a vast number of marketplaces to be sure, but that was so as to set up whorehouses in them. The bathhouses were for your own pleasure. Silver and gold belong to me anyhow: "Mine is the silver and mine is the gold, says the Lord of hosts" (Hag. 2:8). Are there any among you who have been telling of "this," and "this" is only the Torah: "And this is the Torah that Moses set before the children of Israel' (Deut. 4:44)." So they will make their exit, humiliated. When the kingdom of Rome has made its exit, the kingdom of Persia enters afterward." How come? Because they are second in importance. And how do we know it on the basis of Scripture? Because it is written, "And behold, another beast, a second, like a bear" (Dan. 7:5), and in this connection R. Joseph repeated as a Tannaite formulation, "This refers to the Persians, who eat and drink like a bear, are obese like a bear, are shaggy like a bear, and are restless like a bear." The Holy One, blessed be He, will say to them, 'How have you defined your chief occupation?' They will say before him, 'Lord of the world, We have thrown up a vast number of bridges, we have conquered a vast number of towns, we have made a vast number of wars, and all of them we did only for Israel, so that they may define as their chief occupation the study of the Torah.' The Holy One, blessed be He, will say to them, 'Whatever you have done has been for your own convenience. You have thrown up a vast number of bridges to collect tolls, you have conquered a vast number of towns to collect the corvée, and, as to making a vast number of wars, I am the one who makes wars: "The Lord is a man of war" (Ex. 19:17). Are there any among you who have been telling of "this," and "this" is only the Torah: "And this is the Torah that Moses set before the children of Israel" (Deut. 4:44).' So they will make their exit, humiliated. But if the kingdom of Persia has seen that such a claim issued by the kingdom of Rome did no good whatsoever, how come they go in at all? They will say to themselves, "These are the ones who destroyed the house of the sanctuary, but we are the ones who built it." And so it will go with each and every nation." But if each one of them has seen that such a claim issued by the others did no good whatsoever, how come they go in at all? They will say to themselves, "Those two subjugated Israel, but we never subjugated Israel." And how come the two conquering nations are singled out as important and the others are not? It is because the rule of these will continue until the Messiah comes. "They will say to him, 'Lord of the world, in point of fact, did you actually give it to us and we did not accept it?'" But how can they present such an argument, since it is written, "The Lord came from Sinai and rose from Sier to them, he shined forth from Mount Paran" (Deut. 33:2), and further, "God comes from Teman" (Hab. 3:3). Now what in the world did he want in Seir, and what was he looking for in Paran? Said R. Yohanan, "This teaches that the Holy One, blessed be He, made the rounds of each and every nation and language and none accepted it, until he came to Israel, and they accepted it." Rather, this is what they say, "Did we accept it but then not carry it out?" But to this the rejoinder must be, "Why did you not accept it anyhow!" Rather, "This is what they say before him, 'Lord of the world, Did you hold a mountain over us like a cask and then we refused to accept it as you did to Israel, as it is written, "And they stood beneath the mountain" (Ex. 19:17).'" And [in connection with the verse, "And they stood beneath the mountain" (Ex. 19:17),] said R. Dimi bar Hama, "This teaches that the Holy One, blessed be He, held the mountain over Israel like a cask and said to them, 'If you accept the Torah, well and good, and if not, then there is where your grave will be.'" "Then the Holy One, blessed be He, will say to them, 'Let us make known what happened first: "Let them announce to us former things" (Isa. 43:9). As to the seven religious duties that you did accept, where have you actually carried them out?'" And how do we know on the basis of Scripture that they did not carry them out? R. Joseph formulated as a Tannaite statement, "'He stands and shakes the earth, he sees and makes the nations tremble' (Hab. 3:6): What did he see? He saw the seven religious duties that the children of Noah accepted upon themselves as obligations but never actually carried out. Since they did not carry out those obligations, he went and remitted their obligation." But then they benefited – so it pays to sin! Said Mar b. Rabina, [3A] "What this really proves is that even when they carry out those religious duties, they get no reward on that account." And they don't, don't they? But has it not been taught on Tannaite authority: R. Meir would say, "How on the basis of Scripture do we know that, even if it is a gentile, if he goes and takes up the study of the Torah as his occupation, he is equivalent to the high priest? Scripture states, 'You shall therefore keep my statutes and my ordinances, which, if a human being does them, one shall gain life through them' (Lev. 18:5). What is written is not 'priests' or 'Levites' or 'Israelites,' but rather, 'a human being.' So you have learned the fact that, even if it is a gentile, if he goes and takes up the study of the Torah as his occupation, he is equivalent to the high priest."

Rather, what you learn from this is that they will not receive that reward that is coming to those who are commanded to do them and who carry them out, but rather, the reward that they receive will be like that coming to the one who is not commanded to do them and who carries them out anyhow. For said R. Hanina, "Greater is the one who is commanded and who carries out the religious obligations than the one who is not commanded but nonetheless carries out religious obligations." "This is what the gentiles say before him, 'Lord of the world, Israel, who accepted it – where in the world have they actually carried it out?' "The Holy One, blessed be He, will say to them, 'I shall bear witness concerning them, that they have carried out the whole of the Torah!' "They will say before him, 'Lord of the world, is there a father who is permitted to give testimony concerning his son? For it is written, "Israel is my son, my firstborn" (Ex. 4:22).' The Holy One, blessed be He, will say to them, 'The heaven and the earth will give testimony in their behalf that they have carried out the entirety of the Torah.' They will say before him, 'Lord of the world, The heaven and earth have a selfish interest in the testimony that they give: 'If not for my covenant with day and with night, I should not have appointed the ordinances of heaven and earth' (Jer. 33:25).'" For said R. Simeon b. Laqish, "What is the meaning of the verse of Scripture, 'And there was evening, and there was morning, the sixth day' (Gen. 1:31)? This teaches that the Holy One, blessed be He, made a stipulation with all of the works of creation, saying to them, 'If Israel accepts my Torah, well and good, but if not, I shall return you to chaos and void.' That is in line with what is written: 'You did cause sentence to be heard from heaven, the earth trembled and was still' (Ps. 76:9). If 'trembling' then where is the stillness, and if stillness, then where is the trembling? Rather, to begin with, trembling, but at the end, stillness." "The Holy One, blessed be He, will say to them, 'Some of them may well come and give testimony concerning Israel that they have observed the entirety of the Torah. Let Nimrod come and give testimony in behalf of Abraham that he never worshiped idols. Let Laban come and give testimony in behalf of Jacob, that he never was suspect of thievery. Let the wife of Potiphar come and give testimony in behalf of Joseph, that he was never suspect of 'sin.' Let Nebuchadnessar come and give testimony in behalf of Hananiah, Mishael, and Azariah, that they never bowed down to the idol. Let Darius come and give testimony in behalf of Daniel, that he did not neglect even the optional prayers. Let Bildad the Shuhite and Zophar the Naamatite and Eliphaz the Temanite and Elihu son of Barachel the Buzite come and testify in behalf of Israel that they have observed the entirety of the Torah: "Let the nations bring their own witnesses, that they may be justified" (Isa. 43:9).' They will say to him, "Then give it to us to begin with, and let us carry it out.' The Holy One, blessed be He, will say to them, 'World-class idiots! He who took the trouble to prepare on the eve of the Sabbath [Friday] will eat on the Sabbath, but he who took no trouble on the eve of the Sabbath – what in the world is he going to eat on the Sabbath! Still, [I'll give you another chance.] I have a rather simple religious duty, which is called "the tabernacle." Go and do that one.'" But can you say any such thing? Lo, R. Joshua b. Levi has said, "What is the meaning of the verse of Scripture, 'The ordinances that I command you this day to do them' (Deut. 7:11)? Today is the day to do them, but not tomorrow; they are not to be done tomorrow; today is the day to do them, but not the day on which to receive a reward for doing them." Rather, it is that the Holy One, blessed be He, does not exercise tyranny over his creatures. And why does he refer to it as a simple religious duty? Because it does not involve enormous expense [to carry out that religious duty]. Forthwith every one of them will take up the task and go and make a tabernacle on his roof. But then the Holy One, blessed be He, will come and make the sun blaze over them as at the summer solstice, and every one of them will knock down his tabernacle and go his way: 'Let us break their bands asunder and cast away their cords from us' (Ps. 23:3)." But lo, you have just said, "It is that the Holy One, blessed be He, does not exercise tyranny over his creatures"! It is because as to the Israelites, too – sometimes [3B] the summer solstice goes on to the festival of Tabernacles, and therefore they are bothered by the heat! But has not Raba stated, "One who is bothered [by the heat] is exempt from the obligation of dwelling in the tabernacle"? Granting that one may be exempt from the duty, is he going to go and tear the thing down? "Then the Holy One, blessed be He, goes into session and laughs at them: 'He who sits in heaven laughs' (Ps. 2:4)." Said R. Isaac, "Laughter before the Holy One, blessed be He, takes place only on that day alone." There are those who repeat as a Tannaite version this statement of R. Isaac in respect to that which has been taught on Tannaite authority: R. Yosé says, "In the coming age gentiles will come and convert." But will they be accepted? Has it not been taught on Tannaite authority: Converts will not be accepted in the days of the Messiah, just as they did not accept proselytes either in the time of David or in the time of Solomon? Rather, "they will make themselves converts, and they will put on phylacteries on their heads and arms and fringes on their garments and a mezuzah on their doors. But when they witness the war of Gog and Magog, he will say to them, 'How come you have come?' They will say, '"Against the Lord and against his Messiah."' For so it is said, 'Why are the nations in an uproar and why do the peoples mutter in vain' (Ps. 2:1). Then each one of them will rid himself of his religious duty and go his way: 'Let us break their bands asunder' (Ps. 2:3). Then the Holy One, blessed be He, goes into session and laughs at them: 'He who sits in heaven laughs' (Ps. 2:4)." Said R. Isaac, "Laughter before the Holy One, blessed be He, takes place only on that day alone." But is this really so? And has not R. Judah said Rab said, "The day is made up of twelve hours. In the first three the Holy One, blessed be He, goes into session and engages in study of the Torah; in the second he goes into session and judges the entire world. When he realizes that the world is liable to annihilation, he arises from the throne of justice and takes up a seat on the throne of mercy. In the third period he goes into session and nourishes the whole world from the horned buffalo to the brood of vermin. During the fourth quarter he laughs [and plays] with leviathan: 'There is leviathan, whom you have formed to play with' (Ps. 104:26)." [This proves that God does laugh more than on that one day alone.] Said R. Nahman bar Isaac, "With his creatures he laughs [every day], but at his creatures he laughs only on that day alone."

That is what the page, without markings other than commas, periods, and quotation marks yields. I shall argue that a proper reference system displays the cogency and well-crafted character of this piece of writing. But, at this point, anyone with the patience to have read the entire passage will by now have found utterly implausible my allegation that that page is at all coherent. And even were I to paragraph the column of words as the Soncino translation does, it would make little difference to that judgment. Long columns of undifferentiated words simply cannot be analyzed in any manner at all; the absence of a reference system renders the translation gibberish: we understand the sentences, but not the composition that they form.

Without further ado, we reconsider the entire passage, now differentiating the composites by Roman numerals, the compositions that form the components of the composites by Arabic numerals, the

Translating Rabbinic Documents

constitutive parts of the compositions by letters; the sources – Mishnah, Tosefta from everything else – by different type faces; the two languages, Hebrew and Aramaic, by regular type and italics, respectively; and the text – the principal discourse – from footnotes and appendices by indenting and double and triple indenting the latter. In this way – through a simple and visually easily understood reference system – we see precisely what is in play in the page; my comments then will explain what our authors have done to give us everything they thought we had to know. We see that they followed a few simple rules, which we can discern and which guide us in reading their writing.

1:1

    A.   [2A] Before the festivals of gentiles for three days it is forbidden to do business with them.
    B.   (1) to lend anything to them or to borrow anything from them.
    C.   (2) to lend money to them or to borrow money from them.
    D.   (3) to repay them or to be repaid by them.
    E.   R. Judah says, "They accept repayment from them, because it is distressing to him."
    F.   They said to him, "Even though it is distressing to him now, he will be happy about it later."

I.1   A.   [2A] Rab and Samuel [in dealing with the reading of the key word of the Mishnah, translated festival, the letters of which are 'aleph daled, rather than 'ayin daled, which means, calamity]:
    B.   *one repeated the formulation of the Mishnah as, "their festivals."*
    C.   *And the other repeated the formulation of the Mishnah as "their calamities."*
    D.   *The one who repeated the formulation of the Mishnah as "their festivals" made no mistake, and the one who repeated the formulation of the Mishnah as "their calamities" made no mistake.*
    E.   *For it is written, "For the day of their calamity is at hand" (Deut. 32:15).*
    F.   *The one who repeated the formulation of the Mishnah as "their festivals" made no mistake, for it is written, "Let them bring their testimonies that they may be justified" (Isa. 43:9).*
    G.   *And as to the position of him who repeats the formulation of the Mishnah as "their festivals," on what account does he not repeat the formulation of the Mishnah to yield, "their calamities"?*
    H.   *He will say to you, "'Calamity' is preferable [as the word choice when speaking of idolatry]."*
    I.   *And as to the position of him who repeats the formulation of the Mishnah as "their calamities," on what account does he not repeat the formulation of the Mishnah to yield "their festivals"?*
    J.   *He will say to you, "What causes the calamity that befalls them if not their testimony, so testimony is preferable!"*
    K.   *And as to the verse, "Let them bring their testimonies that they may be justified" (Isa. 43:9), is this written with reference to gentiles? Lo, it is written in regard to Israel.*

L. For said R. Joshua b. Levi, "All of the religious duties that Israelites carry out in this world come and give testimony in their behalf in the world to come: 'Let them bring their witnesses that they may be justified' (Isa. 43:9), that is, Israel; 'and let them hear and say, It is truth' (Isa. 43:9) – this refers to gentiles."

M. Rather, said R. Huna b. R. Joshua, "He who formulates the Mishnah to refer to their calamities derives the reading from this verse: 'They that fashion a graven image are all of them vanity, and their delectable things shall not profit, and their own witnesses see not nor know' (Isa. 44:9)."

The foregoing, we see clearly, presents a beautifully balanced dispute form, and the form is used to provide a medium for presenting Mishnah text criticism: how are we to read the text of the paragraph before us. That classification presents no problems. We must now enter a much more difficult question because I maintain that, along with the classification of **I.1**, everything that is attached to **I.1** in a continuous and ongoing manner goes along as a single composite, the whole put together in its own terms, but then utilized by the framer of the Talmud before us – folios 2A-5B – as a continuous (if in our perspective rather run-on) statement. It is obviously a composite. But I classify the entire composite all together and all at once, because it is more than a composite: it also is a composition. And the reason I see it as a coherent and cogent composition is that every item fits together with its predecessor and leads us without interruption to its successor, from the starting lines of **I.1** to the concluding ones of **I.32**.

No. 1 has referred us to gentile idolatry and Israelite loyalty to the religious duties assigned to them by God. We now have a long exposition of the theme of gentile idolatry and perfidy. Everything that follows in **I.2** serves as a play on the theme of **I.1L-M**! The unity of the whole of **I.2** will be readily apparent because of the insets of gloss and expansion, and the further insets of the appendices to the gloss and expansion. We shall now see, through the device of indentations, how much in the expansion of the foregoing in fact serves as gloss, footnote, and appendix; recognizing that fact we see a rather well-crafted and cogent composite, made up of a principal composition – extending to the far lefthand margin – and a variety of subordinated compositions, moving off to the right in progressive indentations. And what we can see, visually, any well-endowed disciple of the document will readily have understood through his thoughtful reading of the document: this is primary, that is secondary and subordinate. In ages past the disciples will not have called what I indent "footnotes" or even "appendices." But they also will not have found confusing the glosses and supplements that, all together, give a full and rich account of any subject introduced in the primary discussion.

Translating Rabbinic Documents 309

True, this is not how Plato and Aristotle set out their ideas; but the great philosophers also did not choose as the medium for writing down their ideas a commentary on a received text, in constant dialogue with yet another received text (the Mishnah, Scripture), with persistent attention to a variety of other received data, all to be provided in a complete and purposeful argument on a point of fundamental importance. They simply set forth a complete and purposeful argument in behalf of a proposition; the evidence and argument were recast by the philosophers into the language required for the proposition they wished to argue, whether in dialogue or in dialectical form. The character of the Judaic sages' system – the inheritance of revelation with which they proposed to enter dialogue – called forth a form that, in itself, expressed the character of the nurturing culture beyond.

I.2 A. R. Hanina bar Pappa, and some say, R. Simlai, gave the following exposition [of the verse,"They that fashion a graven image are all of them vanity, and their delectable things shall not profit, and their own witnesses see not nor know" (Isa. 44:9)]: "In the age to come the Holy One, blessed be He, will bring a scroll of the Torah and hold it in his bosom and say, 'Let him who has kept himself busy with it come and take his reward.' Then all the gentiles will crowd together: 'All of the nations are gathered together' (Isa. 43:9). The Holy One, blessed be He, will say to them, 'Do not crowd together before me in a mob. But let each nation enter together with **[2B]** its scribes, 'and let the peoples be gathered together' (Isa. 43:9), and the word 'people' means 'kingdom': 'and one kingdom shall be stronger than the other' (Gen. 25:23)."

B. *But can there be a mob scene before the Holy One, blessed be He? Rather, it is so that from their perspective they not form a mob, so that they will be able to hear what he says to them.*

C. [Resuming the narrative of A:] "The kingdom of Rome comes in first."

D. *How come? Because they are the most important. How do we know on the basis of Scripture they are the most important? Because it is written,* "And he shall devour the whole earth and shall tread it down and break it into pieces" (Gen. 25:23), *and said R. Yohanan,* "This Rome is answerable, for its definition [of matters] has gone forth to the entire world. [Mishcon: 'This refers to Rome, whose power is known to the whole world.']"

E. *And how do we know that the one who is most important comes in first? It is in accord with that which R. Hisda said.*

F. For said R. Hisda, "When the king and the community [await judgment], the king enters in first for judgment: 'That he maintain the case of his servant [Solomon] and [then] the cause of his people Israel' (1 Kgs. 8:59)."

G. *And how come? If you wish, I shall say it is not appropriate to keep the king sitting outside. And if you wish, I shall say that [the king is allowed to plea his case] before the anger of the Holy One is aroused."*

H. [Resuming the narrative of C:] "The Holy One, blessed be He, will say to them, 'How have you defined your chief occupation?'

I. "They will say before him, 'Lord of the world, a vast number of marketplaces have we set up, a vast number of bathhouses we have made, a vast amount of silver and gold have we accumulated. And all of these things we have done only in behalf of Israel, so that they may define as their chief occupation the study of the Torah.'

J. "The Holy One, blessed be He, will say to them, 'You complete idiots! Whatever you have done has been for your own convenience. You have set up a vast number of marketplaces to be sure, but that was so as to set up whorehouses in them. The bathhouses were for your own pleasure. Silver and gold belong to me anyhow: "Mine is the silver and mine is the gold, says the Lord of hosts" (Hag. 2:8). Are there any among you who have been telling of "this," and "this" is only the Torah: "And this is the Torah that Moses set before the children of Israel' (Deut. 4:44)." So they will make their exit, humiliated.

K. "When the kingdom of Rome has made its exit, the kingdom of Persia enters afterward."

L. *How come? Because they are second in importance. And how do we know it on the basis of Scripture? Because it is written, "And behold, another beast, a second, like a bear" (Dan. 7:5), and in this connection R. Joseph repeated as a Tannaite formulation, "This refers to the Persians, who eat and drink like a bear, are obese like a bear, are shaggy like a bear, and are restless like a bear."*

M. "The Holy One, blessed be He, will say to them, 'How have you defined your chief occupation?'

N. "They will say before him, 'Lord of the world, We have thrown up a vast number of bridges, we have conquered a vast number of towns, we have made a vast number of wars, and all of them we did only for Israel, so that they may define as their chief occupation the study of the Torah.'

O. "The Holy One, blessed be He, will say to them, 'Whatever you have done has been for your own convenience. You have thrown up a vast number of bridges to collect tolls, you have conquered a vast number of towns to collect the corvée, and, as to making a vast number of wars, I am the one who makes wars: "The Lord is a man of war" (Ex. 19:17). Are there any among you who have been telling of "this," and "this" is only the Torah: "And this is the Torah that Moses set before the children of Israel" (Deut. 4:44).' So they will make their exit, humiliated.

P. *But if the kingdom of Persia has seen that such a claim issued by the kingdom of Rome did no good whatsoever, how come they go in at all?*

Q. *They will say to themselves, "These are the ones who destroyed the house of the sanctuary, but we are the ones who built it."*

R. "And so it will go with each and every nation."

S. *But if each one of them has seen that such a claim issued by the others did no good whatsoever, how come they go in at all?*

T. *They will say to themselves, "Those two subjugated Israel, but we never subjugated Israel."*

U.	*And how come the two conquering nations are singled out as important and the others are not?*
V.	*It is because the rule of these will continue until the Messiah comes.*
W.	"They will say to him, 'Lord of the world, in point of fact, did you actually give it to us and we did not accept it?'"
X.	*But how can they present such an argument, since it is written, "The Lord came from Sinai and rose from Sier to them, he shined forth from Mount Paran" (Deut. 33:2), and further, "God comes from Teman" (Hab. 3:3). Now what in the world did he want in Seir, and what was he looking for in Paran?* Said R. Yohanan, "This teaches that the Holy One, blessed be He, made the rounds of each and every nation and language and none accepted it, until he came to Israel, and they accepted it."
Y.	*Rather, this is what they say,* "Did we accept it but then not carry it out?"
Z.	*But to this the rejoinder must be, "Why did you not accept it anyhow!"*
AA.	Rather, "This is what they say before him, 'Lord of the world, Did you hold a mountain over us like a cask and then we refused to accept it as you did to Israel, as it is written, "And they stood beneath the mountain" (Ex. 19:17).'"
BB.	And [in connection with the verse, "And they stood beneath the mountain" (Ex. 19:17),] said R. Dimi bar Hama, "This teaches that the Holy One, blessed be He, held the mountain over Israel like a cask and said to them, 'If you accept the Torah, well and good, and if not, then there is where your grave will be.'"
CC.	"Then the Holy One, blessed be He, will say to them, 'Let us make known what happened first: "Let them announce to us former things" (Isa. 43:9). As to the seven religious duties that you did accept, where have you actually carried them out?'"
DD.	*And how do we know on the basis of Scripture that they did not carry them out? R. Joseph formulated as a Tannaite statement,* "'He stands and shakes the earth, he sees and makes the nations tremble' (Hab. 3:6): What did he see? He saw the seven religious duties that the children of Noah accepted upon themselves as obligations but never actually carried them out. Since they did not carry out those obligations, he went and remitted their obligation."
EE.	*But then they benefited – so it pays to sin!*
FF.	Said Mar b. Rabina, [3A] "What this really proves is that even when they carry out those religious duties, they get no reward on that account."
GG.	*And they don't, don't they? But has it not been taught on Tannaite authority:* R. Meir would say, "How on the basis of Scripture do we know that, even if it is a gentile, if he goes and takes up the study of the Torah as his occupation, he is equivalent to the high priest? Scripture states, 'You shall therefore keep my statutes and my ordinances, which, if a human being does them, one shall gain life through them' (Lev. 18:5). What is written is not 'priests' or 'Levites' or 'Israelites,' but rather, 'a

human being.' So you have learned the fact that, even if it is a gentile, if he goes and takes up the study of the Torah as his occupation, he is equivalent to the high priest."

HH. Rather, what you learn from this [DD] is that they will not receive that reward that is coming to those who are commanded to do them and who carry them out, but rather, the reward that they receive will be like that coming to the one who is not commanded to do them and who carries them out anyhow.

II. For said R. Hanina, "Greater is the one who is commanded and who carries out the religious obligations than the one who is not commanded but nonetheless carries out religious obligations."

JJ. [Reverting to AA:] "This is what the gentiles say before him, 'Lord of the world, Israel, who accepted it – where in the world have they actually carried it out?'

KK. "The Holy One, blessed be He, will say to them, 'I shall bear witness concerning them, that they have carried out the whole of the Torah!'

LL. "They will say before him, 'Lord of the world, is there a father who is permitted to give testimony concerning his son? For it is written, "Israel is my son, my firstborn" (Ex. 4:22).'

MM. "The Holy One, blessed be He, will say to them, 'The heaven and the earth will give testimony in their behalf that they have carried out the entirety of the Torah.'

NN. "They will say before him, 'Lord of the world, The heaven and earth have a selfish interest in the testimony that they give: 'If not for my covenant with day and with night, I should not have appointed the ordinances of heaven and earth' (Jer. 33:25).'"

OO. *For said R. Simeon b. Laqish, "What is the meaning of the verse of Scripture, 'And there was evening, and there was morning, the sixth day' (Gen. 1:31)? This teaches that the Holy One, blessed be He, made a stipulation with all of the works of creation, saying to them, 'If Israel accepts my Torah, well and good, but if not, I shall return you to chaos and void.' That is in line with what is written:* 'You did cause sentence to be heard from heaven, the earth trembled and was still' (Ps. 76:9). If 'trembling' then where is the stillness, and if stillness, then where is the trembling? Rather, to begin with, trembling, but at the end, stillness."

PP. [Reverting to MM-NN:] "The Holy One, blessed be He, will say to them, 'Some of them may well come and give testimony concerning Israel that they have observed the entirety of the Torah. Let Nimrod come and give testimony in behalf of Abraham that he never worshiped idols. Let Laban come and give testimony in behalf of Jacob, that he never was suspect of thievery. Let the wife of Potiphar come and give testimony in behalf of Joseph, that he was never suspect of 'sin.' Let Nebuchadnessar come and give testimony in behalf of Hananiah, Mishael, and Azariah, that they never bowed down to the idol. Let Darius come and give testimony in behalf of Daniel, that he did not neglect even the optional

Translating Rabbinic Documents 313

prayers. Let Bildad the Shuhite and Zophar the Naamatite and Eliphaz the Temanite and Elihu son of Barachel the Buzite come and testify in behalf of Israel that they have observed the entirety of the Torah: "Let the nations bring their own witnesses, that they may be justified" (Isa. 43:9).'

QQ. "They will say before him, 'Lord of the world, Give it to us to begin with, and let us carry it out.'

RR. "The Holy One, blessed be He, will say to them, 'World class idiots! He who took the trouble to prepare on the eve of the Sabbath [Friday] will eat on the Sabbath, but he who took no trouble on the eve of the Sabbath — what in the world is he going to eat on the Sabbath! Still, [I'll give you another chance.] I have a rather simple religious duty, which is called "the tabernacle." Go and do that one.'"

SS. *But can you say any such thing? Lo, R. Joshua b. Levi has said, "What is the meaning of the verse of Scripture, 'The ordinances that I command you this day to do them' (Deut. 7:11)? Today is the day to do them, but not tomorrow; they are not to be done tomorrow; today is the day to do them, but not the day on which to receive a reward for doing them."*

TT. Rather, it is that the Holy One, blessed be He, does not exercise tyranny over his creatures.

UU. *And why does he refer to it as a simple religious duty? Because it does not involve enormous expense [to carry out that religious duty].*

VV. "Forthwith every one of them will take up the task and go and make a tabernacle on his roof. But then the Holy One, blessed be He, will come and make the sun blaze over them as at the summer solstice, and every one of them will knock down his tabernacle and go his way: 'Let us break their bands asunder and cast away their cords from us' (Ps. 23:3)."

WW. But lo, you have just said, "it is that the Holy One, blessed be He, does not exercise tyranny over his creatures"!

XX. *It is because as to the Israelites, too — sometimes* **[3B]** *the summer solstice goes on to the festival of Tabernacles, and therefore they are bothered by the heat!*

YY. But has not Raba stated, "One who is bothered [by the heat] is exempt from the obligation of dwelling in the tabernacle"?

ZZ. *Granting that one may be exempt from the duty, is he going to go and tear the thing down?*

AAA. [Continuing from UU:] "Then the Holy One, blessed be He, goes into session and laughs at them: 'He who sits in heaven laughs' (Ps. 2:4)."

BBB. Said R. Isaac, "Laughter before the Holy One, blessed be He, takes place only on that day alone."

CCC. *There are those who repeat as a Tannaite version this statement of R. Isaac in respect to that which has been taught on Tannaite authority:*

DDD. R. Yosé says, "In the coming age gentiles will come and convert."

EEE. *But will they be accepted? Has it not been taught on Tannaite authority:* Converts will not be accepted in the days of the

	Messiah, just as they did not accept proselytes either in the time of David or in the time of Solomon?
FFF.	Rather, "They will make themselves converts, and they will put on phylacteries on their heads and arms and fringes on their garments and a mezuzah on their doors. But when they witness the war of Gog and Magog, he will say to them, 'How come you have come?' They will say, '"Against the Lord and against his Messiah."' For so it is said, 'Why are the nations in an uproar and why do the peoples mutter in vain' (Ps. 2:1). Then each one of them will rid himself of his religious duty and go his way: 'Let us break their bands asunder' (Ps. 2:3). Then the Holy One, blessed be He, goes into session and laughs at them: 'He who sits in heaven laughs' (Ps. 2:4)."
GGG.	Said R. Isaac, "Laughter before the Holy One, blessed be He, takes place only on that day alone."
HHH.	But is this really so? And has not R. Judah said Rab said, "The day is made up of twelve hours. In the first three the Holy One, blessed be He, goes into session and engages in study of the Torah; in the second he goes into session and judges the entire world. When he realizes that the world is liable to annihilation, he arises from the throne of justice and takes up a seat on the throne of mercy. In the third period he goes into session and nourishes the whole world from the horned buffalo to the brood of vermin. During the fourth quarter he laughs [and plays] with leviathan: 'There is leviathan, whom you have formed to play with' (Ps. 104:26)." [This proves that God does laugh more than on that one day alone.]
III.	Said R. Nahman bar Isaac, "With his creatures he laughs [every day], but at his creatures he laughs only on that day alone."

The shift from language to language signals the presence of a sotto voce observation, a gloss, or a footnote. The movement from the main point to an indented composition does not obliterate the character of the whole as a well-crafted composite – a unity from start to finish.

That the whole of the foregoing constitutes a single essay is readily apparent. When the continuing discussion set forth by Hanina bar Pappa or Simlai is interrupted with a gloss, that is readily apparent. To show how that glossing process in our terms would form a footnote, I indent what I conceive to be footnotes. The interesting point comes at CCC, where we have an appendix to BBB. That is to say, the footnote, BBB, completes the foregoing statement, AAA. Then the additional information is added not to the basic text but to the gloss; it is not filler, the information is valued. But the insertion clearly adds nothing to the basic text – hence it is relegated to an appendix, which, in our technical age, we should simply place at the end of a book. But then HHH forms a footnote to an appendix, therefore is indented still further. The two pages of the Talmud of Babylonia presented here, therefore, are seen, through a proper reference system, to form a coherent and well-crafted essay, text and notes, in which a clear and present proposition governs from beginning to end.[3]

---

[3] I do not claim mine is the best of all possible reference systems, but I have yet to find any alternative one at all – let alone one that provides as much information about the original for analytical purposes as does mine. For an example of the incapacity of colleagues to grasp the simple proposition that a reference system is required, note the stupid remarks of Louis Jacobs in his review of A. J. Avery-Peck, ed., *New Perspectives on Ancient Judaism* volume III. Lanham, 1989: University Press *Studies in Judaism* Series.

16

Mr. Maccoby's Red Cow – and Mine: A Reply to Critics

Mr. H. Maccoby, Richmond, Surrey,[1] has just now advanced discussion of some proposals of mine. A decent respect for the opinions of colleagues requires a proper response to the main points made by him. For despite the rather hateful personal tone that Mr. Maccoby seems unable to avoid in his writing, what is at issue between Mr. Maccoby and me is a fundamental methodological problem: the relationship of a religious system to its own canon. Mr. Maccoby takes the view that if in a received holy book, we may locate support ("prooftexts" or pretexts, depending on one's taste) for a position taken by heirs of that holy book, then we may interpret said position as a "mere" continuation and amplification of the received position. My view is that the canon recapitulates the system, not the system, the canon. Maccoby represents a single, continuous Judaism, the rabbinic one, as though in antiquity there were such a singular, harmonious, unitary, and normative system. But at the time of which he speaks, there was no such thing, but only Judaisms. Not only so, but he imagines that, from Scripture forward, there was a linear and singular progression, his normative Judaism unfolding, generation by generation, out of that same scripture. That is the nub of argument.

In point of fact, just as there cannot be one history of a single Judaism, so also there cannot be a continuous story that tells how first came this, then came that, there can be an exercise of description, analysis, interpretation: examination of system after system. There never has been a single, unitary and linear Judaism, any more than as a matter of mere fact there has been a single, linear and incremental *History of the*

---

[1] H. Maccoby, "Neusner and the Red Cow," *Journal for the Study of Judaism* 21 (1990):60ff.

Jewish People, let alone a single People, "One People."[2] These statements of theological or ideological program do not describe how things have been or are today. But there have been Judaisms, and, as historical entities, there have been groups of Jews. There can be histories of Judaisms and histories of Jewish groups. And these Judaic systems, these Judaisms, we can describe, analyze through comparison and contrast, interpret by locating the ineluctable questions, the self-evidently true answers, and the circumstances and context that imparted urgency to both questions and answers. Accordingly, appeal to Scripture to explain how a given group made the choices that it did – which verses of Scripture to identify, how to read them, with what hermeneutical purpose in mind – is proven post facto by the variety of choices that various Judaisms made for themselves.

Each Judaism invented for itself such past as it found necessary. Part of that invention involved selecting verses of Scripture that would contribute authority to the fully formed system. In the case of the Red Cow, for example, the Judaism represented by the Mishnah devoted attention to that subject and so read with care – as both Maccoby and I have demonstrated – the pertinent verses of Numbers 19. Other Judaisms found nothing in those same verses. The act of selection then is prior to the act of hermeneutics, just as the variety of verses chosen as critical by various Judaisms (Matthew's school's choices, Philo's choices, the Essenes' choices, for example) attests. The fact that many Judaisms, and Christianities as well, appealed to the same Scriptures renders null any claim that all we have in any rabbinic document is a recapitulation and a paraphrase of the plain meaning of Scripture. Accordingly, the invented past of any Judaism has ordinarily consisted of a set of selections not so much of particular events – set into a linear and incremental story of how things came to be what they are – but singular documents, passages in holy books purported to tell the story and therefore also to justify and validate the Judaism at hand.

To be sure, in other work,[3] I account for the shape and character of all Judaisms that have ever flourished and predict the structure of any Judaism that will ever come into existence. Specifically, because the Mosaic Torah's interpretation of the diverse experiences of the Israelites

---

[2] I have expanded on this matter in my review of Michael Meyers' anthology on "Jewish history," reprinted now in J. Neusner, ed., *Essays in Jewish Historiography* [=*History and Theory* Beiheft 27, edited by Ada Rapoport-Albert]. With a new Introduction and an Appendix (Atlanta, 1991: Scholars Press for South Florida Studies in the History of Judaism).

[3] *Self-Fulfilling Prophecy: Exile and Return in the History of Judaism* (Boston, 1987: Beacon Press. Second printing: Atlanta, 1990: Scholars Press for South Florida Studies in the History of Judaism). With a new introduction.

after the destruction of the Temple in 586 invoked – whether pertinent or not – the categories of exile and return, so constructing as paradigmatic the experience of only a minority of the families of the Jews (most in Babylonia stayed there, many in the Land of Israel never left), through the formation of the Pentateuch, the Five Books of Moses, the events from 586 to 450 B.C., became for all time to come the generative and definitive pattern of meaning. Consequently, whether or not the paradigm precipitated dissonance with their actual circumstances, Jews in diverse settings have constructed their worlds, that is, shaped their identification, in accord with that one, generative model. They therefore have perpetually rehearsed that human experience imagined by the original authorship of the Torah in the time of Ezra. That pattern accordingly was not merely preserved and perpetuated. It itself precipitated and provoked its own replication in age succeeding age.

A Judaism – that is, a Judaic system, way of life, worldview, worked out by a distinct social group (an "Israel") – therefore would for time to come represent a reworking of the theme of exile and return, alienation and reconciliation, by an Israel, a group troubled by the resentment of that uncertain past and of that future subject to stipulation. Each Judaism therefore recapitulates the original experience. To state matters in more general terms, religions recapitulate resentment. All Judaisms that have come into being have conformed to that paradigm, and, so long as framers of Judaic systems – ways of life, worldviews, addressed to an Israel subject to particular definition – refer to that same holy scripture, the Five Books of Moses in particular, all Judaisms that will emerge will focus, in one way or another, upon that same generative resentment.

My general theory of the history of Judaism[4] is that a particular experience, transformed by a religious system into a paradigm of the life of the social group, became normative – and therefore generative. Under other circumstances, in other times and places, that experience preserved in authoritative Scripture consequently imparted its form and substance upon Jewish polities that, in point of fact, faced the task of explaining a social world quite different from the one that, to begin with, had generated that original and paradigmatic experience. That is why I maintain that the social world recapitulates religion, not that religion recapitulates that social and political datum, the given of society,

---

[4]My field theory of the history of Judaism beginning to the present rests on a number of completed works, the following in particular: *Foundations of Judaism: Method, Teleology, Symbol* (Philadelphia, 1983-1985: Fortress Press) I-III, *Judaism in the Matrix of Christianity* (Philadelphia, 1986: Fortress Press), *Judaism and Christianity in the Age of Constantine* (Chicago, 1987: University of Chicago Press), and *The Death and Birth of Judaism: From Self-Evidence to Self-Consciousness in Modern Times* (New York, 1987: Basic Books).

economy, politics, let alone of an imaginative or emotional reality. It must follow, of course, that the canon ("verses of Scripture, prooftexts," in context of the debate with Maccoby) recapitulates the system, not the system, the canon.

One may well ask, however, what of the role of the Pentateuch, which by definition is critical to every Judaism. It is a simple fact that the original reading of the Jews' existence as exile and return derives from the Pentateuch, the Five Books of Moses, which were composed as we now have them (out of earlier materials, to be sure) in the aftermath of the destruction of the Temple in 586 B.C. and in response to the exile to Babylonia, the experience selected and addressed by the authorship of the document is that of exile and restoration. So the document itself serves the system that comes to expression in the document; the Pentateuch itself attests to a process of selection and revision. Its framing of events into the pattern at hand represents an act of powerful imagination and interpretation.

The pentateuchal account is fabricated in not only a historical sense, as everyone knows, but also in an existential sense as well. It is an experience that is invented, because no one person or group both went into "exile" and also "returned home." Diverse experiences have been sorted out, various persons have been chosen, and the whole has been worked into a system by those who selected history out of happenings, and models out of masses of persons. I say "selected," because no Jews after 586 actually experienced what in the aggregate Scripture says happened. None both went into exile and then came back to Jerusalem. So, to begin with, Scripture does not record a particular person's experience. More to the point, if it is not autobiographical, writing for society at large the personal insight of a singular figure, it also is not an account of a whole nation's story. The reason is that the original exile encompassed mainly the political classes of Jerusalem and some useful populations alongside. Many Jews in the Judea of 586 never left. And, as is well known, a great many of those who ended up in Babylonia stayed there. Only a minority went back to Jerusalem. Consequently, the story of exile and return to Zion encompasses what happened to only a few families, who identified themselves as the family of Abraham, Isaac, and Jacob, and their genealogy as the history of Israel. Those families that stayed and those that never came back had they written the Torah would have told as normative and paradigmatic a different tale altogether.

That experience of the few that formed the paradigm for Israel beyond the restoration taught as normative lessons of alienation. Let me state with emphasis the lessons people claimed to learn out of the events they had chosen for their history: the life of the group is uncertain, subject to conditions and stipulations. Nothing is set and given, all things a gift: land and life itself. But what actually did happen in that uncertain world – exile but then restoration – marked the group as special, different, select.

There were other ways of seeing things, and the pentateuchal picture was no more compelling than any other. Those Jews who did not go into exile, and those who did not "come home" had no reason to take the view of matters that characterized the authorship of Scripture. The life of the group need not have appeared more uncertain, more subject to contingency and stipulation, than the life of any other group. The land did not require the vision that imparted to it the enchantment, the personality, that, in Scripture, it received: "The land will vomit you out as it did those who were here before you." And the adventitious circumstance of Iranian imperial policy – a political happenstance – did not have to be recast into return. So nothing in the system of Scripture – exile for reason, return as redemption – followed necessarily and logically. Everything was invented: interpreted.

That experience of the uncertainty of the life of the group in the century or so from the destruction of the First Temple of Jerusalem by the Babylonians in 586 to the building of the Second Temple of Jerusalem by the Jews, with Persian permission and sponsorship returned from exile, formed the paradigm. With the promulgation of the "Torah of Moses" under the sponsorship of Ezra, the Persians' viceroy, at ca. 450 B.C., all future Israels would then refer to that formative experience as it had been set down and preserved as the norm for Israel in the mythic terms of that "original" Israel, the Israel not of Genesis and Sinai and the end at the moment of entry into the promised land, but the "Israel" of the families that recorded as the rule and the norm the story of both the exile and the return. In that minority genealogy, that story of exile and return, alienation and remission, imposed on the received stories of pre-exilic Israel and adumbrated time and again in the Five Books of Moses and addressed by the framers of that document in their work over all, we find that paradigmatic statement in which every Judaism, from then to now, found its structure and deep syntax of social existence, the grammar of its intelligible message. I therefore offer these principles by way of generalization:

1. No Judaism recapitulates any other, and none stands in a linear and incremental relationship with any prior one.
2. No Judaism merely recapitulates the canon of Scripture; all make choices therein: which verses, which issues, define the generative problematic of a system.
3. But all Judaisms recapitulate that single paradigmatic experience of the Torah of "Moses," the authorship that reflected on the meaning

of the events of 586-450 selected for the composition of history and therefore interpretation.

Accordingly, a Judaic religious system recapitulates a particular resentment, the one to which the Pentateuch in its general shape and structure precipitates. In this one way each Judaism relates to other Judaisms, religious systems. Each one in its own way, on its own, will address and go over that same pattern, all addressing the same original experience. That is why a sequence of happenings, identified as important history and therefore paradigmatic event, then, is recapitulated in age succeeding age, whether by one Judaism in competition with another or by one Judaism after another. But, as a matter of systemic fact, no Judaism recapitulates any other, though each goes over the same paradigmatic experience.[5] Maccoby errs because he treats the canonical writing as primary to the formation of a Judaic system. But a book is not a Judaism and a Judaism is not a book – except after the fact.[6]

Maccoby thinks that, because he can find some prooftexts for a rabbinic document, he has explained the system to which that document testifies. But his premise, that the framers of the document set about merely to paraphrase the canonical writing they have chosen, answers no question but begs all questions. Recapitulating the story a religious system tells about itself does not help us understand the religious system – let alone account for it. The story – the chosen prooftext – tells not why people made their choices, let alone what happened on the occasion to which the story refers (the creation of the world, for instance) but how (long afterward and for their own reasons) people determined to portray

---

[5] That is the argument of my *Death and Birth of Judaism* (New York, 1987: Basic). There I argue at some length that no Judaism stands in a linear relationship with any other, none forms an increment on a predecessor, and all constitute systems that, once in being, select for themselves an appropriate and useful past – that is, a canon of useful and authoritative texts. And that is the order: the system creates its canon.

[6] The importance of this principle of selection cannot be missed. Let me explain by way of example. I do not see the writings of Philo as a Judaism, though they may represent a Judaism. We have distinctive books that represent social groups, for instance the apocalyptic writings of the Second Temple period, but our knowledge of those social groups – their way of life, their worldview, their identification of themselves as Israel – is imperfect. Consequently we cannot relate the contents of a system to its context or account for the substance of a system by appeal to its circumstance. We therefore know the answers provided by a system – that is, the contents of the book – but have not got a clear picture of the questions that the answers take up, or, still more important, the political or social forces that made those questions urgent and inescapable, in just that place, in just that time.

themselves. The tale therefore recapitulates that resentment, that obsessive and troubling point of origin, that the group wishes to to explain, transcend, transform – and to that formative process in the making of a religious system, the prooftext is post-facto.[7]

If, therefore, in Maccoby's conception a mere narrative of history – discovering prooftexts or pretexts for positions of a later document – is supposed to serve the purpose of explanation, it is because of an evasion, on the one side, and a deep misunderstanding of the character of Judaisms on the other. The evasion represents the easier side to perceive: people find it easier to recite and paraphrase than to analyze and explain. That is why – as in the rather clumsy article of Maccoby in this journal – they play out the conventions of show-and-tell and let the answers come from they know not where: self-evidence, mostly. The incomprehension of Judaisms derives from accepting as fact the claim of a Judaism to constitute Judaism: as it was in the beginning, as it is, and on through time. The linear and incremental story of Judaism that today serves – beginning from Abraham, ending with this morning's events in Jerusalem or Jewish Providence – constitutes a profound theological judgment. It does not record how things really were. For no Judaism – Judaic system made up of a worldview, a way of life, and a particular group of Jews, an Israel, whose collective life is explained by the one and patterned by the other – stands in a linear and incremental relationship with any other. Indeed, none relates to any other at all, except in making selections from a common treasury of historical detritus. But the selections from the rubbish heap of history – the holy books, the customs and ceremonies (so to speak) always follow the inner logic of a system, which, after the fact, makes its choices, pronounces its canon.

Now this brings us back to Mr. Maccoby's point. The principal objection advanced by Mr. H. Maccoby to my account of the red cow in Mishnah-tractate Parah is this:

> His general thesis...is that the Mishnah expresses, through the details of ritual, a philosophy of holiness that is, in significant respects, different from that of the Bible, being a response to the historical circumstances of Jewish political helplessness after the destruction of the Temple. It may be objected, however, that this schema is flawed by considerable special pleading and inaccuracy [sic!] on Neusner's part. Details of rabbinic law which Neusner wishes to attribute to innovative rabbinic philosophy

---

[7]Since all Christianities share the same books, the Torah, that for Judaisms portray the paradigmatic experience of exile and return, Maccoby's certainty about the determinative power of the received canon is not only puzzling, it is incomprehensible. That explains why Maccoby has elicited among specialists in the various areas on which he writes a uniformly negative response. His ignorance of New Testament scholarship has denied him all serious hearing.

turn out, time after time, to be mere responses to the biblical text. The 'myth' which Neusner wishes to extract from alleged rabbinic ritual innovations is constructed out of non-existent materials; while the myth to which the rabbis really subscribed is that of the Bible itself, with its major themes of Exodus, Revelation, Desert, and Promised Land – a myth powerful enough to induce submission to the text of scripture and faith in its ability to provide answers to all possible difficulties. Neusner's offered paradigm case of the Mishnah's treatment of the Red Cow rite may serve to illustrate the above criticisms.

For a critique who claims to contrast his "accuracy" as against his allegation of errors I am suppose to have made, this vague, inaccurate and misleading, précis of my ideas hardly supplies much validation. Maccoby has not proved himself a careful and accurate reader of other people's work.

A brief account of positions of mine, clearly stated and broadly known, suffices to show how slovenly is his précis. In my work, I maintain that the Mishnah took shape after the Bar Kokhba War, not "after the destruction of the Temple." It is represented by me as a response not to "Jewish political helplessness," which vastly understates Judah the Patriarch's power, but to the religious crisis represented by the failure of the scriptural paradigm, destruction, three generations, return and renewal. It is not the destruction of the Temple in 70 that precipitated a crisis, but the debacle of Bar Kokhba's effort to replicate the rebuilding in the time of the second Isaiah, that I think accounts for the distinctive emphases of the Mishnah upon the enduring sanctification of the Land and of the people, Israel.

On the face of it, Maccoby puts forward the claim that the rabbinic system "merely" restated what the Written Torah said to begin with: "the plain sense."[8] That hoary apologetic[9] hardly serves the authentic

---

[8]Maccoby's "Bible," but of course he cannot mean that the rabbis drew also upon the New Testament, which is one half of the Bible. For a defender of the faith such as Maccoby represents himself to be, this Christian usage seems rather odd.
[9]The same apologetic surfaces in the dreadful work of Daniel Boyarin, *Intertextuality and the Reading of Midrash* (Bloomington & Indianapolis: Indiana University Press, 1990), treated in Chapter Seventeen. The difficulty in following Boyarin is that he writes in a strange, turgid jargon. Furthermore, without telling us why this is important, he identifies himself early on as an Orthodox Jew (p. ix); He calls himself a participant observer, so as to win credibility, I suppose; this confuses religious authenticity with intellectual accuracy. But as a matter of fact, the apologetic point of the work is clear: "What in the Bible's text might have motivated this gloss on this verse?" He states at the end (p. 128), "Midrash is best understood as a continuation of the literary activity which engendered the Scriptures themselves." This sounds suspiciously like the familiar claim that Midrash says what Scripture really means, and that *is* the theology of some Orthodox Judaisms. In this book the literary critical frosting covers a stale but

Judaism of the Dual Torah, which alleges that the oral part of the Torah complements and completes the written part, but also is free standing. Since numerous Mishnah tractates take up subjects of which the Written Torah knows nothing, Maccoby's basic allegation is simply ignorant and inaccurate. But – despite his obvious program of theological apologetics for his particular Judaism to accord him a fair hearing – if I understand Maccoby, what he wishes to claim is that "details...turn out...to be mere responses to the biblical text." I gather that his argument is that since the framers of tractate Parah found support for some of their propositions in verses of Scripture, therefore any claim that they did more than state the plain meaning of Scripture must be rejected.

If that is what he wishes to say, then his criticism is simply charming for its naiveté. As my opening remarks have emphasized, every writer from Ezra's closure of the Pentateuch in 450 found in Scripture whatever he wanted, whether Bar Kokhba, Philo, Jesus, or the Teacher of Righteousness, the School of Matthew, or the authorship of a tractate of the Mishnah. Mentioning those six who can well have claimed merely to say what the Written Torah had said ("not to destroy but to fulfill") underlines that people could find not only what they wanted, but also the opposite of what they wanted. So at stake in explaining a piece of writing is not whether verses of Scripture can have been adduced in support of what an authorship wished to say, for they always can and were found, ready at hand, when wanted. At issue, rather, is why someone went looking for proof, chose a given subject to begin with. Maccoby begs the question, of course, unless he can explain why a particular verse of Scripture to begin with attracted attention. Maccoby does not seem to take seriously that the school of Matthew as much as the authorship of Mishnah-tractate Parah found ample support in Scripture for whatever they wished to say.

Precisely what he says about the authorship of Mishnah-tractate Parah can and should be said about Mark, Luke, Matthew (for Isaiah, for instance), and John (among many!). Then are we to dismiss the School of Matthew or the authorship of Mishnah-tractate Parah therefore can be dismissed as mere epigones of Scripture? Not very likely. To the contrary, when we wish to understand a document, the first question (in this context) must be, why this particular topic, as against a vast range of other scriptural topics that are neglected? If the Red Cow, then why not the flight to Egypt. I should be interested in Maccoby's evidence for his allegation that "the rabbis" (I assume in this context he means the

---

kosher cake. Boyarin thus represents in connection with rabbinic exegesis of Scripture that proposition that Maccoby puts forth in the context of the origins and growth of law within the system of the Judaism of the Dual Torah.

authors of the tractate under discussion) have found in "Exodus, Revelation, Desert, and Promised Land" anything pertinent to their Red Cow. I should be curious to know just where, in the tractate under discussion, Maccoby finds his grand themes of "Exodus...," etc. Maccoby persistently exhibits the deplorable tendency to make things up as he goes along. The wide-spread realization that his writings on Jesus and Paul are simply bigoted joins with the broad recognition that he is scarcely a master of the sources.

Whenever I have had occasion to test an allegation on which Maccoby displays his marvelous certainty, I have found no evidence in support of that allegation, but rather, evidence of Maccoby's incomprehension of the sources and also of the considerations that have led scholars to the conclusions that they have reached. There seems to me no reason to pay more attention to Maccoby; I have the impression that colleagues in New Testament scholarship have reached that conclusion as well. In any event the most decisive refutation of Maccoby is given in Jewish Law by E. P. Sanders himself in Jewish Law from Jesus to the Mishnah: "The idea of human intention, greatly and correctly emphasized by Neusner, is original to the Pharisees so far as we know. Thus even when they are only defining or clarifying biblical law, they are operating with some post-biblical categories."[10] What is said in this small context applies throughout, and with that we may dismiss Maccoby as not merely uninformed but, alas, simply uncomprehending.[11]

---

[10] *Jewish Law*, p. 187.
[11] I have replied to Sanders's critique of my picture of the Pharisees in "Mr. Sanders's Pharisees and Mine," *Scottish Journal of Theology*, in press.

17

More Orthodox Apologetics: Boyarin's Version of Midrash

Intertextuality and the Reading of Midrash. By Daniel Boyarin. (Indiana Studies in Biblical Literature. Bloomington & Indianapolis: Indiana University Press, 1990). 161 pp.

This rather thin, first book by the new Taubman Professor at University of California, Berkeley, proposes through examining a tiny segment of the anomalous and probably medieval exegetical text, Mekhilta, to clarify the nature of Midrash. The use of contemporary literary theory to explain Midrash is hardly news; the trend is more than a decade old. The results have proven trivial and dubious, as in Susan Handelman, *The Slayers of Moses: The Emergence of Rabbinic Interpretation in Modern Literary Theory* (Albany: SUNY Press, 1982). So Boyarin's is not a work of pioneering intellect, but of mere application and paraphrase. Unhappily, the application is not very compelling.

To be sure, using a medieval compilation for that purpose is exceedingly odd, and therefore certainly original, if perhaps ill-advised. Boyarin knows but dismisses B. Z. Wacholder, "The Date of the Mekilta de-Rabbi Ishmael," *Hebrew Union College Annual* 39 (1968), pp. 117-144. He maintains that Wacholder's view has been "decisively and definitively disproved by Menahem Kahana, 'The Editions of the Mekilta deRabbi Ishmael on Exodus in the Light of Geniza Fragments' *Tarbiz* 45 (1986):515-520." Indeed Boyarin goes on to state (p. 130, n. 3), "The Mekilta may be in the main, in fact, the earliest of rabbinic midrashic texts, although its final recension seems to have been a little later than some other early midrashim." This murky claim of his – what he means by "final recension" and how he knows what he says – is not spelled out but just tossed off.

Boyarin's ignorance of Mekhilta scholarship, the very text to which he devotes his entire book, is genuinely alarming. First of all, Dr. Mireille Hadas-Lebel's major paper, on loan words from Greek and Latin in Mekhilta, has definitively demonstrated that these loan words are terms that did not come into existence before the third or fourth century C.E. Borrowing these terms into Hebrew necessarily belongs to a subsequent date. That paper was written without reference to Wacholder's thesis but substantiated his views, point by point. Wacholder for his part has furthermore dismissed Kahana's article (which was in *Tarbiz* 55, pp. 489-524, not the pages Boyarin cites!) as based on "insubstantial evidence." Boyarin also does not seem to know that Mekhilta Attributed to R. Ishmael is asymmetrical in rhetoric and logic to the entire corpus of other, demonstrably early Midrash compilations, Sifra, and the two Sifrés, for example, as shown in my *Mekhilta Attributed to R. Ishmael. An Introduction to Judaism's First Scriptural Encyclopaedia* (Atlanta, 1988: Scholars Press for Brown Judaic Studies). How can a work that purports to describe Midrash on the basis of a few passages of a single, atypical text win our confidence when the author does not even know the scholarly literature on the document he claims to describe and interpret?

The book is written in a strange, turgid jargon, for example, "...all of them [interpretations in Midrash compilations] are more or less different from the commentary of the European traditions in that they do not seem to involve the privileged pairing of a signifier with a specific set of signifieds," and again, "I intend to articulate a theory of this text which will explain its hermeneutic moves as hermeneutic – i.e., without reducing them to some other species of discourse." At many points Boyarin seems to be talking mainly to himself. Without telling us why this is important, he identifies himself early on as an Orthodox Jew (p. ix); He calls himself a participant observer, so as to win credibility, I suppose; this confuses religious authenticity with intellectual accuracy. The apologetic point of the work is clear: "What in the Bible's text might have motivated this gloss on this verse?" He states at the end (p. 128), "Midrash is best understood as a continuation of the literary activity which engendered the Scriptures themselves." This sounds suspiciously like the familiar claim that Midrash says what Scripture really means, and that *is* Orthodox Judaism. In this book the literary critical frosting covers a stale but kosher cake.

Lest readers suppose that I exaggerate the oddity of his representation of Midrash, let me give a typical passage (p. 35) among the half-dozen or so that comprise the entire book. This shows us how Boyarin uses the language of literary criticism to tell us what a

More Orthodox Apologetics: Boyarin's Version of Midrash 329

straightforward reading of the text shows without literary criticism of this sort. First the reader must know that the passage we consider is not in the Mekhilta at all, but in the Talmud of Babylonia. So we are introduced to the Mekhilta by other-than-Midrash texts, a fine instance of the intellectually vulgar Orthodoxy of this book: everything Jewish is the same as everything else Jewish, Midrash, Talmud, Bible – whatever. The reason he gives is that the names that occur in one document occur in another – and that's that. For Boyarin that gullibility does not pose a problem: "The Talmud preserves a story about the very rabbis of the Mekhilta which contains a nearly explicit commentary on midrashic intertextuality...."

> For this commandment which I command you today is not too difficult for you or too remote. *It is not in heaven* that one should say, Who will arise to heaven, take it and make it heard that we might do it. And it is not over the sea, that one might say, Who will cross to the other side of the sea and take it for us and make us hear it, that we might do it. Rather, the word [thing] is very close to you in your mouth and heart, to do it (Deut. 30:11-14).

On this passage, Boyarin states the following:

> R. Yehoshua [to whom the passage is attributed (JN)] transforms the verse through his citation into meaning that the Torah is beyond the reach, as it were, of its divine author. The nature of R. Yehoshua's hermeneutic speech act here is vital to understand the text. If we do not perceive what he is doing with the verse from Deuteronomy, we could misunderstand him to be making precisely the opposite claim, namely, that the text is autonomous and sufficient in itself, not requiring the author to guarantee its true interpretation – a version of the New Criticism. By performing an act of tesseration of the language, however, the rabbi disables any such reading of his statement. Without fanfare, R. Yehoshua creates radical new meaning in this verse, simply by reinscribing it in a new context. "It is not in heaven" means not only that the Torah is not beyond human reach, but that it is beyond divine reach, as it were.

The "as it were"s do not help us much in figuring out what Boyarin wants to say here. "Not only that the Torah is not beyond human reach" should mean that the Torah is within human reach. "...but that it is beyond divine reach" means either, [1] "not only that it is not beyond human reach, but that it is [supply: not] beyond divine reach," or, [2] "it is within human reach but it is beyond divine reach." If we do not supply the *not* in version 1, we end up saying that Boyarin thinks that the author of the passage is saying that human beings can master the Torah, but God cannot. That strikes me within the context of the text he purports to interpret as little short of lunatic.

Adherents to the theory he expounds here will maintain that you can say pretty much anything you like about any text, and in the next paragraph of the same passage, Boyarin defends himself:

> This brings us squarely up against the dilemma of any hermeneutic theory that does not allow appeal to author's intention as a curb on interpretation. Once that control is gone, it seems that any interpretation is the same as any other, that anything at all can be said to be the meaning of the text. Such hermeneutic anarchy is clearly *not* the way that midrash presents itself. Within our text both the dilemma and an answer to it are offered.

The sentence that follows, we have a right to expect, will specify the dilemma and the answer. But here is Boyarin:

> Present within the narrative is a commentary on itself, namely: "What is 'it is not in heaven'? Said R. Yermia, Since the Torah has already been given from Mt. Sinai, we do not pay attention to heavenly voices, for You have written already at Mt. Sinai, 'Incline after the majority.'"
>
> R. Yermia's rereading of R. Yehoshua solves the problem of what constrains interpretation. The answer is surprisingly modern: the majority of the community which holds cultural hegemony controls interpretation. To put it another way: correctness of interpretation is a function of the ideology of the interpretive community.

Boyarin is saying that the message of the passage is: the community controls the interpretation of the Torah. That is quite so – but then, why write a whole book to say what we have always known Midrash to mean? If this is what intertextuality has to contribute to the reading of Midrash, it is not even trivial, but merely paraphrastic – just the *peshat*.

Much of the book walks over these same well-trodden paths; when we read his analysis of passage after passage, we know pretty much what we knew before we read his analysis. The publisher's blurb holds: "the best, most cogent and intelligent attempt to date to apply insights from modern literary criticism to the interpretation of midrash." But Indiana University Press appears to have forgotten its own publication of a far more original and compelling work, José Faur, *Golden Doves with Silver Dots* (Bloomington: Indiana University Press, 1986). Those who wish to gain whatever benefit a now-fading theory of literature may offer for the study of Midrash will do far better to dismiss Boyarin's vacuity and turn to Faur.

Epilogue
ON COMPARISON

18

What Does Judaism Teach Us about Religion in General?

World-shaking Middle Eastern and European events of the past two years have demonstrated that in claiming that economic motivations best explain human behavior, Karl Marx was wrong. Two other forces which are not of an economic character take priority in telling us why people do what they do: zeal for nation, and love of God. If we wish to explain the eight-year war of Iraq and Iran, both come into play, for example, since Iranian youth willingly gave their lives for nation and for their particular version of the Islamic religion, and so did Iraqi ones. What can explain the endurance and ultimate triumph over Communism of the Polish people, except for zeal for nation and love of God? And how can we account for the endurance of the Ukrainian and Russian and Byelo-Russian and Lithuanian and Latvian and Estonian peoples, without reference to zeal for nation and love of God? Many, though not all, of the irrepressible conflicts within nations, moreover, draw their power from religion, the division of Ireland, the tensions between the Roman Catholic western and the Protestant eastern parts of Germany, or the Roman Catholic south and the Protestant north of the Netherlands, let alone the Protestant English speaking part of Canada and the Roman Catholic French speaking part. And the catalogue of nations divided by religion must include India and Pakistan and Sri Lanka, not to mention, after all, the State of Israel. So as to religion and nationalism, when joined, no other power or motive or force can ultimately overcome them, and, when divided, religion surely holds its own in the struggle with nationalism, with its demonstrated capacity to destroy nations and rip the fabric of societies.

I need hardly claim that religion is the single most powerful force in human affairs today, therefore, to make the case that religion is something that we must understand if we hope to make sense of the world we know. And yet what all of us know is not religion, but only religions, ordinarily our own religion. And when we speak about religion, it is commonly discourse concerning anecdotes and episodes: religions, not religion. We are in the position of natural scientists lacking a general theory of the data they know so well – astronomy without Copernicus, physics without Einstein, geology without the theory of plate tectonics, to give three striking examples, the third from our very own time.

What is it that we do not know about religion? If I had to identify the single most urgent question confronting us when we want to make sense of a world that is shaped in significant measure by religion, it is, what do religions tell me about religion in general? For if I look at Canada, with the division by language and by religion, or at Germany, with the division by region and by religion, or at Sri Lanka, with the division by ethnic origin and religion, or in the Iran-Iraq conflict, with the division by culture and by religion, or at Poland, with religion a source of national identity, or at the State of Israel, with religion the source at one and the same time of ethnic identity and national disunity – if I look at the examples of the enormous power of religion, I do not know what these examples exemplify. I cannot say how religion has made a difference throughout, only how religion forms a factor case by case. So, as I said, I can make sense of religions, but I do not know how to speak about religion.

Let me give some examples of what we do not know because we cannot explain what we mean by "religion" but only "religions." In the recent past in this country we have found the Supreme Court distinguishing between the "religious" and the "merely cultural" or "secular" aspects of Christmas, which celebrates the birth of Jesus Christ. What then do we mean when we distinguish "religion" from "culture," and what can Christians concede to be "secular" about Christmas? We have debated whether or not Federal funds may finance "blasphemy" and "sacrilege," without a clear definition of what we can mean, in the civil discourse, by "sacrilege," speaking of a flag, for instance; and what "blasphemy" the state can define and penalize. The Supreme Court invokes eighteenth century definitions of religion when it wants to know what is to be categorized as religious, what as secular, and the House of Representatives undertakes to legislate about sacrilege and blasphemy, with no clear notion of what, in the context of this Republic, we can possibly mean by those terms. So to return to the main point, if we have nothing to say about "religion" but speak only of distinct "religions," we cannot only not understand the world abroad and its wars, we also cannot make sense of urgent issues here at home. In the one case, it is because we do not understand how religion works, in the other, it is because we have no language that permits us to speak about religion at all.[1]

Where do we start? At two points, and each is equal in importance to the other. First, we have to start at the bottom, with the comparison and contrast of one religion with another. Second, we have to start at the top, with a theory of religion in general. The importance of starting at the bottom is simple: there we can control our facts, we can speak of some few things, about which we are well informed. But that hardly suffices since our goal is not religions but religion, and that means, more than two. The urgency of starting with some general theory is obvious, too. We have to formulate some sort of generalization, which is to be tested against the facts of the here and the now. We require some sort of pattern that holds together a good deal of information – I began with such a pattern when I pointed out that many unrelated facts all point to religion as the single most important force in human affairs through much of the world. So I theorized, implicitly to be sure, that religion is the single most important force in the social order of many nations and even whole regions of the world, the Middle East and India, Western Europe and North America, for instance. Can we test that theory? Of course we can – once we admit it is a theory.

And what is at stake if we succeed in this fresh thinking about religion? It is the possibility of defining a shared range of conversation, so that, in this-worldly terms, religions may talk together. When, today, different religions meet, in the persons of the faithful, with good will they may speak of God, but conversation falters when they wish too to speak of the here and the now. But when they move onward and downward to this world, wanting to speak not of God in the abstract but of religion in the concrete, they succeed only in illustrating the impossibility of shared speech. For what they mean by "religion" is pretty much a generalization of what they perceive to be their own, particular religions. When, therefore, we frame some theory or theories of religion, encompassing many or even all religions, we shall be able to begin that inter-religious dialogue about the welfare of this planet and this race of ours, this earth, this human race, the future of which so preoccupies us all.

Now being a scholar of Judaism, I have of course to commence within the case of Judaism when I try to make my own contribution to theory– Judaism at the bottom and Judaism at the top alike. That means I have to treat Judaism as an example, not a thing all by itself but as a

---

[1]This paragraph draws upon Jonathan Z. Smith, "Connections," *Journal of the American Academy of Religion* 48 (1990):1-15.

case of something that goes beyond its own limits: an example of religion. I may well discover that what I think exemplary will turn out to be distinctive, a series of one, so to speak. But that is to be discovered at the end, not adduced as an excuse for not taking chances to begin with. So what can I say about Judaism "at the bottom," in comparison with some other religion or religions? And what can I say about Judaism viewed from a distance, as exemplary of "religion in general"? To invoke the title of this address, what does Judaism teach us about religion in general?

If I had to select the single most stunning trait of Judaism in today's world, by comparison with another religion in today's world, what should I choose? Focusing upon not belief, which has always seemed to me post facto, but behavior, which defines the everyday, I have to select the capacity of a single religious tradition to obey the biblical commandment to be fruitful and multiply. That is to say, the world today produces ample evidence that there is not Judaism but only Judaisms, which concur on very few matters indeed. For when I ask myself what Reform Judaism in the USA has in common with one of the many varieties of Orthodox Judaisms in the State of Israel, I have to answer, practically nothing of any interest. To state the question in homely terms, would I, as an American Jew with deeply endogamous commitments, find preferable my daughter's marrying an American Baptist or an Israeli yeshiva-bochur, I should rather not choose. Indeed, Judaism illustrates the dilemma of religion: just as their are Judaisms, but no Judaism, so there appear to be religions, not religion. How, then, I think about the identification of a single Judaism, what would serve as a definition for that Judaism[2] – these define questions that, in a small way, form counterparts to the large question that I asked at the outset.

If then I compare Judaisms with another religion, do I speak intelligibly if I use the counterpart, Christianities? By comparison with Roman Catholic, Anglican, and Orthodox Christianities, not at all, for these form a remarkably cogent religious communion, agreeing on many more things than those on which they disagree. If I compare Judaisms with the various Protestant communions, by contrast, the diversities of the one do find counterparts in those of the other. What, after all, does an Evangelical Baptist have in common with the United Church of Christ in behavior or in belief? No more, I should venture, than a Reconstructionist Judaist has in common with a Lubovitch Hasid, which

---

[2] This paragraph reflects the thinking in my *Self-Fulfilling Prophecy: Exile and Return in the History of Judaism* (Boston, 1987: Beacon Press. Second printing: Atlanta, 1990: Scholars Press for South Florida Studies in the History of Judaism). With a new introduction.

What Does Judaism Teach us about Religion in General? 337

is to say, nothing much. So I find myself forming the theory that some religions are simple, others complex, in the obvious sense that some religions hold together diverse elements, others do not. Moving outward to Islam, with its vast and public warring sectors, Sunni and Shiite, draws us into entirely familiar ground, so long as we do not treat as analogous the wars of the Reformation and the eight year war between Iran and Iraq, and so long as we remember that Iraq and Saudi Arabia and Kuwait all fall within the Sunni camp.

Moving from the bottom to the top, I suppose I should propose as my generalization for all religions that they serve in the end to divide, that their power in society is principally to generate conflict. That certainly would form one valid conclusion to draw from the observation that some religious traditions, the Judaic and the Muslim and elements of the Christian, for instance, comprise scarcely-congruent constituents. Religion then is to be classed as one of the main fissiparous forces of the social order, bringing a message of peace to those near at hand, but of war and destruction to those far away, and, alas, defining those near at hand in ever diminishing circles.

And yet, viewed from above and beyond, religions – and therefore, religion too – may claim to provide the bonds that hold families together and form of families communities, and of communities, whole societies. This is for three reasons. First of all, religions (I would guess, invariably) respond to the human need to mark the turnings of life: birth, puberty, marriage, death, for instance. So they frame the life of home and family. Second, religions impose upon the dreary passage of sunrise, sunset, and the movements of the sages some significance and order, transforming the turning of the winter solstice into Christmas or Hanukkah, the fall and spring equinoxes into (for Judaism) the autumnal month of celebration that culminates in Sukkot, the feast of tabernacles, with its spring counterpart in Passover (for Christianity: Easter). So religions differentiate the course of nature and celebrate its twists and turns. Finally, religions link strangers, people with no other natural bond to one another but a shared belief or a common response to a given body of symbols. There is no given that makes me identify in the other a person like myself, or a person unlike myself. Nothing dictates that I should care what happens to someone I have never seen or known and will never see or know. And yet, my religion, Judaism, imparts the capacity to care for people long dead, on the one side, or today in danger, on the other; and the same is so for other religions. I would then claim that religions invariably impose upon the human imagination a sense of society that otherwise would not find a presence among us.

It follows that we may generalize about religions and speak of religion. We may set forth propositions about what religion is and does, and we may test those propositions against the facts that derive from what religions are and do. In that context, at the end, let me specify three propositions about religion that Judaism in particular offers for people to consider.

1. The first is that religion serves particularly well to help a defeated society endure defeat.³ The Judaism that has predominated for nearly two thousand years is the one that took shape after the destruction of the Second Temple of Jerusalem in the year 70; all of its canonical writings beyond the Hebrew Scriptures took shape from the second century forward, and the power of that Judaism – the self-evident truth that the believers have imputed to it – derives from its capacity to answer a very particular question: what next? Just now the Dalai Lama has called for a consultation a variety of rabbis and scholars of Judaism to ask them about what it means to live for centuries without a homeland; how does a religion continue both to remember where it was – in Tibet, in what we know as not "Palestine" but "the Land of Israel" – and also to acknowledge the here and now. At a religious convocation in Bari, in southern Italy, just now, I found myself addressing a group of Cambodians and telling them hopeful things about their future. I thought I was speaking of us, but discovered that every word struck their hearts as personal, to them. So Judaism tells us that when religion works, it works best because of its peculiar kind of power. That is not to suggest, in the line of Marx, that religion is the opiate of the masses, or of Nietzsche that some religions (he spoke of Christianity) really are for slaves. It is to suggest, to the contrary, that religion explains the human condition better than any other source of explanation, because the human condition, if groups live long enough, is more often one of defeat and disappointment than victory and triumph.

2. The second is that religion explains particularly well the progress of humanity through the cycle of life, from birth to death. Contemporary Judaism in this regard contains a very powerful argument in behalf of that proposition. It is that, in a context of diverse commitments, in a society in which all of us are many things, part of an undifferentiated mass when we want (at mass sports events, for instance, or watching network TV), and different from everybody else when we want, Jews choose to be different on only some very distinctive occasions. And these, we now know, find what defines them in the affairs of home and family: where we live, as we pass through the years allotted to us. Judaism is perceived in the world at large as not a strong religion,

---

³I stated this matter in a simple way in my *Ancient Israel after Catastrophe. The Religious World-View of the Mishnah. The Richard Lectures for 1982* (Charlottesville, 1983: The University Press of Virginia).

because Jews do not go to synagogue in the massive proportions that Christians go to church. But when we realize that when Jews marry other Jews, it is (so far as anyone knows) mostly in a religious rite, that most Jews who reach puberty celebrate a bar or bat mitzvah, that most Jews celebrate those rites of Judaism that involve the home and family, such as Passover, that most Jews who die are buried in accord with the rites of Judaism, we have to see Judaism in quite a different way. What we observe is a religion that works its power of enchantment within the framework of the life of the home and the family.[4] And what that means is that a religion that sets forth dietary laws that some Judaisms reject altogether and most Jews, of whatever Judaism, ignore most of the time, also makes demands that most people obey. The reason, I maintain, is that Judaism explains particularly well the life of the individual and of the family, and from that fact I generalize that religion works well when it comes to living in the here and now.

3. The third lesson I learn from Judaism is that religion never begins this morning, and yet it invariably thrives in the acutely contemporary world. That is to say, what religion accomplishes is the transformation of the past into something memorable, and of the present into an occasion for the celebration of the past. Religion speaks of history but is never historical. Judaism teaches those lessons because, while described as a historical religion, most of the "facts of history" that are supposed to dictate the faith of Judaism either never happened at all, or did not happen in the way in which Judaism says they did, or, if they did, then did not mean to everybody who knew about them what they self-evidently meant to Judaism. So "the facts of history" turn out to be the constructs, out of which the faith is composed.[5] But the composition of the faith forms an acutely contemporary task, for it happens in the intensely-present-tense of this morning. Judaism says that in so many words when it speaks of how, at Passover, each person is to see himself or herself as redeemed, personally, from Egypt: and that can be only in the here and the now. The deepest layers of contemporary Judaic consciousness, bearing the memories of murder and transforming them into "Holocaust," form the foundations of a conception of today's world-order, a conception that dictates how people relate to their neighbors and what they want of their nations as well.

---

[4]This is the argument of my *The Enchantments of Judaism. Rites of Transformation from Birth through Death* (New York, 1987: Basic Books). Judaic Book Club selection, September, 1987. Jewish Book Club selection, October, 1987.
[5]This is the argument, for the matter of "Israel" as a construction and fabrication of the faith, of my *Judaism and its Social Metaphors. Israel in the History of Jewish Thought* (New York, 1988: Cambridge University Press).

That much then: what Judaism teaches us about religion in general is three theses, [1] religion is for the losers, who in time by religion are turned into, if not the winners, then at least the survivors – the ones who get to tell the story later on; [2] religion informs the life of home and family, and, whatever its power in the social order and the life of nations, derives its strength from the intimate and fragile bonds of child to mother and father; [3] religion turns history into the reality of the moment, reshaping a received past into the materials for a usable future. Commonly speaking of events in a long-dead past, religion in fact means to frame a message for this morning and for me in particular. These three lessons that Judaism teaches stand in contrast with the point at which I began: the power of religion in world affairs. I adduced as evidence for my proposition that religion is the most powerful force in humankind on planet earth, the capacity of religion to cause war and disrupt the life of regions and nations. And yet I offered as generalizations about religion propositions about the humble affairs of home and family, community and near-at-hand society.

Were we to speak of Christianity or Buddhism or Shinto or Islam, were we to interrogate religion in Papua Nieu Guini or in the Celebes or in Bali or in Morocco, we might produce other generalizations; but I am confident that wherever we should turn for our facts about religions, we should end up with these generalizations everywhere. And therein lies the fundamental lesson that I think Judaism, in particular, offers: religion matters in the world order – whether as a medium for disruption, as in times past, or as a method for the conduct of dialogue between different persons, as in times to come – because, to begin with, religion makes a difference in the home and family. But Judaism is a religion that, through time, found itself speaking to not a nation in its land, or to a powerful and important social group within society at large, but, mainly, to humble folk: mothers and fathers and their children. So what we learn about religion from Judaism is what a religion is when it speaks in particular to the family in the here and now of their immediate condition: this morning, to an us that assembles around a common table.

Index

Aaron, 99, 202, 204
Abba Saul, 181
Abbahu, 137
Abigail, 71
Abner, 71
Abodah Zarah, 299
Abot, 10-11, 13, 22, 132, 141, 143, 150-151, 263-264, 270, 276
Abraham, 140, 144, 169, 304, 312, 320, 323
Adam, 252, 263
Adda, 44
Adda bar Ahbah, 44, 62
adultery, 206
agglutinative process, 279
Ahab, 182
Ahia, 43-44
altar, 27, 34-37, 40-44, 46-48, 51-52, 58-66, 78, 83-84, 190, 202-204, 206, 212, 246
analogical-contrastive, 2, 33, 41, 77, 79
analogy, 37-39, 42, 47-59, 66, 75-84, 147-148, 169, 206, 210, 228-229, 336
angel, 132, 168
animal-offering, 34

annointed, 48-49, 55, 60, 63, 78, 126, 205, 211, 267
anonymity, 2, 1, 12, 18-19, 21, 76, 279, 283, 291
apocalyptic, 232, 238, 271, 275
appendix, 34, 201, 281, 299, 307-308, 314-315
Aqiba, 36-39, 61-63, 65-66, 76, 123, 181, 184, 209
Arab, 299, 306, 336
Arakhin, 285-286
Aramaic, 48, 286-287, 298-299, 307
argument a fortiori, 44, 51, 55-58, 61-63, 65-66, 79-83
Aristotle, 90-103, 110, 122, 309
ark, 34
atonement, 34, 43-44, 50, 52, 55, 59, 61-65, 70
attributions of sayings, 4
Augustine of Hippo, 2, 10, 111, 142, 143, 156-157, 159-166, 170-171, 190
authorship, 4, 6-7, 9, 11-12, 18-19, 21, 24-25, 29, 59, 67-69, 85, 93, 95-96, 98-99, 101, 155, 159, 199, 205, 207, 209-211, 213-215,

218-219, 224, 280-281, 283, 285-286, 288, 290, 319-321, 325
autonomy, 23, 163, 168, 193, 272
Azariah, 170, 304, 312
B. Ker., 37
Baba Batra, 295
Baba Qamma, 207, 295
Babylonia, 3, 9, 10-11, 13, 22, 133, 190, 218, 248, 260, 265, 272, 279, 281, 285-286, 288-289, 294-295, 315, 319-320, 329
Babylonian, 10, 33, 286, 288, 295, 299
Balaam, 182
Bar Kokhba, 259, 268-269, 273-275, 324-325
Bavli Arakhin, 285
Bavli, 10, 13, 22, 33, 66-68, 73-74, 85, 155, 215, 218, 279-295, 298
Berakhot, 291-292
bereavement, 70
Bible, 3, 10, 111, 148, 155, 158, 165, 214-215, 221-224, 226-228, 231, 233, 236, 262, 271, 275, 297, 323-326, 327-329, 336
bird-offering, 43
blood, 34-36, 40, 43-44, 46-47, 58-66, 78, 83, 202-204, 208-209
Boyarin, Daniel, 3, 11, 327-330
burnt-offering, 35-36, 40-44, 46-48, 52, 58-62, 84, 202-204
Byzantine, 165
Cain and Abel, 161, 163, 165
canon, 6-14, 16, 19-27, 29-30, 67, 90, 107, 148, 154-155, 167, 170-171, 175-177, 190-191, 193-194, 196, 214, 218, 221, 226, 230,
233, 236-237, 250, 252, 255, 264, 270, 276, 278, 279, 285-286, 297, 317, 320-323, 338
carrion, 57
catalogue, 21, 59, 69, 84, 92, 150, 169, 185, 292, 333
category formation, 51, 81, 91, 106, 111, 115, 118, 123, 171, 175
children of Israel, 302, 310
Christianity, 3, 10, 31, 94-95, 99, 111, 142, 152-154, 157-158, 160, 162, 164-165, 175-179, 187, 221-226, 237, 241-245, 247-262, 265-267, 271, 276-278, 318, 334, 336-340
chronology, 10, 15-16, 293-294
Cicero, 160
city of God, 1-2, 10, 87, 111, 143, 146, 157-164
classification, historical, 4
cleanness, 45
cogency, 25, 27, 29, 39, 59, 89-91, 103, 111, 113, 170, 213, 215, 217, 221, 223, 280-281, 283, 285, 287-291, 306, 308, 330, 336
Cohen, Shaye J. D., 191
commandment, 37, 75, 141, 168-169, 272-273, 276, 329, 336
comparative Midrash, 282
comparison, 3, 10, 29-31, 33, 39, 41, 51-52, 59, 68-69, 72-77, 84, 91-92, 101-102, 107, 111-113, 118, 142, 156, 159, 164, 175, 187, 200-201, 205, 208-210, 218, 252, 282, 288, 318, 331, 335-336
compilation, 2, 9, 10-11, 13, 22, 30, 67, 89, 91, 105, 114, 120, 122, 126, 145, 150, 156, 168, 175, 190, 196, 214-215, 217, 227,

233-234, 238, 258, 260, 279, 283-284, 286, 288-290, 294, 297, 327-328
composite, 66, 96, 272, 289-291, 308, 314
composites, free-standing, 291
congruence, 10, 39, 48, 50-57, 66, 76, 79-84, 111, 249, 257, 278
consecration, 42, 45, 50, 57, 161
Constantine, 153-154, 241, 243, 245, 248-252, 254-256, 259-260, 265, 277
continuity, 12, 14, 20, 23-24, 27, 114, 148, 164, 171, 242, 283, 285
contrast, 2, 5, 30, 33, 38-39, 41, 51-52, 59, 68-69, 72-75, 77, 79, 81, 84, 91-92, 95, 97, 99-103, 111-112, 117, 120, 122, 127, 148, 155-156, 175, 177-178, 187, 191-192, 199-201, 205, 208-210, 213, 218, 221, 229, 251, 256, 282, 288, 290, 318, 324, 335-336, 340
counterpart category, 93, 107, 109-111, 113, 115-116, 117-118, 121-125, 129, 140, 142, 175, 178
Creation, 31, 145, 166, 181, 195, 229, 238, 246, 249, 270, 304, 312, 322
Dan., 302, 310
Daniel, 170, 304, 312
David, 71, 123, 231-232, 252, 265, 267, 306, 314
Day of Atonement, 34, 55, 63
Deuteronomist, 191
Deuteronomy, 10, 54, 64, 67, 70-72, 131, 184, 189, 191, 204, 209, 228, 231, 246, 300, 302-303, 305, 307, 310-311, 313, 329

dialectic, 2, 33, 39, 48-49, 74, 76, 79, 81, 84, 293, 309
diaspora, 222
Dimi bar Hama, 303, 311
Divine Name, 181
divorce, 41
doctrine, 3, 12, 16, 21, 110, 148, 150-152, 163, 175, 178, 180, 221, 231, 244, 247-248, 250, 255, 257, 259-260, 262, 264, 267, 272-273, 277-278, 292
documentary method, 2, 3-4, 6, 12, 19, 91
documentary study, 5, 19
drink-offering, 45
Dual Torah, 11, 3-4, 6-7, 11, 18-19, 29, 177, 186, 190-191, 194, 196, 204, 214, 222-224, 226, 237, 243-244, 246-248, 250, 255-256, 260, 262, 264, 267, 269, 277, 297, 325
economics, 31, 89-90, 93-103, 106-113, 115-116, 121-124, 126, 129, 139-140, 142, 143-144, 148, 151, 153
eisegesis, 263
Eleazar, 265, 274
Eliezer b. Jacob, 43
Eliezer, 184, 204
English, 3, 281, 297, 333
Enoch, 263
Epicurean, 181
Erubin, 295
Esau, 277
eschatology, 155, 186, 257, 261, 266-267, 270, 273, 275-277
Essene, 99, 237, 246, 318

Esther Rabbah, 10

eternity, 2, 10, 155, 163-165, 173, 175-181, 186-187, 253, 275, 279

ethics, 30, 89-90, 143, 234, 236

ethnos, 30, 89-90, 143

ethos, 30, 89-90, 143, 270

Euclid, 52

Eusebius, 164, 190

exegesis, 10-11, 13, 22, 27, 36, 38, 41, 48-49, 54, 59, 66-67, 74-75, 79, 106, 108, 114-115, 118, 125-126, 150, 155, 170-171, 175, 193-194, 207, 212, 214-218, 221-223, 227-229, 231, 233-234, 236-237, 243, 258, 260, 265, 275, 285-286, 288, 291-292, 327

Exodus, 10, 181, 189, 200, 209, 246, 265, 302-304, 310-312, 324-325, 327

expiation, 37, 51-52

extirpation, 37, 43-44, 50, 52, 180

Ezra, 19, 189, 246, 263, 319, 321, 325

Faur, José, 330

Festival, 149, 260, 300, 305, 307, 313

firstling, 203

Flood, 182-183

footnote, 34, 190, 281, 287, 299, 307-308, 314-315

forbidden, 256, 300, 307

form-analysis, 33

frankincense, 206

Freedman, H., 36, 40, 42, 44-46, 48, 50, 52, 54-55, 58-66, 79, 83-84

freewill-offering, 203, 206-207

French, 243, 249, 281, 333

Gemara, 300

Genesis, 156, 158, 183, 189, 215, 246, 297, 301, 304, 309, 312, 321

Genesis Rabbah, 2, 10-11, 105, 109, 121, 132, 134, 142, 156, 215, 217, 228, 234, 237, 248-249, 254, 258, 282

gentile, 125-126, 178, 182, 185-186, 205, 247, 275-276, 300-301, 303-305, 307-309, 311-313

genus, 51, 59, 69, 72-74, 81, 91-92, 167-168, 178, 181, 191-192, 203-205, 210, 236

German, 195, 281, 297

Gittin, 295

gloss, 299, 308, 314, 328

gnosticism, 117-118, 129, 131, 134-135, 148

God, 1-3, 10, 19, 29-30, 67, 85, 87, 96, 99-100, 105, 111, 113-115, 119, 124, 129, 131, 134, 141, 143-148, 150-151, 157-165, 167-170, 178, 180-182, 185-186, 194, 199-201, 214, 218-219, 223, 226, 229, 235-236, 238, 245-249, 252-258, 260-264, 266-267, 270-276, 303, 306, 308, 311, 314, 329, 333, 335

Gospels, 18, 223, 267

Goths, 156

Grace, 132, 246, 249, 258

Greco-Roman, 90-91, 95, 98-102, 146

Greece, 90, 92, 175, 234, 328

guilt-offering, 34-39, 43, 46-47, 50-52, 75-78, 202

Hab., 303, 311

Hadas-Lebel, Mireille, 328
Hag., 302, 310
Haggai, 265
hallot, 54
Hananiah, Mishael, and Azariah, 304, 312
Hananiah b. Gamaliel, 212
Hananiah, 170, 304, 312
Hanina bar Pappa, 309, 314
Hanina, 304, 312
Hanukkah, 337
harmonization, 68
Heaven, 70, 99-100, 115, 125-126, 134, 137-138, 141-142, 143-148, 151-152, 156, 161, 163-164, 167, 178, 181, 186-187, 255, 257, 259, 269-270, 272-273, 275, 304-306, 312-314, 329-330
Hebrew, 3, 48, 263, 286-287, 298-299, 307, 327-328
Hebrew Scriptures, 30, 90, 105, 189, 194, 221-222, 226, 237, 249, 255, 257-258, 338
Hellenism, 176
hermeneutic, 74-75, 189, 257, 259, 318, 328-330
hierarchy, 67, 69, 72-73, 79, 85, 91-92, 119, 121, 127, 139, 145, 147, 202, 205, 207-210, 212-214
high priest, 63, 69-70, 72-73, 99-101, 125-126, 303, 311
Hippo, 142, 156-157, 165
Hisda, 301, 309
historiography, 15, 190, 196, 275
history of religion, 3, 13, 22, 27, 171, 298

Holy Land, 142, 152, 247, 251, 256, 261
Holy of Holies, 63
Holy One, 200-201, 301-306, 309-314
Holy Place, 46, 58, 65, 84, 261
Holy Things, 34, 36-38, 40, 43, 46, 54, 202
Hos., 265
Huna b. R. Joshua, 300, 308
hypothesis, 76, 280, 284
idolatry, 42, 48, 78, 300, 307-308
incense, 206
inner sanctum, 36, 61, 63
intentionality, 58, 147-148, 151-152
interpretation, 10, 6-8, 13, 19, 22, 28-29, 61, 65, 89, 113, 170, 216, 229, 249, 275, 282, 317-318, 320, 322, 327-330
intertextuality, 286, 327, 329-330
intratextuality, 286
Isa., 180, 300-301, 303, 305, 307-309, 311-312
Isaac, 140, 144, 169, 305-306, 313-314, 320
Isaiah, 223, 237, 324-325
Ishmael, 10, 51, 55-57, 61-63, 81-83, 209, 327-328
Islam, 31, 242, 253, 279, 333, 336-337, 340
Israel, 2, 9, 9-11, 13, 16, 22, 25, 28, 30-31, 69, 89-91, 94, 99, 101, 105, 109, 115, 118-120, 124-127, 129, 131-132, 134, 140, 142, 143-144, 146, 152-159, 161-165,

167-170, 178-180, 182, 185-187, 189, 192, 194, 199-200, 215, 221, 224-226, 230, 232, 234-238, 242-250, 252-262, 264-278, 285-286, 292-293, 300-305, 307-312, 319-321, 323-324, 333-334, 336, 338

Israelite, 7, 127, 135, 145-146, 152, 169, 180-182, 185-186, 200-201, 209, 211, 223-225, 237, 257, 267, 271, 275, 294, 298, 300, 303, 305, 308, 311, 313, 318, 336

Jacob, 1, 12, 140, 169, 277, 320

Jastrow, Marcus, 139

jealousy, 150

Jer., 304, 312

Jerome, 157

Jerusalem, 45, 101, 154, 157, 160, 167-168, 182, 252, 256, 269, 320-321, 323, 338

Jesus, 95, 221, 223, 225, 249, 254-255, 257, 267, 325-326, 334

Jew, 9, 12, 14, 16, 20-21, 23, 31, 90, 101, 142, 152-154, 190, 229-231, 241-246, 248-250, 252-256, 258, 262-263, 266, 268, 271-272, 276-278, 318-321, 323-324, 326, 328-329, 336, 338-339

Job, 59, 138, 228

John of Patmos, 177-178, 186-187

Jonathan, 170

Josephus, 191

Joshua b. Levi, 65-66, 300, 305, 308, 313

Joshua, 168, 189, 191, 246, 263

Judah, 42, 45, 57, 65-66, 70-71, 182, 300, 306-307, 314

Judah the Patriarch, 324

Judaism, 1-3, 9-12, 3-8, 10-14, 15-23, 25-26, 29-31, 87, 89-94, 97, 99-100, 102, 105, 107, 109-110, 113, 116, 117-118, 127, 132, 135, 139, 142, 145-148, 151-157, 160-165, 167-168, 171, 173, 175-179, 186-187, 189-191, 193-196, 199, 214-215, 218, 221-226, 230, 237-238, 241-269, 271-272, 277-278, 279, 282-286, 288-290, 297, 309, 317-323, 325, 328, 333, 335-340

Judges, 70, 126, 189, 191, 246, 306, 314

Julian, 153-154, 157, 260

Kahana, Menahem, 327-328

Kgs., 209, 301, 309

king, 69-73, 99-101, 123, 125-126, 182, 185, 189, 191, 246, 249, 252, 255, 257, 259, 274-276, 301-302, 309-310

knife, 43

Lamentations Rabbati, 10

Land of Israel, 2, 9, 10-11, 13, 22, 91, 99, 101, 105, 109, 120, 126, 132, 142, 144, 154-158, 164, 180, 215, 234, 237, 246-250, 252-260, 262, 264-266, 269, 271-273, 275-276, 285-286, 319, 338

Latin, 328

law, 36-38, 41-43, 46-50, 52-54, 59-62, 64-65, 67, 70, 77-79, 98, 100-101, 126, 136-137, 149, 180-181, 207, 228, 232, 234-235, 238, 247-249, 252, 254, 259, 262, 265-266, 268-270, 272, 275, 279, 289-292, 323, 326, 339

laying on of hands, 42, 45, 77

Levi, 130

Index 347

levirate marriage, 70-71

Levite, 125, 303, 311

Leviticus, 10, 35-42, 46-48, 50, 53-54, 59-61, 63-65, 67, 70, 77-78, 84, 97, 156, 200-201, 204, 206, 208-209, 211, 215, 218, 227-228, 231, 234, 237, 246, 248-249, 285, 303, 311

Leviticus Rabbah, 2, 10-11, 105, 109, 121, 123, 132, 142, 156, 227-231, 233-234, 236-238, 248-249, 254, 258, 282, 286

liability, 36, 38

list making, 68-69, 171, 193, 236

Listenwissenschaft, 72, 92, 167, 191-192, 195, 199-200, 205, 209, 213

literature, 3, 8-9, 12-13, 15, 21-24, 30, 116, 155, 167, 191, 247, 275, 283-284, 294, 298-299, 327-328, 330

logic, 3, 23-24, 27, 33, 39, 41, 52, 64, 72-73, 84, 108, 167-168, 191, 195, 199, 202-203, 206-210, 213-215, 218, 221, 223, 226-229, 232-233, 235, 241, 267, 289-291, 293, 323, 328

Lord, 36-38, 71, 130, 161-162, 181, 183-184, 200-201, 206, 265, 274, 301-304, 306, 310-314

M. B.Q., 207

M. M.S., 45

M. Men., 205, 210-212

M. Q., 149

M. San., 149

M. Suk., 149

M. Zeb., 57

Maccoby, H., 3, 11, 317-318, 320, 322-326

Manasseh, 182

Mar b. Rabina, 303, 311

Mar Zutra b. R. Mari, 42, 45, 47-48, 54, 78

marital rite, 70

Matthew, 18, 223, 237, 318, 325

meal-offering, 205-207, 210-212

Meir, 57, 70, 303, 311

Mekhilta deRabbi Ishmael, 10, 328

Menahot, 295

Messiah, 155, 249, 252, 254-255, 257, 259-261, 265-268, 270, 273, 275-277, 302, 305-306, 311, 314

metaproposition, 33, 36, 66-68, 74-76, 85, 295

method, 2-3, 9, 1, 3-6, 8-9, 12, 19, 26, 29, 68, 84, 90-94, 108-111, 119, 171, 234, 239, 244, 270, 273, 281, 287, 293-295, 340

mezuzah, 169, 306, 314

Midrash, comparative, 282

Midrash compilation, 2, 9, 30, 89, 91, 105, 114, 120, 145, 156, 175, 190, 196, 214-215, 217, 227, 233-234, 238, 297, 328

Midrash, 2-3, 9, 10, 89, 91, 105, 114, 120, 145, 156, 175, 190, 196, 214-215, 217, 233-234, 238, 285, 297, 327-330

Mishael, 170, 304, 312

Mishcon, 301, 309

Mishnah, 2, 9-10, 10-13, 21-22, 30, 33-34, 36, 41, 44-46, 49, 59,

66-69, 72-74, 85, 89-103, 105-106, 108-110, 113-115, 117-119, 121-127, 130, 132-134, 145, 148-151, 155-156, 175, 177-180, 184, 187, 199, 204-205, 207-208, 210-218, 225-228, 230-231, 234-235, 237-238, 247-248, 255-257, 259-271, 273, 275-276, 281-283, 285-286, 288-289, 291-294, 297, 299-300, 307-309, 318, 323-326

monotheism, 145

Moore, George F., 3, 8

Moses, 19, 67, 85, 99-100, 105, 156, 200-201, 214, 221, 223-224, 231-232, 238, 246-248, 255, 257-258, 261-265, 302, 310, 319-321, 327

Mount Paran, 303, 311

Nahman bar Isaac, 306, 314

Nahshon, 42

Nathan b. Abetolomos, 50

Nazir, 35

Nebuchadnessar, 304, 312

Nehemiah, 66, 183

Neusner, Jacob, 1, 12, 323-324, 326

New Testament, 222, 224, 234, 326

Niddah, 295

nomothetic, 69, 72, 145

Num., 42, 50, 183-184, 206

oath, 293

Old Testament, 30, 90, 175, 189-190, 221-222, 226, 238, 247, 257-258

Omnipresent, 113

Oral Torah, 4, 29, 175-176, 196, 218, 222, 225, 247-248, 264-265

Orthodox Judaism, 328, 336

paganism, 153-154, 157, 249, 256, 259, 276

Palestine, 101, 142, 152, 154, 157, 247, 256, 338

Pappa, 37, 49, 55-56, 62-63, 82

Parah, 323, 325

Passover-offering, 43, 45

Paul, 18, 325

peace-offering, 35, 45, 48, 53-54, 78, 202

Pentateuch, 19, 97, 99-102, 148, 189-190, 196, 218, 237, 246, 258, 263, 319-322, 325

pericope, 207

Persia, 302, 310, 321

Pesiqta deRab Kahana, 10-11, 105, 109, 121, 132, 156, 282, 286

Pesiqta Rabbati, 282

Pharisee, 326

Philo, 27, 318, 325

philology, 175, 298

philosophy, 2, 9, 31, 69, 72, 87, 89-102, 106-116, 117-119, 121-124, 127, 129, 129-130, 139, 142, 143-145, 147-149, 151, 153-155, 158, 175-179, 187, 191, 195, 214, 234-236, 238, 247, 259, 266-271, 280, 309, 323

phylactery, 168-169, 306, 314

Pirqé Abot, 263

Plato, 95, 97, 99-101, 309

Platonism (neo-Platonism), 90-92

Plotinus, 92

Polanyi, Karl, 96

Index

politics, 9, 12-13, 16, 20-22, 24, 26-27, 29, 31, 69, 89, 95-103, 106-113, 115-116, 117, 122, 124-127, 129, 133, 139-140, 142, 143-144, 146, 148, 151-153, 155-157, 164, 178-182, 184-186, 229, 234, 236, 241-245, 248-254, 256-257, 259, 262, 266, 276-278, 319-321, 323-324

prayer, 136-138, 145, 168-169, 267, 292, 304, 312

Presence of God, 168-169

priest, 35, 40, 43-44, 46-49, 55, 58-60, 63-64, 66, 69-70, 72-73, 78, 97, 99-101, 125-126, 202, 204-206, 211-212, 246, 252, 267, 303, 311

priestly code, 97, 246

proposition, 10, 4, 33, 38, 42, 48, 59, 61-62, 66-69, 72, 75, 78, 84, 90-92, 110, 114-115, 118-119, 130, 139, 145, 168, 185, 189-190, 192-193, 199, 215, 224-228, 230-231, 233, 236, 238, 264, 273, 281, 288, 298-299, 309, 315, 325, 337-338, 340

proselyte, 306, 314

Protestant, 195, 333, 336

Proverbs, 228

Psalms, 123, 133, 183-184, 221, 228, 274, 304-306, 312-314

Qiddushin, 295

Qohelet, 228

Qumran, 99, 221, 237, 246

Rab, 133, 300, 306-307, 314

Raba bar R. Shila, 44

Raba, 48-49, 54-55, 65, 78-79, 81, 305, 313

Rabbah, 2, 10-11, 105, 109, 121, 123, 132, 134, 142, 156, 192, 215, 217, 227-231, 233-234, 236-238, 248-249, 254, 258, 282, 286

Rabbi, 9, 4-5, 8-10, 37-39, 55, 60, 65, 67, 75-76, 85, 90, 126, 132, 135-138, 141, 211, 221, 223-224, 227-228, 232, 238, 255, 259, 261, 265, 267, 324-325, 327, 329, 338

rabbinic, 3, 11, 3-4, 7-8, 12, 14, 18, 20-21, 23, 132, 136, 155, 221, 224-225, 228, 230, 233-236, 247, 255, 259, 263, 266-267, 270, 273, 276, 284, 286, 297-299, 317-318, 322-324, 327

Rabina, 42, 44-45, 47-48, 54-55, 57, 78-79, 81, 83

Rami bar Hama, 54-56, 64, 81-82

red cow, 3, 317-318, 323-325

redaction, 4, 8, 214, 290, 294

reference system, 3, 11, 297, 299, 306-307, 315

Reformation, Protestant, 195

refuse, 58

religion, 2-3, 9-10, 12, 1, 3, 6-9, 13, 15, 18-20, 22-28, 30, 40, 44, 63, 87, 89, 91, 93, 95-96, 105-111, 113-115, 117-119, 121-122, 129, 132, 134, 139-140, 142, 144-145, 147, 150-155, 163-164, 167, 171, 175, 189, 194-196, 221-223, 225-226, 228, 238, 241-242, 244-246, 248-249, 251-252, 257, 259, 261, 267, 271, 285, 294, 298, 300, 303-306, 308, 311-314, 317, 319, 322-324, 328, 333-340

Revelation, 10, 29, 79, 100, 105, 130-131, 158, 177-178, 199, 208,

214, 222-223, 226, 238, 247, 252, 255, 257-259, 261-264, 270, 309, 324-325

rhetoric, 23-24, 72, 106, 108, 115, 162, 227, 236-237, 242, 289, 291, 293, 328

rite, 35, 40, 44, 46-48, 59, 62-66, 70-71, 77-78, 211, 226, 273, 324, 339

Roman Empire, 153, 243, 248-249, 252, 254, 256, 260, 276

Rome, 90-91, 95, 98-102, 146, 154, 156-158, 160, 163, 165, 249, 251-252, 256, 272, 277, 299, 301-302, 306, 309-310, 333, 336

Ruth Rabbah, 10

Sabbath, 305, 313

sacrifice, 34, 37, 42-45, 47-48, 50, 52-53, 58-60, 64-65, 78, 83-84, 144, 154, 184, 260

sacrilege, 35-38, 75, 334

sage, 2, 9-10, 4, 6, 8, 17-19, 37, 52, 59, 68, 90, 92, 99-102, 106, 117, 125-126, 129, 129-136, 138, 142, 143, 154, 156-166, 168, 213-214, 216, 223, 225, 232-235, 244, 247-249, 253-256, 258-269, 273-278, 293, 309, 337

Sahlins, 169

salvation, 111, 113, 118, 120-121, 129-132, 134, 152, 155, 234, 238, 247, 253, 255, 257, 259-260, 267-268, 273, 275

Sam., 71, 184

Samaritan, 274

Samuel, 189, 191, 246, 300, 307

sanctification, 45, 52, 96, 99, 101, 113, 115, 124, 126-127, 129, 147, 168, 179-181, 185, 234, 246, 253, 259-261, 268, 271, 273, 275, 324

sanctuary, 37, 70, 302, 310

Sanders, E. P., 11, 326

Sanhedrin, 69, 98, 180, 184, 291-292

Saul, 71, 181

Sayings of the Fathers, 263

Schechter, Solomon, 3

scribe, 67, 123, 301, 309

Scripture, 3, 7, 9-13, 21-22, 30, 35-36, 38-44, 46-52, 54-55, 59-68, 72-79, 81, 90-91, 99-100, 102, 105, 114, 118, 126, 148, 150, 152, 155, 171, 189, 194-195, 199-218, 221-238, 248-249, 254-255, 257-258, 260-264, 266-267, 270, 275, 277, 283, 285-286, 291-292, 301-305, 309-313, 317-321, 324-325, 328, 338

Shema, 168-169

show bread, 212

show fringe, 168-169

Sier, 303, 311

Sifra, 3, 10-11, 199, 202, 207-208, 210, 213-215, 217-219, 227, 234, 237, 258, 285-286, 328

Sifra to Leviticus, 67, 248

Sifré to Deuteronomy, 67, 228, 231

Sifrés, 10, 258, 328

Simeon b. Laqish, 304, 312

Simeon, 42, 71, 201, 205, 211

Simlai, 309, 314

sin-offering, 34-37, 39-44, 46-48, 50-52, 60-64, 75-76, 78, 203-204

Sinai, 7, 67, 85, 105, 167-169, 192, 200, 214, 244, 247-248, 252-253, 255, 257-258, 261-265, 303, 311, 321, 330

sinner, 205-207

skin ailment, 34-35, 47, 50, 77

slaughter, 37, 40, 43-44, 46, 52, 57-58, 83

slave, 229, 269, 338

Smith, Jonathan Z., 170-171

social entity, 6, 16, 19, 25-27, 30-31, 89-90, 93-94, 98, 101, 106-107, 109-111, 122, 125, 129, 140, 148, 162, 164, 189, 235

sociology, 15

Solomon, 3, 246, 301, 306, 309, 314

Soncino Press, 300, 306

Song of Songs Rabbah, 10, 192

Song of Songs, 194

Spanish, 10, 133, 281, 297

Spinoza, 85

sprinkling the blood, 64

Stock, Brian, 18

storyteller, 3, 17, 136

substitute, 45

successor system, 91, 106-108, 110-111, 113-114, 116, 117, 121-125, 127, 129, 129-132, 134, 144-145, 147, 151, 164, 171, 261

Sukkah, 282-283

Sukkot, 337

syllogism, 92, 114, 118, 227-228, 236, 264

synagogue, 9, 12, 14, 20, 23, 133, 222, 339

T. Menahot, 211

T. Zebahim, 204

Tabernacle, 168-169, 305, 313, 337

Talmud of Babylonia, 3, 9, 10-11, 190, 218, 248, 260, 265, 279, 281, 285-286, 288-289, 294-295, 315, 329

Talmud of the Land of Israel, 2, 9, 10-11, 91, 105, 109, 120, 126, 132, 142, 155-156, 164, 215, 234, 237, 248-250, 254, 257-260, 262, 264-266, 269, 271-273, 275-276, 285-286

Talmud, 7, 10, 33, 41, 59, 105, 114, 132, 155-156, 175, 190, 196, 215-216, 231, 248, 260, 262, 264, 266-267, 273, 275, 286-290, 293-294, 297, 299, 329

Tanakh. *See Written Torah*, 189

Tannaite, 2, 10, 34-37, 40-43, 46, 51, 54-57, 59-60, 62-67, 81-84, 89, 302-303, 305, 310-311, 313

Tarfon, 122-123

taxa, 92, 119, 131, 165, 168-169, 194, 199, 202, 205, 207-208, 213, 217-218, 291

taxonomy, 3, 68, 72, 127, 147, 167-168, 170, 176, 199, 202, 207-208, 213-217, 229, 267-270, 286-287, 291

teleology, 100, 120, 155, 178, 180, 186, 244, 252, 255, 257, 259-261, 266-268, 270, 272-273, 275-277

Temple, 58-59, 84, 97, 101, 126, 153-154, 168-169, 229, 246, 252, 256, 259-260, 268-269, 272, 319-321, 323-324, 338

Temurah, 291

Ten Commandments, 168-169

tent of meeting, 59, 61, 65, 168, 200-204

terefah, 57

text criticism, 298, 308

textual community, 18, 168, 194

thank-offering, 211

thanksgiving-offering, 53-54, 202

Theodosian code, 153

Theodosius, 154

theology, 2-3, 9-10, 3, 10, 16, 18, 24, 26, 29, 89, 113, 118-119, 142, 146, 150, 152, 157-158, 163-164, 170-171, 175-178, 186-187, 189-196, 197, 213-214, 222, 241, 243-244, 249, 254, 267, 277, 279, 285, 291-292, 318, 323, 325

tithe, 45, 53-54

topic, 4, 8, 11-14, 20-24, 29, 37, 90, 95-96, 106, 108, 111, 115, 118, 155, 179, 217, 227-228, 233, 248, 254, 285-286, 291-293, 325

Torah study, 106, 124, 129, 132-136, 139, 148, 192

Torah, 3, 11, 3-4, 6-7, 11, 16-19, 29, 39, 50, 59, 67, 71, 84-85, 105-106, 111, 116, 117-124, 129, 129-136, 140-141, 145-146, 148, 164-165, 167-168, 175-177, 181, 186, 189-192, 194, 196, 199, 201, 204-205, 208-209, 211, 213-214, 218-219, 221-228, 233, 236-238, 243-250, 252-253, 255-267, 269-270, 273, 275-277, 297, 301-306, 309-312, 314, 318-321, 324-325, 329-330

Tosefta, 2, 10-11, 13, 22, 89, 105, 132, 155, 211, 230, 234, 237, 248, 283, 285, 288-289, 291, 297, 299, 307

translation, 3, 9, 33, 113, 280, 297-300, 306

uncleanness, 37, 57, 260

unit of thought, 281, 284, 298-299

Urbach, E. Ephraim, 3, 8

vandal, 157

verbal analogy, 37, 39, 47-53, 56, 75, 78-82, 84

verbal congruence, 54-57, 81-83

voice, 18, 165, 226, 233, 279, 281, 287, 290-291, 293-294, 330

Wacholder, B. Z., 327-328

Weber, Max, 30-31, 113

Western (civilization), 6, 30-31, 156, 176-177, 187, 194, 222, 243, 250, 252-253

whole-offering, 34

Wilson, H. Jackson, 15-16, 21

woman, 137-138, 142, 184, 205, 208-209, 245

wrath, 272

Written Torah, 85, 175, 189, 214, 218, 221-222, 225-226, 247-248, 255, 257, 265, 324-325

Y. Hagigah, 265

Y. Taanit, 130, 133, 136, 273

Yannai, 136

Yebamot, 295

Yerushalmi, 10, 13, 22, 91, 108, 113-114, 117, 120-121, 126, 129, 145, 150-151, 155, 214-217, 282, 286, 288

Yohanan, 50, 56, 65-66, 82-83, 265, 273, 301, 303, 309, 311

Yosé, 57, 305, 313

Yosé the Galilean, 212
Zebahim, 33-34, 68, 74, 295
Zech., 274
zekhut, 132-142, 143-144, 146, 148, 150-152, 155, 164-165, 167

Zion, 259, 320
Zutra b. R. Mari, 42, 45, 47-48, 54, 78

South Florida Studies in the History of Judaism

240001	Lectures on Judaism in the Academy and in the Humanities	Neusner
240002	Lectures on Judaism in the History of Religion	Neusner
240003	Self-Fulfilling Prophecy: Exile and Return in the History of Judaism	Neusner
240004	The Canonical History of Ideas: The Place of the So-called Tannaite Midrashim, Mekhilta Attributed to R. Ishmael, Sifra, Sifré to Numbers, and Sifré to Deuteronomy	Neusner
240005	Ancient Judaism: Debates and Disputes	Neusner
240006	The Hasmoneans and Their Supporters: From Mattathias to the Death of John Hyrcanus I	Sievers
240007	Approaches to Ancient Judaism: New Series Volume One	Neusner
240008	Judaism in the Matrix of Christianity	Neusner
240009	Tradition as Selectivity: Scripture, Mishnah, Tosefta, and Midrash in the Talmud of Babylonia	Neusner
240010	The Tosefta: Translated from the Hebrew: Sixth Division Tohorot	Neusner
240011	In the Margins of the Midrash: Sifre Ha'azinu Texts, Commentaries and Reflections	Basser
240012	Language as Taxonomy: The Rules for Using Hebrew and Aramaic in the Babylonia Talmud	Neusner
240013	The Rules of Composition of the Talmud of Babylonia: The Cogency of the Bavli's Composite	Neusner
240014	Understanding the Rabbinic Mind: Essays on the Hermeneutic of Max Kadushin	Ochs
240015	Essays in Jewish Historiography	Rapoport-Albert
240016	The Golden Calf and the Origins of the Jewish Controversy	Bori/Ward
240017	Approaches to Ancient Judaism: New Series Volume Two	Neusner
240018	The Bavli That Might Have Been: The Tosefta's Theory of Mishnah Commentary Compared With the Bavli's	Neusner
240019	The Formation of Judaism: In Retrospect and Prospect	Neusner
240020	Judaism in Society: The Evidence of the Yerushalmi, Toward the Natural History of a Religion	Neusner
240021	The Enchantments of Judaism: Rites of Transformation from Birth Through Death	Neusner
240023	The City of God in Judaism and Other Comparative and Methodological Studies	Neusner
240024	The Bavli's One Voice: Types and Forms of Analytical Discourse and their Fixed Order of Appearance	Neusner
240026	Precedent and Judicial Discretion: The Case of Joseph ibn Lev	Morell
240030	The Bavli's One Statement: The Metapropositional Program of Babylonian Talmud Tractate Zebahim Chapters One and Five	Neusner